M000167110

BUDDY

THE BIOGRAPHY

By the same author:

Fiction

Slip on a Fat Lady
Plumridge
Wild Thing
The Skaters' Waltz
Words of Love
Everyone's Gone to the Moon

Biography and Journalism

Shout! The True Story of the Beatles
The Stones
The Road Goes On For Ever
Tilt the Hourglass and Begin Again
Your Walrus Hurt the One You Love
Awful Moments
Pieces of Hate
The Age of Parody
The Life and Good Times of the Rolling Stones
Elton
Days in the Life: John Lennon Remembered

Plays

The Man That Got Away
Words of Love

BUDDY
THE BIOGRAPHY

Philip Norman

MACMILLAN

First published 1996 by Macmillan

an imprint of Macmillan Publishers Ltd
25 Eccleston Place, London SW1W 9NF
and Basingstoke

Associated companies throughout the world

ISBN 0 333 68099 5

Copyright © Philip Norman 1996

The right of Philip Norman to be identified as the
author of this work has been asserted by him in accordance
with the Copyright, Designs and Patents Act 1988.

The excerpt from 'American Pie' by
Don McLean is reproduced by kind
permission of MCA Music Ltd

All rights reserved. No reproduction, copy or transmission
of this publication may be made without written permission.
No paragraph of this publication may be reproduced, copied
or transmitted save with written permission or in accordance
with the provisions of the Copyright Act 1956 (as amended).
Any person who does any unauthorized act in relation to
this publication may be liable to criminal prosecution
and civil claims for damages.

1 3 5 7 9 8 6 4 2

A CIP catalogue record for this book is available from
the British Library

Typeset by CentraCet Limited, Cambridge
Printed by Mackays of Chatham plc, Chatham, Kent

To the Lailey family, Trevor, Anne, Anne-Marie
and Suzannah.
Good companions on the road to Lubbock.

AUTHOR'S NOTE

This book could not have been written without the help of Buddy's widow, Maria Elena Holly, and his eldest brother, Larry Holley. I am grateful to both for suspending their usual low opinion of would-be biographers and trusting me to write a book that would do justice to its subject at long, long last. I owe a huge debt of gratitude to Trevor Lailey, co-founder of Britain's Buddy Holly Appreciation Society, for opening the first doors to me in Lubbock and Clovis. However devoted, a biographer is only as good as his luck, and I must here record two strokes of luck well beyond the ordinary. The first was enjoying the help and guidance of the meticulous Bill Griggs, Holly archivist and researcher par excellence. The second was making the acquaintance of the remarkable Dr Jerry Fisher and being permitted to share his penetrating observations about the character and motivation of Norman Petty.

Heartfelt thanks also, for their assistance, kindness and patience, to Tommy Allsup, Tony Barrett of Rockstar records, John Beecher, Kenneth Broad, David Bryce, Jim Carr, Carley Clark, June Clark, Bill Clement, Jerry Coleman, Des O'Connor, Sonny Curtis, Jack Davis, Murray Deutch, Don Everly, Phil Everly, Jake Goss, Echo and Ron Griffith, Tommy Hancock, Ben Hall, Ronnie Keene, Buddy Knox, Shirley Kornegay, Robert Linville, Little Richard, Pansie McGuire, Alice Maddox, Edith

Massey, Joe B. Mauldin, Bob Montgomery, Jack Neal, Barbara O'Nions, Harold Orenstein, Terry Noland, Bill Pickering, Peggy Sue Rackham, Jimmy Self, Sharon Sheeley, Pappy Dave Stone, Niki Sullivan, the late Bob Thiele, Gary and Ramona Tollett.

My gratitude, as always, goes to Michael Sissons and Peter Matson for their unfailing encouragement and enthusiasm, and to my wife, Sue, the best editor any writer could have.

Philip Norman
London, May 1996

CONTENTS

LIST OF ILLUSTRATIONS

Prologue

LISTEN TO ME

BUDDY HOLLY is buried almost within sight of the modest
street where he was born in Lubbock, Texas. Despite the
thousands who have come to visit his grave these past
thirty-seven years, no tour-buses run to it; there are no sonorous-
voiced guides, no Disney-style working models nor souvenir
stalls. His home city may have been slow to recognize his
enormous fame, but at least that has prevented any hint of the
tacky opportunism with which Elvis Presley is memorialized at
Graceland. In death, as in his brief life, Buddy remains untainted
by vulgarity.

Those who would do him homage must make their own way
by rented car from the new Civic Center where he is belatedly
commemorated by a lanky bronze statue and a 'Walk of Fame'.
You drive past the La Quinta Inn along Avenue Q, make a right
on to 4th Street, then another right on to Martin Luther King Jr
Boulevard, which Buddy knew as Quirt Avenue. Beyond the
railroad-tracks, in a desolate hinterland of granary yards and
container-depots, is Lubbock's municipal cemetery. It is wholly
typical of this star of uttermost magnitude that his last resting-
place should be on public land, accessible to any and every
visitor.

Lubbock cemetery is a pleasant place, tranquil and under-
stated in a way which seems hardly Texan yet somehow evokes

the spirit of Buddy everywhere you look. In defiance of year-round sun, the interconnecting lawns are a fresh spring green. The memorials are unpretentious and set generously wide apart. Small trees lend dappling shade to vases and pots whose flowers are regularly replenished and arranged with loving care. The only noise is the steady roar of a neighbouring grain-silo, as huge and sombrely magnificent as a medieval cathedral. Beside one newly turfed hillock, a little black and white dog keeps vigil with its nose resting miserably on its front paws. Its air of baffled disbelief that a much-loved voice could be extinguished with such cruel suddenness is doubly appropriate here.

A female clerk in the nearby administration office points out 'the Holly grave' with a courteous smile, despite the wearisome familiarity of the inquiry. It lies barely 100 yards from the main gate, beside a dusty roadway where the cars of one or two latercoming mourners are usually parked. There is no fancy memorial, not even an upright stone – just a simple oblong of granite, embedded in the stubby grass. The red dust that blows from the cottonfields, winter and summer, has illuminated the letters of the inscription in dusky orange. This commemorates Buddy under the surname he was born with and would have kept throughout his life had not a typing mistake on his first recording contract decided otherwise:

In loving memory
of our own
Buddy Holley
September 6, 1936
February 3, 1959

To the right of the inscription is a bas-relief of a Fender Stratocaster guitar, that once-astonishing two-horned silhouette, set about by musical notes and holly-leaves. Across the guitar's granite contours lie a scatter of small coins like so many extra volume-knobs in pristine silver and copper. It has become a tradition that the fans who find their way here from all over the world leave behind good-luck tokens of nickels and new-minted 'pennies', as well as red carnations, plastic toy crickets, children's drawings of Buddy and pairs of black horn-rimmed spectacles in case there should be no oculists in Heaven.

In the distance, the grain-silo temporarily abates its roar, turning up the volume of birdsong. The sad little dog still lies and waits for a voice that can never come. The sun glances off the scatter of nickels and pennies, transforming them to brilliant treasure under the giant Texan sky whose stillness now might be of conscious remembrance.

On a basis of simply counting heads, rock music surpasses even film as the most influential art form of the twentieth century. By that reckoning, there is a case for calling Buddy Holly the century's most influential musician.

Elvis Presley and he are the two seminal figures of fifties rock 'n' roll, the place where modern rock culture began. Virtually everything we hear on record or tape and see on video or the concert stage can be traced back to those twin towering icons – Elvis with his drape jacket, sideburns, pout and swivelling hips; Buddy in big black glasses and buttoned-up Ivy League jacket, brooding over the fretboard of his Fender Stratocaster.

But there is no question as to whom posterity owes the greater debt. Presley's place in rock 'n' roll is no more than that of a gorgeous transient; having unleashed it on the world, he soon forsook it for slow ballads and schlock movie musicals. Holly by contrast was a pioneer and a revolutionary; a multi-dimensional talent which arrived fully-formed in a medium still largely defined by fumbling amateurs. In the few hectic months of his heyday, between 1957 and 1959, he threw back the boundaries of rock 'n' roll, gave substance to its shivery shadow, transformed it from a chaotic cul-de-sac to an highway of infinite possibility and promise. To call someone who died aged twenty-two 'the father of rock' is not as incongruous as it might seem. What has always set his persona apart from others in the rock 'n' roll pantheon is its air of maturity, sympathy and understanding. To successive generations of fans he has seemed less like an idol than a teacher, guide and friend; a 'buddy' in every sense of that unassuming yet so-comforting word.

The songs he wrote and performed are classics of rock 'n' roll; two-minute masterpieces that remain as fresh and potent today as when they were recorded going on forty years ago. 'That'll Be The Day', 'Peggy Sue', 'Oh Boy', 'Rave On' – the titles have become synonyms for a drape-suited, pink-Cadillac *belle époque* which we have come regard almost with the same misty-eyed nostalgia as the golden years of Hollywood.

His voice is the most imitated, yet imitable, in rock music. Dozens of other singers down the decades have borrowed its inflection and eccentricities of pronunciation and phrasing. None has ever exactly caught the curious lustre of its tone, its erratic swings from dark to light, from exuberant snarl to tender sigh, nor quite brought off the famous hiccupy catches of breath with which he could fracture even the word 'Well' into six stuttering syllables. It was a voice able effortlessly to run the whole gamut of pop, from rock 'n' roll in maximum overdrive to thoughtful love songs whose warm intimacy stays in bloom year after year. As I write this, in London on 6 March 1995, the radio is playing a commercial for Home Comfort garden conservatories and storm windows. The jingle is a breath-for-breath copy of Buddy singing 'Everyday': as usual, like him yet nothing like him.

One crucial detail above all sets him apart from Presley and the other primal rock genii. Whereas they had all become solo performers by the time they burst on the world, Buddy Holly came to stardom fronting a group, the Crickets, whose guitar/bass/drums line-up was the protype of every rock band there has been or will be. Unlike Presley and other guitar-toting idols of the period, he was a gifted player, responsible for most of the luminous guitar breaks that became a hallmark of his records. His playing-style is as widely copied as his voice – the moody drama he could conjure from a shifting sequence of four basic chords, his incisive downstrokes and 'rhythm-lead' solos. The deification of the rock guitarist, the enduring sex-appeal of the solid-body guitar, the pre-eminence of the Fender make: all were set in train, on the stage of the New York Paramount and the London Palladium, by Buddy and his sunburst Stratocaster.

As a songwriter, performer and musician, he is acknowledged as the progenitor of virtually every world-class rock talent to emerge in the sixties and seventies. The Beatles, the Rolling Stones, Bob Dylan, the Byrds, Eric Clapton, Pete Townshend, Elton John, Bruce Springsteen, all freely admit that they would never have started to play music without having had the way shown to them by Buddy Holly and the Crickets. The uncount- able imitators and derivatives of those artists, whether they know it or not, owe the same elemental debt. However rock may have seemed to advance or mutate over the past twenty years, one performer above all remains ineradicably part of its spirit and soul. Listen to the newest record by the latest 'original' singer- songwriter: you're almost bound to hear an echo of Buddy in there somewhere. Look at Jarvis Cocker, gangly, big-spectacled star of the hit nineties band Pulp. What else but a Buddy for the digital age?

His time on the world stage was pitifully short, lasting only from September 1957, when 'That'll Be The Day' became a hit, to the snowy, disillusioned February of 1959. But in those sixteen months he created a blueprint for enlightened rock stardom that every modern newcomer with any pretence at self- respect still aspires to follow.

He was the first rock 'n' roll performer both talented and strong-minded enough to insist on the artistic control which his successors now take for granted. He was the first not only to write his own songs but also to arrange them and supervise his own studio-sessions, directing his back-up musicians to his own exacting standards. He was the first to master the studio's technical resources, achieving effects with echo, double-tracking and overdubbing which to this day have never been bettered.

He was the first rock 'n' roller not to be a simpering pretty-boy; to be, in fact, rather plain and nerdy-looking, with glasses that did not assume their stylish black frames until the very last months of his life. He was the first to make it on solid ability, energy and personality; appealing to a male public as much as to a female one; redefining the perception of good looks and enviable style much as John Lennon and Mick Jagger would in later years; making rock 'n' roll audiences listen and reflect as well as jive and jump about; endowing teenage fan-worship with the grown-up properties of liking and respect.

Whereas other great rock music talents have needed years of trial and error to reach fulfilment, Buddy's took only a few sure-footed months. Just a few weeks after recording the wonderful but elementary 'That'll Be The Day', he was taping 'Words Of Love', a ballad with which the rest of pop still has only barely caught up. In a time where repetition was believed the key to success, each of his releases was utterly different from its predecessor, a policy he maintained even when it began to cost him success in the charts. He used wacky percussion like an empty cardboard box beaten with drumsticks ('Not Fade Away') and hands slapping on denim-clad knees ('Everyday'); extended the vocabulary of the rock 'n' roll guitar to flamenco ('Well ... All Right') and Hawaiian ('Heartbeat'); and worked with arcanely non-rock sound-effects like Hammond organ, celeste and, finally, massed violins. He rebelled against the apartheid which had hitherto divided white rock 'n' roll artists from black, cutting one track ('Early In The Morning') with a gospel choir, another ('Reminiscing') with the blues saxophonist King Curtis.

He anticipated how the record market of later decades would be dominated by albums rather than singles, and foreshadowed the 'Live Aid' spirit of the eighties, when superstars would form *ad hoc* duets and even play on one another's records anonymously, just for the fun of it. He was the first pop performer to make the now familiar transition to record producing and talent-spotting, and the first with ambition to become a businessman and impresario as well as a creative artist, planning his own publishing company, recording studios, record-label and even retail business almost a decade ahead of the Beatles' Apple organization.

His death in a plane crash on 3 February 1959, with fellow tour artists Ritchie Valens and J.P. 'The Big Bopper' Richardson, is the most famous tragedy in rock music history. Numerous songs have been written about it, notably Don McLean's 'American Pie', which immortally called it 'the day the music died'.

It was yet another of Buddy's long series of 'firsts', darkening rock 'n' roll's brassy face with the twin concepts of death and irony – his career apparently in decline, he had just recorded a song called 'It Doesn't Matter Anymore' – and creating the definition of pop musical genius as something tragic, self-consuming and short-lived. Here, too, imitators were to abound in the years that followed: Eddie Cochran, Patsy Cline, Sam Cooke, Jim Reeves, Janis Joplin, Jimi Hendrix, Jim Morrison, finally even Elvis himself.

But once again, the copies never could quite match the original. There was always to be something uniquely poignant about Buddy's death, a quality both sad and satisfying. For this was no rock 'n' roll tearaway, hell-bent on self-annihilation, but an amiable young Texan, whose life seemed to bear not the least taint of scandal, discredit or unkindness; who had recently married and was soon to become a father; who took that fatal plane flight with his two fellow artists only to gain a few hours' rest and get his laundry done.

Desperately sad, of course, to think of such a talent

extinguished at twenty-two, when it might have gone on to achieve so much more. But satisfying to have a hero who can never be made otherwise. For Buddy, unlike Elvis Presley, there had been no grisly unmasking. For him, unlike the Beatles, there has been no bitter, disillusioning anticlimax. For him, unlike Dylan and the Stones, there has been no grotesque, undignified senescence. To his millions of original devotees, and the millions more who join them each year, he is pure music incarnate, as immaculate and irreproachable as one of his own songs, his sufficient eulogy spoken time and again in the bittersweet regret of 'American Pie':

> *I can't remember if I cried*
> *When I read about his widowed bride*
> *But something touched me deep inside*
> *The day the music died.*

Buddy Holly, in short, is the perfect modern myth.

I was sixteen when he died. I can remember for certain that I didn't cry: sixteen-year-olds don't really do that. True to my generation, what touched me deep inside was not much stronger than resigned dismay. So it was over already, even though it had only just begun.

Like John Lennon, Paul McCartney, Mick Jagger, Keith Richards and Eric Clapton, I was a British boy whom Buddy Holly rescued from monotony, boredom and pessimism, and pointed towards a dazzling better way. At his tacit encouragement, I took up playing the guitar, nerved myself to perform his songs in public, tasted the heady nectar of applause, even fancied myself endowed with some of his unostentatious glamour. Like first love, first daydreams never quite die. Here in deep middle age, there is still a part of me that longs to wear a high-buttoning suit and a flat, two-horned guitar, and be able to play every twist of the wonderful back-spiralling electric intro to 'That'll Be The Day'.

But crying is difficult when you have no idea whom you're crying for. Buddy Holly was my idol, hero and exemplar, but at the time of his death, like all his other British fans, I knew next to nothing about him. If the most brilliant, he was also the vaguest of rock 'n' roll deities. Unlike Elvis and other youth idols of the period, no marketing campaign, what today we call 'hype', came with him. There were no souvenir badges, no fan magazine interviews, no starring nor even cameo roles in movies. The few photographs of him that I'd seen all showed him integrated into the Crickets' line-up – tall, lean, smilingly vague. While every breath and tongue-click of his singing voice was familiar to me, I had no idea what his speaking voice might sound like. The only clue was to be found mingled with, perhaps, his most hypnotic molten-silver guitar solo: that soft, encouraging murmur of 'Listen . . . listen to me.'

In March of 1958, he and the Crickets toured Britain (a favour Presley was never to confer), bringing him face to face at last with many of his disciples. His itinerary included Southampton, which is separated by only six miles of choppy water from the Isle of Wight, where I then lived. But I had no money for a concert ticket and the ferry fare. His famous television appearance on *Sunday Night at the London Palladium* was for me just a glimpse . . . three numbers dashed off at the very end, then gone. For ever, as it would turn out.

Death is, anyway, an incomprehensible subject to a sixteen-year-old. It really did not seem all that terrible, especially when one listened to Tommy Dee's 'Three Stars', the 'tribute record' made for him, Ritchie Valens and the Big Bopper together:

> *Buddy, I can still see you*
> *With that shy grin on your face*

Seems like your hair was always mussed up
And kinda outa place.

Not many people really knew Buddy
Or understood how he felt.
But a song from his lips
Could make the coldest heart melt.

Buddy's singing to God now . . .

Despite the sadly appropriate title, his last single, 'It Doesn't Matter Anymore', contained none of the weary resignation it suggested. The voice was as airy and full of optimism as ever, skipping above the unfamiliar pizzicato strings. And how could something which had brought him back to the top of the charts possibly be the end?

To us fifties teenagers, the concept of a 'posthumous' hit record was a completely new one; it was as morbidly fascinating to hear dead Buddy Holly's voice still singing as to see James Dean, the very first teenage icon to perish at his zenith, still up there in living Technicolor on the CinemaScope screen. Until then, we had innocently supposed that pop singers went into the recording studio to make one double-sided single at a time. But with the success of 'It Doesn't Matter Anymore', we learned that Buddy Holly had left behind a cache of finished tracks which could be released as further posthumous singles. By this means, it was calculated, his career might be prolonged for another year, possibly even two.

A month after his death came an LP (as we called them then), *The Buddy Holly Story*, its unusually black-and-white cover showing a face which I for one had never seen before. Sleekly barbered, with an airbrush-smooth face and new, modishly sculpted black spectacle-frames, he looked like someone whose career had been just launched rather than just extinguished.

That July came a new single, 'Peggy Sue Got Married', a

playful sequel to the darkly tom-tomming love-chant of November 1957. The Crickets also continued to put out records, admittedly without Buddy leading them on vocal and guitar, but with a glancingly similar singer added to the same rhythms, the same chord-changes, the same blurry 'Mmms', 'Ooohs' and 'Aahs' as on all his living hits. The Crickets had always seemed such a part of him and he of them that just the rhythms, the chords, the 'Ooohs' and 'Aahs' were enough to turn our minds away from the reality yet again.

Nor was it any coincidence that 1959 was the year in which British pop music finally started to amount to something. Cliff Richard became the nation's top star fronting the Shadows, a group of the same composition as the Crickets whose lead guitarist, Hank B. Marvin, was as wand-thin as Buddy had been, wore thick black horn-rimmed glasses exactly like his and played a Fender Stratocaster. At the year's end, a struggling vocalist named Adam Faith borrowed Buddy's inflection of a single word on 'It Doesn't Matter Anymore' ('Buy-bee') and had a number 1 single with 'What Do You Want?', couched in the same shivery pizzicato strings. Repetition of the formula made Adam Faith the first home-grown performer to have three consecutive British number ones.

In the new decade of pop music, Buddy Holly wasn't just there. He *was* the new decade of pop music. Among the rising American generation of American pretty-boy crooners, none was more successful than Bobby Vee, who sang with an uncanny tremor of Buddy's voice (he had deputized for him at a concert after the fatal plane crash) and who used his vocal style to appeal directly to girls in a way that Buddy himself had always seemed too grown-up and well-bred to do. Bobby Vee also recorded and performed with the post-Buddy Crickets, and once again it was almost enough.

Buddy's way, if not his voice, could be anyone's, however flat the emotion or limited the range. Between 1960 and 1963, it notched up fleeting success for John Leyton, Mike Sarne, Joe

Brown; there were two unabashed British Buddy clones, Mike Berry (whose 'Tribute To Buddy Holly' made the Top 20 in 1961) and the horn-rimmed Buddy Britten. In America, Bobby Vee's impersonation was rivalled by that of Tommy Roe, whose 1962 US number 1 'Sheila' used the same rolling drum-beat and chafing guitar as 'Peggy Sue', and featured the ultimate in Buddy-style flattening of a single vowel:

Sheila says she loves me, she says she'll never leave me.
True love will never dur...

One British songwriter, Geoff Goddard, even claimed direct imput from Buddy beyond the grave on the 'Peggy Sue'-inspired 'Johnny Remember Me', which was a hit for John Leyton in 1961. A devout spiritualist, Goddard claimed to be in psychic contact with Buddy and to have been assured by him that the record was bound for number 1.

Meanwhile, releases kept on coming from the authentic and irreplaceable voice itself – 'Reminiscing'; 'Brown-eyed, Handsome Man'; 'Bo Diddley'; 'Wishing'. So regular were the posthumous singles and so vibrant was the presence on them that many began to wonder if he really was dead after all. There were rumours that the plane crash had been no more than a highly successful stunt to boost his sales, and that he could make a Lazarus-like return to his fans at any moment. Another widely circulated and fervently clung-to story had it that he'd survived the crash, but with terrible disfigurements which prevented him from appearing in public ever again, and that he was now living as a recluse in, of all places, Scotland.

These repeatedly profitable resurrections also focused attention for the first time on Buddy's former manager and producer, Norman Petty, in whose Clovis, New Mexico, studio most of the hits took shape and who shared credit with him as writer of 'That'll Be The Day', 'Peggy Sue', 'True Love Ways' and many more. Producers and managers in the late fifties did not aspire to the celebrity they were later to enjoy, and thus far little had been known of Petty beyond that regularly appearing other surname on Buddy's records. But now he began to be a talking point in his own right. Since many of the tracks left behind by Buddy had been voice-only demo's, Petty was having to ovedub them with instrumental backing – not by Buddy's Crickets, for some reason, but by a sixties group called the Fireballs. As time went on, these doctored releases seemed to have less and less of the authentic Buddy sound. But we accepted them unquestioningly, presuming that if anyone had Buddy's best artistic and financial interests at heart it must be his former manager.

The British 'Beat Boom' of the middle sixties is credited with having changed the face of pop music and transformed its audience from an embattled minority to a world-wide move-ment. But in its essentials, it was not British at all; merely Buddy Holly's students coming to maturity. The Beatles had founded themselves on his vocal style and repertoire. John Lennon and Paul McCartney's vocal harmony, in its first incarnation at least, was a northern English version of Buddy's double-tracked solo voice from 1957. It was the fact that he wrote his own original material which encouraged Lennon and McCartney to try to do likewise, and so to become the most prolific and successful songwriting team in pop music history. They acknowledged their comprehensive debt on their 1964 *Beatles For Sale* album with a near-perfect facsimile of 'Words Of Love', the greatest Buddy song never to become a hit during his lifetime.

In 1963, the Rolling Stones transformed themselves from backwoods R & B group to commercial chart-toppers with a pounding, harmonica-ridden version of Buddy's '57 B-side, 'Not Fade Away'. Britain's third most popular new group were called the Hollies. The fourth most popular, the Searchers, named themselves after the John Wayne movie which provided the inspiration for 'That'll Be The Day'. The ninth or tenth most popular could have had nothing but holly on their minds when they called themselves the Rockin' Berries. He was there in (bespectacled) Peter and Gordon (who made both the US and UK charts with their 1965 cover version of 'True Love Ways'); in Herman's Hermits (one bespectacled), the Ivy League (named after the style of his suits), the Moody Blues, the Barron Knights, the Fortunes, the Applejacks; in a hundred more who got into the charts for five minutes, plus thousands more who never made it beyond their local pub or youth club.

He was there, too, in the American backlash – in Bob Dylan's new 'electric' voice, the harmony and echo of the Byrds, the chord-patterns of new-look attractions like Neil Diamond, Mitch Ryder and the Detroit Wheels, the Fireballs, the Bobby Fuller Four, even the Monkees. He was there in the time of psychedelia and acid, when the smartest thing for any rock star to do was put on a pair of little 'granny-specs'. He was still there in London's Hyde Park in the Moon-shot summer of '69, when the hippy multitudes gathered to see rock's first 'supergroup', Blind Faith, least recognizable mutation yet of Buddy's Crickets, whose sacred solitary album included his most brilliant non-hit of 1958, 'Well . . . All Right.'

For year after crowded year, all that went with this huge creative National Debt was the same life story of barest essentials. A nice young guy had come out of Texas, made wonderful music, got married, died. It was a legend in the purest sense, carried mostly in the head, passed on from mouth to mouth. Even after all this time, one saw no images of Buddy other than the half-dozen or so familiar ones in photographs or on his album-covers. Few articles were written about him, and those that were merely repeated the same one or two facts. There seemed to be no film clips of him, nor even records of his speaking voice.

I had become a journalist with the London *Sunday Times Magazine*, writing extended profiles of major rock and soul music figures like James Brown, Johnny Cash, Stevie Wonder, Wilson Pickett, B. B. King; travelling to interview them in New York, Los Angeles, Memphis and Nashville. In all that time, though he remained my hero of heroes, I never wrote a word about Buddy Holly, nor contemplated doing so. My assumption was the one of which every reporter should beware: if there were any story to tell, surely it would have been told already.

In 1972, I interviewed the Everly Brothers, Don and Phil. Though a major revival in rock 'n' roll music and style was then under way in America, it did not yet encompass rock 'n' roll's original stars, all of whom remained in unfashionable obscurity in their native land. The surviving big names, Bill Haley, Little Richard, Chuck Berry, Carl Perkins, Jerry Lee Lewis, Neil Sedaka and the Everlys, worked mainly in Britain, where the loyalty of their original following remained undiminished.

Both Don and Phil Everly talked at length, and with great warmth, about Buddy Holly, with whom they had toured extensively during 1957 and 1958. Don remembered first meeting him and the Crickets in the basement of an arena in Toronto, Canada, and how the badly-dressed Texas boys' eyes lit up at the sight of the Everlys' sharp Ivy League clothes. Recalling the Crickets' lack of sophistication in those early days, he added what then seemed a bizarre detail: 'At the time, the only publicity picture they had was of them down in Lubbock, in Levis and T-shirts setting tiles on a roof.'

Phil Everly's memories were more emotional: he and Buddy had evidently been real friends, not merely joshing companions on 'the road'. 'He wrote "Wishing" for Don and me. It burns me up when I read about "Wishing" being "reportedly written by Buddy Holly for the Everly Brothers". I remember Buddy putting me into bed with a girl one night . . . and how he laughed! But I can remember him in New York, right at the end, playing all his songs for me and asking me why he couldn't get a hit, he was so low. Then he said "Will you put me to bed?"'

I was the *Sunday Times*'s 'Atticus' columnist in 1975 when Paul McCartney began his secondary career as pop music's most astute businessman with another gesture of homage to his most formative influence. Thanks to the lack of interest in Buddy Holly in America, McCartney's MPL company was able to acquire publishing rights to all his greatest hits in the US and Canada for a knockdown price, rumoured to be less than a million pounds. McCartney also inaugurated the annual 'Buddy Holly Week' of memorial concerts and fan-fests, coinciding with Buddy's birthday on 6 September which continues to this day. In my capacity as Atticus – that is, in no very serious or reverential spirit – I attended the launch of that first Buddy Holly Week, for which McCartney had taken the trouble to fly Norman Petty over from Clovis, New Mexico. At the lavish lunch which marked the occasion, Petty presented McCartney with a pair of Buddy's gold cufflinks, allegedly the very ones he'd been wearing when the plane crashed. I remember thinking it odd that a dead rock 'n' roll star's ex-manager should possess such an intimate souvenir, let alone feel free to hand it out as a business gift.

In the late nineteen-seventies – when Elvis Costello dominated the post-Punk charts, wearing black horn-rimmed spectacles and playing a Fenderish solid-body guitar, and when Linda Ronstadt found 'That'll Be The Day' and 'It's So Easy' no less accessible to the voice of a country and western chanteuse – I switched from journalism to writing biographies of pop music stars: the Beatles, the Rolling Stones, Elton John. My aim was to get behind the mythology and the hype; turn superstars and legends into creatures of flesh and blood; discover who and what had made them what they eventually became; savour all the absurd accidents and wrong turnings that led them to their stupendously right destination; above all – and most challengingly – translate the excitement of great pop music into words. When I first thought of applying this formula to the Beatles, friends and editors alike urged me not to waste my time. 'It's all been said already,' they told me. 'Everyone knows everything there is to know.'

During my research for all three biographies, Buddy cropped up time and again. I learned the full story of how he had encouraged Paul McCartney and an unhappily bespectacled John Lennon to write their earliest songs on truant afternoons in Allerton, Liverpool; how Buddy tracks like 'Crying, Waiting, Hoping' and 'Mailman, Bring Me No More Blues' bolstered the Beatles' early repertoire around the Liverpool dance-halls and helped get them through all-night club sessions on the Hamburg Reeperbahn; how the first record they ever made, at their own expense, was 'That'll Be The Day'; how their very name evolved from a desire to be as much as possible like Buddy's group, the Crickets.

In the annals of the supposedly hard and unsentimental Stones, he occupied a similarly warm niche. I learned how Mick Jagger still remembered seeing him perform 'Not Fade Away' in Woolwich during his one and only British tour; how Keith Richards's original guitar-playing technique was modelled on his; how, to be sure, the name 'Buddy Holly' was almost the only one in Creation with the power to soften Keith's vampire-like physiognomy. Later on, I learned how the great flashy four-eyes of seventies rock had acquired the look from the same role model as inspired Hank B. Marvin's horn-rims and John Lennon's (and Roger McGuinn's and John Sebastian's) granny-glasses. Reg Dwight, alias Elton John, was born with normal vision but during his schooldays took to wearing black horn-rims in imitation of Buddy Holly, so ruining his eyesight for ever.

I was as ravenous as ever for information about Buddy but, after all these years, still had almost nothing to chew on beyond that basic formalized fifties legend. The one existing biography, *Buddy Holly, His Life and Music* by John Goldrosen, published in 1975, was a sincere effort by a painstaking, level-headed fan, but one which sacrificed almost all colour and vividness in favour of dry musical analysis. In 1978, America's rekindling appreciation of Buddy's talent was marked by a Hollywood film, *The Buddy Holly Story*, with Gary Busey in the title role. Though a self-evident travesty (Buddy's two fellow Crickets, Jerry Allison and Joe B. Mauldin, were given fictitious names) it nevertheless became a box-office success and even received an Oscar for Busey's clumpy renditions of Buddy's songs.

The first real television documentary about him was not seen in Britain until 1986, on the fiftieth anniversary of his birth. The maker was Paul McCartney's MPL, a company by now grown hugely wealthy on the back of its presciently acquired Holly song-copyrights. McCartney had been deeply offended by the shallow and semi-fictional Hollywood portrayal of Buddy's life, and had now resolved to employ both his commercial and personal clout to set the record straight.

McCartney's film was shown on BBC 2, in the *Arena* arts programme's series on great names of rock 'n' roll. I sat through it spellbound. Here at last was film of Buddy and the Crickets, performing 'That'll Be The Day' and 'Peggy Sue' on the Ed Sullivan television show – the original four of them, all in tuxedos, and featuring a rhythm guitarist who, confusingly, also wore glasses. It was a surprise to see how weedy and uncharismatic Buddy looked, especially in those original un-chic half-frames, and how hard he had to work with the indifferent sound-system. To the learner guitarist of thirty years previously, a great unresolved question was settled at last: he played 'That'll Be The Day' in the key of A, with a capo over the Stratocaster's fretboard to save his index finger the labour of forming a six-string 'bar'.

Here, for the first time, was a walking, talking Buddy Holly, long-necked and almost one-dimensionally thin, summoned for a few impromptu front-of-curtain words with Ed Sullivan;

answering his host's perfunctory question about the Crickets' ages in what one always should have guessed must be a huskily melodious tone ('Well, there's two eighteen, one twenty and I'm twenty-one'), saying 'Sir' punctiliously and at the end, rather to Sullivan's surprise, thrusting out his hand in that American manner with the palm flat and the thumb stuck up at right angles.

Here was a highway between the Texas cottonfields, and a speeding truck with 'Holley Tile Co., Lubbock' printed on its cab. Here were his two brothers, Larry and Travis, reminiscing about his early childhood, and the amiable Sonny Curtis, one of his earliest musical partners, remembering him as a teenage bluegrass wizard on a four-string banjo. Here was Jerry Allison, the Crickets' once fair-haired, wolf-eyed drummer, now bald and with a bushy Apostle beard, describing him as a student at Lubbock High School, and playing after hours at the seamy 16th and J Club. Here was Vi Petty, Norman's widow, in the tiny studio in Clovis where the greatest hits were made. Here, even, were scraps of conversation between takes: Buddy's voice saying 'Are we rolling?' 'Can you go like that? . . .' then, commandingly, 'OK, let's do it . . .'

Here were his song-publisher, Murray Deutch, and his A & R man at Coral records, Bob Thiele. Here was his 'widowed bride', Maria Elena, describing how he proposed marriage to her on their very first date. Here was the apartment building in Greenwich Village where they settled for the few months they were to enjoy together. Buddy Holly in Greenwich Village among beatniks and coffee houses . . . it was a thought somehow almost too exotic to handle.

Here was Tommy Allsup, the lead guitarist he brought in on his final great run of rock 'n' roll singles, and his companion on the last fatal tour. Here was Allsup's account of the cold and misery of it, and the bizarre twist of fate that led Ritchie Valens and the Big Bopper to join Buddy on the fatal flight. Here was

Phil Everly, still as impassioned as when we had spoken about his old friend, giving added weight to a thesis tentatively raised in John Goldrosen's biography. This was that Buddy's royalty earnings had been tied up in some way by Norman Petty; that in early '59 he had meant to stay in New York until he got another hit, but was forced out on the road again by the need to provide for his pregnant young wife.

In a one-hour documentary, of course, all these matters could be only touched on with tantalizing brevity. One moment on the soundtrack stuck in my mind as revealing tremendous niceness, tact and power of understatement on its subject's part. In some or other rain-sodden far-northern city, an interviewer asked Buddy what the weather in Lubbock would be like just now. 'Oh, it's not quite this cool,' he replied. 'And it's a little bit drier.'

The new information in the documentary, added to the legend, inspired me to write a play, *Words of Love*, which contrasted the last hours in Buddy's life with the existence of a teenage boy like myself at sixteen, for whom his music is a respite from parental repression and dreary hopelessness. The play was transmitted on BBC 2 in 1988. That same year, the musical *Buddy* opened in London, combining the usual vestigial life-story with a reprise of all his greatest hits (plus a couple he never did perform). *Buddy* has since become a theatrical phenomenon to rival anything by Rodgers and Hammerstein or Lloyd Webber, breaking box-office records in the US, Australia and Germany; in London playing at the Victoria Palace, a theatre previously sanctified to wholly British institutions like Max Bygraves and the Crazy Gang. Now in its seventh year, and transferred to the Strand theatre, it is taking bookings until the year 2000.

In 1990, a startled British public had learned that its new Prime Minister, John Major, relaxed by listening to Buddy Holly. But it was not until there had been a bespectacled Buddy Holly fan at 10 Downing Street for almost four years that the idea finally came to me. Might there be even more to be learned about Buddy than the Paul McCartney documentary had uncovered? Might the way to obtain the facts I had been hungering for since the age of sixteen be to go out and look for them? I had vowed never to write another pop music biography, but this was not quite the same as Elton John, the Rolling Stones or even the Beatles. Those books had been motivated by the promise of a good story. This one would be motivated by three decades of love, fascination and gratitude.

When I mentioned the idea to friends, the general reaction was much as in 1978 when I had first thought of investigating the Beatles: 'It's all been said. Everyone already knows everything there is to know.' That was all I needed to hear.

During the filming of my television play I had got to know Trevor Lailey, co-founder of the British Buddy Holly Appreciation Society and an enthusiast since his schooldays. With Trevor, his wife Anne and their daughters Anne-Marie and Suzannah (all three also devout Buddy fans), I travelled to Lubbock in the summer of 1994. Within a couple of days of arriving, I was holding Buddy's Fender Stratocaster. Spread before me on a table lay a selection of his stage clothes – a mustard-coloured tweed jacket; a pair of Floresheim 'Tuxedo' shoes in black suede with red piping; charcoal grey slacks, still shiny-seamed from their last dry-cleaning in his lifetime. And the real Buddy Holly story was flying at me from every direction, sometimes almost too fast for me to write down.

Part One

BLUE DAYS,
BLACK NIGHTS

L OOK AT A map of the nation-sized expanse that is the
state of Texas, move westward from Dallas a couple of
hundred miles, then northward, and you eventually light
upon Lubbock. Far away from all the buzz-names, Houston,
San Antonio, Laredo, El Paso, shut away in the narrowing
corridor between the Oklahoma and New Mexico state-lines
that becomes the Texas Panhandle, it proclaims itself as much a
backwater as any hot, dry inland place can be. Its nearest
substantial neighbour is Amarillo, 120 miles to the north, where
Interstate 40, the successor to famous old Route 66, flings endless
silver ribbons of traffic west to Los Angeles and east to Chicago.
Except for one brief, brilliant period in the late nineteen-fifties,
the ebb and flow of national events has seemed equally intent on
passing Lubbock by.

The city stands, alone and self-contained, on huge vistas of
flat farmland. The principal crop is one which has nurtured so
much American music and mythology that the foreign visitor,
seeing it for the first time, is disconcerted by how ordinary it
looks. Surely those meagre melting snow-white pods, set in
Roman-straight rows of vermilion earth to the horizon, can't
possibly be all there is to cotton!

For nine months of each year in these Texan South Plains,
the climate is an ideal one of strong, steady sunshine, hard blue

skies and almost zero humidity. But spring and fall bring a more complex, erratic time when the temperature can drop twenty degrees in a few seconds and ferocious gales called 'Blue Northers' come sweeping over the high plateaux that extend uninterruptedly to Canada, buffeting each unsheltered hamlet in turn with their Arctic onslaught. Other days bring a vague, directionless turbulence – Lubbockites call it 'blowin' dust' – when the whirling red grit from the cottonfields stings eyes and nostrils and stains the whole immensity of the sky a delicate rose-petal pink. Most alarming is the tornado season, between April and June, when up to seven of the deadliest black cones, the kind which reach to the ground, can be counted out there, whirling around the cotton and wheat like some ghastly square-dance of monsters out of M. R. James. Every year brings its crop of 'just fancy that' tornado stories – of hens stripped of every feather, cattle picked up and carried miles across country, straws driven inches deep into wooden telegraph poles, entire hamlets hammered flat. As it happens, the biggest tornado ever recorded – in 1970 – chose to cleave its mile-and-a-half-wide path with almost geometrical precision right through the centre of downtown Lubbock.

In Abilene, 160 miles to the east, you can stand in the main street and instantly visualize the frontier town it once was. But Lubbock has no such romantic origins. First settled in the eighteen-nineties well after the old West was tamed, named in honour of the Mexican War hero Tom S. Lubbock, it did not become a city proper until shortly before the Great War. Together with cotton, farming and some limited light industry, its principal *raison d'être* is Texas Technical College, founded in 1923, granted university status in the early sixties, attended today by 29,000 students and boasting the largest campus in the country. 'Texas Tech' gives Lubbock somewhat the air of an Oxford or Harvard, out there on waving seas of grass. The broad thoroughfare that passes the campus is called University Avenue, lending a vision of gowns and mortar-boards to the scene of Buddy Holly's earliest triumphs as a musician. But, despite this whiff of academe, there is never any doubt that you are in deepest Texas, where long-legged men settle at breakfast-counters without troubling to remove their ten-gallon Stetsons, and every other vehicle in the traffic-stream seems to be a prairie-dusted Dodge or Chevrolet pick-up truck.

From well-watered verges in the downtown area, crosses of many styles signal Lubbock's original claim to celebrity. It possesses more churches per head of population than any other city in America. If West Texas is 'the Buckle of the Bible Belt', then Lubbock is that belt's most deeply-worn notch; a place where worship is still as regular and vociferous as in pioneer days, and where notions of good and evil, Heaven and Hell, have much the same stark simplicity they did a century ago. Here in teeming display can be found all the usual outwardly similar, inwardly irreconcilable banners of Presbyterian, Episcopalian, Lutheran, Church of Christ. Here, as everywhere throughout the South, Baptists predominate, not as a unified creed but in innumerable, hotly competitive subdivisions: the First Baptist Church, the Second Baptist Church, the Trinity Baptist Church, the Bethany Baptist Church, the Wayne Avenue Baptist Church, the Lyons Chapel Baptist Church. Here, too, churches do not hold themselves aloof from the ebb and flow of secular life but stand along all the busiest commercial strips; sober, one-storey temples to God democratically cheek-by-jowl with bright-coloured ones to McDonald's, Arby's and Whataburger. Among the largest and most prosperous of all Lubbock's churches is the Tabernacle Baptists' on 34th Street, a vermilion hangar of a place which Buddy's money helped to build, where his funeral took place, and where his two brothers, Larry and Travis, are still pillars of the congregation.

To Lubbock, the virtue next to godliness has always been sobriety. In Buddy's time, and right up to 1972, the city was 'dry'; although today one can buy a drink in bars and restaurants, it is impossible to obtain liquor by the bottle within the city limits. When men of a certain age foregather over their long-necked beer bottles, the talk will often turn to those comparatively recent Prohibition days; to famous bootleggers whose congregations were larger than any pastor's; to the speakeasies and 'joints' – and the equally illicit music – that once flourished on the raffish edges of town, beyond the jurisdiction of church elders or police.

The face which Lubbock turns to the visitor has all the Southern virtues of courtesy, helpfulness and openness, sweetened with that peculiar, slow-smiling Texan charm. 'Where y'all from?' is a question which people here ask with genuine interest, often on a note of flattering incredulity. They imply you have done them honour to seek them out, across all those tracts of corn and cotton. A sign at the city's threshold, only lately taken down, used to say 'Welcome to Lubbock for all reasons'.

But the courtesy and smiles can have limits, as strictly defined as the city's own, and can vanish with the abruptness of sunshine in the face of a Blue Norther. 'Don't mess with Texas' – a caution printed even on dry-cleaners' plastic garment-covers – underlines how carefully it is advisable to tread in some company hereabouts. One must remember not to be even glancingly flippant about God, the Flag or the Republican party, nor show too much enthusiasm for contemporary concepts like feminism or gay pride. One remembers that, despite all those crosses and public texts about forgiveness and brotherly love, this is a part of America where to carry firearms is not merely a constitutional right but the *sine qua non* of manliness and self-respect. On the subject of brotherly love, one remembers that when Buddy was growing up, and until almost a decade after his death. Lubbock practised racial segregation as stubbornly ruthless as any in Alabama or Tennessee. The old ghetto-boundaries remain to this day: blacks to the east of town, hispanics to the north. A great change of heart has been forced to take place, epitomized by the metamorphosis of Quirt Avenue into Martin Luther King Jr Boulevard. Even so, there are still some older citizens who persist in such traditional usages as calling east Lubbock 'Coloured Town' and a child's slingshot a 'nigger-shooter'.

Off the wide boulevards are intersecting back streets of one-storey houses, some showy, some simple, all bound into the familiar idyll of communal front lawns, family-named mailboxes, sprinklers, sunlight and dappling shadow. In its essential ways of life, America has a continuity that makes Britain seem a land of mad flux by comparison. Looking down 6th Street, where Buddy was born, you feel that little can have changed in sixty years, other than the shapes of the cars parked there.

There is one great change, however: a mystifying one to the fans who arrive here on their circuit of devotion, between Buddy's statue and his grave. Number 1911 6th Street, where he was brought into the world (at 3.30 pm on 7 September 1936) has vanished. The only trace of the house is the narrow grass strip it once occupied, gaping like the cavity of a lost tooth between its former next-door neighbours. There is no alternative but to turn up a photograph taken during the early seventies by that most devoted of all Holly archivists, Bill Griggs. It looks a fitting enough birthplace for an all-American hero – a narrow wooden dwelling with a sloped roof, not much more elaborate than a pioneer cabin, its front door situated at one end, beneath a small slope-roofed porch. The solitary visible decorations are cut-out shapes like playing-card clubs on its window-shutters.

Buddy's parents, now also years dead, must likewise be sought in photographs. Here is his father, Lawrence Odell Holley, a tall, black-browed man, thin and sinewy in a way that has almost vanished from these obese modern times, and with a familiar lantern-jawed amiability of expression. Here is his mother, Ella, a tiny, fine-boned woman, barely reaching to Lawrence's shoulder, but a patent ball of fire whose robustness, energy and humour leap out of the orangey early-fifties Kodachrome. There is a chemistry which attracts lanky and easygoing men to small, feisty women, and in this Buddy was destined to take after his father, although not, alas, with the same reward of a lifetime's happiness and harmony.

'L.O.', as Lawrence Holley was always called, grew up in Honey Grove, near Paris, Texas, far away to the north-east, near the Oklahoma border. He was twenty-five and working as a short-order cook in nearby Vernon when he met Ella Drake, whose family traced their lineage from the Elizabethan adventurer Sir Francis Drake and whose father was part Cherokee Indian. The couple married in 1924 and, a year later, moved to Lubbock, a community then in the throes of frenetic expansion around Texas Tech. By the time Buddy arrived in 1936, Ella Holley was thirty-four, and believed her childbearing days to be past. She already had two sons, Larry (born in 1925) and Travis (born in 1927), and a daughter, Patricia (born in 1929). But the six-and-a-half-pound baby boy was greeted with joy by both his parents and his elder siblings. He was named Charles Hardin Holley, after his two grandfathers, Charles Wesley Drake and John Hardin Holley. As this seemed absurdly long and formal for a little baby, it was quickly abbreviated to Buddy, a traditional American nickname for the youngest boy of a family and one which his mother had always liked. Foreshadowing the indifference it would show to Buddy throughout his short life, Lubbock's morning paper, the *Avalanche*, recorded his birth as that of a girl, weight eight and a half pounds.

He entered the world in the mid-season Depression years, when America's eastern cities were vistas of weary, work-starved men, its westbound highways teemed with migrant jalopies, and miserably firelit 'hobo jungles' lined its railroad-tracks. L. O.

Holley kept in work by turning his wiry arms to many trades and by his tireless industry and conscientiousness. 'There never was a worker like Daddy,' his eldest son Larry remembers. 'If folks couldn't pay him, then he'd work for nothing.' In Lubbock he had been fortunate in finding a good long-term employer, an entrepreneur named L. D. Thomas, universally known as 'Little Dog' or 'Pup' Thomas. L.O. held down a variety of jobs in Pup Thomas's various enterprises down the years: café-cook, tailor in a menswear store, even timekeeper at the boxing-booth where Thomas presented nationally famous pugilists like Max Baer. On Buddy's birth certificate L.O.'s surname is given as 'Holly', not 'Holley' and his occupation as 'tailor', but his main activity thereafter was work for Pup Thomas's construction company as a carpenter and house-framer.

When Buddy was a year old, L.O. Holley moved his brood from the little plank house on 6th Street to Wolfforth, in those days a rural hamlet just to the west of Lubbock, where they read by the light of oil lamps, used an earth closet and burned 'cow-chips' for fuel. Over the next twelve years, the family would have five further addresses in and around the city – on Avenue O; on 28th Street; in the 'Loftland addition' beyond east Lubbock; on Acuff Road and then Mulberry Road. Shortage of money kept them permanently on the move; the one house they owned rather than renting had to be sold after eighteen months.

But despite their straitened circumstances, L.O. and Ella were the epitome of 'decent folks', respectable, sober, public-spirited and, of course, godfearing. Their church – where L.O. served for many years as deacon – was the Tabernacle Baptists', in those days situated at 15th Street and Avenue N. The Tabernacle Baptists are a sect based on almost 100 per cent literal reading of the Bible, yet in matters of teaching and procedure set apart from other Lubbock Baptist congregations almost as vehemently as from competing sects like the Episcopalians or the Church of

Christ. In common with most Southern churches, Tabernacle Baptists are expected to pay a 'tithe', or regular contribution, from their earnings, usually fixed at 10 per cent.

The Holleys might have been 'pretty much behind the eight-ball financially' as Larry now puts it, but thanks to the unremitting sweat of L.O.'s brow and the blessed egalitarianism of the educational system, Buddy lacked few of the ingredients for a classic American boyhood. Like his better-off schoolfriends, he played baseball, joined the Cub Scouts and entered local fancy-dress contests in fancy cowboy clothes, riding on a pony. L.O. had not hesitated to chastise his two older boys with a double-thickness leather razor-strop, but Buddy received no such dire punishment for the juvenile misdemeanours he committed as readily as any other small boy. Most third sons have to resign themselves to the existence of 'tail-end Charlie' as far as their parents' affections are concerned, but Buddy might have been L.O. and Ella's only child. His tiny, strong-minded mother, in particular, petted, indulged and watched over him almost obsessively.

Like most devout and self-sufficient Southern families, then and now, the Holleys loved music and were adept at making it, both as an expression of faith and to amuse themselves, their relations and friends. Ella sang duets with her twin sister, Buddy's Aunt Allie. His two older brothers performed as a twosome in local hoedowns and talent contests, Larry on violin and piano, Travis on accordion and guitar. Their sister Pat had a sweet singing voice, and at family get-togethers would harmonize with Ella and Allie. The one exception was the head of the family: as Travis Holley remembers, L.O. 'couldn't carry a tune in a bag'.

When Buddy was five, his parents bought him his first musical instrument, a toy violin. He made his first stage appearance soon afterwards when he accompanied his two elder brothers to a talent contest in the school house at County Line, about thirty miles north-east of Lubbock. Peeved at being 'slowed up' onstage by a toddler, Larry smeared grease on Buddy's violin-bow so that no one would hear it. But the song he sang so captivated the judges that they awarded him the $5 first prize. 'I can see him doing it now,' Larry Holley says. 'It was that old song that goes "Have you ever gone sailing down the river of memor-ees?"'

In character, these two elder brothers could hardly have been more different. Travis Holley, though 'as good-looking as a movie star', his family thought, was shy and unassuming while Larry was a tough, humorous character, sharing his father's dedication to hard work but also with an adventuring, roistering bent recalling his famous ancestor Sir Francis Drake. As Buddy grew up, Larry became a combination of surrogate father and role model; whatever his big brother did, he would gamely try, although his nature back then was anything but confident. 'He was just an insecure, scared little kid,' Larry remembers. 'When I'd just got married, Buddy was about ten and my wife and I took him with us on a hunting trip. We slept out in the open, and late at night, you know, the coyotes would get to howling. Buddy crawled into the sleeping-bag with my wife and me, right in between the two of us.'

The Holleys' quest for cheaper accommodation outside Lubbock city limits uprooted Buddy from his first elementary school, Roscoe Wilson, at the age of ten, and transferred him to Roosevelt Elementary School in Lubbock County, where he had no friends and to which he had to make a long, wearisome journey by bus each morning. A year later, he began having formal piano lessons. His teacher reported him to be a promising pupil with a natural ear, but after a few months Buddy announced that the piano wasn't for him. On the school bus he'd seen a boy named Wayne Maines strumming a guitar and singing. His parents started him on steel guitar, the kind played on the lap like a zither, but that did not do either: he said he wanted an

acoustic 'flat-top' model 'like the one Travis has'. L. O. Holley
bought him a cheap Harmony model from a pawnshop; brother
Travis, who'd learned to play during wartime service with the
Marines, showed him the first one-finger chords; from there on,
Buddy was seldom seen without a guitar in his hands. He'd
strum and sing in his room, on the front steps of his house and
on the long daily journey to and from school.

For a Texas boy with his first guitar in the late nineteen-
forties there was only one kind of music to play and sing. It was
country music (in Texas, more commonly known as 'Western'
music), the folk songs of the American frontier, ballads of the
prairie, the cattle-range and the campfire. Forged inside the
circled wagons of the first pioneers, it was music that knew no
barriers of age or class. 'Country-style' meant family, friends and
neighbours; the community spirit, harmony and togetherness
which were the youthful nation's most cherished virtues. Its
quintessential form was the hoedown, barn-dance or 'jamboree',
with straw bales for seats, pies and lemonade set out on red-and-
white gingham cloths, fiddles sawing, hens clucking, grandpap-
pies and small children clapping along together. Two Saturday-
night radio shows, hugely popular throughout the South in
Buddy's childhood, were presented in this homely manner before
a live audience – the *Louisiana Hayride*, transmitted by station
KWKH in Shreveport, Louisiana; and the famous *Grand Ole
Opry*, transmitted by station WSM from country music's capital,
Nashville, Tennessee.

But first and foremost, country was white man's music, as
bare-faced a declaration of white supremacy as the drinking-
fountains, lunchrooms and public benches available to some and
not to others throughout the unreformed South. Like their
housing, drinking, eating and transport, black people's music was
subject to rigid segregation. The whole panoply of blues genius,
from Blind Lemon Jefferson and Robert Johnson to Muddy
Waters and John Lee Hooker, was lumped together under the

same condescending classification of 'specialty' or 'race' music', ferociously corralled off from the ears of white people, especially women and children; allowed to be retailed only to black audiences in black-owned clubs and halls, and broadcast only over black-operated radio stations. Country music, with its formality and decorum, epitomized white civilization and refinement to godfearing Southern minds, just as the blues, with its simplicity, humour, sexual frankness and insidious rhythm, epitomized every possible nuance of the word 'sin'.

For all country music's huge popularity, it had barely begun to be commercialized when Buddy came to it at the tail end of the forties. The public at large knew it mainly as incidental music for cowboy movies, warbled by buckskinned heroes like Gene Autry or Roy Rogers and the Sons of the Pioneers. Its single splash of contemporary glamour was Hank Williams, whose idiosyncratic yodelling vocal style managed to suggest youth rather than late middle-age, and whose songs, like 'Your Cheatin' Heart', 'Hey, Good Lookin'' and 'Jambalaya', regularly 'crossed over' from the purely country sphere to become international pop hits. Williams is regarded as the first true pop singer-songwriter, not least for creating an image that was tantalizingly aloof, yet troubled and vulnerable. He was to die of drugs and drink in 1953, aged only twenty-nine, one of the earliest intimations that fame, wealth and adulation need not necessarily be beneficial to one's health.

The style of country music varied according to the regional psyche which fostered it. From the eastern South came 'bluegrass', a frenetically fast and nimble banjo-led sound, popularized far and wide by Bill Monroe and the Bluegrass Boys, and the duo of Lester Flatt and Earl Scruggs, who picked together as competitively as if their banjo and guitar were duelling rapiers. Along the paranoiacally guarded frontier with Mexico, it became chilli-flavoured 'Tex-Mex'; down around the Louisiana bayous, it took on the accordions and accent of the French colonists to become 'Cajun'; to its detractors it was 'hillbilly', redolent of remote mountain regions where families still carried on blood feuds with shotguns. The open, windy Texas plains, and the restless energy of its people, had fostered a further zestful subdivision called 'Western Swing', whose chief exponents, Bob Wills and Hank Thompson, fronted groups augmented by brass and drums – similar to what a later era would term 'showbands' – and made music specifically for energetic dancing.

The songs which Buddy learned to sing and strum as a twelve-year-old were his parents', and grandparents', favourites – sentimental cowboy ballads, folk songs, spirituals handed down from tent-meetings on open prairies a century earlier. Like many young people, he was fascinated by Hank Williams and would gamely try to copy the way that Williams's yodel pulverized simple words like 'do' and 'cry' into half a dozen or more breath-jerking syllables on 'Lovesick Blues', the jukebox hit of the hour. He followed the same stars that every adult country fan did: Jimmy Rodgers, 'the Singing Brakeman', the Carter Family and Hank Snow, whose 'train songs' were the first in Western music to introduce a driving, finger-snapping beat. 'He started learning the banjo, too,' Larry Holley remembers. 'Seems like he picked that up in just a matter of days.'

At his first elementary school, Roscoe Wilson, he had got to know another guitar enthusiast, a plump, rather matronly-looking boy named Bob Montgomery whose parents ran the Gin Café (named after the cotton-processing machine, not the liquor) on the south side of town. Buddy and Bob spent long hours practising at each other's houses, modelling themselves on blue-grass duos like the Louvin Brothers and Johnny and Jack, whose high tenor harmonies suited their unbroken voices. They even managed to get hold of a wire-recorder, precursor of the tape-recorder, and put down middle-aged country tracks like 'Foot-prints In The Snow', 'I'll Just Pretend' and 'Take These Shackles

From My Heart'. At the beginning, and for some time to come, Bob Montgomery seemed the more talented of the pair: he would usually sing lead while Buddy supplied the harmony. 'I didn't have any brothers or sisters, and Buddy's two brothers and his sister were much older than he was, so we became kind of like brothers,' Montgomery says now. 'I don't really remember him having any personality in those days. He was just a scrawny, gangly kid.'

When Buddy was thirteen, his family moved back into Lubbock, settling at 3315 36th Street. This meant he could attend J. T. Hutchinson junior high school with many of the city friends he had made at Roscoe Wilson. They included Bob Montgomery and two others who were to be crucial in his early musical development, Don Guess and Jerry Ivan Allison. Out of school hours, he found a further kindred spirit in Jack Neal, a diminutive seventeen-year-old with a quiet voice and wide smile, then working with L. O. Holley as a carpenter's helper. 'At lunchtime, I'd get my guitar out of the car and set and play out in the sun,' Neal remembers. 'One day, Mr L. O. Holley saw me and said "My boy Buddy plays guitar, too. You all ought to get together."'

The two boys formed a duo, 'Buddy and Jack', and started appearing in the talent shows which continually cropped up in the little towns round about Lubbock: Meadow, Whiteface, Abernathy, Levelland. Jack Neal sang lead while Buddy supplied the guitar riffs that are to country music what vegetable 'florettes' are to modern haute cuisine: decorative, painstaking and about as exciting as puréed carrot or tomato. 'We started writing songs together, too,' Jack says. 'Only in those days, you didn't call it that. You just called it makin' up songs.

'Buddy was real quiet and shy – but not all the time. He could be a cut-up, too. He loved the car I used to have, an off-yellow and brown '48 Fleetline Chevrolet. 'Cause the only thing

Buddy had to drive at the time was his Daddy's Dodge flatbed truck. The old Fleetline had a throttle-lever and a choke-lever. One of Buddy's favourite things to do while we were driving along was to suddenly reach over and pull on the throttle. The car'd leap forward; I'd slap his hand away. Then he'd lean and pull on the choke. That car'd be leaping and jumping down the highway like some ol' firecracker.'

In September 1952, along with Bob Montgomery, Buddy began his first semester at Tom S. Lubbock High School. The school is still there on 19th Street, a long biscuit-coloured façade whose formal high windows and terracotta roof give it somewhat the appearance of an oversized Spanish hacienda. Once more, the timelessness of an American institution contrasts with the neurotic impermanence of a British one: while our education system is endlessly overhauled and fiddled with, theirs remains unchanged in structure from generation to generation. At Lubbock High, you can walk the same grey-shiny passageways that Buddy would have done forty-four years ago; past the same high-ceilinged classrooms and bulky staircases and the rows of steel lockers, any one of which might have contained his books and had his class timetable taped inside its louvred door.

One of the more agreeable American high school traditions is the Yearbook, an expensively bound annual volume – so much classier than the smudgy samizdat magazines and newsletters of British schools – containing a miniature photograph of each student as well as news about staff appointments and academic and sporting achievements. You can go to Lubbock High's administrative offices today, and a kindly, boyish old man in a bow tie will show you the Yearbooks back to Buddy's time and before. Here he is in the 1953 edition, pictured among the Class of '55 (i.e. the year they are due to graduate). At sixteen, he is hardly recognizable as the person he will become; chubby-faced,

big-eared, with slicked-flat hair, a rather anxious, uncertain smile
– and no glasses. He did not take to wearing those until his
senior year, 1955, when one of his teachers sent a note to his
parents, urgently recommending them to have his eyes tested.
The subsequent examination, by Lubbock opthalmologist Dr J.
Davis Armistead (another unsung but crucial link in the Buddy
Holly story), revealed his vision to be 20/800, four times the
minimum requirement for certification as legally blind. His first
pair of glasses, unveiled with no visible pleasure or pride in that
fall's Yearbook, had lightweight plastic frames with an ostentatious zigzag design on the earpieces. These were soon exchanged
for 'half-frames', a classic piece of fifties design which, with their
transparent lower area, seemed to give the wearer an additional
pair of thick, dark eyebrows.

For the mid-fifties adolescent, particularly in America, most
particularly in Texas, wearing glasses meant saying goodbye to
any hope of being thought good-looking or interesting, and
accepting relegation to a risible subspecies of over-bookish
weakling. The only bespectacled figure in popular culture was
Clark Kent, the 'mild-mannered reporter' who was the alter ego,
and antithesis in every way, of Superman. But that was, alas, not
Buddy Holley's only physical demerit. The chubby cuteness of
his toddlerhood had given way to almost painful skinniness;
though he was tall enough, almost a six-footer eventually, when
he turned sideways you could hardly see him. Ever-ready and
winning though his broad smile might be, it revealed an extreme
case of what were called 'West Texas teeth', not only crooked
but dulled and stained brown by the region's over-fluorided
water. It hardly helped that his complexion was good, his face
almost free of adolescent spots and blackheads. 'He was what
today we'd call a nerd,' a Lubbock High classmate, Jane Liver-
more, remembers. 'I don't think any of us took him seriously in
those days.'

At all three of his previous schools he had been a diligent

student, and at Lubbock High he kept up the good work. His report cards show a steady stream of A's and B's, though there could be lapses when his guitar beckoned more strongly than home-study. His best subject was English: he had been a reporter on his junior high school's newspaper, learning to type in the process, and had once won a decorative pin in an essay competition organized by a paper in Fort Worth. In essays and letters, as later in his songs, he expressed himself with unfailing clarity and succinctness. His handwriting was neat and legible, though little like standard American italic. His signature had a particular flourish – almost as if anticipating the autograph-signing to come – with its elongated capital B and H, its long-tailed, slightly wavery d's, l's and y's.

If resigned never to be the class Adonis, he was fussy about his clothes and personal grooming. Jerry Allison, who had also followed him to Lubbock High from J. T. Hutchinson, noticed how an indulgent mother provided him with a clean, crisply starched and flawlessly ironed shirt each day; how his white socks shone and his black loafers sparkled; how even his Levis always had a knife-edge crease in them. 'His hair bothered him more than anything else,' Jack Neal remembers. 'It was always real curly, and he didn't care for that. He wanted it to be straight so he could comb it right back like the smart guys. He used to say he'd never have had curly hair like that if his folks hadn't made him wear a toboggan [woollen hat] when he was a little kid.'

Music loomed large in Lubbock High's curriculum. The school had two mixed a cappella choirs and a band which performed at sports events and 'assemblies' (regular impromptu concerts in the assembly hall). Buddy joined both choirs, the sophomore Choralaires and the junior-senior Westernaires, but seemed content to remain just another voice among many. The school also cultivated a strong cowboy flavour, naming its students and sports teams 'Westerners' and holding an annual

'Westerners Round-up', with suitable dress and music. One Round-up souvenir programme records that Bob Montgomery had written a song called 'Flower Of My Heart' especially for the occasion. Bob's name figures prominently on the list of 'Wranglers' (participants) but Buddy's isn't mentioned.

The drippy, nerdish look of his early teenage years was in fact wholly misleading. Although totally uninterested in organized sports, he enjoyed the outdoor life, going on regular hunting and fishing trips with his brothers and cousins. In August 1952, while on vacation in Colorado, he wrote his big sister Pat that he'd enjoyed swimming in both the Pecos and Rio Grande rivers, despite the icy coldness of the water.

From his father he had inherited both a versatile practical streak and a capacity for hard manual work belied by his beanpole physique. His eldest brother, Larry, had augmented the family's meagre income by starting a tiling business a couple of years earlier: during vacation times, Buddy would help L.O. on house-framing contracts and go out on tiling jobs with Larry, who taught him to set plain red tiles on roofs and fancy ceramic ones around kitchens and bathrooms. 'When I laid tile, I took a lot of care but went real slow,' Larry remembers. 'Travis went fast, but sometimes used to skimp the work. Buddy could go fast *and* take care.'

The principal of his several hobbies was leatherwork. He would make wallets and purses as gifts for his family and friends, hand-tooled with intricate Western-style curves and swirls. He also drew and painted and, as he grew older, became interested in industrial drafting and blueprint-making, an occupation which so suited his neat, painstaking nature that he began to think of it as a possible career.

At Lubbock High, his main extra-mural activity was membership of the school's Industrial Co-Operative Training chapter, a social club designed to introduce students to prospective employers from local industries. Buddy and Bob Montgomery were stalwarts of ICT's Chapter 95, which also provided a willing audience for their country music partnership. They would perform at chapter-meetings as well as at more formal occasions like the banquet for the Lubbock Real Estates Board. Buddy was elected a vice-president of Chapter 95, and also served on its entertainments committee. At parties and barbecues, he would be put in charge of the games: balloon-bursting, pillow-stuffing and the like.

His nature was genial, considerate and endlessly obliging, but with an edge of self-assurance – almost cockiness – the result of growing up the adored and petted 'baby' of the Holley family. In particular, his brother Larry remembers, patience was a concept almost unknown to him. 'With Buddy, everything had to be right now. If he wanted to write a song, he'd just pick up his guitar and get right on with it. If he felt like doing some leatherwork, even if the family wasn't through with Thanksgiving dinner, he'd go get all his tools and materials and spread them out on the floor. It was almost like he knew he didn't have much time to do all the things he wanted.'

For all his glasses and gawkiness, the lottery of teenage romance seemed to have dealt him a winning ticket. At his first elementary school, Roscoe Wilson, he had met a tiny girl with glossy dark eyebrows, a captivating smile and the equally captivating name of Echo McGuire. Echo came from a prosperous background: her father owned McGuire's drive-in dry-cleaners, and her house on 20th Street, close to the Texas Tech campus, was considerably grander than the Holley family's rented one on 36th. There was also a great religious divide. While the Holleys were Tabernacle Baptists, the McGuires were Church of Christ, a sect if possible even more zealous in its scriptural observances and sterner in its definition of worldly sin. Larry Holley had once dated a Church of Christ girl, but had been forced to break up with her by the extreme disapproval of their respective ministers. 'Our two churches just don't see eyeball to eyeball about anything.'

Buddy and Echo became friends at Roscoe Wilson, losing touch for a couple of years when Buddy's family moved outside the Lubbock school system and he had to transfer temporarily to Roosevelt Elementary. They met up again at Hutchinson Junior High, by which time Buddy had begun playing music with Bob Montgomery. Buddy, Bob and Echo became a threesome, spending long hours playing ping-pong together at Echo's house. It wasn't until well into their sophomore year at Lubbock High that Buddy put the relationship into different gear by asking Echo for a date. They went to a football game together, and afterwards to the Hi-D-Ho drive-in at College (now University) Avenue and Second Place, which in those days was the favourite meeting-place of Lubbock's teenage crowd. From an archetypal round, flat-roofed servery, 'Hidey burgers', 'Hidey fries' and 'Hidey pies' were sped to the semicircle of parked cars by waitresses, or carhops, in scarlet and white uniforms with military-style pillbox hats. For Buddy and his friends, the favourite evening amusement was what they called 'circling the Ho' – driving their borrowed family cars round and round the Hi-D-Ho, exchanging pleasantries or challenges through their wound-down windows, periodically stopping to continue the dialogue over yet another round of cheeseburgers and malts.

Echo McGuire was a catch in anyone's terms, barely five feet tall, with an aureole of fluffy hair and a more than usually seductive West Texan drawl. An exceptional student, she quickly went on to Lubbock High's honour-roll with straight A's. She was also a deeply serious girl who unquestioningly accepted the rigorous teaching of her church, even though it cancelled one of teenagerdom's chief pleasures. The Church of Christ used no music in its services and forbade dancing.

Echo's father, O. W. 'Mac' McGuire, had initially thought

her too young to go steady, but he and his wife, Pansie, were won over by Buddy's respectfulness, good manners and charm. Though the McGuires were much better off than the Holleys, and Echo had grown up with many luxuries Buddy had lacked, the two families became on amicable terms. Even their opposing religious creeds did not present the obstacle that might have been expected. Buddy regularly accompanied Echo to services at the Church of Christ's richly endowed establishment on Broadway, and took part in get-togethers and expeditions organized by its youth group. For her sake, he even gave up Lubbock High's annual Prom, the dance where she would have been a scripturally enforced wallflower, instead escorting her to the banquet and entertainment which the Church of Christ provided as an alternative. Echo still has the frothy white 'formals' (evening gowns) she wore at two such functions.

Back at her family's old home in 1996, she demonstrates how she'd watch for Buddy from her bedroom window above the neat front garden with its white picket fence. He'd always come in, say 'Hello' to her parents and sit for a while on the ottoman that still stands among the antique vases and marble surfaces in Pansie McGuire's drawing-room. Then the two would set off together in Buddy's family car, bound for a football or basketball game, or a session at Lawson's roller-skating rink on College Avenue, near the Hi-D-Ho. Echo owned a horse, a mare named Gipsy, and Buddy and she would go riding together on the Texas Tech campus – which then, as now, encompassed large tracts of open countryside – or hike together in Palo Duro Canyon, a scenic area in the Texas Panhandle, south of Amarillo. Their relationship was easy, humorous, understanding, above all perfectly chaste. As Echo remembers now, 'Buddy didn't even kiss me until we'd been going together for a year.'

Even in his decorous wooing of Echo McGuire, the impudent and anarchic side of Buddy's nature was apt to break out. She remembers once accompanying him to a Tabernacle Baptist service, so much looser than the Church of Christ's with its music and informality. 'The Minister was asking for donations for missionary work and he looked at Buddy and said, "How about you, Buddy, will you give ten dollars?" Buddy said, "Do you think I'd be here if I had ten dollars?" I turned several shades of pink and almost crawled under the pew.'

The most illuminating glimpse of him as a sixteen-year-old, however, comes down to us in his own words. Early in 1953, his English class at Lubbock High was asked to write an essay entitled 'My Autobiography'. Buddy's effort (written on pages from a jotting-pad given out by the Morrow Thomas Hardware Co., Amarillo) is mainly a rueful inventory of his current academic and personal problems. However, it reveals in passing that his musical ambitions are already quite serious. There is also a whisper of the personality we recognize from his music – modest, unpretentious and confiding; doubtful about what the future will bring, but resolved to hope for the best:

... Little did I know what the last nine weeks of my sophomore year held in store for me. This will make the second time I have given my English theme for my test; I got kicked out of Plane Geometry class in the last week of school; I am behind with my Biology work and will probably fail every course I'm taking. At least that's the way I feel. But why quit there? I may as well go ahead and tell all. My father's out of town on a fishing trip, and he is really going to be proud of my latest accomplishments when he gets back. As of now I have these on the list. When I was driving our pickup Sunday afternoon against a hard wind, the hood came unfastened and blew up and now it's bent so that it won't fasten down good. Before I got home, I stopped at a boy's house and he knocked a baseball into the front glass, shattering it all over me. As if that wasn't enough, I had an appointment to apply for a job with a drafting firm yesterday afternoon and when my mother came after me, she let me drive on towards town. I had bought a picture of the choir and she was looking at it. She asked where I was, and I pointed to my picture. Just as I looked back up we hit the back of a Chrysler and tore the front end of our car up. So you see, I hope my father gets to catching so many fish that he will forget to come back for a little while.

Well, that's enough of bad things for a while. I have many hobbies. Some of these are hunting, fishing, leather-work, reading, painting and playing western music. I have thought of making a career out of western music if I am good enough but I will just have to wait and see how that turns out. I like drafting and have thought a lot about making it my life's work, but I guess everything will just have to wait and turn out for the best.

Well, that's my life to the present date, and though it may seem awful and full of calamities, I'd sure be in a bad shape without it.

It's hard to believe today, tuning one's car radio through teeming bands of steel guitars, violins and plaintive, Stetson-shaded voices, but in the mid-fifties America possessed not a single radio station devoted exclusively to country music. All it had were general music stations which might or might not feature country in their programming. Even deep down here in its Tennessee – Texas – Louisiana heartlands, country could seldom be heard for longer than a couple of hours each day, usually early in the morning to reach the farmers who were presumed to be its main audience. Hence the enormous interstate popularity of the two live radio jamborees, the *Grand Ole Opry* and the *Louisiana Hayride*. Nashville's WSM and Shreveport's KWKH were both 'clear channel' stations, well apart from their rivals on the radio-dial and supposedly audible for hundreds of miles. But the West Texas plains harboured iron deposits which interfered with radio reception: on Saturday evenings, Lubbock country fans had to cluster close around their crackling sets to catch the precious draughts of sentiment, jollity and togetherness.

Lubbock's station KSEL had always maintained the usual broad-banded policy of easy listening pop and talk. In 1953, its general manager and chief announcer was a genial man named Dave Pinkston, better known over the air as 'Pappy Dave Stone'. Although subject to the usual prejudice against country music from KSEL's owners and advertisers, Pappy Dave remained convinced of its commercial potential, and strove to give his listeners as much of it as possible. Under his aegis, KSEL acquired its own miniature *Grand Ole Opry*, the *Saturday-Night Jamboree*, with local country acts performing to a studio audience. Pappy Dave Stone found a willing ally in his assistant manager and co-star disc jockey, an immensely tall and long Levi-legged man, known, with impeccable Western logic, as 'Hi Pockets' Duncan. Hi Pockets both compèred the *Saturday-Night Jamboree* and did comic monologues as a hayseed character called 'Herkimer Torsnoff'.

KSEL had recently acquired another disc jockey, Ben Hall from Breconridge, Texas, a talented country singer and guitarist who played and sang on his own nightly record show. Early in 1953, Ben Hall heard that a licence for a new radio station in the Lubbock area was about to come up for grabs. Hall had long pined to see a station that would play country music exclusively, rather than shoehorning it in here and there. Unable to do anything himself on a deejay's salary, he persuaded Pappy Dave Stone to bid for the licence on the unprecedented basis of an all-country playlist. Pappy Dave – still alive today, and living on Kissing Camels Drive, Colorado Springs, Colorado – remembers the incredulous horror of the local businessman he approached to finance the enterprise. 'He said, "You mean every time I turn on this new station, I'm gonna hear a gitar plunkin'?" I said, "Yes, that's just what I mean!"'

The new station, KDAV, was established at the southern end of Quirt Avenue, a rural setting which allowed its founders to style its one-storey stone shoebox 'the KDAV Country Farm'. It went on the air in September 1953, transmitting in daytime hours only, 'sun-up to sundown', with programmes whose names richly reflect the combination of music, talk, homespun humour and worship: *Sunset Trading Post, Old Camp Meeting, Corral Club, Bethel Chapel, Easy the Janitor*. Both Hi Pockets Duncan and Ben Hall defected from KSEL to join the announcing staff. Pappy Dave Stone insists – and no one has ever come forward to contradict him – that this was America's first-ever all-country station.

One of KDAV's earliest attractions was an afternoon live music show called the *Sunday Party*, intended to showcase various local country singers and groups. Hi Pockets Duncan combined the roles of disc jockey, talent scout and entrepreneur, putting on shows in and around Lubbock with the object of finding performers good enough to broadcast on KDAV. In October, he ran across a lanky seventeen-year-old Lubbock High boy and a smaller, older partner, performing as 'Buddy and Jack'. Their playing impressed Hi Pockets sufficiently to include them in a show he was promoting out at the old glider aerodrome. There they acquitted themselves so well that Hi Pockets offered them a fifteen-minute (unpaid) slot on KDAV's *Sunday Party*. They made their début on 4 November 1953 with four numbers: 'Your Cheatin' Heart', 'Got You On My Mind', 'I Couldn't Keep From Crying' and 'I Hear The Lord Callin' For Me'.

That first appearance brought such favourable response from the station's fledgling audience that Pappy Dave Stone gave Buddy and Jack the half-hour *Sunday Party* spot to themselves, renaming it *Buddy and Jack's Sunday Party*. They performed in a tiny room, not much more than ten feet square, with their audience, twenty to thirty strong, watching them from the corridor through a glass partition. Many more people turned up to see the show than could be accommodated, and the overflow would sit outside in their cars, with radios tuned to the show going on a few feet away.

From now on, Buddy's classmates at Lubbock High were forced to regard him as something more than an amiable, forgettable nerd. He was a radio star, in the same firmament as Hank Snow, Ernest Tubb and other great strumming deities of the *Grand Ole Opry*. When he and Jack Neal arrived at KDAV each Sunday, they would find a pile of letters, requesting favourite numbers both from the standards they copied and the songs they had 'made up'. There would also be straight fanmail, albeit more often addressed to 'Jack and Buddy', and from people of their parents' generation. 'I think you boys are doing better each week. Keep up the good work ...' '... Jack has the best hillbilly voice with the most distinctive style that I have heard among local musicians ...' 'Buddy, tell your mother hello from me, Loretta ...'

For someone with Buddy's technical mind it was thrilling to be given virtual free run of a brand-new radio station, to sit in with Hi Pockets and Ben Hall as they did their work, observing the complexities of its desk controls, turntables and large-spooled professional tape-recorders. The most exciting discovery was that KDAV possessed facilities for converting the choicer items it put on tape into the more permanent form of a 78 rpm acetate disc. In other words, the station could double as a basic recording studio.

On 10 November 1953, less than a week after their début on the *Sunday Party*, Buddy and Jack paid KDAV a nominal couple of dollars to cut a double-sided acetate containing the spiritual 'I Hear The Lord Callin' For Me', and Jack Neal's song 'I Saw The

Moon Cry Last Night'. Jack (who hung on to the acetate, and possesses it to this day) remembers how ambition and determination kindled in his junior partner at their very first mild taste of celebrity. 'He often used to say after that: "Jack, it's that I want to be in the lamplight, it's not that I want to be rich. I just want the world to remember the name Buddy Holley."'

While performing with Jack Neal on KDAV, Buddy also kept up his partnership with his childhood friend and high school classmate, Bob Montgomery. Before long, Bob was invited to join *Buddy and Jack's Sunday Party*, as was another ex-J. T. Hutchinson boy named Don Guess, who could play both steel guitar and double bass, and whose triangular, shaggy-browed face was like that of a Steven Spielberg extra-terrestrial thirty years before its time. This larger group were known as the 580 Ranch Hands (580 being KDAV's spot on the radio-dial). Buddy took on the role of PR man, composing a two-page release in his painstaking capital letters, from his family's latest change of address, to be circulated among other local high schools that might offer the group an engagement:

DEAR SIR

WE ARE A GROUP OF HIGH SCHOOL BOYS THAT HAS
ORGANISED ONE OF THE LEADING HILLBILLY &
WESTERN BANDS IN LUBBOCK. WE ARE INTERESTED IN
HELPING NEIGHBORING HIGH SCHOOLS TO RAISE
FUNDS AND AT THE SAME TIME RAISE MONEY FOR US
TO PAY OUR WAY THROUGH COLLEGE.

I KNOW YOU WOULDN'T WANT TO LET JUST
ANYONE PLAY AT YOUR SCHOOL, SO IF YOU HAVE NOT
HEARD OF US, WE ARE THE 580 RANCH HANDS AND
BUDDY AND JACK, AND WE HAVE TWO RADIO
PROGRAMS EVERY SUNDAY AFTERNOON AT 3:15
O'CLOCK AND 3:30 O'CLOCK RESPECTIVELY. THE RADIO
STATION WE ARE ON IS KDAV (580 ON YOUR RADIO

DIAL). IF IT WOULD NOT BE ASKING TOO MUCH, WE
WOULD LIKE TO REQUEST YOUR LISTENING TO OUR
PROGRAMS AND SEE IF YOU LIKE US . . .

. . . I KNOW THAT IF YOUR SCHOOL IS LIKE OUR
SCHOOL, IT CAN ALWAYS USE SOME EXTRA MONEY. WE
HAVE HELPED QUITE A FEW SCHOOLS AROUND AUSTIN,
TEXAS, TO GATHER MONEY IN THIS WAY AND THEY
WERE QUITE SATISFIED WITH THE RESULTS. IF YOU
ARE AT ALL INTERESTED IN THIS, WE WOULD
APPRECIATE IT VERY MUCH IF YOU WOULD WRITE TO
ME, BUDDY HOLLEY

3204 1ST ST
LUBBOCK, TEXAS

At the time, the idol and role model of most teenage country
musicians in the Lubbock area was a fiddle-player named
Tommy Hancock, sometime owner of the Glasserama Club and
leader of a seven-piece Western Swing dance band, the Roadside
Playboys. Adding another junior schoolfriend, Larry Welborn,
KDAV's group changed their name to Don Guess and the
Rhythm Playboys. On 4 May 1954, temporarily minus Don
Guess, the Rhythm Playboys performed for the 'Distributive
Education class' at Brownfield High School. The contract for the
appearance has survived – a letter written in Buddy's careful,
long-tailed hand, confirming that their fee will be 50 per cent of
the evening's receipts.

Such paid engagements were rare. The far more usual thing
would be for someone to 'invite' them, and their instruments, to
a party or social where the only rewards, it was mutually
understood, would be soft drinks, cake and heartfelt appreciation. For Buddy, Bob, Jack, Larry and Don, the important thing
was being asked to perform. They would play anywhere – youth
clubs, church groups, school halls, in the boxing-ring at the
centre of Lawson's Skating Rink, or to swell the Saturday-

morning trade at food stores like Sewell's Country Market on East Broadway. Ever eager for an advertising tie-in, Pappy Dave Stone would send KDAV's outside broadcast truck to put them on the air 'live', competing for shoppers' attention with special offers on watermelon or hamburger.

For all its many-steepled piety and state of strict prohibition, there was a side to Lubbock as rowdy and boozy as anywhere on the West Texas frontier. With no legal liquor store nearer than Amarillo, 120 miles to the north, bootleggers did a roaring trade, shipping in beer by the illicit truckload or compounding lethal 'home-brew' in back-yard stills. The most famous local bootlegger was a man named 'Frenchy' who lived out on Slaton Highway in a cabin with a stuffed two-headed calf standing on its front porch. The city's music clubs – the Glasserama, the 16th and J, the Cotton Club – had a reputation for being the most violent for miles around. 'There's several reasons for that,' Tommy Hancock says. 'First, the liquor folks were drinking in those clubs was so raw and bad, and they had to drink it back real quick, thinking there might be a raid at any minute. And anyway, country music always does seem to get folks fighting worse than any other kind.'

As Buddy's group became better known, they began playing in clubs, even though all of them were too young to be on premises where liquor could be bought. 'The 16th and J booked us a lot of times,' Jack Neal remembers. 'It was a big barn of a place at Avenue J and 16th Street – I think it may have been a church some time before. Trouble there used to come just like a twister out on the plain. One minute it'd be quiet, the next there'd be bottles flying. We'd carry on playing and try to calm things down with our music. If we were playing a real jumpy number, we'd cut it to something more mellow like a two-step.'

Inevitably, the boys made their own experiments with the Falstaff bootleg beer which Frenchy sold at a dollar per quart bottle. Buddy downed his share, but never became the serious drinker that most self-respecting West Texans aspire to be. Since childhood, he had suffered mysterious stomach pains for which doctors could find no cause other than 'nerves', and which redoubled agonizingly if he over-indulged in alcohol or too-spicy food, like the ubiquitous Mexican tamales and taquitos. In common with almost every fifties teenager, he took up smoking at the earliest possible age, choosing Salem cigarettes from the myriad soft-pack brands available. Although L. O. Holley was a heavy cigarette smoker, as his gaunt frame betrayed, and brothers Larry and Travis both smoked pipes, Buddy was obliged to indulge the habit in elaborately underhand ways until he became legally entitled to smoke at eighteen. Even then, devout young Baptist that he was, he always took care never to do so in front of his parents or church minister and never, if he could help it, in photographs. Only in rare, unguarded shots can the Salem pack be seen in ghostly silhouette through the breast pocket of his crisp white shirt.

Six musicians and instruments proved ticklish to fit into Jack Neal's '47 Fleetline Chevrolet. Then, on Fenner Tubbs's used-car lot in Lubbock, Buddy and Jack spotted a more commodious vehicle. 'It was a '37 Packard hearse, two tone red and yellow,' Jack remembers. 'I had to persuade my Dad to stand guarantor if I traded in my Chevrolet, though he told me I was crazy to do it.

'We used that ol' hearse as a bandwagon and to take us on hunting-trips, too. One time, me and my Dad and Buddy were heading for Tahoka, Texas, to go duck-shooting, and by the side of the road we saw this dead cow with a coyote feasting on it. We turned right round and headed back, and Buddy took a blast at the coyote with the 4.10 shotgun he had. "Did you hit it?" my dad and I yelled. "Sure I hit it!" Buddy said, but I don't believe he did. The thing just gave a jump up in the air with the noise, and ran right off into the brush.'

Despite the burgeoning talent in their line-up, and their eye-catchingly macabre band-wagon, the Rhythm Playboys never did quite get off the ground. But Don Guess and Larry Welborn were to remain part of Buddy's intimate circle and, with Bob Montgomery, to accompany him to the lower foothills of fame.

In any case, no single group or partnership could satisfy the appetite he now had for performing. He had got to know Ben Hall, the dapper, dignified KDAV disc jockey and country singer, when Hall was new in town and still working at radio KSEL. Buddy admired Hall's musicianship and songwriting abilities, and often backed him onstage, together with his other teenage protégé, steel guitarist Weldon Myrick. Wherever a group found itself short of a musician, or invited volunteers for a jam session, he would be straight up there with his guitar slung over his starched sport shirt, and his unfailing snaggly grin of 'Don't mind if I do.' To take a random instance, 9 October 1954 found him and Bob Montgomery at the high school in Borger, Texas, still ostensibly preparing for their postgraduate commercial life by attending a chapter-meeting of the school's Vocational Industrial Club. The minutes record that entertainment was supplied by the Borger Metal Trades Hillbilly Band, with Buddy sitting in on guitar.

He had by now switched from acoustic guitar to his first solid-body electric model, a Gibson Les Paul Gold Top. It was a handsome instrument for a high school boy to possess; semi-cutaway, with an inlaid fretboard, studded with volume-knobs and bearing the signature of Les Paul himself, the great pioneer of electric guitar-playing and double-track recording. Buddy had always loved Paul's gentle, fluid 'talking guitar' style and the intimate close harmonies he sang with his wife, Mary Ford, and was to be greatly influenced by them when he began to make records of his own.

Around the time he got his Les Paul Gold Top, a kind of music very different from country, bluegrass and Western Swing began itching at Buddy's fingertips. But this was not one which could be played, or even talked about, to his family, his church elders or his grown-up fans at KDAV's *Sunday Party*. This was black people's blues music: the fatal mixture of pigments which in all correct white Southern minds still produced apoplectically purple contempt, revulsion and fear.

Since the 'race' and 'specialty' euphemisms of Buddy's prewar toddlerhood, black music had, in artistic terms at least, taken a major step forward. The postwar migration of rural Southern blacks to Northern industrial cities had produced a new version, very different from the 'country' blues of Robert Johnson and Blind Lemon Jefferson. Amended to 'rhythm 'n' blues', it hymned the racier pleasures and pressures of metropolitan life with crudely amplified guitars, braying saxophones and a driving drum-beat. It was performed by solitary voices no longer but by groups who, rather like city street-gangs, cultivated a unified personality and named themselves with eccentric and self-mocking collective nouns – the Drifters, the Moonglows, the Spiders.

From the beginning, 'R & B' had attracted a following among white teenagers who, on their side of the racial divide, had nothing more visceral to listen to than big bands and crooners. Nineteen fifty-four was the first year that America's mainstream music industry realized its dollar-earning potential. Formerly segregated artists, like Antoine 'Fats' Domino from New Orleans, and the Drifters with their sighing, twittering lead vocalist Clyde McPhatter, began to infiltrate the white airwaves and have hits on the white record-charts.

Buddy and his cronies were by then already long-time surreptitious listeners to R & B radio shows, beamed across the cotton-plains from stations far away in the teeming hothouse of southern Louisiana. To add to the sense of something forbidden and deviant, the disc jockeys who played R & B were generally not allowed on the air until late at night. Buddy's secret circle of addicts used to listen in one or other of their cars, partly to avoid parental interference and partly because a car-radio's DC frequency provided better reception of long-distance signals. 'You'd have to put the antenna right up,' Ben Hall remembers. 'Even then, the signal often used to fade, and you'd have to turn the car around to make it louder. You'd keep turning the car this way and that through the number, the way people today keep turning the portable aerials on their TV sets.'

Buddy loved R & B with its driving drumbeat, so unlike the restrained amble of country music, and the raucous electric guitar breaks constructed around chords and chiming pairs of strings rather than single notes. His great favourites were Hank Ballard and the Midnighters, a Chicago group who combined raunchily tongue-in-cheek songs about the same recurring character, 'Annie' ('Work With Me Annie'; 'Annie Had A Baby'; 'Annie's Aunt Fanny') with intoxicating 'half-chord' guitar-licks. He also had a taste for the hardcore urban blues of Muddy Waters, Elmore James and Howlin' Wolf, whose stylish plectrum-downstrokes served as a counterpoint to anger or mordant humour, and for Lonnie Johnson, whose voice was deceptively mild, and who picked guitar notes as soft as kittens' paws as he sang about syphilis, alcoholism and murder.

Many white teenagers in the American South during this period enjoyed black people's music in the abstract without feeling obliged to treat black people in the flesh as human beings on the same level as themselves. Buddy had grown up in a city of rampant and pettifogging segregation, most of whose Bible-quoting men and women would have felt physical nausea as well as moral outrage if ever compelled to share a lunch-counter, bus-seat or drinking-fountain with a black person. For all his mildness and tolerance in other directions, L. O. Holley was a man of his time and place, and might well have reconsidered the use of that double-thickness leather razor-strop had he ever learned what his youngest son was listening to after midnight.

With his usual impatience Buddy blanked out the social and

academic consequences of playing R & B music, and with his usual all-out thoroughness set about educating his voice and fingers in it by every possible means. On nights when he and his group were not playing country and bluegrass, he would lead them determinedly across Lubbock's racial frontier, to the ghetto-ized sector east of Avenue A. 'They had little cafés and joints over there, where Buddy loved to sit and listen,' Jack Neal remembers. 'Sometimes it'd just be someone's yard or front porch. There'd be one guy with a guitar, another with horn, and usually barbecue cookin' in a pit. You could get a sandwich for fifty cents.'

Inevitably, Buddy got talking to these amateur bluesmen, asking them about the chords and single-string licks they played. Under their good-humoured tutelage, the wispy, bespectacled white boy began to develop a guitar style as lean and aggressive as any to be heard around T-Bone or Leadbelly. Most importantly, he discovered that the language of music makes race irrelevant. From here on, Buddy Holley wanted no truck with Southern apartheid and, in his own way, would do much to chip away at its foundations. As an act of domestic subversion, he even named his cat after the black hero Booker T. Washington.

At the end of 1954, though himself still barely twenty, Jack Neal decided to get married. Faced with new grown-up responsibilities, he told Buddy regretfully he could no longer play on KDAV's *Sunday Party*. His place was taken by Bob Montgomery and bass-player Larry Welborn, though to preserve continuity the trio called itself 'Buddy and Bob'. 'Kay-dave' was by now so much a second home that they gave it as their address on their business cards.

The station was also important for the increasing role of its general manager, Pappy Dave Stone, and its star deejay, Ben Hall, as entrepreneurs and concert-promoters. From 1954 onwards, Stone and Hall put on regular country music spectaculars at Lubbock's Fair Park Coliseum, a covered arena recently purpose-built for the annual South Plains agricultural fair. They also developed close ties with the Cotton Club, an establishment which, atmospherically as well as geographically, was as far as could be imagined from its glamorous namesake in New York. The Lubbock Cotton Club was a place of no frills and little refinement; a 1,400-square-foot ex-military Quonset hut with an awesome reputation for bootleg boozing and brawling. Unlike Fair Park Coliseum, it lay outside the city limits and so could allow black and white spectators to mingle as equals. The two venues in tandem made Lubbock a worthwhile stopping-place for the major country stars and the multi-act tours promoted by the *Grand Ole Opry* in Nashville. On the north-westerly swing from Dallas to Amarillo or Albuquerque, everyone who was anyone could be guaranteed to pass through, sooner or later.

Through the good offices of Pappy Dave Stone, Buddy and Bob would get the opening spot on the country spectaculars which KDAV presented at Fair Park Coliseum and the Cotton Club. Their set might be brief and barely heeded, but at least it allowed them to mingle backstage with their country idols, like Ferlin Husky and Tommy Collins. Country music then had a tradition of informality, and the stars were usually accessible and friendly to the gawky Texan boys who plied them with questions about the music business. One who went out of his way to encourage and advise them was Marty Robbins, a rising talent still half a dozen years away from his cowboy classic, 'El Paso'. Robbins was much impressed by Buddy's singing and also by his skill at leatherwork. 'Buddy made Marty a billfold,' Larry Holly remembers. 'He liked it so much, he wrote saying, "Can you make me a hundred more to give away as gifts?"'

Every dollar Buddy and Bob earned from playing and from vacation jobs as carpenter's helpers with L. O. Holley was poured into financing demos of their songs, either at KDAV or at Nesmans Recording Studios at Wichita Falls, a drive of over 100 miles away. It was at Nesmans, for example, that they cut

'Flower Of My Heart', the song written by Bob for their high school 'Round-up', together with other tracks of a doleful cardiovascular nature: 'Door To My Heart', 'Soft Place In My Heart', 'I Gambled My Heart'.

Late in 1954, having long been their unofficial manager, Hi Pockets Duncan proposed that he should take on the job officially. As Pappy Dave Stone remembers, it was an offer inspired less by thoughts of personal gain than annoyance at the way the boys still often found themselves conned into playing for nothing or next to nothing. Buddy himself was so short of cash at Christmas time that he had to pay for his $11.70 high school class-ring (the one he hoped Echo McGuire would wear on a chain around her neck) in two instalments of $3.00 and $8.70. Every entrepreneur who ever takes on a group of teenage musicians claims to have only their interests at heart, but in Hi Pockets's case it was true. The contract he made with Buddy and Bob promised that if they ever became famous outside the Lubbock area, he would give up all managerial claim on them.

Although Jack Neal and Don Guess were no longer in the line-up, they continued to go around in a bunch with Buddy, Bob and Larry, sitting in on guitar and 'steel' respectively whenever the spirit moved them. By the year's end, this same easy companionability had turned the duo-named trio into a quartet. The new recruit was Sonny Curtis, a farmer's son from Meadow, a few miles north of Lubbock, who brought with him impressive talents and antecedents. Two of his uncles had formed the Mayfield Brothers, a well-known bluegrass act, and one in addition had played with the revered Bill Monroe's Blue Grass Boys. Though two years Buddy's junior, Sonny was proficient on violin and guitar, a good singer and an aspiring songwriter, and possessed the almost unheard of distinction of having appeared on local television.

A mutual friend arranged for him to come in to Lubbock and meet Bob Montgomery. 'I sat waiting in Bob's folks' place, the Gin Café – I remember, it was kind of a cloudy, sand-stormy afternoon. Bob arrived home on the school bus, then we got in the car and went straight over to Buddy's house. We skipped all the small talk, took our instruments out and got right to playing. I was accepted into the group right there and then.

'At that time, they were still playing mostly bluegrass. Buddy had a banjo – a four-string, not the five-string that bluegrass people use – and he played the mandolin some, too. With him and Bob, it was like playing cowboys and Indians, seeing which one of them could pick faster, Buddy trying to be Earl Scruggs and Bob trying to be Lester Flatt.' But when Buddy switched to guitar, Sonny noticed a different style altogether, infused with the blues and R & B influence he had been absorbing through every pore. 'I was getting into jazz at that time. I was studying under a jazz guitarist and learning real difficult chords. But Buddy wasn't too interested in chords. He cared more about the feel of it.'

The first gig Sonny played with them was at a school near Austin, where Bob Montgomery's uncle was superintendent. Bob's mother drove them all down in her open pick-up with one riding alongside her, the other four lounging on a mattress spread in the back.

Sonny, too, loved black music, and soon became a confederate in Buddy's secret listening sessions. Their favourite source was KWKH in Shreveport, the *Louisiana Hayride* station which after dark changed character as radically as Jekyll into Hyde, putting out a blues and R & B show sponsored by Stan's Record Shop and hosted by a black-sounding white deejay named Frank 'Gatemouth' Page. 'He didn't come on until midnight,' Sonny remembers. 'So I'd go to Buddy's house to spend the night, and at midnight we'd creep out into the drive, get into his folks' car, turn on the radio, sit back in the front seat and listen ... to Elmore James ... Howlin' Wolf ... Lonnie Johnson. Boy, was he terrific!'

Sprawling back on the leatherette bench with the churchy stillness of Lubbock all around them, and those hot, angry, hilarious sounds pouring from the dashboard's glimmer into their bloodstream, Buddy and Sonny would be torn between bliss and despair. For there seemed no way on earth that two white boys could get to be a part of such music.

Towards the end of 1954, together with other radio stations throughout the South-west, KDAV–Lubbock received a new single from a small record-label in Memphis, Tennessee, offering an elixir which none before had ever dared concoct. One side was a country song, 'Blue Moon Of Kentucky', written by the bluegrass giant Bill Monroe; the other was a R & B song, Arthur 'Big Boy' Crudup's 'That's All Right, Mama'. The big, breakable 78 rpm disc bore a label decorated with the two-tone rays of a rising sun; the name on it was 'Elvis Presley'.

It was clearly meant to be country music, otherwise why would it have been sent to KDAV? But the voice was like none ever heard in country: not measured and melodious but urgent and breathless, high where it should be low, low when it should be high, hitting notes sideways instead of dead straight-on, reducing one of country's most sacred images to an insistent, almost clownish mumble of 'Blue moon, blue moon, blue moon ...' It was in short, and unbelievably, somebody white singing in the style of somebody black.

Elvis at that point was not yet twenty, a year and three-quarters older than Buddy. Although he hailed from an exotically distant and different city and state, his background was similar to Buddy's in several essential respects. Born in Tupelo, Mississippi, the son of poor migrants, Elvis too had been brought up within a devout fundamentalist sect, the First Assembly of God, and had been performing in public since early childhood. The great edge he possessed was having grown up in Memphis, a city which is to urban blues what New Orleans is to jazz, and one whose more relaxed interracial atmosphere allowed a white boy open access to its famous music quarter, Beale Street. He had been spotted by Sun Records as an eighteen-year-old-truck-driver, using the studio's record-your-voice booth to sing a birthday greeting to his mother. To his first professional session he brought the phrasing and body-language he had absorbed first from black gospel choirs, then from Beale Street's R & B dives. Sun's boss, Sam Phillips, was prescient enough to let the kid do it his way.

Combustible as this stylistic cocktail was, it did not make Elvis notorious overnight. Quite the contrary, he made his initial impact on the middle-aged country music audience who accepted him as one of their faction, reassured by the endorsement of radio stations like KDAV. Though the phrase 'rock 'n' roll' did exist by then, it was not even mentioned around Elvis at the very beginning. Billed, with deliberate imprecision, as the 'Hillbilly Cat' or the 'King of Western Bop', he toured in conventional country spectaculars and appeared on the *Louisiana Hayride*.

Thanks to their friendship with KDAV's Ben Hall, Buddy and his group received an early preview of Elvis's début record. 'Buddy loved this new sound, like we all did,' Hall remembers. 'But it was mysterious to us. All we had was this name, "Elvis Presley". We had no idea where he came from or what he looked like.'

They found out on 2 January 1955, when Elvis appeared in a country music show promoted by KDAV at Fair Park Coliseum. Buddy was still two weeks away from being prescribed his first pair of glasses, but even his unassisted 20/800 vision could not miss the moment when the 'Hillbilly Cat' first exploded on to the stage. Forty years on, Sonny Curtis can still picture the dazzling vision. 'He had on an orange sport coat, red pants, white bucks. Tell you what boy, he looked like a motorsickle headlight comin' right at you!'

The Texan boys, with their neat poplin shirts and pressed blue jeans, sat mesmerized by this performer in brilliant Technicolor whose every song tore down the immemorial law and custom of country music, and trampled it under white buckskin shoes. Instead of staying rooted to centre stage, as even Hank Williams always had, the Hillbilly Cat bobbed and ducked and wove continually, twisting his midriff, buckling at the knees, flinging out his arms and jerking his head so that a spray of his over-long oily hair flopped over his pale, sullen face. Instead of 'picking' the respectable country guitar slung around his neck, he beat on it with his hands, spun it by the fretboard or pushed it contemptuously behind his back; instead of articulating the words that respectable country fans hungered to hear, he mumbled and slurred them with almost drunken irreverence; instead of smiling cordially upon all ages, he grimaced, glared, pouted, sneered, smirked and smouldered in a manner that did not spell 'barnyard' half so eloquently as it spelt 'bedroom'.

If the Texans had initially felt disposed to laugh at this extraordinary burlesque, their minds were soon changed by the sheer wicked joy of the music, and also by something even more alien to normal country music practice. While the grown-up portion of the audience watched in speechless horror, the normally undifferentiated teenage portion reacted with roaring delight, the girls in particular forgetting the starchy decorum required of a mid-fifties Southern miss, and bouncing up and down in their seats, screaming in the strangest mixture of pleasure and anguish.

From that moment on, Buddy's group abandoned bluegrass music and adopted a role model very different from Lester Flatt or even Earl Scruggs. 'The day after Elvis left town, we turned into Elvis clones,' Sonny Curtis says. 'And we was bookin' out as an Elvis band.'

It helped to have a leader with a draughtsman's eye which could instantly render down the new style to its essential blueprint. Elvis camouflaged himself within a traditional country trio, backed only by a lead guitarist, Scotty Moore, and a stand-up bass-player, Bill Black; as yet even he had not dared include the giveaway R & B touch of a drummer. In total contrast with the vocalist's unbridled lunacy, Scotty Moore played an angular and stylish guitar riff invented by the doyen of country pickers, Chet Atkins: starting as an upward slide along the thickest bass string, it then leapt crossways to make pairs of treble notes swing and knock against each other like windchimes. And Bill Black did not pluck his bass fiddle in the usual discreetly muffled way, but belaboured it with a foreground-grabbing 'thunk-thunk-thunk' or slapped the amazed old spinster silhouette percussively with the flat of his hand.

So Sonny Curtis put his fiddle aside, took up his big Martin D-28 acoustic guitar and mastered the Scotty Moore riff. Don Guess gave up steel guitar and played 'slap bass' in the Bill Black style. As for Buddy himself, the transformation was as complete, and astonishing, as chrysalis into butterfly. Sonny Curtis remembers how his singing voice seemed to change in an instant, soaring from the drab husk of that restrained, even rather self-conscious country 'tenor'; initially just copying the Hillbilly Cat's tricks of intonation and phrasing but soon lighting on a variety that were all his own. Physically, too, his stage presence was transformed. 'Buddy had never moved around much up till then,' Sonny remembers. 'In country, you just stood still and did your thing. But after seeing Elvis, there was no holding him. Soon as he picked up a guitar, he was way out front and all over the place.'

On 13 February, yet another country music spectacular played Fair Park Coliseum with the 'Hillbilly Cat' half-buried in its bill. The day was a Sunday, the show began, promptly, at 4pm, and this time the local group who opened for the out-of-towners were Buddy and Bob. KDAV's Ben Hall had just bought an 8 mm movie camera which he tried out by filming the performers in their communal dressing-room. Here is the first-ever movie sequence of Elvis, the famous features poignantly carefree and unused, laughing and joshing with his two avuncular sidemen, Scotty and Bill. Over here, a little apart, not wishing to intrude but tickled pink to be there, are the Texas boys: Buddy in his half-frame glasses, a smart blue sport coat and matching shawl-collar shirt; beside him the rubicund Sonny Curtis and the ET-faced Don Guess.

'When we saw the way Elvis was onstage, we couldn't imagine what he'd be like as a person,' Sonny Curtis says. 'But he was real nice and quiet and unpretentious, just sitting by himself with a Coke.' After the show, its country headliners were besieged by autograph-hunting fans, but Elvis could still leave via the front entrance, bothered by no one.

Over the next nine months he returned to Lubbock several times more, and always that reverent posse of Texan boys would never be far away. When he appeared at the Cotton Club on 29 April, they had to be content with seats in the audience, but when he returned to Fair Park Coliseum on 3 June, Buddy's group once more were the warm-up act. They had done the same earlier that same evening for Elvis's (unpaid) appearance on the back of a flatbed truck at the gala opening of the Johnson-Connelly Pontiac car showroom at Main Street and Avenue O. Before long, they were on friendly enough terms to be driving Elvis around Lubbock on a tour of what interesting sights the city could offer. Buddy's boyhood crony Jack Neal, who also went along, remembers that Elvis had nothing special to do afterwards, so they invited him to the movies. They all trooped off to the Lindsay theatre together to see *Gentlemen Prefer Blondes*, starring Marilyn Monroe and Jane Russell.

According to Larry Holley, Elvis had been so lonely on the night of his first Lubbock appearance that Buddy volunteered to find him a date. 'It was just someone to go around with,' Larry stresses. 'Buddy wasn't fixing him up or anything.' However, it is recorded that the girl in question accompanied Elvis to his next gig, in Odessa, Texas. Now in her fifties, and still living in Lubbock, she has always firmly declined to reminisce about the matter.

Elvis expressed friendly enthusiasm for Buddy and Bob's music, and promised to use his influence to get them a booking on the *Louisiana Hayride*. Taking him at his word, they all piled into Buddy's parents' car, a Hudson Hornet, and drove the 1,000 miles to Shreveport, expecting to be welcomed with open arms. But on their arriving at the *Hayride* studio, they were told Elvis was out on tour again, and the show's producer hadn't even heard of them. As Bob Montgomery recalls, 'We couldn't even get through the door.'

All this time, Buddy was still a senior at Lubbock High School and – in theory at least – studying hard to complete the courses necessary for his graduation the following May. He was also still going steady with Echo McGuire, the five-foot-nothing beauty whose surname adorned Lubbock's principal drive-in dry-cleaning establishment. Though Echo preferred not to wear his class-ring round her neck in time-honoured style, there was no doubt about the depth of their relationship. A gifted seam-stress, she tailored shirts for Buddy to co-ordinate with her dresses; he had made a Western belt to encircle her twenty-four-inch waist with 'Echo' printed on the back; one of his Western boots bore the initials 'BH', the other 'EM'. After their joint graduation from Lubbock High, they planned to marry; indeed, they seemed so happily engrossed in one another that some of their friends suspected they might already have become secretly engaged.

Buddy loved Echo deeply and devotedly, and strove with all his might to live up to her high ideals and devout religious convictions. As their relationship had deepened and his fascina-tion with rockabilly music intensified, he had found himself increasingly leading an almost schizophrenic double life of bootleg liquor and boogie with Bob, Larry and Sonny by night and devoutness and teetotalism by day with Echo. About this time there occurred another of the periodic moves by local businessmen to put an end to Prohibition in Lubbock. Buddy and Echo were among a group of Christian students who went around collecting signatures with a petition – successful, as it turned out – to keep their city 'dry'.

Echo loved Buddy just as much as he loved her, and was more than ready to brave the displeasure of her church for even contemplating 'marriage out' to a Tabernacle Baptist. But of late the serious-minded young woman had begun to worry about just what kind of married life she could expect with Buddy, she whose inflexible religion forbade her even to dance. As her mother, Pansie McGuire, recalls: 'She said, "I can't go with him into those clubs, Mother, and I don't want to spend half my life sitting at home and waiting for him."'

In mid-1955, Elvis threw away the last remaining figleaf of country music by adding a drummer, D. J. Fontana, to his back-up band. Among *Grand Ole Opry* and *Louisiana Hayride* purists, the outrage was roughly comparable to a modern rock star's being exposed as a child-molester. And in Lubbock, Texas, the former Hillbilly Cat's faithful acolytes, sight-seeing guides and movie companions once again followed the revolutionary blueprint to the letter.

The only possible drummer for the Buddy and Bob trio was sixteen-year-old Jerry Ivan Allison – even then known to his friends with orotund Southern formality as 'J.I.' – whom Buddy had first met at J. T. Hutchinson junior high. Slightly built, with the triangular face and slant-eyes of a Burmese tom-cat, J.I. was two years Buddy's junior but so academically bright as to be only just behind him at Lubbock High. Since their first school-yard encounters he had developed into a gifted percussionist and was currently undisputed star of a country group named Cal Wayne and the Riverside Ranch-hands, with whom Buddy sometimes sat in at dives like the 16th and J Club.

J. I. Allison and his drums were on board when Buddy, Bob Montgomery and Larry Welborn returned to cut more demo records, at their own expense, at Nesman's Wichita Falls studios during the late spring of 1955. They came away with two tracks, Elvis Presley's 'Let's Play House', and a number called 'Down The Line' which Bob had composed in his head while driving to see his girlfriend in Albuquerque. Listened to with hindsight, it is very much R & B in bluegrass style, with still traditional close-harmony voices taking turns in its frantic 'Go! go! go!' refrain. But Buddy's guitar solo is a straight 'lift' from a new record at the top of the charts, Bill Haley's 'Rock Around The Clock'.

Hi Pockets Duncan, their long-legged saint of a manager, had recently taken a furlough from KDAV to try his hand at running a Western Swing hotspot called the Clover Club just outside Amarillo. The Clover Club thus became a regular gig for Buddy and Bob as well as somewhere they could always find a free meal and words of encouragement in Hi Pockets' reassuring deep-velvet drawl.

Whatever Buddy's parents thought about his sudden aban-donment of country music, they too remained tirelessly suppor-tive. The Holleys' home was always open to his friends as a rehearsal room, flophouse, free café and now, too, as a permanent parking-bay for J. I. Allison's drums. When L. O. Holley bought a new car, a black-and-white '55 Oldsmobile, he virtually gave it to Buddy's group as a band-wagon on condition that Buddy helped keep up the payments. Around this time, his doting mother wrote proudly to a friend that he was now giving several shows per week in the Lubbock area, as well as continuing to appear on KDAV's *Sunday Party*, and sometimes shared as much as $40 per appearance with his three sidemen. However late he rolled home in the Olds, Ella would always be waiting up for him with peanut butter sandwiches and milk, and his cat Booker T. Washington on her lap, avid to hear everything about the night's gig and how well he had 'gone over'.

His elder brother Larry, the member of the family who knew him best, happened to be off on a three-month tiling job in Arizona during this whole period of conversion to rock 'n' roll. When Larry returned home he was amazed to see what a great leap Buddy had made, both in musicianship and self-confidence.

'I had gotten a contract to work on a new school here in Lubbock, and I had to go down to San Angelo to pick up a load of tiles. I rented this big eighteen-wheeler flatbed truck to carry 'em in, and took Buddy along with me. I'd never driven a rig that big, and I had to learn how on the way. Buddy drove it some, too. He'd never chicken out of anything I was going to do.

'We got to San Angelo too late in the day to pick up the tiles, so we went into this place to get a hamburger. We thought it was a diner, but it was really more of a coloured joint. It was the deadest little old place you ever seen, and in the corner of it there was a black combo getting ready to play that evening. Buddy got to watching them real intently, then he went up and started talking to 'em, and of course they could tell he was a musician 'cause he knew their lingo. So these guys said, 'Hey man, how about playing us a number?' and Buddy, who'd been dying to, says, "Don't mind if I do!"

'Well, he picked up that guitar and hit the chords, and it made a clean sound, like it was a different instrument. He played 'em that song "Sexy Ways", that he'd heard Hank Ballard do. While he's playing, people start crowding round him, and I see the owner get on the phone, and then more and more people start coming in. Suddenly little old joint isn't dead any more. Buddy made the whole place came alive!

'Then I saw him again in a thing they called 'the Battle of the Bands' at the Tower Theater here in town. I was way at the back, and there was a bunch of crazy kids in front of me, shouting and yelling and stepping on paper cups to pop 'em. There'd been a lot of real good-looking singers up on that stage and when it was Buddy's turn to come on, all these kids started laughing at him and yellin' out things at him, like "Ol' Turkey-neck!" I was starting to get real aggravated about it all. But Buddy came from the side of the stage to the middle in one movement without seeming to move his feet at all, and hit his guitar, and right away that whole crowd went hog-wild.'

On 27 May, the Lubbock High School Class of '55 lined up in their gowns and mortar-boards to receive their graduation scrolls. Buddy was among them, albeit only by the skin of his teeth. A month earlier the school principal, Floyd Honey, had written to L. O. Holley warning that his son might not qualify for graduation owing to consistently poor marks in solid geometry. So, for a few nights at least, the Les Paul Gold Top had to be put aside in favour of set-squares, protractors and compasses.

That spring was a customarily brilliant and busy one in an America where every day still represented another measurable step towards perfection. The United States Supreme Court had just ordered the Southern states to end racial segregation, although omitting to specify a date when this should come to pass. The Salk vaccine had been pronounced effective against polio, so removing another deadly disease from the ever-shortening list. In movie houses across the continent, audiences sat transfixed behind their parti-coloured red and green '3-D' glasses, periodically ducking to avoid the express trains, Grand Prix cars and Apache tomahawks that seemed to fly out of the screen into their faces. Ike was in his White House, Ricky loved Lucy, a dollar was a dollar and Pepsodent toothpaste made you wonder where the yellow went. To be sure, in the whole Vista-

Vision expanse of progress, stability, enlightenment and shiny chronium plating, the only unsightly blot was this thing called rock 'n' roll.

Though horrifically novel and unspecific to adult whites, the term had of course been familiar for years within America's parallel black culture. From earliest blues days the twin verbs to 'rock' and 'roll' had meant to dance, have sex or enjoy oneself uninhibitedly. Postwar R & B had teemed with double-entendre invocations of one or the other, from Roy Brown's 'Good Rockin' Tonight' to Big Joe Turner's 'Shake, Rattle And Roll'. The first tautologous coupling of the two is generally agreed to have taken place in 1952: Alan Freed, a white disc jockey on station WJW in Cleveland, Ohio, realized that as many white teenagers as black were listening to the R & B music he played and, to banish racial distinction from his late night show, renamed it *Moondog's Rock 'n' Roll Party*.

Its evolution into a music, and a movement, began a year earlier, when a country musician named Bill Haley, from Chester, Pennsylvania, had a minor hit with an R & B-flavoured song called 'Rock The Joint'. For all his respectable, podgy whiteness, Haley sang with the humorous ebullience usually found only in black performers; for a time, indeed, his record company encouraged the misconception by issuing no publicity photographs of him. In 1955, his song 'Rock Around The Clock', already once released, was used on the soundtrack of *The Blackboard Jungle*, a film about delinquent teenage pupils at a big city high school. Its raucous speaking clock of a theme tune produced uproar among teenagers wherever *The Blackboard Jungle* was shown: from all over America – and, subsequently, Europe – came reports of demented screaming, wild cavorting in the aisles and wanton vandalism of seats. 'Rock Around The Clock' stayed at number 1 in the American charts for twenty-two weeks and Bill Haley and his group, the Comets, were rocketed to international stardom. Thus did the term 'rock 'n' roll' achieve wide currency, linked – as it would prove, irredeemably – with visions of adolescent rebellion and riot.

This initial phase, from mid-1955 to early 1956, can be classified as rock 'n' roll's Phoney War. Hysterical outbreaks of juvenile fan-worship might be distasteful but they were hardly new, having occurred in the twenties over silent movie stars like Rudolf Valentino and in the forties over crooners like Frank Sinatra. Against such sex-saturated icons, Bill Haley cut an unthreatening figure with his chubby cheeks, receding hairline and query-shaped kiss-curl. The general adult view was that, like sheikh movies and swing before it, rock 'n' roll was a fad which would quickly pass.

Throughout that first year, Bill Haley and the Comets were the only visible white rock 'n' roll stars. The rest were mainly R & B performers, like Fats Domino and Johnny Otis, who had honed their styles for years around the blacks-only 'Chittlin' Circuit', and now for the first time tasted the heady mixture of white audiences and serious money. In the R & B tradition, there were also vocal groups: the silky-voiced Platters, the multi-harmonizing Penguins, whose 'Earth Angel' had sold 2 million copies by the beginning of 1955. From New York came the Teenagers, fronted by a vivacious boy soprano named Frankie Lymon, and, from the Chess label in Chicago, a spindle-shanked young man named Chuck Berry – sometimes alternatively known as 'Berryn' – who sported a thin moustache like a 1930s tango champion, played a cherry-red guitar down around his knees and sang about the real life of attending high school, dating girls and driving cars with a clear enunciation and darting wit not heard in black music since the days of Louis Jordan. From the wash-up of a Georgia bus station came a youth baptized Richard Penniman but known since infancy as Little Richard; a wild-haired, wide-eyed, drape-suited whirling dervish whose shriek of 'Awopbopaloobopalopbamboom!' would take the new culture to its delicious, drivelling apotheosis.

As jukeboxes blared, new employment spread, profit margins quintupled and factories and pressing-plants worked overtime, the moral debate continued to rage. Young performers who, to a man (for they were all men), had been raised by devout Christian families and learned their first performance skills in church were denounced from pulpit and pamphlet as emissaries of the Devil. In particular, the spectacle of such as Little Richard, Chuck Berry, Bo Diddley and Fats Domino wearing good clothes, driving expensive cars and being treated as heroes by white boys and girls caused anguish below the Mason–Dixon Line. As one typical *ad hoc* moral guardian, the North Alabama White Citizens Council, noted of rock 'n' roll with quivering, quasi-literate disgust: 'It is sexualistic, unmoralistic, and brings people of both races together.'

'NOTICE! STOP!' ran another leaflet distributed to restaurants and stores throughout the South. 'Help save the Youth of America. Don't buy Negro records. If you don't want to serve Negroes in your place of business, then don't have Negro records on your jukebox or listen to Negro records on the radio. The screaming, idiotic words and savage music of these records are undermining the morals of our white youth in America. Call the advertisers on radio stations that play this type of music and complain to them ...' Black rock 'n' roll stars on tour in the South routinely faced the affront of segregated theatre audiences; in many cities, white and black musicians were not to share the same bill; hotels, motels and restaurants could with impunity refuse service to people of the wrong skin colour. Had it not been for the rapid rise of the fast food outlet in this era, there would often have been nowhere for them to get a meal on the road.

The piety and conservatism of Lubbock had not inhibited its two radio stations from swiftly moving with the times. KDAV was now the Elvis Presley station, proud of its role in bringing the Hillbilly Cat to West Texas. Despite having alienated the pure country music audience, Elvis was still not classified as a rock 'n' roll artist. Yet another new term, 'rockabilly', had been welded from 'rock' and 'hillbilly' to keep him in the approximate domain of hay-bales and hoedowns. The same term defined the other young white performers now following Elvis from the Memphis Sun label – Carl Perkins, Johnny Cash, even a recruit from Wink, West Texas, named Roy Orbison. KDAV's arch-rival KSEL, by contrast, had moved from easy-listening pop to all-out rock 'n' roll, spiced by hardcore blues and R & B. It also had acquired a formidable new weapon in the airwaves-war: a hotshot teenage disc jockey named Jerry Coleman whose Hi-D-Ho Hit Parade, sponsored by Lubbock teenagers' favourite drive-in ('Don't just say "Hello", say "Hi-D-Ho"'), went out between nine and eleven every night.

Jerry Coleman became aware of Buddy Holley as 'a real ugly young guy in glasses' who was infatuated with R & B stars like the Drifters and Smiley Lewis, and loved to hang out at KSEL, when he wasn't performing over at KDAV, watching the hyper-active 'Jerry-bo' at work. 'I'd put him on the air sometimes, talking about the records I was playing,' Coleman remembers. 'And I'd go see the group play at the Cotton Club. Boy, that place was rougher 'n a stucco bath-tub. That was the kind of place where they'd stab you goodnight! At six o'clock, you'd see the bouncers wrapping gauze around their hands so as not to injure them when they started hitting folks. One time, two bouncers had a fight, and one of them bit off the other one's ear!'

Graduation from Lubbock High, which should have been an exciting threshold, instead seemed to have left Buddy in limbo. Despite all that assiduous wooing of local employers through ITC's Chapter 95, he had not, after all, found a well-paid white-collar job in the drawing-office of some local company like Panhandle Steel. Nor had he carried out his second long-nurtured life-plan, that of going straight from graduation ceremony to church, to marry his childhood sweetheart, Echo McGuire. Thanks to the combination of her academic record and high spiritual seriousness, Echo had won a place at the Christian University in Abilene, 100 miles east of Lubbock. Buddy and Echo were still pledged to one another, and kept constantly in touch. But, as his family – especially his mother – noticed, a light seemed to have gone out of Buddy's life.

During that first rock 'n' roll summer, with Echo in Abilene and his classmates dispersed to college, traineeships or the armed forces, the only conventional work Buddy could find was as a casual builder's labourer. Between tiling jobs, his elder brother Larry was building the house on 17th St, West Lubbock, which he occupies to this day. Buddy spent most of the sweltering June days stripped to the waist, digging out foundations for Larry's storm cellar and helping to lay the tile floor in the front hall.

His KDAV mentor Pappy Dave Stone was now bringing black rock 'n' roll acts to Lubbock – not to Fair Park Coliseum, where the city's segregation laws would have caused difficulties, but to the geographically immune Cotton Club. Buddy was there with J. I. Allison or Sonny Curtis every Saturday night as the rackety stage, with its fringe of coloured fairground lights, revealed yet another magical presence, once available only via car-radios after midnight: Fats Domino with his gently rolling bulk and tiny Oriental face; Ivory Joe Hunter, a dignified man of forty-one, bemused at suddenly finding himself a teenagers' icon. For Buddy the greatest excitement of all was seeing Little Richard swagger out with his baggy suit and wild Medusa mop, and have to do nothing but open his Clara Bow lips to unleash ear-shattering, heavenly mayhem.

Offstage, he was just as spectacularly outrageous, garlanded with chunky gold jewellery, reeking of scent and comporting himself in a manner for which the term 'screaming camp' had yet to be invented. This concatenation of all the South's most hated taboos, blackness, effeminacy and rock 'n' roll, made Richard a prey to constant official persecution and harassment. His début appearance at the Cotton Club was brought to a premature halt by Lubbock's police department on the excuse that it was causing fights outside. In Amarillo the previous night, he had been arrested for 'vagrancy', despite having $1,200 in cash in his suitcase. In El Paso the following night he would be arrested again, this time for failure to carry his military draft-card.

Meeting Richard in the Cotton Club's backstage mêlée, Buddy was captivated – as many others would be – by the self-knowing wit which leavened his preposterous vanity and promiscuity. At this point in his career, he travelled with a stripper named Lee Angel, whose bust measured fifty inches and whom he encouraged to have sex with any of his fellow performers who fancied her. He also freely admitted being attracted to men, and boasted of his ability to masturbate 'seven or eight times each day'. As for his conversation, an ear-assaulting, almost schizophrenic mixture of the sacred and profane, well might Richard himself affirm that while other young men may have 'majored in math' at high school, he 'majored in mouth'.

Buddy was to spend many hilarious hours in his company and, after a later Cotton Club gig, invited him home to dinner, blissfully unmindful of L. O. Holley's inevitable reaction. 'When Buddy's Daddy saw who his son had brought home, he wouldn't let me in,' Little Richard writes in his memoirs. 'But Buddy told his Daddy "If you don't let Richard in, I'll never come back to this house again." So they let me in but they weren't very happy. I'll bet they washed them dishes I ate off about twenty times after we'd gone." Ella Holley later confirmed that L.O. truly had been reluctant to admit Richard to their home and that, as a compromise, dinner was a barbecue in the back yard.

Buddy's summer of marking time coincided with J. I. Allison's high school vacation and the two began spending long hours together, J.I. to some degree filling the void left by Echo. As well as rock 'n' roll, Buddy and he had every taste in common

– cars, motorcycles, hunting, guns. J.I. had a lazily humorous wit
and love of wordplay that appealed to Buddy; despite his squat
build and poor complexion, he was also enviably successful with
girls. Apart from rehearsing with the group still called Buddy
and Bob, they spent hours practising as a duo at each other's
houses, Buddy singing and playing rhythm and lead guitar
together, J.I.'s energetic drum-sticks filling in every other crack.
'They were *the* perfect combination,' remembers a fellow
musician who'd known Buddy since Sunday School days. 'Just
the two of them could make a bigger and better sound than my
whole five-piece band.'

J. I. Allison was more than willing to kick against authority
wherever it might raise its head. But for all Buddy's seeming
quietness and shyness, he could be rash and reckless in a way
that even J.I. sometimes found alarming. Such was his blithe
disregard of traffic-tickets that at one point, in late 1954, the
City of Lubbock was at the point of issuing a warrant for his
arrest. A classic Buddy toe-curler occurred when he was driving
the band to a gig at the South Plains Fair, the annual showcase
for local agriculture and industry. 'A cop pulled us over for
speeding,' J. I. Allison later remembered. 'If it'd been me, I'd
have said, "Sorry, sir, won't do it again . . ." But Buddy gets real
argumentative with this cop, like, "Hey, I'm on my way to do
something that's going to benefit this county, and now you want
to give me a ticket . . ." '

Like many teenage boys, he went through a phase of aggress-
iveness towards his parents, so much so his brother Larry had to
take him aside and say, 'They're my parents, too, and I don't
think you should talk to them that way.' With most adolescents,
such an elder-brotherly dressing-down would have been
counter-productive. But Buddy was mortified to think he'd
upset L.O. and Ella, and vowed to be nicer in future.

J.I. discovered, too, that despite his outward good nature and
love of laughter, Buddy had a dark and strange and unknowable

side. In the middle of the most enjoyable get-together with his cronies he would suddenly get up and, without a word to anyone, go out to the family Oldsmobile and drive away. Next day, when the others saw him, he would be back to his old genial, easygoing self; if they asked where he'd been, he just grinned and said, 'For a drive.' In fact, he might have gone hundreds of miles alone to Dallas or Carlsbad, New Mexico, non-stop and often through the night.

They knew he was missing Echo, worrying about what handsome young Christians she would be meeting in Abilene, struggling to reconcile his ambitions in music with being the kind of person she required as a husband. That winter of 1955, she gave him a copy of a currently celebrated religious novel, inscribing it in a way which left no doubt about her faith in his deeper spiritual qualities: 'Dearest Buddy, I hope you will receive as much inspiration from this book as I have. I also hope it will help you to see things more clearly after carefully reading it and comparing it with your Bible. Love always, Echo.' The book had a title that now seems horribly prophetic: *Must the Young Die, Too?*

But at nights, as Buddy was pounding his Les Paul Gold Top in some club or hall outside Lubbock's ring of godliness, Abilene and Echo could seem very far away. He had discovered with incredulity how rock 'n' roll banished his physical shortcomings in the eyes of the opposite sex; how his scrawny build, his too-curly hair, his 'West Texas teeth', even the hated half-frame glasses, all were instantly magicked away as soon as he leapt onstage and started giving out like Elvis or Little Richard. Girls screamed for him just as loudly as they did for the out-of-town rock 'n' rollers and, after every show, clustered around him in equal numbers, ready and willing for any late-night adventures he might suggest. 'Buddy was sure no little plaster saint like people try to make out,' his deejay friend Jerry Coleman remembers. 'He was an average hard-on good ol' American boy.

He liked pussy as much as any other guy his age. He ran his traps, the same way all of us did.'

Little as might be happening in his life, he remained buoyant, optimistic, confident to the point of cockiness. He was sure that, although his only regular gig might be at a windswept local radio station and his management no more influential than a kindly local deejay with 'high pockets', he was destined, sooner or later, to be gathered up by the same Blue Norther that was already whirling Elvis, Little Richard, Fats Domino and Chuck Berry into the big time. 'There was never any question in Buddy's mind that he was going to make it,' Bob Montgomery says. 'The rest of us thought he deserved to, but none of us could see how he was going to do it.'

On 14 October 1955, Bill Haley and the Comets appeared at Fair Park Coliseum, supported by Jimmie Rodgers Snow and Buddy, Bob and Larry. Travelling with the show was a Nashville agent named Eddie Crandall whose clients included Marty Robbins, that long-time fan of both Buddy's music and his leatherwork. Crandall was impressed by Buddy's performance and watched him carefully the following night when he opened another KDAV-sponsored show, headlined by Elvis Presley and featuring 'rockabilly' newcomers Johnny Cash and Floyd Cramer.

Elvis, that previous August, had acquired a new manager, a former carnival huckster and municipal dog-catcher named 'Colonel' Tom Parker – who, indeed, was destined to develop Rock's great founding genius as a cross between a fairground freak and a captive poodle. Crandall knew Parker well and suggested to him that there might be as promising a new client in the boy from Lubbock, Texas, as in the one from Tupelo, Mississippi. The Colonel said he was too busy with Elvis to launch another newcomer but agreed that Buddy had possibilities and suggested Crandall himself should have a shot at promoting him.

On 2 December, Crandall wrote to Pappy Dave Stone: 'Dave, I'm very confident I can do something as far as getting Buddy Holly [sic] a recording contract. It may not be a major but even a small one would be beneficial to someone who is trying to get a break ... Col. Parker suggested I try and help Buddy as he's pretty well tied up, and with your friendship I'll try my darndest to help him. Marty Robbins also thinks Buddy has what it takes. So all we can do is try, OK?' On the same day that Pappy Dave received the letter, a telegram arrived from Crandall requesting a demo of four original songs by Buddy post-haste, and urging, 'Don't change his style at all.'

By mid-January, Crandall was on the telephone with exciting news. He had taken Buddy's demo to a Nashville talent agent named Jim Denny who specialized in booking acts for the Grand Ole Opry show and also owned a publishing company called Cedarwood. Denny was prepared to offer him a songwriter's contract with Cedarwood and also to try to get him a recording deal.

The moment was a providential one. Nashville's recording industry was just then awakening to the challenge being offered to it as 'Music City, USA' by the Memphis Sun label. In the race to make up ground, the RCA-Victor label had forged ahead, buying Elvis Presley's contract from Sun, in a deal brokered by Colonel Tom Parker, for a staggering $35,000 – plus a Cadillac. Both the two other major labels with operations in Nashville, Columbia and Decca, were now agitatedly seeking their own young, white rockabillyists. Jim Denny could not interest Columbia in Buddy, but was able to convince Decca's Nashville director of A & R, Paul Cohen, to offer him a recording contract. Decca were a hugely powerful and prestigious label, boasting country music 'greats' like Red Foley, Kitty Wells and Ernest Tubb, the 'Texas Troubadour', as well as the single extant white rock 'n roll star, Bill Haley. Of no small assistance in exploiting Haley's monopoly was the fact that Decca controlled roughly 40 per cent of the jukeboxes in America.

The snag was that Paul Cohen wanted just Buddy; he did not want Bob Montgomery, the other half of the musical partnership which had existed since their elementary school days. The painful choice between loyalty and ambition was one Buddy did not have to make, however, since Bob instantly and amicably stood aside. He had always been far too deep-dyed a country musician to feel comfortable with rock 'n' roll, and was to go on to his own fulfilling career as a songwriter and, later, a music-publisher. Hi Pockets Duncan, too, behaved with a gentlemanliness hard to imagine today, instantly honouring his longstanding pledge to relinquish all managerial claim once Buddy was on the road to success.

Paul Cohen's offer, however, was a long way from promising that. Like every other major record-label at that moment, Decca were subjecting dozens of young singers to a quick X-ray examination in hopes of discovering another Presley. Cohen expressed no wild enthusiasm about Buddy, and promised no commitment to making him a star nor investment in developing him beyond the costs of a recording session early in 1956.

Buddy himself had no doubt that the great moment had arrived for which he had been actively preparing since the previous spring. He had long been itching to trade in his Les Paul Gold Top for a classier instrument, and the previous April, at the Adair music store in Lubbock, had found one classy beyond his dreams. Fender solid-body guitars even then were nothing new: it was in 1948 that the electronics wizard Leo Fender marketed his revolutionary prototype, the Broadcaster. But to most guitarists, especially ultra-conservative country ones, the idea of a guitar that had no acoustic resonance, and was entirely dependent on amplification to give it voice, belonged in the same daunting sci-fi realm as the H-bomb, 3-D films and the research into space travel going on at Houston and Cape Canaveral.

That made it all the more remarkable that Adair's had got hold of a Stratocaster, the latest and most expensive Fender; on the market barely a year, named for the new age of space-travel, and the perfect craft to explore the virgin galaxies of rock 'n' roll. Fortunately the Adair's salesman, Clyde Hankin, was a friend of Buddy's and a guitar buff who had once given him lessons. He had already been allowed to savour the contoured snugness of its black-to-brown 'sunburst' body against his, testing the new freedom which its double-cutaway shape gave to fingering in the high treble register, experimenting with volume-changes between its three electric pick-ups. He loved everything about it but the tremolo-lever, worked in the palm of the strumming hand, which bore down on all six strings at their root, or 'bridge', dragging a note or chord into drawn-out, shivering echo. In the hard all-downstroke style Buddy had learned from R & B soloists, he preferred all his notes to be ringingly clear and clean.

As a recording star in Elvis's footsteps, he knew he would also need clothes of very different kind from his usual starched white shirts, Levis and loafers. The price-tag for this combined musical and sartorial makeover, when he reckoned it up, far exceeded the modest savings he had managed to accrue from music and manual labouring, so as always in time of emergency he turned to his eldest brother. 'He came up to me one day, all eager and patting his hands together,' Larry Holley remembers. 'He said, "Larry, I knew good and well I could make it if only I had me a decent guitar and some decent clothes." I said, "Make it as what?" He said, "Why, make it in the music business." So I said, "OK, how much do you need?", thinking he was going to say about fifty dollars. But Buddy says, "How about lending me a thousand dollars?"

'Well, I was pretty amazed, because that was a pile of money back then, but I reckoned he knew what he was about, so I scraped up the thousand bucks from somewhere. And he bought some of the gaudiest clothes you ever did see! I wouldn't have worn 'em to a bullfight! There was a red coat ... a green sport jacket ... some blue shoes that were suede. Then he brought over the guitar and showed it to me. I said, "How much did you give for that?" and he said, "Six hundred." I was flabbergasted. "Six hundred dollars for a guitar!" I said. "You can get one for fifty at Huber's."'

To accompany him and the Stratocaster on their triumphal entry into Nashville, Buddy recruited the two back-up musicians who had crossed over with him from country to rock 'n' roll: guitarist Sonny Curtis and slap bass-player Don Guess. Naturally he also wanted Jerry Allison on drums, but J.I. had now returned to Lubbock High for another semester and even he dared not play hookey on such a scale. The three travelled in Buddy's family's black-and-white '55 Oldsmobile, with Don Guess's bass strapped to the roof.

The producer to whom Decca had assigned Buddy was Owen Bradley, a veteran in the country music field who ran his own studio on Music Row, Music City's famous boulevard of publishing and recording establishments. An ex-military Quonset Hut, not much less cavernous and spartan than that which housed the Cotton Club back in Lubbock, it bore the wholly appropriate nickname 'Bradley's Barn'.

From the moment that the Texan boys walked in to Bradley's Barn, on 26 January 1956, chill disillusionment set in, To begin with, Buddy was informed, his backing group did not measure up to the requirements of professional recording. To augment Sonny and Don Guess, Owen Bradley had brought in two session musicians, Grady Martin on rhythm guitar and Doug Kirkham on drums – both highly accomplished, but self-important and condescending to the young out-of-towners as only Nashville session-men know how to be. To make matters worse, Buddy was told that singing and playing guitar simultaneously, as he'd been used to doing since the age of nine, was contrary to recording-practice. Sonny Curtis, therefore, had to take charge of the Fender Stratocaster while its owner stood at the silver stand-mike, his long arms dangling uselessly beside him, feeling as naked as if he'd forgotten to put on his Levis.

There were also difficulties about the material to be recorded. Of the original songs Buddy had submitted to Paul Cohen, the A & R man chose only 'Don't Come Back Knockin'' and 'Love Me', both of them written in collaboration with a Lubbock girl named Sue Parrish. Two further numbers by other writers were added to the list: 'Midnight Shift', by Earl Lee and Jimmy Ainsworth, an uptempo number featuring the sportive 'Annie' of Hank Ballard's R & B hits; and 'Blue Days, Black Nights', written by Buddy's disc jockey friend Ben Hall and taught to him by ear one hot afternoon in the sheltering shade of the KDAV building.

All four titles were recorded at a single evening session at Bradley's Barn, starting at 7.15 and finishing at 10.15 p.m. To give Owen Bradley due credit, he made no attempt to turn Buddy into something he wasn't or cramp his style. 'Blue Days, Black Nights' stands comparison with any of his later work, a well-crafted if rather staid country song, performed with a skipping lightness of touch, yet total sincerity and involvement. But on the other three tracks, he shows palpable tension and lack of confidence, reflecting his own uncertainty about what Decca expected of him. Even the slap-bass beat and saucy lyrics of 'Midnight Shift' produced little more than an exhibition of how well he could take off Elvis. (So familiar was this masquerade around the Holley home that when L. O. Holley first heard Elvis on the radio he remarked innocently, 'That boy sounds just like Buddy.')

As if to underline Decca's vagueness of purpose, the contract that eventually came through on 8 February 1956 spelt Buddy's surname 'Holly' instead of 'Holley'. Since 'Holly' seemed to have a more professional, showbizzy ring to it – and since any objection would doubtless have produced further glitches in Decca's administrative machinery – he decided to let it stand. Paul Cohen had also requested some biographical details for publicity purposes, and on 2 March Buddy sent off a neatly typewritten letter that reads more like the CV of an aspiring invoice-clerk than a rock 'n' roll singer: 'I started taking music lessons on the violin at four years old and won an amateur contest when I was five. I also took lessons on the piana [sic] but as I didn't care for these instruments, I discontinued studying them ...' The signature on the letter shows he had not yet fully adjusted to his new persona: 'Appreciatively, Buddy Holley.'

Throughout that February and March, as Buddy anxiously watched the mailbox and listened for the phone, only one sound seemed to come from America's jukeboxes, radios and speeding, shark-finned cars. It was the first single to be released from Elvis Presley's Nashville sessions; a song called 'Heartbreak Hotel' which combined a classic X-rated R & B style with the self-dramatizing angst of a lovelorn white street punk. In January, Elvis had made his first national television appearance, performing two songs on the CBS network's *Stage Show*, hosted by former bandleaders Tommy and Jimmy Dorsey. The resultant deluge of complaints from viewers about his voice, hair, face, clothes – above all, his 'obscene' bodily mannerisms – was promotion which the canny Colonel Tom Parker could not have bought. By mid-March 'Heartbreak Hotel' had become the first record ever to reach number 1 simultaneously on all three record charts, pop, R & B and country.

No one in Decca's A & R department was under any illusion that a similar whirlwind had been unleashed at Bradley's Barn. After several weeks' agonized waiting, Buddy was unceremoniously informed that his début single would be the Ben Hall song

'Blue Days, Black Nights', coupled with 'Love Me'. Catchy and polished as the A-side was, it clearly stood no chance in the 'Heartbreak Hotel' league. But Buddy's buoyant optimism remained undented. As proof of his high hopes for 'Blue Days, Black Nights', he spent hours in painstakingly tooling a blue and black leather overjacket for his Gibson J 45 acoustic guitar, stamping his new name in bold white capitals on the body, and his initials in medieval calligraphy, flanked by miniature guitars, on the shoulder-strap.

Thanks to this new status as a Decca recording artist, he had been offered his first professional tour: a week on the road with Faron Young's 'Grand Ole Opry Show', visiting spots as breath-takingly far afield as Tulsa, Oklahoma. With him he took his Decca sidemen, Sonny Curtis and Don Guess, although once again not J. I. Allison, who was still fumingly imprisoned in high school. They were billed as 'extra added attractions' along with Tommy Collins and Carl Perkins. The pay was $10 per day each, plus food and accommodation.

A last-minute hitch arose when Don Guess, who did not own his own double-bass, was unable to borrow one as he usually did for the group's one-night appearances. Then Buddy remembered a Lubbock High boy named Terry Noland who rented a bass from the school for $2 per semester. 'He called up the high school, saying he was my dad and needed to speak to me urgently,' Noland remembers. 'I got pulled out of history class to take the call ... only to discover that it's just Buddy, wanting me to let him have this bass. The voice that he'd put on as my dad couldn't have been that good because while we were talking, my teacher picked up an extension-phone and listened in on us. Boy, did Buddy get an earful for that!'

The Texan trio did not travel on the tour-bus with the country stars, but had to follow behind in Buddy's family's '55 Olds. 'We had to drive hundreds of miles, and never got much sleep between gigs,' Sonny Curtis remembers. 'To stay awake late at night, we used to tell each other ghost stories. Buddy had some pretty good ones about the Mark of the Beast from the Book of Revelations. Sometimes we all used to get so scared that no one wanted to ride in the back seat of the car. We all used to squash up together in front.

'We'd gone on the road pretty unprepared, without any stage uniform like the other bands had, or even a name to call ourselves. When we stopped off in Oklahoma City, we went to a haberdasher's and bought some white pants and two shirts each, a blue one and an orange one. So when we went onstage that night, we told 'em to announce us as the Two-Tones.' For the Texan boys, the biggest thrill of the tour was when one of its stars, Tommy Collins, rode with them in the Olds. 'We was flipped out about that,' Sonny remembers. 'Riding down the road with a guy who made records! And, because we had our accommodation paid, we could order steaks all the way.'

Buddy spent the tour on a wave of extrovert high spirits that frequently embarrassed the polite and civilized Sonny. 'When we went into a restaurant, Buddy would fill up all the water-glasses to different heights, and start playing tunes on them. I remember once we all went to see this movie *Wuthering Heights*, with Laurence Olivier and Merle Oberon. There's a line in it, "If you come over to my house, I'll let you hold my hand beneath my fan." Buddy leans back in his seat, throws out his arms and says, "Ha-ave MERCY!" Well, the whole place just broke up.'

The release of 'Blue Days, Black Nights' in April brought his spirits down to earth with a crash. Decca spent nothing on promoting the record and organized no publicity beyond a few handout pictures of Buddy tense and unsmiling in his half-frame spectacles, clutching his acoustic guitar defensively to his chest. With no indications to the contrary, the record was treated as pure country. *Billboard* magazine's country and western reviewer gave it a good rating and also had the acumen to spot the rock 'n' roll singer trying to get out: 'If the public will take more than one Presley or [Carl] Perkins, as it well may, Holly stands a strong chance,' *Billboard* concluded. Apart from on KDAV–Lubbock, radio airplay was never other than desultory. Buddy was clearly grasping at straws when he wrote to a booking agent a few weeks later: 'I have talked to some friends that were travelling up around the north-eastern part of the country, and they said my record was very popular around Washington DC and through Missouri.' Decca's final estimate of sales was 18,000 copies, which at the standard 2.5 per cent royalty – and after deducting the publisher's 50 per cent – meant that Buddy and his co-writers, Ben Hall and Sue Parrish, would have shared $225.

The horribly unflattering Decca publicity photographs made one thing abundantly clear. No one who aspired to be like Elvis Presley could possibly go on being seen in glasses. On the Faron Young tour, Buddy tried leaving them off while he was performing, but with his 20/800 vision could barely see his fellow musicians, let alone the audience. During one show, he dropped his guitar-pick and had to crawl around the stage looking for it with his nose only a couple of inches from the floor.

On 14 May, the day after he returned from the tour, he went to see his ophthalmologist, Dr J. D. Armistead, and announced that he wanted contact lenses. This further miracle of fifties consumer technology had at the time been available only for a year or two, and was something more usually associated with fashionable city women than with six-foot beanpole young Texans. The hard lenses of 1956 were hugely expensive and, by modern standards, enormous and unwieldy; as tricky to insert under the eyelid as miniature magnifying-glasses. Buddy paid $125 for the lenses prescribed for him by Dr Armistead, but found them so uncomfortable he could wear them only for about ten minutes each day.

On 22 July, he was back in Nashville for a second Decca

recording session at Bradley's Barn. Jerry Allison was on vacation by now, and so could take the place of the session drummer, Doug Kirkham. Buddy had persuaded Owen Bradley to let him, rather than an outsider, play rhythm guitar, so now at least he would be backed by the same band on record as on stage. For further moral support, his cast-off partner, the generous-spirited Bob Montgomery, had also driven up from Lubbock in the jam-packed black-and-white Olds.

The tracks on this session were angled far more to rock 'n' roll and mainstream pop. There was a Buddy song, 'I'm Changing All Those Changes', a Don Guess song, 'Girl On My Mind', a Sonny Curtis song, 'Rock Around With Ollie Vee' (named after an old black lady who helped Sonny's mother around the house), and 'Ting-A-Ling', a bluesy number by the future head of Atlantic Records, Ahmet Ertegun. Almost by way of an afterthought, there was also Buddy's first casual attempt at songwriting in partnership with Jerry Allison.

A week or two previously, they had been to the State theater in Lubbock to see *The Searchers*, the darkest and most complex of all John Ford Westerns, starring Buddy's hero John Wayne, for once, as a not wholly good or admirable figure. The searchers are a posse in pursuit of Indians who have kidnapped two white girls. Throughout the picture, whenever anyone asks Wayne's character, Ethan Edwards, if he's ready to abandon the chase or otherwise disconcerted, he growls the same laconic response: 'That'll be the day.'

It became a catchphrase among Buddy's circle, though none was quite as good at reproducing Wayne's slurry monotone as Buddy himself. 'A little while after we saw the movie, we were over at my house,' J.I. later remembered. 'Buddy had a tune in his head, and he said, "Hey, why don't we two write a song?" I said, "That'll be the day." He said, "Hey, that's a good idea . . ."' The song was knocked off in less than half an hour, with the two improvising alternate lines and Buddy stirring in a jangly guitar riff borrowed from one of his favourite R & B records, Hank Ballard and the Midnighters' 'Switchie Witchie Titchie'.

Owen Bradley was perfectly willing for a new original song called 'That'll Be The Day' to be added to the morning-long session. But, even at the nineteenth take, the result was hardly exciting. Buddy sang it without any back-up chorus, in a just-too-high key which robbed his voice of its normal range, suppleness and humour. The cavernous echo which Bradley added was obviously intended to create the same dramatic, angst-ridden atmosphere it had for Elvis Presley's voice on 'Heartbreak Hotel'. But here it merely emphasized the unsteadiness of Buddy's delivery and the unsympathetic ambience of Bradley's Barn.

Though Buddy got along with Owen Bradley well enough, the more crucial rapport with Decca's A & R Director, Paul Cohen, had failed to materialize. The protocol of recording in 1956 was quite clear: A & R men were God Almighty, and singers followed their instructions to the letter in humble grati-tude. But Buddy had been cutting records on his own initiative since early boyhood, and had strong and clear-cut ideas about how his music ought to sound. Moreover, when it came to protecting his work, as he saw it, from the indifference of Nashville's ruling élite, his usual Texan courtesy and respectful-ness went out of the window. Jim Denny, his mentor at Cedarwood Music, several times found himself called on to act as peacemaker in hot disputes between Buddy and Paul Cohen. Yet for all that, and his unspectacular results to date, Decca still felt he had something about him, and told him to come back to Nashville for a third session later in the year.

All through the high summer months, as Buddy helped Larry to lay tiles or worked on house-framing jobs with his father, there was still nothing to see or hear but Elvis, Elvis, Elvis. Instead of blowing over as predicted, rock 'n' roll was raging stronger than ever, but now with something which had not been there in the simple, cinema-smashing days of 1955: it was simple, straightforwardly unpleasant juvenile delinquency no longer, but juvenile delinquency packaged with neon-bright, flaunting glamour and soaked to the eyebrows in sex.

The cohesion of American family life, its chief pride for a century and a half, was gone for ever. To the young generation, Elvis was a rock 'n' roll hero in their own image at long last – an idol more dangerously fascinating than Marlon Brando in *The Wild One*, more tantalizingly unfathomable than James Dean in *Rebel Without A Cause*; the incarnation of all modern teenagerdom's volatile moods, randy energy and tumultuous self-pity. To their parents, he was a spectre of disruption and subversion more terrible than any conjured up by the late McCarthy era; a figure of blatant physicality not shut away in a burlesque house as tradition demanded, but able to penetrate and defile any home with his too-oily hair, his too-long sideburns, his too-garish clothes, his too-sullen face, the too-effeminate twirls and preens of his too-loose head, shoulders, legs and hips, but worst of all the too-suggestive forward jerks and thrusts of his far-too-tautly-enclosed crotch. The dim realization that both his material and performing style derived from 'Negro' music reactivated all the horrified superstitions and complexes of the white race concerning the sexual powers of the black one. So that was what rock 'n' roll and its new mumbling, glowering figurehead were about! Initiating clean-cut young American manhood and pure young American womanhood into the mindless, shameless rhythms that promoted rutting rituals in the jungle!

The war between the states, ninety years earlier, was hardly more bitter and unrelenting than that which Elvis had started between America's teenagers and their elders. High schools and colleges, the Federal side, poured forth virulent anti-rock 'n' roll propaganda in the form of pamphlets and even films, showing how to recognize the rebel 'enemy within' – the males by their sideburns and blue jeans, the even more reprehensible females by their ponytails and ankle-bracelets. Elvis himself could have been Robert E. Lee, reincarnated with hair-dye and a pout. And as any beginner in psychology could have predicted, the more furiously adults condemned, deplored and ridiculed him, the more ardently teenagers formed lines to buy his records and flocked, shrieking, to his concerts. After the monster success of 'Heartbreak Hotel', RCA Victor took the unprecedented (and unrepeated) step of releasing seven of his songs simultaneously, thereby keeping him at number 1 in the charts every single week from August to December. Meanwhile, the media pursued him back and forth across America as if he were some ghastly erotic evangelist, faithfully reporting from each new city-gone-berserk where demented girls had besieged his dressing-room, obliterated his car, tried to tear the clothes from his back or kissed him until his mouth bled.

Buddy as a rule was too wrapped up in his music and hobbies, and far too restless, to sit around watching television. But on 9 September, even he was anchored before the flickering grey-and-white screen to see Elvis's first appearance on NBC's *Ed Sullivan Show*. Sullivan was the most unlikely of all TV music-hall hosts, a former sportscaster with hunched shoulders, a long-jawed, misanthropic face and a corncrake voice with which he managed to make even his best-known guests sound like denizens of outer space. Compelled to exploit the ratings opportunity that rock 'n' roll presented, he barely troubled to conceal his incredulous disgust for the music, its performers or the noisy teenagers who increasingly dominated his studio audience. His introduction of Elvis to the nation was quintessential Sullivan – a self-absolving wave of the hand and the words: 'America . . . judge for yourselves.'

Elvis that night performed four numbers: 'Don't Be Cruel', 'Houn' Dog', 'Love Me Tender' and Little Richard's 'Rip It Up'. He drew an audience of 54 million, setting a record that would remain unbroken until February 1964, when another reluctant wave of Ed Sullivan's little hand introduced the Beatles.

The ensuing national furore signalled open season on rock 'n' roll musicians and enthusiasts wherever they should chance to be found. In October Lubbock's morning paper, the *Avalanche*, published a picture of Buddy playing with his group at the Cotton Club, as if that were a wholly new and noteworthy circumstance. The faces of the musicians and the dancers below them were blacked out in the style of scandal magazines like *Confidential* and *Whisper*.

The city's evening *Journal* followed up the story on 22 October by interviewing the rock 'n' roll player whom Lubbock still hardly realized it had in its midst. Headlined YOUNG SINGER IS LUBBOCK'S ANSWER TO ELVIS PRESLEY – BUDDY HOLLY PACKS 'EM IN, the article broke the ten-month-old story of Buddy's Decca recording contract and mentioned his remarkable drawing-power on weekends at venues like the American Legion Youth Center. *Journal* readers were no doubt relieved to read that their home-grown rock 'n' roller resembled Elvis only in the most superficial way, and in private conducted himself with a restraint and decorum entirely appropriate to the 'City of Churches'. While Buddy confessed to playing music in 'fancy' sport coats, he emphasized that he never wore such garments offstage, not even 'for publicity purposes'.

A better reporter could have winkled out some more interesting facts – for instance that Buddy was by now such a star in the Lubbock area that his brother Larry, the tough ex-soldier, had to go to gigs with him, to stop him being mobbed and to stave off occasional attacks by irate boyfriends of the girls who now screamed for him. Or that the one-time high school nerd whom no one took seriously had become a figure of such glamour and magnetism that the Hi-D-Ho drive-in employed him to attract teenage customers by performing on its circular flat roof.

On 15 November he had his third and, it would prove, final session for Decca in Nashville. This time at Bradley's Barn, Don Guess was the only one of his band allowed to take part; the rest were session-men, including Floyd Cramer on piano and E. R. 'Dutch' McMillin on tenor saxophone. The most promising track was agreed to be 'Modern Don Juan', a lacklustre joint composition by Guess and Jack Neal. It was released on 24 December – a date which, even though America's Christmas holiday is far shorter and less disruptive than Britain's, amounted to marketing suicide. This time, Don, Jerry Allison and Sonny Curtis received billing on the record: not as the Two Tones, much to their chagrin, but as the 'Three Tunes'. Once again *Billboard* reviewed the song as country, and gave it mild praise, but this time sales were negligible.

Relations between Buddy and Paul Cohen, meanwhile, had deteriorated beyond repair. Infuriated by his refusal to kowtow, Cohen told him flatly that he hadn't the kind of voice that could ever sell pop records and, to a third party, called him 'the biggest no-talent I ever worked with'. For all his buoyancy and native stubbornness, he had no choice but to concede defeat by Nashville's music mafia. It was mortifying, but no real surprise, when, early in January 1957, a letter arrived from Decca, terminating his contract.

So was this to be the zenith of his career as a rock 'n' roller – floodlit on the flat roof of the Hi-D-Ho drive-in, singing and playing his heart out to a semicircle of parked cars while the carhops in their scarlet tunics and pillbox hats scurried to and fro under his feet with orders of Hidey burgers, Hidey fries and Hidey pies?

Part Two

LOOKING FOR SOMEONE TO LOVE

CLOVIS, NEW MEXICO, is some ninety miles to the north-west of Lubbock, a two-hour drive in a modern small car under modern speed-restrictions. Although Route 84 is no longer the undivided two-lane blacktop of Buddy's era, its milestones and incidental sights remain much the same that he would have seen from behind the wheel. On your left are infinite cotton- and wheatfields; to your right run the banked-up tracks of the Sante Fe Railroad. Shabby one-street towns along the way – Sudan, Shallowater, Muleshoe – vainly attempt to beguile the eye with knock-down gas-prices, real estate offices, mobile-home parks, truck-wrecking yards and silver grain-elevators as huge and fancy as Las Vegas casino-hotels. Occasionally a freight train swings into view to relieve the monotony; half a mile or so of boxcars, hauled by squads of dark blue locomotives, each with SANTE FE emblazoned on it in gold Victorian script.

At the state-line, the time-zone changes from Central to Mountain, setting clocks and watches back one hour. You can thus proceed to Clovis, six miles further on, with the pleasant illusion that your journey from Lubbock took only half the time you thought. The view may appear much the same as back in Texas, but do not suppose you are anywhere half so candid and straightforward. Even to Western Americans New Mexico is an enigma, the so-called 'Secret State' whose vast interior deserts are thickly planted with top-secret nuclear research establishments, crack military bases, missile-pads and legends of close encounters with UFOs.

Were it not for Buddy Holly, Clovis would be known merely as a relic of America's great railroad age. Originally named Riley Switch (after the man who once dwelt there, switching trains from one line to another) it grew up in the late nineteenth century as the railhead for herds driven in mainly from a huge ranch in the Texas Panhandle called the XIT. Even the city's mellifluous European name – that of a fifth-century Frankish monarch and a character in Saki's short stories – was bestowed by the scholarly daughter of a railway official stationed there. It reached its zenith in the early 1900s as a rail terminal for livestock, freight and passengers, and, later, a staging post for the first transcontinental air-journeys, which originally were made jointly by train and plane.

That busy, purposeful era was already fading when Buddy first came here in the mid-fifties, and now has practically vanished. All that remains of the once splendid passenger terminal is the Harvey House hotel, where travellers would once alight from the 20th Century or Superchief to lunch or dine at their leisure. The once bustling freight depots and repair shops have been closed or been ruthlessly 'downsized'. Looking along cobbled Main Street, with its washed-out colours and permanent air of weekend quiet, you would not think that much of anything goes on in Clovis any more. Even the ripe odour from the remaining active stockyards has something nostalgic, at night a little ghostly, about it.

Before 1957, other than in railroad schedules, Clovis had only one substantial claim to fame. Just south of the city is the archaeological site which, in the late forties, yielded up the earliest evidence of human habitation in the Americas. This 14,000-year-old culture is known for short among pre-historians as 'Clovis Man'. We have come to disinter another species of Clovis Man, however; one which may date from a more recent era, but is hardly less mysterious and unfathomable.

At 1313 West Seventh Street, his neat blue sign still rears over the sidewalk as if half-hopeful of enticing passing trade: 'Norman Petty' in two diagonals of white script, 'RECORDING STU-DIOS' in businesslike capitals. Below are two flat-roofed yellow buildings, picked out in vermilion, nestling in lush foliage and connected by a short strip of wire-fenced garden. The larger, two-storey building, to the right, has a decorative façade on which spreading greenery partly obscures the raised letters NOR VA JAK MUSIC INC.

In the smaller, single-storey building, to the left, the studio where Buddy created his greatest music is preserved intact, its period fitments and artefacts as fascinating to the modern eye as any pristine cave paintings or unplundered pharaoh's tomb. Here is the tiny reception area with its serried rows of framed Golden Discs, and the old-style red-and-white vending machine which dispensed Coca-Colas in thick green sculpted bottles, ten cents apiece. Here, beyond, is Norman Petty's control-room with equipment still in place – the black-boxed, silver-studded Ampex tape-recorder, the lathe which used to convert Buddy's tapes into demo discs. Here are glass-fronted cabinets containing headphones, maracas and recording-wire, and Petty's own grey leather armchair pushed up to the veiny black work-surface with its heavy-based RCA microphone.

And there, through the glass, the studio itself, a place no bigger than an average-size living-room, where Buddy made 'That'll Be The Day', 'Peggy Sue', 'Oh Boy', 'Not Fade Away', 'Words Of Love', 'Listen To Me', 'Love's Made A Fool Of You', 'Heartbeat', 'It's So Easy' and every other classic track bar one or two. Pushed up to the left-hand wall is the Baldwin grand piano that played the rolling bass solo on 'Think It Over'; opposite is the celeste that tinkled through 'Everyday'. Here is the heavy stand-mike Buddy used on every session, and the Fender Pro amplifier into which he used to plug his Stratocaster. Amazing to see how small is its yellow cabinet and compare its 20-watt capacity with the almost 4 million watts needed to project the Rolling Stones' stage version of 'Not Fade Away' in 1995.

Down a short passage from the studio is the kitchen where Buddy and the Crickets would wolf down inter-session snacks, and the room with two dark-blue-covered-beds, folding out into four, where they would sometimes snatch a couple of hours' sleep after dawn. No mummy's tomb was ever packed more densely with precious relics than is this long-unused guest suite with iconography of the mid-fifties American Raj – lamps with hand-stitched vellum shades, supported on barley-sugar twists of gold and black; fish-shaped clocks; narrow-necked vases of dark blue Murano glass; sets of fancy iron fire-tongs; swan-necked black cats; pomanders in the shape of straw-hatted donkeys; gilt-racked sets of coaster-mats; sage-green Picasso-print curtains; top-of-the-range Grundig valve radios and radio-grams; splayed white table- and chair-legs and orange synthetic leather.

The two-storey building across the garden houses the apart-ment where Petty lived with his wife, Vi, and his elderly parents, and the loft space where Buddy's father and brothers built the echo-chamber that was to be used with such effect on 'Peggy Sue'. At the rear is the barbecue area where Norma Jean, the Pettys' secretary/bookkeeper, would serve picnics of Mexican taquitos, and the white truck – Air Force blue in Petty's time – which used to take his cocktail lounge trio to its engagements and which Buddy, that incurable auto-nut, frequently drove.

Inside this bizarre little compound, almost everything a pop record could ever say was definitively said between February 1957 and the summer of 1958. It is all now history as distant as Clovis Man; yet, in common with all thrilling archaeological sites, one has a sense of life interrupted rather than extinct. The fish-shaped clocks, the swan-necked cats, the dime-slot Coke machine, the Fender Pro amp, all seem to await a crunch of Oldsmobile tyres on the forecourt, a yell of Texan laughter, a clatter and ruffle of drums being set up, then a voice, melodious but commanding: 'OK . . . let's do it.'

Our particular species of Clovis Man left behind such contradictory evidence of his existence, and took such pains to cover his tracks in all crucial areas, that building up a definitive archaeological profile would, in the ordinary way, be next to impossible. You can talk to a dozen people who knew Norman Petty well, and from each vantage-point see a totally different character. To some, he was a technical wizard whose inspired know-how shaped raw talent into glossily-finished genius; to others, he was simply a button-pusher who just happened to be in the right place at the right time. To some, he was a model of generosity, altruism and square dealing; to others, a shameless opportunist, thief and cheat. To some, he was the person who made it possible for Buddy Holly to come alive; others feel he could hardly be more to blame for Buddy's death if he'd gone out into the Iowa snows with a machine-gun and pointed it straight into the sky.

The many photographs of himself that Petty left behind are scarcely more illuminating than the autobiographical symbols and effigies scratched on stone by original Clovis Man, 14,000 years earlier. Most of these date from his own years as a performing musician; the kind of glossy portrait meant to be displayed on scalloped boards outside cocktail bars and supper clubs with 'TONITE' printed slantwise in one corner. The face is a blandly good-looking one, its well-oiled hair forming a slight peak, its cheekbones curving with the symmetry of a ventriloquist's dummy's, its complexion airbrush-smooth, its butterfly bow perfectly tied. The expansive smile is professional rather than humorous, and kindles no warmth in the eyes, which are narrow, opaque and calculating.

Here is a later study, taken at the height of the Buddy Holly era, when Petty (it's easy to forget) was himself still barely into his thirties. He is turning round from his wall-mounted Ampex recorder, wearing what looks like a short-sleeved shirt but what those who knew him say was more likely a one-piece jumpsuit in cotton or voile. He looks – and no one denies he was – meticulous, efficient, quiet and polite. One can almost smell the antiseptic fragrance of British Sterling aftershave lotion and perfumed soap that hung around him even in New Mexico's most punishing summer heat, and hear the softly mellow voice, full of long, reflective pauses, that Buddy did so often over the studio intercom. Can this really be the same creature Buddy's brother, Larry, is talking about in a Lubbock coffee ship, rubbing his bare arms as if to ward off an attack of goose-pimples? 'During World War II, when I was with the military over in Saipan, I remember falling asleep one night in a fox-hole with water up to my chin. Over there, you know, you get snails, measuring about ten inches to a foot across. When I woke up in the foxhole, there was this giant snail crawling right across my face ... Well, I tell you, I used to get just the same kind of feeling every time I was around Norman Petty.'

It so happens that our investigation into modern Clovis Man has turned up an archaeological find even richer than his crowded sarcophagus on West Seventh Street. By January 1959, when Buddy set out on that fatal tour of the blizzardy Midwest, he had fired Petty as his manager and record-producer and begun legal action to recover the recording royalties which Petty had been 'holding' for him. In the face of this lawsuit, to reassure himself that his business dealings could stand impartial scrutiny, Petty turned over all the correspondence and financial records relating to Buddy and the Crickets to his banker in Clovis, with instructions to retain them for the three years required by the US Internal Revenue Service, then destroy them.

But the banker did not destroy these intimate papers and, after Petty's death in 1984, passed them on to a former friend and associate of the Petty family, who possesses them still and has agreed to open them for our inspection. We can, therefore, shine a light on to the innermost cave-walls of our modern, secretive Clovis Man. We can examine contracts, cash-books and tax-returns, read lawyers' angry letters and cables, go through receipts for Buddy's guitars and clothes, handle the tickets and boarding passes for his famous British tour in 1958, see the cashed cheques for his cars, dental work and wedding-ring, even read the heartbreakingly polite last letter he sent to Petty a couple of weeks before his death. To the self-seeking professional biographer, hungry for the 'real' Buddy Holly story, it is a wildly exhilarating experience. But to the one-time English schoolboy, whose adolescence Buddy both brightened and soothed, it is horribly sad.

As so often with those who cloak themselves in ostentatious secrecy, there was little about Petty's life that could be called exotic or dangerous. His father, Sydney, had originally been a migrant from the Oklahoma oilfields, stricken with tuberculosis and seeking a cure in New Mexico's high altitudes. Norman Eugene Petty was born in Clovis in May 1927, and brought up in the same spot where his studio complex later stood. The two-storey building on the right used to be a garage-cum-gas station, kept by a once more hale and vigorous Sydney and his wife, Margaret; the studio building was originally a small general store, run by Margaret's sister, Eula, and her husband.

Despite its busy railroad life, Clovis in the nineteen-thirties was a small, closely knit community, more village than city. Sydney and Margaret Petty were prominent local characters who made their garage a community focal-point straight out of a

Saturday Evening Post cover by Norman Rockwell. In addition to mending cars, 'Pa' Petty, as he was universally known, repaired domestic appliances, radio sets and cameras; 'Ma' Petty kept the books and pumped gas out front, in addition to raising a brood of four. As well as Norman there were two daughters, Edith and Shirley, and an older boy, Billy, who died aged eighteen of leukaemia – the same disease that would claim Norman at the age of fifty-seven. After Billy's death, both Ma and Pa Petty, but especially Ma, doted excessively on their 'Normie'.

Both his parents were keen amateur musicians, Pa Petty playing the 'harp' (mouth organ) and Ma playing guitar at regular get-togethers with their neighbours. As a small boy, Normie astonished his parents by climbing up on to a piano-stool and picking out tunes, like 'Under The Double Eagle', after having heard them only once. As well as being able to play anything instantaneously by ear, he had such abnormal sensitivity to tone and pitch that he was soon getting lucrative work as a part-time piano-tuner. A friend remembers: 'He'd walk into a hall or a room before a concert, look round it once, and say, 'An octave up from middle C, about F sharp, there's a dead spot.' When they checked it on the piano he'd always be right. And if he ever heard a bad note, it almost brought him out in a rash.'

His technical ingenuity also revealed itself when he was very young. His sister Shirley remembers how, when he was only eight or nine, he wired a microphone into the family radio set so that he could broadcast his own shows through its speaker. In his teens he became a disc-jockey, presenting a twice-daily programme called *Musical Mailbag* on Clovis's station KICA. He formed his first musical group, the Torchy Swingsters, and would record them on a wire-operated machine to see how better to polish up their performance. He also invested his savings in a disc-cutter, the only one in the Clovis area, and developed a profitable sideline in recording greetings from

servicemen to their families and putting local politicians' cam-
paign-messages on disc, for broadcast by the area's radio stations.

At Clovis High School, he met a curly-haired, buxom girl
named Violet Ann Brady, a carpenter's daughter who lived only
a block or two away from the Petty garage. A year younger than
Norman, Vi was an accomplished classical pianist, good enough
to play duets with the school's Director of Music, and able to
read – and write – the notes which Norman played by ear. He
had never before shown much interest in girls, but Vi's skill on
the piano, her talent as a singer, the impressive fact that her uncle
had been Professor of Music at Oklahoma University, all helped
create a bond. They began dating when he was 18 and she was
17; they continued to go steady while Petty did his military
service in Norfolk, Virginia, and Vi completed her musical
studies at Oklahoma University; in 1948, when he was 21 and
she 20, they married.

The marriage was cemented by a successful artistic partnership. Shortly after dropping out of East New Mexico University,
Petty had formed a musical trio consisting of himself, Vi and a
friend named Jack Vaughn, a former star pitcher in the Texas
baseball league. Petty played organ, Vaughn played guitar, Vi
played piano and sang in the lush mid-Forties big-band style of
Dinah Shore and Margaret Whiting. They were a self-contained
unit, voyaging far and wide from Clovis in a smart blue truck,
always accompanied by Speedy, the Pettys' doted-on black
chihuahua.

This was the era of pre-Rock 'n' Roll pop music, of Guy
Mitchell's 'Red Feathers', Rosemary Clooney's 'Come On A-
My House', Kay Starr's 'Wheel of Fortune', Frankie Laine's
'Jezebel'. The Norman Petty Trio never made the premier league,
but carved out a profitable niche: they recorded on the Columbia
label and had two hits – one in 1954 with a close-harmony vocal
version of Duke Ellington's 'Mood Indigo' (which Ellington
himself publicly praised), the other in 1957 with an instrumental

written by Petty, 'Almost Paradise'. Petty, too, could sing, but chose to do so only rarely. One of the few surviving examples on record is a version of Hank Williams's 'Jambalaya', in which he makes the Creole-accented call to 'crawfish pie' and 'ol' fruit-jar' for 'son-of-a-gun' high-jinks on the bayou sound about as seductive as an impending dental check-up.

Recording for a major label, even one so large and prestigious as Columbia, was an unhappy experience for Petty. His technical perfectionism was affronted by the sloppiness with which the Trio's sessions were often conducted, and the poor acoustics and reproduction quality grated on his fastidious musical ear. Most of all he hated the way that recording sessions were ruled by the clock. When a track had used up its scheduled studio-time, finished or not, the house producer would often simply shrug and let it go out as it was.

The royalties from 'Mood Indigo' in 1954 helped Petty to realize his ambition of building a studio where, as well as recording his trio to his own pernickety standards, he could be his own producer and engineer, and even cut the 'master' copies of his own records. The studio duly took shape on West Seventh Street, Clovis, on the site of his Aunt Eula's old store, helped by a mortgage taken out on the adjacent family garage. Petty invested in state-of-the-art technology, ordering one of the new Ampex reel-to-reel tape-recorders, the type developed in Germany during World War II and until the early fifties used principally as a tool of the US Military. Petty's Ampex was only the second to be supplied for music-recording, the first having gone to the double-track guitar wizard Les Paul.

Elsewhere he had no choice but to use the primitive studio equipment of the day. His Altec single-channel recording board, for instance, was years away from modern custom-built, multi-track 'desks'. A bulky grey object shaped rather like a Gladstone bag with thick black switches and single Geiger-counter dial, it was standard equipment at most radio and television stations.

Where Petty could excel was in the acoustics of his single, small recording space, whose polycylindrical walls reflected sound to and from each other to infinity, ensuring no distortion or 'dead spots' in any part of the room.

At first the studio was used exclusively by Petty's own trio for rehearsal and recording between extended spells on the road. Petty had developed close links with that ubiquitous New Mexico employer, the United States Air Force, and as time went on, more and more of the Trio's live appearances were at USAF bases like White Sands or Las Cruces – lucrative, undemanding engagements that could last up to two months each as they moved round the various officers' and NCO clubs. If the Trio had a concurrent recording commitment, Petty would take along his Ampex machine and, with the Air Force's indulgence, rig up an improvised studio in the corner of some officers' club lounge. With the studio, he also established a music publishing company, NOR VA JAK Inc., formed from the Trio's Christian names, Norman, Violet Ann and Jack. He continued to record local politicians' campaign messages, supplied the Air Force with prepackaged music programmes and also worked out of 1313 West Seventh as a professional photographer, covering weddings and civic functions.

No children came along to disrupt this industrious existence. Although Petty and his wife, Vi, were still only in their mid-twenties, both always maintained they were too busy for the distractions of parenthood. While they were undoubtedly fond of each other, their friends believed it to be primarily a professional relationship – that Petty had married Vi to secure assets for his trio, her keyboard skills, her singing voice; the fact that she could read music, rather than simply playing by ear as he did, and so could write out the lead-sheets.

And Vi Petty, for all her assured musicianship and warmly sensuous singing voice, was a troubled, vulnerable soul. Her mother had suffered from schizophrenia and had to be institutionalized for several years during Vi's childhood. She herself manifested all the symptoms of the disease in its low-level, 'episodic' form: hyper-activity, anxiety, squirrel-like acquisitiveness, chaotic disorganization. She was completely under Petty's control: he chose the gowns and shoes, even the hairstyles, she wore for her appearances with the Trio. In their photographs together, Petty usually has a hand on Vi's shoulder in an almost conscious gesture of keeping her down. Between musical engagements, Vi left Norman to take care of all business matters and spent most of her time working in the flower garden she had established around the studio and lavishing affection on Speedy, their chihuahua, and a long-haired cat named Squeaky.

The first outsider to cut a demo record at Petty's studio was a pixie-faced country singer named Jimmy Self, with his group the Sunshine Playboys. Thanks to the contacts Petty had built up in the East Coast music industry, he was subsequently able to get Self a recording deal with Elvis Presley's future label, RCA Victor. Word of this success quickly spread among other local musicians, and Petty found himself with a queue of other singers and groups wishing to avail themselves of his studio's perfect acoustics and his own engineering expertise. The Western Union clock, accurate to the millisecond, which hung on his control-room wall, was the least used item of Petty's equipment. Remembering how his own creativity had been stifled by clock-watching, he did not rent his studio facilities by the hour, but instead charged a flat fee for recording each song. The musicians could thus feel free to hone and polish their compositions without constant fear of someone calling 'time'. To maintain creative flow at the maximum, there was a kitchen with a well-stocked refrigerator where they could eat, rather than dispersing to restaurants or drive-ins, and a comfortable bedsitting-room where they could unwind or sleep.

All this was not quite the open-handed philanthropy it might appear. Petty, in fact, operated on much the same contingency basis as do beady-eyed modern lawyers. If any record made in his studio, with his help and expertise, and networked through his New York contacts, turned out to be a success, it was understood that he'd expect a lion's share of its profits, taking some of the composer's royalties, even if he had not written a word of it, and also publishing it via his NOR VA JAK company. In his defence, Petty could – and did – argue that he was gambling time and money; that in the East Coast music world appropriating a writer's credit was a standard producer's perquisite; and that, anyway, most of the songs were unlikely ever to earn a cent.

Musicians also had to accept that recording at the Norman Petty studio meant a suspension of their normal manners and customs. A regular and vociferous worshipper at Clovis's Central Baptist Church, Petty did not allow drinking or swearing on the premises and, though he could not actually ban smoking, frigidly disapproved of that also. He kept a Bible near him at all times and, after a good studio take, was liable to suggest that the musicians put down their instruments, form a circle, join hands and offer up an impromptu prayer of thanksgiving.

The dawn of the rock 'n' roll era initially made little impression on Petty, even though two of its earliest pioneers materialized under his very nose. Early in 1956, a wispy, chinless teenager named Roy Orbison, from the tiny hamlet of Wink, Texas, came to Clovis with his group the Teen Kings to demo several tracks including a rock 'n' roll number called 'Ooby Dooby'. Orbison subsequently moved on to join the rockabilly stable of Sun Records in Memphis along with Elvis Presley, Carl Perkins and Johnny Cash; he had a minor chart-hit with 'Ooby Dooby', but was not to achieve international success until turning to high-decibel ballads like 'Only The Lonely' in 1960.

Later in 1956, Petty's studio and engineering services were booked by another West Texas group, the Rhythm Orchids, who had recently appeared in concert with Elvis Presley and been advised by him to get in 'on the ground floor' of rock 'n' roll. The Rhythm Orchids produced their own demo tracks, which included a song called 'Party Doll' written by their singer, Buddy Knox, a handsome youth who'd grown up on a farm in Happy, Texas. Since the studio drummer David Alldred, alias 'Dickie Do', could not muster a full kit, the beat for 'Party Doll' was produced by beating drumsticks on a cotton-filled cardboard box.

Petty recognized that the Rhythm Orchids had potential but the lyrics of 'Party Doll' (which included the refrain 'I'll make love to you') offended his religious sensibilities and he preferred not to try to market 'a dirty song' among the New York record companies. He was to rue this decision for, having released a single locally at their own expense, the Rhythm Orchids were offered a deal by a brand-new East Coast label called Roulette. Instead of marketing them as a group, Roulette cleverly conjured two separate hit-making vocalists from their line-up. 'Party Doll' by Buddy Knox, with its catchy box-bashing beat, went to number 1 in March 1957; 'I'm Sticking With You', by his colleague Jimmy Bowen, reached number 11 a month later.

Despite Petty's growing reputation throughout New Mexico and West Texas, the ménage at 1313 West Seventh Street, Clovis, continued to be a picturesque one. His parents' garage still functioned in the building next to his studio, with Pa Petty repairing cars, Ma pumping gas out front and the couple living in a ground-floor apartment at the rear. Ma also oversaw the studio accounts, and was even empowered by her son to sign cheques on his behalf with a shaky counterfeit 'Norman Petty' that only such a tolerant home-town institution as the Clovis National Bank would have honoured. The fifth member of the household was Petty's secretary/bookkeeper, Norma Jean Berry, a one-time local journalist who'd originally come to the studio to do a newspaper story about him and, somehow, had never left. Burly of build and masculine of dress, with a deep, gruff voice, Norma Jean was devoted to Petty and the faithful, unquestioning executant of his every command.

Petty's rather effeminate looks, his fastidious manners, his addiction to strongly-scented toiletries and hand-lotions, his taste for collarless shirts decorated with little elephants – above all, the fact that the raw material of his business was relays of young men – inevitably produced rumours that he might be homosexual. Even wilder speculation was generated by the burly figure of Norma Jean, who conformed in almost every way to the most obvious stereotype of the 'butch' lesbian, and whose relationship with the Pettys was clearly far more than simply clerical. Intermittent rumour had it that Vi Petty and Norma Jean carried on a lesbian relationship; that Norma Jean and Petty had once had an affair; even that the three participated in troilistic sexual acts. The truth appears to have been that all three, for different reasons, were virtually sexless, and that Norma Jean clung to the Pettys as her surrogate family.

If Petty was not gay, he certainly behaved like someone with some similar deep, dark secret, continually baffling even so close a personal and business associate as his original country music protégé, Jimmy Self. 'I knew Norman for something like twenty-five years,' Self says. 'And every day I spent with him, I seemed to find out something new about him.'

Partly as a result of living with the frantic and chaotic Vi, Petty developed a parallel secret life which would have done credit to a Soviet spy or fugitive Nazi war criminal. 'When Norman was working with musicians in the studio, he'd be there all the time, taking care of every detail,' Jimmy Self remembers. 'But in between sessions, he'd disappear completely. He had bolt-holes all over town, some of them offices for corporations he'd set up without telling Vi, with their own phone-numbers, headed stationery and chequebooks. Norman would be in one of these secret offices, doing gosh-only-knows what, for hours on end. Sometimes we'd find he'd just take off to New York, the West Coast ... even to Europe. The first Vi knew about it would be when he'd call her up, saying, "I'm in LA," or "I'm in London."'

So we may begin to construct an archaeological profile of modern Clovis Man – technically brilliant but creatively mediocre; a visionary in some respects but in others a blinkered small-town wheeler-dealer; ostensibly a self-effacing boffin and back-room-boy, yet with a ravening ego, watchful for any chance to use the talent of the young musicians who passed through his hands for his own profit and advancement; in his own small, rarefied sphere, a figure of absolute power and knowledge, surrounded by people who never questioned his authority and judgement and so able to dwell in his own moral universe, beatifically convinced that in all his dealings, however questionable, he was the very soul of reason and rectitude.

And, let us not forget, very, very mean. Petty was never frugal, especially not with himself, and was capable of generosity to his wife, parents and friends. But he was one of those people who value money beyond any power or luxury it can buy and who suffer real anguish when forced to part with it. The various local friends and acquaintances co-opted to work at the Petty studios as session musicians or back-up singers mostly had to resign themselves to doing so for nothing. Among these were two brothers named John and Bill Pickering who sang as a duo and had known Petty since high school. 'Norman would always be as nice as pie,' Bill Pickering remembers. 'He'd talk to you, encourage you, praise you and feed you – I mean real good food, steaks and everything. But he'd never give you a dime.'

Dr Jerry Fisher, who worked as an engineer with Petty in later years, and got to know him well, believes him to have been a classic case of arrested development. 'Norman missed out a crucial stage in his evolution: he went straight from being a baby to being an adult. That explains his sexlessness. Like a child he regarded everyone else as there to validate and accommodate

him. Like a child, all he wanted to do was play with his toys –
his studio and his equipment. He couldn't – and didn't – deal
with anything which got in the way of that. How else could
a businessman and impresario like Norman claimed to be let
his mother sign his cheques? All his life he was just "baby
Norman".'

One day towards the end of January 1957, Jimmy Self was at
the Petty studio, recording a radio spot for a local politician,
when he noticed yet another group of young musicians rehearsing in the studio. 'Their leader stood out because he wore a
maroon shirt and because his legs were so long that his Levis
flapped above his ankles,' Self remembers. 'And he wore glasses,
which was kind of unusual to see a young musician in those
days.

'Norman forgot what we were working on and said, "Oh,
gosh, I have to go and see that guy, Buddy Holly. I'm going to
record him." I said, "Norman, he doesn't look like he can afford
it." "No, he can't," Norman said. "So I guess I'm going to have
to finance him."

'I said, "He plays great guitar, Norman. But I don't think
he'll ever make a singer."'

Buddy had known about the Norman Petty studio since his
earliest semi-pro country music days. In March 1954, Don Guess
wrote him an enthusiastic four-page letter from El Paso, suggesting that their then group, the Rhythm Playboys, should try out
this new place in Clovis the next time they scraped up enough to
finance a demo. Instead, as their style mutated through bluegrass
to rock 'n' roll, the habit stuck of using radio KDAV or
Nesman's studios at Wichita Falls. It was not until the early
spring of 1956, between his first two sessions for Decca in
Nashville, that Buddy finally decided to see what the Petty
studio had to offer. Backed by Don, Sonny Curtis and J. I.

Allison, he cut six of his own compositions, 'Baby, Won't You Come Out Tonight?', 'I Guess I Was Just A Fool', 'Because I Love You', 'I'm Gonna Set My Foot Down', 'I'm Changing All Those Changes' and 'Rock-a-Bye Rock'. According to Petty, he hoped to persuade Decca to let him record for them in Clovis rather than at Bradley's unsympathetic Barn in Nashville.

The person who aroused Petty's interest at that first session was not Buddy but his group's second featured guitarist, the chubby and personable Sonny Curtis. It so happened that the guitarist in Petty's own trio, Jack Vaughn, had just announced his resignation, so putting many lucrative Air Force bookings in jeopardy. A couple of days later, Sonny was surprised to be telephoned by Petty and asked to return to Clovis on his own. 'Norman invited me up to that apartment he had above the garage, and gave me cookies and milk. I'm sitting there, eating these macaroons, feeling as uncomfortable as a hog upstairs. Norman's telling me that if I'll be in his trio, he'll buy me my own electric guitar and I'll be headed for the big time, and I'm thinking "Hey! Great gig man!"

'Then he takes me across to the studio for an audition, and I realize that if I join up with him, I'll have to spend my life playing slow old things like 'Honeysuckle Rose'. Buddy begged me not to quit as well, so I turned it down. And after that, I don't believe Norman liked me until the day he died.'

The thought of Petty as a possible saviour did not seriously cross Buddy's mind until the end of 1956, after his second Decca single had flopped and he was kicking his heels around Lubbock, resigned to the idea that his contract would be terminated any day now. In the tight, mutually supportive circle of West Texan rockabilly, he had become good friends with the Rhythm Orchids and Roy Orbison, and from both quarters had heard how recording at Petty's studio had been a kick-start to bigger and better things. Further encouragement came from his old Sunday school classmate Terry Noland, who now worked with

Larry Welborn in a group called the Four Teens, but whose distinctive voice and good looks had inspired Petty to promote him as a solo singer. Noland remembers Buddy riding up to his house on a motorcycle, sunken in gloom over the Decca business. 'I said, "Why don't you go see Norman? He's got me a recording contract. Maybe he can get you one."'

Amid the encircling despondency, that January of 1957 contained one bright spot. Back in hopeful 1956, when Buddy and the Two Tones still enjoyed the prestige of Decca recording artists, a concert promoter named A. W. Bamford had signed them up for their second professional tour, a major roadshow featuring Hank Thompson, Wanda Jackson, Hank Locklin, Mitchell Torok and Cowboy Copas, and visiting fourteen cities scattered through Arkansas, Louisiana, Georgia, Alabama, Tennessee and Florida. The entire bill was country with the exception of Mitchell Torok, who had a novelty hit single entitled 'When Mexico Gave Up The Rumba To Do The Rock And Roll'. But at least Buddy's group were featured artists rather than just fill-ins, though they also had the job of backing other acts on the bill. Afterwards, in his usual punctilious way, Buddy wrote to the promoter, apologizing for the fact that they'd been 'a little green', but saying he thought the experience had helped them.

In fact the Hank Thompson tour saw the end of the quartet which had struggled so hard to make it on the Decca label. When they returned home, both Don Guess and Sonny Curtis decided to quit. Don had never been able to afford his own bass fiddle, and the one on loan from Lubbock High had been so badly knocked about by travelling on car roof-racks that its scroll was now completely broken off. And Sonny, despite his genial nature, was miffed by Buddy's growing tendency to play lead guitar as well as singing. Offered a further tour, this time with the country music giant Slim Whitman, he jumped at the chance and joined Whitman's caravan, destined for his own glory as a performer and songwriter, but never to play in a group of Buddy's again, at least not during Buddy's lifetime.

As a replacement for Don Guess, Buddy turned to Larry Welborn, who had played bass for Bob Montgomery and him back in schoolboy country days on radio KDAV. Larry agreed to fill in, but was not always available for gigs since he also was still playing rhythm guitar in the Four Teens. There was also the problem of finding a new guitarist content to play rhythm chords in Buddy's – and the Stratocaster's – lengthening shadow. The solution materialized in nineteen-year-old Niki Sullivan, who happened to turn up with his brand-new semi-cutaway 'cello guitar at one of their living-room jam sessions. A distant cousin of Buddy's – though they only found this out much later – Niki had much the same lanky build and also wore glasses, albeit with slightly more modish transparent frames. He did not consider himself musically talented and was amazed to be asked to join Buddy's group without any kind of formal audition.

At the tail-end of January, with the Hank Thompson tour behind him and no other prospect ahead, Buddy returned to the Norman Petty studio with Jerry Allison and Larry Welborn. This time they recorded just two tracks: Chuck Berry's 'Brown-Eyed, Handsome Man', and 'Bo Diddley', the only song which a composer ever had the hubris to name after himself. Black rock 'n' roll performers had by this point become resigned to the taming and homogenization of their songs by bland white balladeers like Pat Boone. Buddy's interpretations both respected the originals and lifted them to his own plane of humour and exuberance:

> ... *Milo de Venus was a beautiful lassie, had the world in the palm of her hand.*
> *She lost both her arms in a rasslin' match*
> *To win a brown-eyed, handsome man ...*

By now, the cold-eyed, not-quite-handsome man watching through control-room glass had ceased to be merely an impassive technician. 'I was amazed at the intensity and at the honesty and sincerity of [Buddy's] whole approach to music,' Petty remembered afterwards. 'Of course, it was completely foreign to what I had known ... our trio had played mainly in hotel dining rooms and country clubs. And so to see someone so honest and so completely himself was super-refreshing. He wasn't the world's most handsome guy, he didn't have the world's most beautiful voice, but he was himself ...' Vi Petty, too, who had initially thought the quartet 'real gangly' in their T-shirts and Levis, was impressed by their professionalism as well as charmed by their old-fashioned Texan politeness. The end result was everything that Buddy had hoped. Petty told him to write a couple of new songs, bring his group back at the end of February, and they'd work together on putting together a single.

The crucial factor in getting the Rhythm Orchids their deal with Roulette Records had been the sister of their guitarist Donnie Lanier, a glamorous girl named Tuddie who worked as a shoe-model in New York and mixed socially with Roulette's boss, the gangster-like Morris Levy.

Donnie's other sister, June Clark, also had the face and figure of a mannequin, but had opted to stay in Lubbock, get married, have a son and work on the cosmetics counter at the Hull drugstore. In early 1957, June, too, found herself being drawn into a Lubbock music scene which suddenly seemed full of burgeoning talent. June's cousin Gary Tollett was also a singer, ambitious to follow the Rhythm Orchids on to the Roulette label. On 21 February Gary booked a recording session at radio KDAV, recruited his wife Ramona and June Clark as back-up singers, and asked June if she could find a drummer and a guitarist to accompany them. 'I was advised to call Jerry Allison, who said he'd do the session, and did I mind if he brought his own guitarist along?' June remembers. 'And the guitarist he brought was Buddy Holly.'

The session went well, producing tracks that did ultimately help Gary Tollett to a recording contract on a subsidiary of Roulette. As a quid pro quo, Gary and his wife Ramona offered to be back-up singers for Buddy's session at the Norman Petty studio, four days hence.

The problem immediately arose of where to rehearse this new, augmented group line-up. Both Buddy's and J.I.'s parents had always made their living-rooms freely available, but even they were likely to jib at the presence of six people. Then June Clark made a fateful suggestion. With her husband, James, and herself both out at work all day and their eleven-year-old son, Carley, at school, their house on Second Place was empty but for June's grandmother, Ada. 'And we had this big den with not much furniture in it, which I told them would be great as a rehearsal-room.'

Buddy, meantime, had been running through the dozen or so songs he had written and recorded over the past year, and arguing with Jerry and Larry Welborn about which might be the most commercial. They kept coming back to the least promising out-take from Buddy's second Decca session, the song he and J.I. had knocked off in half an hour, inspired by John Wayne's laconic catchphrase in *The Searchers*. For all that its title now seemed an all-too-apt commentary on Buddy's struggle to succeed, they decided to try again with 'That'll Be The Day'.

Over four days of intensive rehearsal in the Clarks' den, the song underwent drastic revision. Where Buddy's Decca version had been strained and over-echoey, this one was lower in key and a little slower, allowing his voice to be both more relaxed and more polished, hinting at rather than showing off the gymnastics of which it was capable. His word-fracturing hiccup was used only once, but to effect, transforming an other clichéd 'bridge': 'Well, you give me all your lovin' and your tu-HIC-

urtle-dovin . . .' His Fender Stratocaster moved to the foreground
with a janglier version of the 'Switchie Titchie Witchie' riff, and
a middle solo, borrowing the two-note bass riff from another of
his Decca out-takes, 'Ting A Ling'. The most crucial new element
was the background chorus of Gary and Ramona Tollett and the
new rhythm guitarist, Niki Sullivan, chiming with Buddy's voice
on the refrain, then supplying a blurry undertow of 'Oooh' and
'Aaah' that owed something to rhythm and blues but rather
more to the choirs that could be heard in any of Lubbock's
numerous churches.

In the late afternoon of 24 February 1957, a bright red '55
Cadillac bowled along the two-lane blacktop from Lubbock to
Clovis, beside the hotel-size grain elevators and the tracks of the
Sante Fe. The Caddy was Buddy's latest bandwagon, largely
financed by his elder brother, Larry – and destined to be returned
to Furrs Auto, 'shot', inside six months. With the barely
restricted speeds and tolerant police of those days, the game was
to maintain an average speed of 90 mph-plus so that, with the
hour gained at the New Mexico border, they would reach Clovis
at the same time, or even a couple of minutes before, they had
left Lubbock. On this momentous trip, Larry also went along to
do the driving and keep order as best he could. 'Buddy and Jerry
together were quite a handful,' he remembers. 'They'd holler or
make signs at guys in other cars, then the other guys'd chase us,
wanting to fight. I'd have to get out there and calm things down.
One of two times, I'd end up having a fight myself.'

At the last moment during rehearsals, Buddy had come up
with another new song to submit to Norman Petty, a jaunty
country-flavoured number called 'I'm Looking For Someone To
Love'. He had not finished it when they set off for Clovis, and,
Larry remembers, spent most of the journey in the back seat
with his guitar, busking lines which were a light-hearted comment on his own emotional predicament, separated from Echo
McGuire, wondering whom she might be dating in Abilene,

'playing the field' himself in pre-emptive retaliation, but unable to get her out of his mind. 'Caught myself . . . thinkin' of you . . . You can't love me . . . and another one, too . . .' When they crossed the railway tracks at the 'City of Farwell' that mark the state line with New Mexico, he was still stuck for a final verse. 'The bump-bump of our tyres over the railroad tracks gave me an idea,' Larry remembers. 'I said, "Why don't you use that saying of Uncle Henry Drake's: 'Drunk man/Street-car/Foot slip/There you are'?" Buddy says, "Yeah, that might do pretty good . . ."'

Recording sessions at the Petty studio could not begin until late evening, when Ma Petty had closed the gas-pump on the forecourt outside and trucks had ceased to rumble along West Seventh Street. Buddy and his six-person ensemble spent the first three or four hours purely in rehearsal, the first-comers noting with surprise that Petty's control-desk did not overlook the studio but was set sidelong to it, as if to remove all distraction from the exercise of his hyper-sensitive ears. By the time Petty was in his grey leather chair, ready to flip the switch on his Altec board for take one, 'I'm Looking For Someone To Love' had superseded 'That'll Be The Day' as the A-side of the projected single. With more churchy back-up vocals by the Tolletts and Niki Sullivan, and Buddy's wild, two-chiming rockabilly guitar break, it seemed to have everything, not least the virtue of being brand-new rather than a tarted-up out-take.

They worked on 'I'm Looking For Someone To Love' for the greater part of the session, ending up with a jaunty, polished rockabilly romp that tailed off in the mock-melancholy 'Waaa' of an old-fashioned glee-club. Not until almost 3 am did they finally get around to 'That'll Be The Day'. 'There was a party atmosphere by that time,' Tollett remembers. 'We were having fun, not concentrating real hard, like we had with "I'm Looking For Someone To Love". At about the fourth take, Norman said, "Right, that's it." I couldn't believe we had finished

Main picture: Buddy aged about fifteen, already an auto nut (*Holley family*)

Left: The 'baby' of the Holley family with his mother Ella (right), grandmother and sister Pat (*Holley family*)

Buddy at Lubbock High in his first pair of glasses (*Griggs Collection – Bill Griggs*)

Right: Echo wearing the western belt Buddy made for her – and his high school ring around her neck (*Echo Griffith*)

Below: Hi Pockets Duncan, the gentlemanly Lubbock deejay who became Buddy's first manager (*Griggs Collection*)

June Clark, the older woman with whom Buddy had a tempestuous affair during 1957, pictured at the El Morocco night club, New York (*June Clark*)

Above: Buddy flight tests the new Stratocaster with steel guitarist Don Guess (left), bass-player Larry Welborn (far right) and the 'wonderfully envy-free' Bob Montgomery (*Kevin Terry/Bill Griggs*)

Below: Buddy, J. I. Allison (left) and new bass player Joe B. Mauldin give it their all in the den at June and Nig Clark's Lubbock home (*Griggs Collection*)

Above: The day in 1955 that changed Buddy's life. The newly launched Elvis Presley meets his Lubbock fans. Buddy is on the extreme right of the picture (*Steve Bonner*)

Left: Clovis man and wife (*Jerry Fisher*)

Right: Vi Petty
writes lead sheets,
guarded by ceramic
gnome and real-life
chihuahua, Speedy
(*Jerry Fisher*)

Below: Norman
Petty: 'A bad note
could bring him
out in a rash'
(*Jerry Fisher*)

Petty listens
to a playback
(*Jerry Fisher*)

a record. I thought it was more like a demo he could send to New York to show some record company what potential the song had.'

For the free use of his studio, his technical expertise and his flawless ear for pitch, and for the East Coast connections he would now bring into play, Petty demanded the customary quid pro quo. Not only must 'I'm Looking For Someone To Love' and 'That'll Be The Day' be published by his NOR VA JAK company, giving him 50 per cent of their publishing revenues, but his name must appear on both songs as a co-composer, giving him a third share of the writers' royalties also. No matter that Buddy had finished 'I'm Looking For Someone To Love' before even reaching Clovis that day; no matter even that 'That'll Be The Day' had not only been written by Buddy and J. I. Allison months before Petty agreed to take them on, but had already been recorded for Decca with their two names as the sole composing-credit.

Petty's argument was blandly simple, as Niki Sullivan remembers. 'He said that people in the music industry knew him because of his trio, so record companies and disc jockeys and people would be more likely to take an interest if they saw the name "Norman Petty" instead of just some unknown kid from West Texas. And anyway he claimed he had helped to write the songs in a way, by getting them to sound right in the studio and making suggestions all along the line. Buddy didn't care; he was just delighted to think that the songs were going to be published, and that someone like Norman believed in him and was going to push him in New York. And Norman told us that was the way it always happened. We had no choice but to take him at his word.'

What cannot be gainsaid was the acuteness of Petty's ear. Untutored though he was in rock 'n' roll, he instantly realized that the polished and catchy 'I'm Looking For Someone To Love' was not half so strong a track as was the casually dashed-off 'That'll Be The Day'. Before the song could be offered on the open market, however, two ticklish contractual matters needed resolving. The first was that Buddy had co-written 'That'll Be The Day' while under contract to Jim Denny's Cedarwood publishing company, which gave Cedarwood an automatic, pre-emptive claim on the new version's publishing revenues, if any. Petty later talked Denny into trading his 50 per cent of 'That'll Be The Day' for full rights in another, much less valuable Buddy song, 'Think It Over' (which Denny must have done with extreme resentfulness many times afterwards).

A more serious problem was that, although Decca had never shown the slightest desire to release their version of 'That'll Be The Day', Buddy was still bound by his contract with them not to re-record any of the material from the Nashville sessions for a period of five years. On 28 February, with the new Clovis version already four days in the can, he made a long-distance call from Jerry Allison's parents' house in Lubbock to Milt Gabler, vice-president at Decca, New York, hoping that, since Decca seemed to have no further use for him, they might release him from this final obligation. But Gabler was not available, and Buddy had no choice but to plead for clemency with his old adversary, Paul Cohen. For mysterious reasons, the call was tape-recorded at Buddy's end; one can thus share the instant crushing of his hopes, the change in Cohen's manner from indifference to suspicion, and the obvious discomfort of a good Baptist boy trapped into telling a lie:

COHEN: No . . . anything you made for Decca, even if they never released . . . You can't make it for five years for anyone . . .
BUDDY: Hm, well . . . okey dokey then. I guess that . . .
COHEN: Don't feel bad about it.
BUDDY: I can't hardly keep from it, Paul . . . It seems sorta a heck of a way to do a guy . . .

COHEN: You haven't made any of these yet, have you? I mean cut 'em for anybody?

BUDDY: No, sir.

COHEN: Well, before you do, let me know. Maybe we can work out something . . .

BUDDY: Well, we was wanting to just about any time now.

COHEN: Huh?

BUDDY: We was wanting to cut a master like you said on our own, pay for it ourselves and see if we could sell it to somebody.

COHEN: Let me hear it first . . .

Petty was equally incensed by Decca's dog-in-the-manger attitude, and offered a solution of appealing deviousness. If 'That'll Be The Day' were to be marketed as the work of a group, like the Inkspots or the Platters, and the record did not mention Buddy's name, chances were that Paul Cohen might never realize he was the vocalist. One of Buddy's favourite black R & B groups was the Spiders, and a few nights later he, J. I. Allison and Niki Sullivan sat in Jerry's bedroom, going through the entymological section of an encyclopaedia in the hope of finding some other creepy-crawly with which collectively to baptize themselves. They thought, prophetically, of 'The Beetles', but discarded it when J.I. protested that he didn't want to be named after 'a little black bug you'd step on'. Eventually they decided on 'The Crickets', liking the definition of a cricket as 'an insect romantically referred to as making music by rubbing its hind legs together.'

The initial reaction to 'That'll Be The Day' was anything but encouraging. And, for a while, it appeared that Norman Petty's much-vaunted New York connections were not so very much help after all.

An early, resounding slap in the face came from the Roulette label, which had not yet had its two hits with Buddy Knox and Jimmy Bowen of the Rhythm Orchids and had no wish to take a chance on a second group from faraway West Texas. Knox tried to soften the disappointment by suggesting that the Rhythm Orchids might do their own cover version of 'That'll Be The Day'. But, while appreciating that kind thought, the less successful of the two Buddys was determined it would be his rendering the American public heard first.

Actually, Buddy Knox, Jimmy Bowen and a good many others around the West Texas music scene wondered if Roulette's indifference to the Crickets might not be something to do with their new name. 'Everyone kept telling us what a dumb thing we'd decided to call ourselves,' Niki Sullivan remembers. 'It was kind of embarrassing even for the people who had to introduce us on shows. "What, crickets . . . like the bug?" they'd say. "Are you guys really serious?"'

Petty, meanwhile, was having no better luck with Columbia, the label on which his own trio recorded. Columbia's head of A & R was the orchestra-leader Mitch Miller, a bald, black-bearded cross between virtuoso and vampire, famous for his 'singalong' albums and for the oracular pronouncement: 'Rock 'n' roll is just a passing fad. I give it six months.' It proved of no help whatever that Petty was on friendly terms with Mitch Miller – nor even that the Miller orchestra's big 1955 hit had been 'The Yellow Rose Of Texas'. The singalong Prince of Darkness hated 'That'll Be The Day', and advised Petty not to waste his time by offering it elsewhere.

After Miller's rebuff, Petty gave up on record companies and decided to try the more roundabout music publishing route that had got Buddy his original break in Nashville. Petty's NOR VA JAK company had for some years had a tie-in deal with Peer-Southern Music, a New York publishing firm with an international reputation and an impressive, though largely non-rock 'n' roll catalogue. Travelling to New York, where he maintained both an office and an apartment, Petty called on Peer-Southern's general manager, a stocky, humorous man named Murray Deutch. 'He brought me this demo, which he said nobody wanted, and asked me if I could do anything to help,' Deutch remembers. 'That was Norman all over. He only came to you when he needed you. I'd done business with him for a number of years, he fed me some good songs but I can't say there was any warmth between the two of us. Warmth wasn't something you got with Norman Petty. He was the kind of a guy who'd give you ice in the wintertime.'

On hearing 'That'll Be The Day', however, Murray Deutch's frostiness evaporated. 'I could tell immediately that it had something totally special. Rock 'n' roll ... rockabilly ... whatever it was, I just flipped out for it.' A deal was instantly struck. Deutch agreed to take over the job of getting the Crickets a recording deal; in exchange Peer-Southern Music would receive half the publishing rights to 'That'll Be The Day' and 'I'm Looking For Someone To Love',

Murray Deutch was well known as an expert talent-spotter, having brought, among others, the era's top black vocal group, the Platters, into Peer-Southern's fold. But even with Deutch behind it, 'That'll Be The Day' continued to run into blank walls. Larry Newton, the head of A & R at ABC records, passed on it without a qualm, as did Jerry Wexler, the usually unerring creative genius behind the Atlantic label. 'Even to this day, whenever I meet Jerry, he always comes up with the same line,' Deutch says. "You were right, you bastard!"'

The one response that was anything like positive came from Bob Thiele, head of A & R for the Coral label and husband to one of Coral's main female singing attractions, Teresa Brewer. Ironically, Coral was a subsidiary of Decca, the company which – unknown to Murray Deutch – had already run Buddy through the X-ray machine and rejected him. Bob Thiele, likewise, had no idea about this unhappy past history since Coral functioned quite separately from the main Decca label, as well as at a considerably lower level of prestige.

Though primarily a jazz enthusiast, Thiele was not anti-rock 'n' roll and had already worked with another pioneer country-rock act, the Johnny Burnette Trio. But Coral's roster consisted largely of mainstream and exceedingly 'square' pop names like Debbie Reynolds, the McGuire Sisters, the Lawrence Welk Orchestra and Teresa Brewer. While agreeing with Murray Deutch that 'That'll Be The Day' had an unusual and compulsive sound, he knew he could expect trouble from his superiors if he were to attempt such a radical departure from Coral's house-style. 'But I knew Bob liked the song, so I kept on and on at him,' Deutch remembers. '"Bob – get outa here! Go press a thousand copies! How could that hurt anyone?"'

When Thiele played 'That'll Be The Day' to a bevy of senior Decca executives, the reaction was unanimously hostile. The jury did not include Paul Cohen; consequently, no one present had the faintest inkling that the lead voice of 'The Crickets' belonged to a solo singer whom their organization had unceremoniously dumped a few months earlier. Still less was it dreamed that the song itself had already been recorded for the Decca label, and was legally prohibited from being hawked around in this revamped version. It was as theoretically brand-new material that it made Decca's high-ups wince. The company's president, Milt Rachmil, warned Bob Thiele that to issue such a single would not only damage Coral's image but also have all its greatest treasures, like Debbie, the McGuires and Larry Welk, up in arms.

With Murray Deutch still good-humouredly riding him, Thiele came up with a solution which would respect the sensitivities of his superiors and still give 'That'll Be The Day' a crack at the charts. A Decca subsidiary label even more marginal than Coral was Brunswick, once famous as the mouthpiece for Bing

Crosby, but now catering mainly to the unfashionable and barely profitable jazz market. Thiele proposed he should release 'That'll Be The Day' on Brunswick, so keeping Coral's precious image intact, and pressing only a hyper-cautious 1,000 copies. 'They agreed to let me do it, but no one else in the company thought it was really serious,' Thiele remembered. 'It was more like "Oh, Bob wants to do this . . . Let him get his kicks."'

That this whole tortuous saga should have been compressed within less than three weeks gives some idea of the frenetic pace at which America's record business operated in the rock 'n' roll fever of early 1957. 'That'll Be The Day' and 'I'm Looking For Someone To Love' had been recorded on 25 February: by 19 March, Norman Petty had Bob Thiele's written agreement to purchase the two master recordings on Brunswick's behalf for a $100 advance. It was the kind of derisory sum which most labels would have paid an unknown signing on account of royalties, but the royalty-rate itself, just over 2 cents per record sold, was generous in the circumstances. Many newcomers in that era would have received 1 or 1½ cents, and been ecstatic about it.

The four Crickets summoned to Clovis for the signing ceremony were not, however, the same four who had recorded 'That'll Be The Day'. On 3 March, their stand-in bass-player Larry Welborn had been unable to make a $65 gig at the Elks Club in Carlsbad, New Mexico. To take his place Buddy borrowed the Four Teens' bass-player, a diminutive, round-faced sixteen-year-old named Joe B. (for Benson) Mauldin. Compared with Larry and the departed Don Guess, 'Joe B.' was anything but a wizard on bass, 'faking' at least as many notes as he played. His great virtue was possessing his own instrument, rather than having to rent or borrow one each time a gig came up. It was to bring that impressive piece of furniture into the Crickets, more than for anything Joe B. was likely to conjure from it, that Buddy asked him to fill Larry Welborn's place.

'Buddy was real confident about the way things were going,'

Joe B. remembers. 'He told me the group had just made a record … they were headed straight for the big time. Of course, I'd heard that one so many times before. I said, "Oh yeah? How long d'you think it'll take you?" Buddy said, "How long'd it take Elvis?"'

So Joe B. let himself be persuaded, on the understanding that playing for the Crickets would not interfere with his day job as a butcher's assistant at a Lubbock supermarket.

The Bible which never lay far from Norman Petty's right hand played its part in the contract-signing. J.I., Niki and Joe B., like Buddy himself, came from devoutly religious families, and all readily accepted Petty's suggestion that they should each pay 10 per cent of their earnings, the customary 'tithe', to their respective churches. Before the signing, Petty placed his hand on the Bible, the four Crickets laid their hands on top of his, and all joined in a silent moment of thanksgiving and prayer for the future.

The signatures were then ceremonially appended: 'Jerry Allison', 'Niki Sullivan', 'Joe B. Mauldin', the latter somewhat bemused at thus receiving shares in a record on which he hadn't played. But not 'Buddy Holly'. To keep Decca in the dark about his involvement for as long as possible, Buddy's name did not appear on the Crickets' first contract. So far as Bob Thiele knew at this stage, the group consisted of three young men named Allison, Sullivan and Mauldin. Buddy accepted his anonymity willingly enough, still nervous that Paul Cohen or some other Decca high-up would see he had broken his original contract with the company, and veto the release of 'That'll Be The Day'. But it was a decision that would cause him much trouble and grief in months to come.

Between the signing of the contract and the release of the record there was to be a wait of almost three months. During that strung-up spring and early summer, Buddy and the Crickets did little else as a group but record at the Norman Petty studio, under Petty's supervision and at Petty's expense. Whatever faults history may impute to Clovis Man, short-sightedness was not among them. Convinced now of Buddy's potential, he was prepared to go on investing time and resources in him, irrespective of whether or not his début single became a success.

Barely a fortnight after recording 'That'll Be The Day', and before the faintest breath of encouragement from New York, Buddy, J.I. and Niki scooped up their new bass-player, Joe B. Mauldin, from his supermarket butcher's counter and hurtled out along Route 84, as usual trying to make it to Clovis a couple of minutes before the time they'd left Lubbock. Under Petty's supervision they began working on a song called 'Maybe Baby', written – or, at least, started off – by Buddy's mother ('Just to prove I can write a song, too') and destined to be an international hit more than a year later.

Petty's motives were, of course, hardly altruistic. Having lit on yet another bright recording prospect, he was not about to let it slip through his fingers the way Buddy Knox, Jimmy Bowen and the Rhythm Orchids had a few months earlier. Giving young Buddy Holly and his group free studio-time, cutting master discs from their tapes, feeding them generously, even occasionally letting them stay overnight in the musicians' dormitory room, all cost Petty little enough in real terms. As he accurately sensed, this atmosphere of open-handed hospitality was deeply impressive to the young Texans, especially after their Nashville experience, binding them to the Petty Studio with ties more irresistible than any formal contract. For, as their new producer confided to his friend Jimmy Self in an unguarded moment, he could 'almost smell dollars bills here'.

Yet there is no doubt that Petty genuinely liked his four new protégés and in their company became a person very different

from the cool, detached technician who normally occupied his
grey leather swivel-chair. Indeed, the exhilaration of working on
early tracks like 'Maybe Baby' and another new Buddy composition, 'Last Night', had the effect of making Clovis Man
positively skittish. Though only nine years older than Buddy, he
took to addressing the Texans as 'boys' and characterizing
himself as 'Papa Norman' as if he were some grizzled Heming-
way figure or garrulous old sidekick to John Wayne. This could,
of course, be interpreted as another subtle way of underlining
his power and authority, and giving weight to his ban on
drinking and 'cussing', his abhorrence of cigarette-smoking and
ever-ready recourse to corroborative passages in the Scriptures.
To his friend Jerry Fisher, it was yet another symptom of
arrested development. 'Treating Buddy and the others like
children was easier than having children of his own. And they
could all be kids and play games together.'

With Buddy he had a special rapport from the beginning.
Despite Buddy's youth, there was an authority, a maturity, about
him that the older professional musician recognized and
respected. Accustomed though Petty was to having things all his
own way in the studio, he would always ask Buddy for his views
on how a song should be arranged and engineered, adopting
Buddy's ideas and deferring to his objections. The gawky Texan
in his simple Levis and T-shirt and the chubby-faced New Mexican in his effete 'lounging clothes' also had more in common
han might at first meet the eye. There was, for example, that habit
of getting up abruptly from among a crowd of friends or colleagues and disappearing for hours on end – Buddy on his solitary
night-time car-drives, Petty to his various secret bolt-holes
around Clovis. 'The two of them were bound to hit it off well,'
says Jimmy Self. 'They were both perfectionists – and both
loners.'

Even on days when Petty was not working with them,
Buddy, J.I., Niki and Joe B. would still make that clock-cheating

drive to Clovis and hang out at the studio, sprawling on the couch in its tiny reception area, feeding dimes into the red and white Coke machine and gossiping with Petty's gruff-voiced secretary, Norma Jean Berry, or wandering around the grassy compound where the Petty Trio's blue truck awaited its next foray to distant Air Force Bases and Vi Petty tended her strawberry bed in dungarees and bandanna, as ever lost in a world of her own. Clovis Man's recently excavated paperwork reveals that Buddy took advantage of one visit to have the group's long-suffering red Caddy looked over by Pa Petty in the adjacent family garage. Norma Jean, the one-time journalist, also took what would be their earliest publicity photographs, in their white T-shirts looking more like Pa's supernumerary mechanics than rock 'n' roll hitmakers-in-waiting.

In part-payment of their mounting debt to Norman Petty, they became the studio's unofficial house band, backing other West Texans who came to cut demos, like their friend Gary Tollett, country singers Billy Walker and Jim Robinson, and Jack Huddle, a personality from local television. And if any visiting group was short a lead guitarist, Petty had only to glance at Buddy and he'd be on his feet with his big, snaggly smile of 'Don't mind if I do!' Many a mundane rockabilly song that never came within a mile of the late-fifties charts would have a Buddy 'rhythm-lead' solo gleaming out of it like a diamond set in suet pudding.

The Holley family naturally had been curious, and not a little uneasy, about this new benefactor their baby boy had discovered across the state line. West Texans are traditionally suspicious of New Mexicans, regarding them as scarcely less weird and unpredictable than the extra-terrestrial beings reputedly given to crash-landing in their midst. But one meeting with Petty was sufficient to reassure L.O. and Ella Holley that Buddy could not be in safer, more responsible hands if his recording sessions were supervised by the minister at their own Tabernacle Baptist Church. L.O. was particularly impressed – 'mesmerized', Larry

Holley says now – by Petty's dapper appearance, his air of influence and importance and the devout Christian sentiments with which his conversation was liberally sprinkled.

Petty also showed keen interest in the tiling firm which Larry had started and for which L.O., Travis and Buddy himself periodically worked. Indeed, it would not be long before the Holleys discovered Papa Norman's knack of turning everyone around him into dedicated, unsalaried employees.

At Petty's studio, the feature most noticeably lacking was a 'live' echo-chamber – i.e., one to which he had instant and unlimited access via his Altec board during sessions rather than depending on the taped echo effects which had made Buddy's Nashville version of 'That'll Be The Day' sound so eerily unnatural. Until now, all the studio's output, including 'That'll Be The Day' mark 2, had been one-dimensionally 'dry'; if he needed a more cavernous sound, Petty would transfer his recording equipment to a movie theatre called the Lyceum in downtown Clovis.

A few weeks after recording 'Maybe Baby' and 'Last Night' with Buddy and the Crickets, Petty began building an echo-chamber to his own design in the A-frame attic space above the family garage. Larry Holley, accompanied by L.O. and Travis, drove over from Lubbock with a truckload of tiles, remnants from various contracting jobs, and laid them on the attic-floor as a highly effective means of soundproofing. It did not occur to Papa Norman to offer payment for their hours of manual work, nor would the Holleys have dreamed of accepting any. 'We figured it was the least we could do,' Larry says, 'because of all that Norman seemed to be doing for Buddy.'

Petty's own oft-repeated definition of Buddy in this period was 'a diamond in the rough'. From that, history was to infer Petty's own crucial role as a polisher and sculptor of precious stones which, but for him, might never have come to light. The truth is that Buddy's talent developed at its own momentum, and at a speed that makes the maturing of John Lennon and Paul McCartney, half a dozen years later, seem slow by comparison. More often than not, by the time the diamonds reached Clovis, they would be fully-fashioned and polished; all Petty had to provide was the setting.

Those long solitary drives by car provide our best clue to the sudden, huge forward leap in Buddy's talent. Before he began recording in Clovis, he had been used to writing songs with one or more partners: Jack Neal, Bob Montgomery, Don Guess, Sue Parrish. But the songs he brought to Norman Petty from March of 1957 onward were generally his work alone, and drawing on emotions far deeper than he would ever have revealed to his friends as they sat around together, tinkering with words and chords. L. O. Holley was later to recall how, after the family's evening meal – sometimes even in the middle of it – inspiration would suddenly hit Buddy and, with his usual impatience, he would jump up from the table, get into the red Caddy and roar away. Two or three hours later, he would return, go straight to his room and pick up the Gibson guitar with its blue and black Western-tooled leather jacket. Out on the highway, *en route* to Abilene or Amarillo, yet another new song – its words, its chords, its whole arrangement – would have worked itself out in his head.

In early 1957, pop lyric-writing was in its infancy. Teenagers at that time bought records to dance to, not listen to, which explains why so many primal rock 'n' roll classics, if not pure gibberish, were simple declarations of how brain-explodingly wonderful the music itself was. Most were the work of middle-aged Tin Pan Alley hacks with no liking for rock 'n' roll and the lowest possible opinion of their public's intelligence. Such were the insatiable demand and the minuscule supply that one could get a million-selling hit by shoehorning a two-four beat and the word 'rock' into such a hoary old Scottish chestnut as 'Comin'

Through The Rye'. To be sure, some inspired rock 'n' roll songwriters, white as well as black, had emerged by 1957, notably Chuck Berry, Carl Perkins and the New York-based partnership of Jerry Leiber and Mike Stoller. But these tended to be in their mid- or late twenties; young enough to be caught up in the teenage revolution, but mature and sophisticated to comment on, even gently satirize, the culture it produced.

Buddy was only twenty and, thus far in his life, nothing much had happened to him. For a creative muse he could not draw on the nervy, neon excitement of Chuck Berry's Chicago nor Leiber and Stoller's view down Broadway: only horizonless wheat and cottonfields, the lawns and churches of Lubbock, the archetypal young American's life-cycle of high school, dating, movies and drive-ins. It was when he stopped pretending otherwise, when he found the nerve, the encouragement and the space to be himself, that raw talent suddenly blossomed into fully-finished brilliance.

The era of profound or meaningful pop-lyrics was, of course, still far in the future. Buddy wrote about what his peers expected him to – falling for girls, pursuing girls, winning girls, losing girls and feeling blue. If simple or predictable, his lyrics were always accomplished, phrased with the neatness of the one-time amateur journalist, adding up with the logic and precision of the draughtsman he had almost become. From Hank Williams first, then the Chicago bluesmen and finally Elvis, he had learned that words were less important than what one put into them. In the perfect environment of Norman Petty's polycylindrical studio walls – and with no one waiting to call 'Time' on the Western Union clock – he began to use his voice with ever more adventurousness and audacity, refining the ebullient tongue-waggles, pulverized vowels, swooning sighs and word-fracturing hiccups that would become his multitudinously imitated trademark.

While the lyrics he wrote and performed were never remotely autobiographical, they were always suffused with his personal characteristics: friendliness, modesty, humour and what can only be called instinctive good taste. Most have the same quality as that English essay he wrote as a Lubbock High School sophomore, on sheets torn from a hardware company's scribbling-pad. Beneath the ostensible high spirits and self-confidence can be felt a qualm of insecurity; a fear that the sunny dream he has expressed may not turn out as he hopes; but a resolution to hope for the best and keep smiling regardless.

Finding a producer with Norman Petty's peculiar combination of talents and obsessions had, creatively speaking, been a lucky break in a million. In 1957, the number of independent record producers could be counted on the fingers of one hand. Even rarer, especially in a far-flung place like New Mexico, were studios well enough equipped to supply major record labels with fully-finished masters that could be put straight into production. Buddy therefore would be spared all the bureaucracy and conformity to house style that had made his Decca sessions so miserable. What Petty gave him was a place to make records in peace and at his own pace, free of distraction and interference, and working to his personal standards rather than committee or corporate ones. In the 1990s this is something any pop musician of original talent takes for granted: four decades ago, it was unprecedented.

Teaming with Petty was important in another crucial respect. For all his dedication to country first, then rock 'n' roll, Buddy had never shut his mind to other musical styles; he enjoyed classical music, and his record collection included all the mainstream 'greats' like Frank Sinatra and Ella Fitzgerald. Nor, unlike the others, did he find the staid cocktail lounge music of the Norman Petty Trio laughably old-fashioned and 'square'; he respected the Trio's polish and professionalism, listening attentively to their records to see what might be learned from them. Later on, when one of the Trio's own recording sessions for Columbia fell due, Buddy joined them on rhythm guitar to demo' a sub-Mantovani composition by Petty called 'Moondreams'. These soft, sweet draughts of mainstream pop were as important as the high-octane input of Elvis and Little Richard in lifting his talent into the stratosphere.

By late spring of 1957, the kindergarten simplicity of 'That'll Be The Day' already seemed years in the past. April 5 saw the taping of a song originally inspired by Mickey and Sylvia's 'Love Is Strange', and already tried out in various styles, one of them featuring Norman Petty on organ. But the final version was Buddy on his own – or, rather, Buddy performing with Buddy, since both his vocal and his guitar were double-tracked, and the most attentive listener was never to know, still less care, that there had been anyone else in the studio.

'Words Of Love' would have been a remarkable production in any era, but is the more remarkable for having been created in the very eye of the rock 'n' roll hurricane, when the only resonance expected from young people's music was soulless, one-dimensional uproar. The double-tracking technique itself was nothing new, having been a feature of Les Paul and Mary Ford records since the early fifties. But the aural cloning process had never before, and has never since, created an effect quite like this. Buddy's lead and descanting voice are so much in the foreground that they seem to whisper directly into one's ear. The words are of tender adoration edged with uncertainty – 'Hold me close and ... tell me how you feel ... tell me love is real' – the dual voice humming confident affirmation in the same breath as it wistfully seeks reassurance. The Stratocaster features not in its usual show-off solo but in a leitmotif that intensifies the two-minded mood, its rhythm track firmly-rippled down-strokes, its lead a tearful Hawaiian phrase, dissolving into icy-sharp, wind-chiming single strings.

The B-side could hardly have been more of a contrast, either in style or interpretation. Just before the session, Petty had received the demo' of a song called 'Mailman, Bring Me No More Blues', one of whose three writers, 'Stanley Clayton', was the pseudonym of Coral Records boss Bob Thiele. Buddy did not have to be persuaded of the wisdom in recording a song by the man who'd given the Crickets their recording contract. And the number itself, a traditional twelve-bar blues, was in the nature of a challenge: 'See what your boy can do with this' had been Thiele's patronizing message to Petty. Clearly, Thiele doubted whether Brunswick's new signing had the talent to perform anything beyond elementary rock 'n' roll.

By the time 'Words Of Love' had been polished to Buddy's and Petty's satisfaction, there remained only the pre-dawn tail-end of the session to work on 'Mailman, Bring Me No More Blues'. To give it an authentic blues feel, and also the lift of professional musicianship, Petty got his wife Vi out of bed to augment the Crickets on piano. Buddy by this time was almost dropping with fatigue, but still managed a bravura performance, his single-tracked voice as soaked in schmalzy melodrama as his double-tracked one had previously been subtle and restrained. Standing at the keyboard of the Baldwin grand in her hair-curlers, robe and slippers, Vi rolled out a raunchy twelve-bar figure that would not have disgraced Fats Domino. After that first, go-for-it take, the mellow voice over the studio-intercom told them it would do just fine.

The two-sided master subsequently posted to Bob Thiele in New York demonstrated beyond argument that here was something more than just the grunting mouthpiece of a rock 'n' roll group. A singer who could perform a complex love song in one breath and a raucous adult blues in the next did not deserve to be hidden away on Brunswick, but could safely be elevated to the Coral label to join the rarefied likes of Debbie Reynolds, Teresa Brewer and Lawrence Welk. With 'That'll Be The Day' still awaiting release under the Crickets' name, Thiele proposed that 'Words Of Love' would come out on Coral under Buddy's name alone.

Behind the apparent compliment to Buddy lay hard-headed

commercial logic. In 1957, the career of a new rock 'n' roll attraction was reckoned in only months, or even weeks. Having a group and solo singer-plus-backing who were identical and interchangeable gave Thiele a double bite at the cherry. Teenagers who liked groups might buy the Crickets' records, those who preferred solo singers might buy Buddy's 'own-name' ones; more gullible or tone-deaf souls might not even realize the same vocalist was featured, and buy both. It was also a ploy to grab extra seconds of vitally important radio airtime: a disc jockey might well play a Crickets record and a Buddy Holly one on the same programme where he could never dream of playing two by the same performer. Talented solo singers emerged from groups commonly enough, but no one before had supposed that a group and its lead vocalist might enjoy successful careers in parallel.

Buddy's signing to Coral under his own name, on 16 May, also had the effect of resolving the awkward situation created by his original Decca contract. The main Decca label now recognized Bob Thiele's new solo artist as the same Buddy Holly who'd had two unsuccessful singles with them a year earlier, and was legally bound not to re-record any material from their sessions until 1961. That undertaking had clearly been breached by his new version of 'That'll Be The Day', for all that he sang it anonymously within a group. On the other hand, since the re-recorded version was to be issued by one of Decca's subsidiary labels, the organization could hardly be said to be the loser. Even so, there were some angry corporate mutters inside Decca, even talk of legal proceedings against Buddy until Bob Thiele successfully pleaded the futility of such a course. In return for being released from the old contract's five-year clause, and not being sued, Buddy had to waive his right to any royalties from the Nashville version of 'That'll Be The Day'.

His relief at the sorting out of the contractual mess and elation at his solo Coral signing was tempered by unease at being so clearly marked out from the other Crickets, especially from his best friend Jerry Allison. Norman Petty had already made the tentative suggestion that, as lead singer and instrumentalist as well as principal songwriter, Buddy could claim a larger share of the group's earnings than J.I., Niki and Joe B., or even get away with paying them a wage as mere 'sidemen'. 'Buddy almost got mad over that,' Niki Sullivan remembers. 'He told Norman we were all part of the team, and we all had to get the same equal share.'

'That'll Be The Day' was released on 27 May. Buddy and the Crickets had not been told in advance of the release-date, and discovered it was finally in the stores only by pure accident. 'Buddy was helping me on a tile-job,' his brother Larry remembers. 'We were out at the new city-county health unit, putting down these big green tiles, and he was real depressed, saying how he and the others had cut their record six weeks ago, and they'd heard nothing more from the record company and couldn't find out anything from Norman about when it was supposed to come out. He said, "Larry, I know good and well I could make it," and I said, 'Well, you and the guys had your chance. I lent you money for a guitar and clothes and all. Looks like maybe that's it."

'Later on, we were working inside, and Buddy was still real blue, so I said, "Why don't you call up the guy in New York and just ask him? You got his number, don't you?" So we went to Mother's and Buddy called up the record company. And the guy there says, "Hey, baby! They're playing your record on the streets of New York City!" So Buddy says, "Well, can you send me five hundred dollars? 'Cause I'm broke!"'

The first test for any new record in 1957, whether rock 'n' roll, country, pop or calypso, was what the music trade press thought of it. The era of music papers with a general readership, let alone a specifically youthful one, had still barely dawned. The two all-powerful arbiters were *Billboard* and *Cash Box*, both of which spoke mainly to the industry itself – and neither of which, as their flat, jaded prose indicated, could muster a single reviewer under the age of about forty. Even so, *Billboard's* capsule notice of 'That'll Be The Day' on 10 June was generally favourable: 'Fine vocal by [the Crickets] on a well-made side that should get play. Tune is a medium beat rockabilly. Performance is better than material.' The B-side, 'I'm Looking For Someone To Love', was described with slightly more warmth ('bright, vigorous treatment') but received the same lukewarm 72 out of 100 rating.

A new rock 'n' roll act making its début that summer faced formidable competition indeed. Not only America but now Britain and most of Europe were gripped by Elvis Presley mania. The mumbling million-sellers continued to congest the tops of every chart, their titles a shorthand summary of the havoc being wrought on family life across the hemispheres: 'Too Much' . . . 'All Shook Up' . . . 'Paralysed'. But if the shrieks of teenage girls were still as appalling as ever to grown-up ears, they also were now recognized as a force to move the giant mills of American industry. A name which, a year ago, had seemed almost too bizarre to articulate had unleashed a marketing and merchandise bonanza on a scale hitherto known only to the Walt Disney Corporation. Thanks to a thousand and one spin-off deals by Colonel Tom Parker, the Elvis handmaiden could display her master's supercilious likeness on her blouse, her jeans, her purse or her bobby-socks; she could buy Elvis cosmetics, with lipstick-shades including 'Tutti-Frutti Red' and 'Houn' Dog Orange', even play her records on an Elvis gramophone upholstered in the same blue suede as his sacrosanct shoes.

The world's fascination was heightened by the contradictory images which Elvis himself presented to the media. It was the same paradox that had astonished Buddy and his friends back-stage at Lubbock's Fair Park Coliseum: the shameless posturing rabble-rouser of the concert stage was in private a shy, modest

Southern boy, amazed and shocked that people should find his performing style objectionable and anxious to reassure that he meant no harm to anyone. If not yet dubbed 'the King', he could already claim undisputed status as a form of deity. For the New York opening of his first film, *Love Me Tender*, ecstatic crowds filled Times Square to watch the covers ceremonially drop from a guitar-toting, sideburned cardboard effigy in 3-D, forty feet high.

No such ambiguity surrounded Little Richard, whose outrageous performances were equalled, if not surpassed, by his behaviour offstage, and whose sparkle-suited, piano-punishing, whooping figure seemed to exult in its power to jangle grown-up sensibilities beyond endurance. The clergy and media-led equation of rock 'n' roll with unbridled sex had been confirmed by *The Girl Can't Help It*, a movie in glorious Technicolor rather than the dingy black and white of previous Rock exploitation pictures, and starring the 'blonde bombshell' Jayne Mansfield, whose gigantic, pointed bosoms resembled a dead-heat in a Zeppelin race. Intended as a satire on rock 'n' roll, the picture somehow turned into a celebration of it, perhaps the best ever created on celluloid. The most memorable sequence shows Mansfield tripping top-heavily along a city street while Richard performs the title song in voice-over; at the combined assault of gigantic breasts and lip-smacking soundtrack, milk bottles explode as if in spontaneous orgasm and the spectacles of a male onlooker splinter in their frames.

The Girl Can't Help It featured cameo performances by other rock 'n' roll hitmakers of the hour, like the Platters and Fats Domino, plus a bevy of rising newcomers. Here was seventeen-year-old Eddie Cochran, singing 'Twenty Flight Rock' with knocking knees and a guitar slung around his neck, for the moment looking and sounding like nothing more than yet another Presley clone. Here was a former merchant seaman named Gene Vincent, partially disabled by a motorcycle accident and with a misshapen palate that gave his singing voice a tremulous castrato pitch. For hard-core rock 'n' roll fans, the film's highlight was Vincent performing a piece of sublime gibberish called 'Be-Bop-A-Lula' with his backing group, the Blue Caps (strictly speaking the prototype rock 'n' roll band in their matching 'cheese-cutter' caps, though too undefined and charmless to produce any direct imitators).

The fact that Elvis was already turning to slow ballads and beginning to carve out a career in Hollywood, together with the dying fall of Bill Haley and the Comets, seemed to indicate that rock 'n' roll's detractors could have been right: maybe after all it was just a nine days' wonder. Certainly, what had begun to dominate the American charts by mid-1957 was not rock 'n' roll so much as rock-flavoured pop, sung by young whites who mirrored the clean-cut high school image of their audience. The two newest chart arrivals, Ricky Nelson and the close-harmonizing Everly Brothers, were devastatingly good-looking boys with a dewy, unused air that in each case belied long experience in the business. Nelson had started as a child actor with his parents on their television sitcom, *The Adventures of Ozzie and Harriet*. The Kentucky-born Everlys, Don and his younger brother Phil, had begun singing together as toddlers on their parents' country music radio show.

That spring the Everly Brothers had their first US number 1 with 'Bye Bye Love'. Ricky Nelson was climbing fast with his cover version of Fats Domino's 'I'm Walkin''. On the strength of his cameo spot in *The Girl Can't Help It*, Eddie Cochran had made number 18 with a sugary teenage idyll called 'Sitting In The Balcony'. Yet week after week, in *Billboard*'s Top 100 chart, there still was no sign of 'That'll Be The Day' by the Crickets. Only one nice thing had happened to the song; yet another 'first' for Buddy, though of little comfort in the circumstances. A black R & B group, the Ravens, had snapped it up through Norman

Petty's publishing partners, Peer-Southern music, and covered it as the B-side of their new single, 'Dear One'.

While everyone else seemed to be going places, the only road that stretched before Buddy Holly and the Crickets was the two-lane blacktop to Clovis. Two more future classics, 'Not Fade Away' and 'Everyday', were already 'in the can' at Petty's, with no idea yet that there would ever be a chance to release them. Both songs exemplify the way Buddy's music evolved in the studio, and how off-the-cuff improvisation – and even outright plagiarism – could be transmuted into something unique. 'Not Fade Away' originally belonged to the second category. Largely written by Jerry Allison, it borrowed the shuffling stop-beat of 'Bo Diddley', which Buddy had demo'd six or seven months earlier. Another idea was cribbed from that much envied Buddy Knox hit, 'Party Doll', J.I. forsaking his drums and beating out the staccato rhythm with sticks on an empty cardboard box. Petty's artful use of volume and echo gave the song a fragile, almost haunted quality: Buddy might be singing it alone in the centre of some wide Texas plain while his and Niki's dubbed back-up voices and the thumping box are borne faintly on the wind.

'Everyday', by contrast, was all Buddy's own, a love song imbued with his special mixture of confidence, uncertainty and steadfast hope: 'Ev'ryday ... it's-a-gettin' closer ... goin' faster than a rollercoaster ... love like yours will surely come my way ...' Among the instruments standing around Petty's studio was a celeste, a distant cousin to the harpsichord whose tinkling notes most familiarly signified time passing or autumn leaves falling in radio soap-operas. In a break from rehearsing 'Everyday' with straightforward Crickets back-up, Buddy went over to the celeste and began fooling around on it. The dainty, old-fashioned sound, Petty realized, exactly matched the mood of the song. Vi Petty was summoned to work out a formal arrangement, though

Norman made it clear that he'd be the one to play on the record. As she tried it through, Jerry Allison sat nearby, beating an extempore rhythm with his palms on the knees of his jeans. 'That sounds pretty good, too!' Petty said. So J.I.'s knee-slapped percussion joined the celeste in an almost non-existent accompaniment which gave Buddy's voice maximum scope to work its alchemy on hitherto unelastic one-vowel words:

> *Love like yours will surely come my way*
> *A-hey*
> *A-hey-hey.*

With 'That'll Be The Day' still nowhere in the charts, Buddy had switched his hopes to 'Words Of Love', his first 'own name' release for the Coral label, twinned with 'Mailman, Bring Me No More Blues'. As with 'That'll Be The Day', the publishing rights had been chanelled by Petty's NOR VA JAK company to Peer-Southern in New York, who put 'Words of Love' on the open market for anyone who wished to make a cover version. And as with 'That'll Be The Day', it was snapped up by a rival vocal group, in this case the Diamonds, who recorded it as a follow-up to 'Little Darlin'', their number 2 hit of the previous March. The Diamonds' unsubtle, unimaginative 'Words Of Love' appeared in the charts on 20 June, the very day that Buddy's version was released, thereby virtually guaranteeing its eclipse.

Though 'Words Of Love' had seemingly joined 'That'll Be The Day' in oblivion, Norman Petty's confidence appeared unshaken, and Buddy and the Crickets were allowed to keep on recording. On 30 June, when the temperature in Clovis stood at 106 degrees Fahrenheit, they returned to Petty's for a session destined to last three days and nights and, among other things, to create a rock 'n' roll goddess.

J. I. Allison's current date was a seventeen-year-old Lubbock High School sophomore named Peggy Sue Gerron. Sharply pretty, with an hourglass figure and short blonde hair, she played alto saxophone and also twirled a drum-majorette's baton in the school's Ruritanian-uniformed marching band. Though Buddy's graduation from Lubbock High now seemed ages past, he would still occasionally sing and play guitar at the school's socials, or 'assemblies'. 'The first time I met him I was on my way to the band-room,' Peggy Sue remembers. 'Buddy came rushing through the door so fast, he almost knocked me over. As he went on, he called over his shoulder, "I'm real sorry I don't have time to stop and apologize."

'Then a few days later, Jerry said to me, "Would you come out on a double-date with me and my best friend." When he came to my house to pick me up, there was Buddy sitting in the back seat of the car with his girl, Echo. When he saw who I was, he laughed and said to Jerry, "I've already overwhelmed your Peggy Sue." The four of us double-dated quite a few times after that. Echo wasn't allowed to dance, so Buddy and I would dance together. He was a real good dancer, very graceful. And he always made me laugh.'

Among the new songs which Buddy brought to Clovis on 30 June was one which he'd originally called 'Cindy Lou' – 'Cindy' after his sister Pat's small daughter, and 'Lou' after Pat's own middle name – and which already featured in the Crickets' stage repertoire, played to a light Latin beat. As they began rehearsing J.I. warmed up, as percussionists often do, with a pounding, cymbal-less paradiddle beat on his snare-drum. Buddy liked the sound and suggested they should use it on 'Cindy Lou', even though the noise rebounded so fearsomely off the polycylindral walls that Petty had J.I. and his drum-kit moved out to the tiny reception area, in company with Norma Jean's vacant desk and the red-and-white Coke machine.

After several attempts, the new tempo still did not seem quite right and, as a spur to his banished drummer, Buddy agreed to drop 'Cindy Lou' as a title and substitute the name of J.I.'s girl.

With this change of vision, from toddler in pigtails to svelte high school majorette, the song finally cohered. In a flash of inspiration, Norman Petty flicked his new echo-chamber's control-switch continually between 'Off' and 'On', so that J.I.'s paradiddles sounded like two drummers pounding out a dark, undulating Voodoo beat against Buddy's relentless plectrum-clicking downstrokes. Rudimentary, undeveloped words heightened the trance-like effect, prophesying the disco and rap age thirty years later. About this mythic Peggy Sue, the words revealed nothing other than that she made her moody paramour feel 'blue', yet still love her 'with a love so rare 'n' true'. Where she came to life was in the ever-changing shades and shifts of Buddy's voice, her name repeated over and over like a mantra – now murmured in tongue-tied bashfulness, now stretched to a six-syllable school-yard taunt ('Sue-oo-oo- oo-oo- oo'), now hiccuped as if it brought on acid indigestion ('Uh-oh, Peg-gy!') now sighed in rapture, now transmuted into a ringing four-chord eulogy, perhaps the simplest, most infallibly nerve-tingling solo in all rock 'n' roll.

That weekend saw a record heatwave in Clovis, with temperatures rising to 107 Fahrenheit and dust-storms gusting to 90 m.p.h. One can visualize it almost like the opening sequence of a black-and-white B-movie – a huge, lowering sky; racketing store-signs and whirling tumbleweed; faint sounds of rock 'n' roll magic drifting from that air-conditioned, alcohol-free bunker on West Seventh Street.

By the time Buddy and the Crickets started back for Lubbock, at 3 am on 3 July, three more tracks had joined 'Peggy Sue' in the can. 'Listen To Me' was a new Buddy song in the same wistful mood and call-and-response style as 'Words Of Love', but with dramatically heightened echo on his double-tracked vocal and guitar. 'Oh Boy' was a tear-'em-up rock 'n' roll number, recently sent in to Norman Petty on spec' by a young writer from Levelland, Texas, named Sonny West, who'd got the idea from seeing cheerleaders jumping up and down at a college football game. 'I'm Gonna Love You Too' was a frisky rockabilly throwback on which the Crickets found themselves augumented from an unexpectedly appropriate quarter. As the last notes of the playback died away, a real cricket, which had somehow found its way into the echo-chamber, gave a reverberant double chirrup. Since the noise happened to be exactly in beat, they decided to leave it on the record.

Although Buddy's contractual difficulties with Decca had been resolved, he was still not quite free of worries arising from his false start the previous year. There remained a residue of disagreement with Cedarwood, the Nashville publishing company whose owner, Jim Denny, had got him his original Decca contract in exchange for signing him as a songwriter. Technically Buddy was no longer bound to Cedarwood, but he was afraid they might find some reason to claim a share in the new songs he was now turning out so prolifically. To prevent Jim Denny realizing just how full was the crop, Petty suggested that Buddy publish some under a pseudonym. He chose one formed from his own real Christian names, 'Charles Hardin'.

'Not Fade Away', 'Everyday' and 'Listen To Me' bore two writer-credits, 'Charles Hardin' and Norman Petty. It was the same as had already happened to 'That'll Be The Day', despite its having been written months before Petty had even met Buddy and the Crickets; the same as also had happened to 'Maybe Baby' – and, for that matter, to 'Oh Boy', the composition of young Sonny West in Levelland, who still did not even know that Buddy and the Crickets had recorded it.

Buddy himself seemed quite unconcerned by the continual appearance of Petty's name on songs which, more often than not, were his own unaided work. He accepted that, without Petty's studio, engineering expertise, power, light, food, beds, toilet facilities and running water, the songs would not have been created; that Petty's name on a record-label really and truly would increase its chances of radio airplay; that for all these manifold benefits, giving up a share of his publishing royalties was no more than fair. 'It wasn't just to Norman,' Larry Holley says. 'Buddy'd give a song away to anyone. 'Cause he knew he could write a new one every night.'

Most times, as a track evolved, Petty would make a suggestion that proved crucial, usually about instrumentation and arrangement, sometimes about tune or lyric, very occasionally both together. His most significant contribution, J. I. Allison has said, was the 'bridge' in 'Peggy Sue' where Buddy switches to a minor key to sing 'Pretty pretty pretty pretty Peggy Sue'. For that Petty took half the song, giving the other half to Jerry for providing its hypnotic paradiddle beat. Buddy received no credit, even though he had written the song and even specified what kind of beat J.I. should play.

While the 'second division' Crickets, Niki Sullivan and Joe B. Mauldin, had no ambitions to become composers on their own account, both frequently contributed ideas to Buddy's songs which – Buddy himself was the first to say – entitled them to some share in the publishing royalties. Unable to keep track of who (apart from himself) had contributed what, Petty would dole out writers' credits in a totally arbitrary way, conceding that the apportionment might not be strictly accurate, but saying that at least this way everyone would get 'a piece of the action'. Niki and Joe B. both claim to have contributed to 'Maybe Baby', but neither found himself listed as writer with Buddy and Petty. Their consolation prize was an undeserved credit (along with Petty's) on 'I'm Gonna Love You Too'. 'Well, Alright', a much later song, eighteen-carat Buddy through and through, ended up with Joe B.'s name on it as well as Buddy's, Jerry's and, of course, Petty's.

After 'Peggy Sue', the most bizarre example of this lucky dip method involved Jerry Allison, who wrote most of the lyrics for 'Not Fade Away' only to find it attributed to 'Charles Hardin /

Norman Petty'. Lines like 'My love is bigger than a Cadillac / I try to show it, you keep drivin' me back' are as hard to identify with Clovis Man as they are redolent of J.I.'s quirky wit. Yet he was talked into giving up his share of the song, a fact which he bitterly resents to this day.

The suspenseful midsummer months of 1957 also produced an interlude not even hinted at in the few formalized stanzas of the Buddy Holly legend. Something happened to Buddy so devastating as to make even his career as a rock 'n' roll star – if he really and truly was to have one – seem unimportant by comparison. He fell head over heels in love with June Clark.

In the recording studio Buddy might show maturity, authority and self-command way beyond his years. But outside in the sunshine again, he reverted to being an ordinary young man, not yet twenty-one and as emotionally unformed, confused, vulnerable, impulsive and foolhardy as anyone else of his age in that time. Apart from the tension of waiting and hoping, there was a particular reason why he should have been so susceptible at this particular moment; why, in his own light-hearted words, he was 'lookin' for someone to love'.

Echo McGuire, his childhood sweetheart, the tiny, radiant girl he had been planning to marry since they were together at high school, was fading gradually but inexorably from his life. Echo's departure to the Christian University in Abilene had been a parting bad enough. But in the autumn of 1956, her church had formed a missionary group to found a new college in York, Nebraska. Echo's academic record and her sparkling social skills made her a natural choice to join this group of pioneers.

Her unofficial engagement to Buddy continued nonetheless: they phoned and wrote to another regularly and at the end of the year Buddy made the daunting eleven-hour road trip to Nebraska to see her. How much he missed her he confided to no one: not his best friend, J. I. Allison, not even his mother. But Echo was clearly the inspiration for all those love songs composed on solitary night-time drives, with their chaste innocence, their prevalent moods of pining and uncertainty, their repeated attempts to convince an unnamed third party ('Listen to me . . . hear what I say . . .') that true love always wins through in the end.

While keeping Echo's image like a chaste altar in his mind, however, Buddy had the normal sexual drive of any heterosexual male just out of his teens. During Echo's absence he had dated numerous, far less respectable girls and, by the age of twenty, was fully sexually experienced. Older women, too, tended to find his combination of hyper-energy and vulnerability highly attractive: according to Niki Sullivan, he even enjoyed a brief fling with Norman Petty's wife, Vi. 'We were over at the studio quite early in the evening, around seven o'clock. Norman had totally disappeared, the way he often did. Buddy suddenly comes and tells us that Vi's phoned over and invited him to their apartment. So he got washed and shaved and went over there. He wasn't gone all that long, and when he came back he could hardly believe what had happened. Neither could we. But we said, "Cool." '

Admittedly the story contradicts everything else known about Vi – her scrupulous Christian upbringing, her unassertive, anxious nature, the almost zero sexual quotient in her relationship with Clovis Man, most of all her delicate mental state. 'For the kind of episodic schizophrenic Vi was,' the Pettys' friend Dr Jerry Fisher says, 'it would have been impossible for her even to contemplate having sex with anyone but Norman.' But Niki Sullivan is adamant. 'Buddy was never a braggart about that kind of thing. If Buddy said it happened, it happened.'

Away from Clovis, Buddy, J.I., Niki and Joe B. spent most of their time rehearsing and hanging out at the home of their main Lubbock friends and supporters, James and June Clark. James Clark, universally known as 'Nig', was a wholesale supplier of snack foods to stores and supermarkets. He and June were themselves only in their late twenties, young enough to be rock 'n' roll fans, yet old enough to seem like surrogate parents in this time of tense uncertainty, offering Buddy and his group sympathy and sanctuary which even their own long-suffering families could not.

June had married Nig when she was only sixteen, and had a son of eleven, Carley, for whom the Crickets' almost live-in presence was undiluted bliss. 'They were always real nice to me,' Carley Clark remembers now. 'They'd take me along with them to gigs, in places like Dumas and Littlefield, riding in that red Cadillac of theirs. I remember on one trip, the wind blew Joe B.'s bass right off the roof and we had to go back along the road, looking for it. They had their own special logo which they called 'Pa', like a circle with two feet, painted on the side of the car. They'd draw it on notes and letters, too; it was like a secret sign, a lucky charm to help them get a hit.'

Despite the Crickets' air of four Texan Musketeers, one for all and all for one, tensions and personality clashes were developing within the group. They had spent more than three months living in one another's pockets for days and nights on end, in alternating moods of euphoria and disappointment. They were all hard up, down at heel and under varying degrees of pressure from their families and friends to forget this silly rock 'n' roll and settle down to some real work. As the scorching weeks dragged on, and 'That'll Be The Day' still did not even make it into the Top 100, nerves frayed and tempers boiled over.

Their newest recruit, at least, caused little disruption. Joe B. Mauldin might not be God's gift to bass-playing but he fitted into the line-up perfectly, being good-tempered, humorous, obliging and, most important, endlessly willing to follow wherever stronger characters led. 'Anything anyone else wanted to do was fine with Joe B.,' Buddy's brother Larry says. 'He was just like a bump on a log.'

But Niki Sullivan, Buddy's third cousin by marriage, was a very different proposition, strong-minded, outspoken and far tougher physically than his lean face and glasses made him appear. Niki was beginning to resent having been pressed into the Crickets when they clearly had so little use for him. He had sung back-up vocals only twice, on 'That'll Be The Day' and 'Not Fade Away'; with Buddy's Stratocaster filling every crack, his duties as rhythm-guitarist were virtually non-existent. On the 'Peggy Sue' session he had not played at all, but had instead been given a job as menial as it was marginal. At the point where Buddy changed from playing rhythm to his ringing chord-solo, he found he hadn't enough time to flip the Stratocaster's tone-control switch. So on the final take, Niki knelt by his side, waiting to do it for him.

'I remember a lot of rows with Niki,' Carley Clark says. 'He and Jerry Allison never did seem to like each other. And Niki made Buddy lose his cool a few times, too. I saw one real bad tiff at our house where the two of them would have come to blows if my Dad hadn't gotten in between them and told them to stop. I can hear Buddy's voice now saying, "OK ... but only because this is your house, Nig."'

That Buddy should have fallen headlong for June Clark was no great surprise. Both emotionally and professionally he was at a low ebb; his records still getting nowhere; Echo hundreds of miles away; the songs on which he'd lavished such passionate care simply gathering dust in Norman Petty's vaults. June was a highly attractive woman, slim and wavy-blonde, with snub, big-eyed features glancingly like those of Brigitte Bardot, the French 'sex kitten'. Her job on the cosmetics counter at Hull's drugstore gave her an aura of glossy, nylon-crisp untouchability. But in fact she was the very opposite: down-to-earth, warm and switched on to everything that Buddy and his friends considered most important.

For all her good looks and sophistication, June, too, stood in dire need of love and consolation. Her marriage to Nig Clark was not a happy one; she persevered with it only for eleven-year-old Carley's sake. Filling the house with young rock 'n' roll musicians had seemed no more than an innocent distraction. But she found herself increasingly drawn to Buddy for his charm, his kindliness, his single-minded ambition and the dark, lonely depths in him which now and then revealed themselves. 'I knew he liked me because he was a normal young guy,' June says now. 'But the thing he always wanted to do most when we were together was just talk to me.'

They began a risky, on-the-wing romance, stealing kisses over coffee-cups in the kitchen with the other Crickets, Nig and Carley only a few feet away in the den. To further complicate matters, June had begun to suspect that J. I. Allison was also 'sweet' on her. 'I felt I should tell Buddy that because Jerry was his best friend. Buddy acted like we were the only two grown-ups involved. "Jerry's young," he said. "He'll probably get over it."'

June had been prepared for a superficial flirtation. But the intensity of Buddy's feelings began to alarm her. Forgetting the need for discretion, he phoned her constantly, and also took to hanging around the Hull drugstore. 'He wouldn't even pretend he'd come in to buy anything. He'd just stand there staring at me while I waited on customers, till it got to be really embarrassing and unnerving.'

Afraid that Nig would discover what was going on, she told Buddy they must cool down and underlined the point by going away from Lubbock for a few days. 'When I got back, Buddy's brother Larry came by the house and told me Buddy was in a terrible way and he wanted to see me. We met in the parking lot at the drugstore. Buddy asked me to leave Nig and go away with him. He said if I would he'd do anything . . . break up the

Crickets, even forget about trying to make it in the music business.'

In an attempt to defuse the situation, Larry Holley persuaded Buddy to go with him on a fishing trip to Colorado. But even that didn't succeed in taking Buddy's mind off his troubles. While they were away, the pop music charts produced yet another sensation – a wailing puppy-love song called 'Diana', sung by its composer, sixteen-year-old Paul Anka.

'One day in this little Colorado town, we passed a record store and there was Anka's picture in the window, and a caption saying how "Diana" was shooting up the Top 10,' Larry Holley remembers. 'After that, Buddy couldn't keep his mind on catching fish at all. "I know I can beat this Paul Anka kid," he kept saying. "I *know* I can beat him."'

Exactly why 'That'll Be The Day' took so long to get into the charts never has been satisfactorily explained. For most rock 'n' roll classics, success has appeared soaringly effortless: for this one it entailed a foot-slog up Mount Everest, fighting headwinds and blizzards every inch of the way.

The blend of sounds, which has seemed unimprovably right for almost forty years, was an unusual, even eccentric one in mid-1957. Though the electric guitar might be the quintessence of rock 'n' roll, no chart hit up to then had featured one quite so heavily and uproariously. And the voice sounded unlike that of a potential teenage idol, being totally lacking in sexual suggestiveness, self-pitying angst or any other clue that its owner belonged to the same generation as Elvis, Ricky, Eddie, Don and Phil. The parents of 1957 might believe their teenage children to lack all discrimination, but in fact they were already showing themselves to be deeply conservative and suspicious of change. The novel sound of 'That'll Be The Day' and the difficulty of pigeonholing it – not quite dance tune, not quite love song, not quite fast, not quite slow, not funny yet not quite serious – were factors rather more likely to make a failure than a success.

In a continent as vast and disconnected as North America was thirty-nine years ago, a new single could not be expected to 'break' everywhere simultaneously unless it bore some established name – ideally that of Elvis Presley – and was accompanied by a massive advertising and promotional blitzkrieg. For an unknown act like the Crickets, the best their record company could hope for was 'regional breakout' – success in a specific state or city which, with a fair wind, might fan outward to other cities and states. Not only the geographical size of the continent but its cultural and ethnic diversity stacked up the odds against conquering every one of the 'territories' where records were bought. What might delight sun-kissed Californians might be totally lost on the weatherbeaten denizens of the far Midwest. What might be rejected by New England sophisticates might go down a storm around the Great Lakes or beside the Gulf of Mexico. Regional breakout in just one or two of the possible key markets would have shown Coral-Brunswick a decent profit. But it would not have made Buddy Holly a star.

The crucial stepping-stones to regional breakout were disc jockeys on local radio stations. The odd thing about 'That'll Be The Day' was that initially it received very little radio airplay yet, despite this lack of vital exposure and endorsement, could be seen to be selling steadily, if not spectacularly. Part of the reason may have been the Ravens' cover-version on the Argo label, which had been extensively played on 'black' stations. It's entirely possible that some people heard the Ravens' version on the radio, then went out and bought the Crickets'. Since the Crickets' faces were unknown, and their lead singer's voice had a timbre which, to 1957 ears, seemed more 'black' than 'white', few of these misdirected customers can have thought it worthwhile to demand a refund. To compound the confusion, there was also a black group called the Crickets, whose existence had been unknown to Buddy, J.I. and Niki when they picked out their name from Jerry Allison's encyclopaedia. People buying the wrong group, as well as people buying the wrong version of the song, undoubtedly contributed to these puzzlingly respectable sales.

The much-despised Hollywood movie version of Buddy's life offers a cartoon version of how 'That'll Be The Day' finally achieved regional breakout. A disc jockey in Buffalo, New York, adores the record so much that he barricades himself in his studio and plays it nonstop over the air until his employers break down the door and restrain him. The scene contains a germ of truth: 'That'll Be The Day' did show a surge in the Buffalo area after a disc jockey named Tom Clay, working under the pseudonym 'Guy King' on station WGR, took to playing it, not around the clock but with unusual frequency, every fifteen minutes or so. A still more spectacular surge came from the Philadelphia area, thanks mainly to the enthusiasm of deejay Georgie Woods on the city's leading black station, WDAS. Bob Thiele remembered being at a Decca sales conference in Cincinnati and hearing, to his amazement, that 'Philly' had just sent an order for 16,000 copies.

Many other regional disc jockeys began to show genuine enthusiasm for 'That'll Be The Day', once they'd worked out the white Crickets, not the black ones, were performing it. And many more still were willing to enthuse for a consideration. To the American music industry of 1957, bribing disc jockeys to give preferential treatment to this or that new release was a natural and normal part of the marketing process. Buddy and the Crickets were left in no doubt that some payola, at least, had helped their record along. Niki Sullivan remembers a figure of $200 being mentioned. 'It was kind of reproachful ... like, "You guys have just cost me two hundred bucks."'

With orders still mounting steadily, the Decca organization finally began to add some promotional muscle. Buddy and the

Crickets were summoned East to New York to meet their label boss, Bob Thiele, and their publisher, Murray Deutch, and make a personal appearance at one of the Manhattan record stores where they were selling best. Buddy made his first-ever flight from Lubbock's old Regional Airport in one of the elderly propeller planes with which Trans World Airlines then served such far-flung regional outposts. 'It was an old military plane, a C47 I think,' Niki Sullivan remembers. 'The ride up to New York was pretty rackety. But we could care less! We were all on top of the world.'

The size and garish splendour of New York City, as it honked and sizzled in the midsummer heat of 1957, took the four young Texans' breath away. 'We were too young to be frightened,' Sullivan remembers. 'But we kept saying the same thing over and over. "Man! Did you ever see so many people in one place before!"' They checked into the Edison Hotel at 46–47 Street, west of Broadway, and spent a couple of days being introduced to executives and marketing men at Coral-Brunswick and wandering the streets and avenues in a state of pop-eyed wonderment, visiting famous tourist spots like Jack Dempsey's Broadway restaurant and sampling their very first big-city cocktails (bourbon and Coca-Cola). Their innocent high spirits and old-world Texan courtesy so charmed the dour Bob Thiele that he threw a party for them at his home in upstate New York, introducing them to his wife, Teresa Brewer, and other stars of the Coral label like Steve Lawrence and Eydie Gorme.

By the end of June, sales of 'That'll Be The Day' had reached 50,000 copies – still a long way short of a national hit, but evidence that, after more than a month, the record had eventually begun to 'move'. A congratulatory wire from Murray Deutch reached Clovis while Buddy and the Crickets were grabbing some sleep during the scorching, dust-stormy weekend of the 'Peggy Sue' session. 'Norman woke us up to tell us,' Niki

Sullivan remembers. 'We were all so tired, we could hardly be bothered to listen to him.' At Petty's suggestion next day they made two jingle-sized versions of 'That'll Be The Day', one 'personalized' to Deutch, the other to Bob Thiele. Buddy's improvised vocal bubbled over with gratitude for his visit to Thiele, 'the Brunswick record compan-ee' and the man who had started the ball rolling. 'That was Norman's idea ...' he sang amid a chorus of Rebel yells from the others. 'Oo-oo ... That was Norman's idea ...'

On 15 July, *Billboard* carried a full-page advertisement for current releases on the Coral label by Debbie Reynolds, the McGuire Sisters, Teresa Brewer, the Dick Jacobs Orchestra and Don Cornell (who had made a deeply square cover version of 'Mailman, Bring Me No More Blues'.) At the bottom was a thumbnail picture of Buddy, Jerry, Niki and Joe B., under the legend 'BREAKING ON BRUNSWICK'. Bob Thiele also quickly exercised his option to renew their contract, offering what seemed a stunningly higher advance – $600 – for the master of 'Peggy Sue' and 'Everyday'.

The growing buzz around the Crickets' name also brought an offer from an East Coast promoter to book them on their first-ever national tour. Headlined by Clyde McPhatter and featuring Otis Rush, Edna McGriff, Oscar and Oscar and the Hearts, the show was to open at the Howard Theater, Washington, DC, on 2 August, moving on to the Royal in Baltimore and finally to the Apollo in New York.

Buddy and Co., in other words, were the victims of an unfortunate mistake. The bill they had been invited to join otherwise consisted entirely of black singers and groups and was booked into theatres at the heart of inner-city ghettos where white people could no longer even walk in safety. The dearth of publicity photographs in advertisements for 'That'll Be The Day', the record's raw R & B sound and the existence of a black vocal group called the Crickets had all proved a fatal combination. The tour-promoters believed they were hiring the black Crickets, not the white ones.

Nonetheless, Buddy, J.I., Niki and Joe B. unanimously agreed to take the booking. They knew what they might be walking into, but were prepared to risk it in exchange for their first exposure on the national tour-circuit. Buddy, in particular, was supremely confident of his power to win over any audience, and laughed off the idea that their fellow performers might regard them with as much hostility as did disappointed paying customers. 'We'd always gotten along so well with the black acts that played the Cotton Club, and been so into their music,' Joe B. Mauldin says. 'We were always in the front row, cheering, every time they came through town.'

Although Norman Petty had been the Crickets' constant adviser, as well as their producer and engineer, for the past five months, it was not until this point that he officially became their manager. According to J. I. Allison, Petty was not seeking the job and, as their success began to snowball, told them they'd better find a manager to handle it all. Whereupon Buddy looked at him, aghast, and said, 'Heck Norm . . . YOU'RE our manager!' Niki Sullivan confirms that Petty did not want the job, saying that he knew little of the rock 'n' roll business and that, with his commitments in Clovis, he'd be unable to travel with them on tour. But Buddy overruled him with words to the effect: 'You've brought us this far. We're not going with anyone else.'

Petty's immediate concern was to outfit them for the tour they insisted on making, despite his own deep reservations, three weeks hence. Until now they had been unconcerned with their image as a group and possessed no stage uniform so to speak of, usually going out to gigs in the same unmatched sports clothes, Levis, T-shirts or Bermuda shorts they wore to studio-sessions. For the immaculate, fastidious Clovis Man that would not do at all; nor would the Technicolor pseudo-cowboy threads that Elvis Presley had made the standard rock 'n' rollers' wardrobe. On 8

July, Petty met Buddy and the Crickets in Lubbock, escorted them to the S & Q menswear store on Broadway and helped them select a stage wardrobe more appropriate to his own trio's milieu of cabarets and USAF officers' clubs – boxy pale grey suits, white linen jackets, grey slacks, plus white shirts, ties, shoes and socks.

He also opened an account on their behalf at the Clovis National Bank, where he himself had been a customer for many years. Into this, they understood, would go their joint income, after deduction of Petty's 10 per cent management commission and the 10 per cent tithe to each of their respective churches in Lubbock; from it would be paid the costs of their clothes and instruments, recording sessions and travelling expenses.

The complete records of this 'Buddy Holly and the Crickets' account are among Clovis Man's recently unearthed records – account-books, receipts and every single cashed cheque, helpfully filled in with the purpose of its encashment. We can see that the account was opened on 24 July 1957 with a deposit of $500. The first withdrawal, a day later, was $175, 'For payment on Buddy's automobile'.

The signature on the sage-green cheque is that of Norman Petty. Since Buddy and the Crickets would clearly be away from Clovis a great deal of the time, but bills would constantly come in, it seemed sensible to give their manager power of attorney over their collective bank account, empowered to pay in all their income and write cheques for such disbursements as might be necessary.

This moment when his fame was about to dawn also may have brought the darkest episode of Buddy's brief life. If it truly did happen, it was not so very dark, goodness knows; hundreds of young men down the centuries have found themselves in the same predicament and behaved no better and no worse. It is shocking only in the context of the Buddy Holly legend, which promulgates a chastely shining, one-dimensional saint rather than a being of flesh and blood.

For many years a story has circulated around Lubbock that, just as Buddy's long-delayed breakthrough finally seemed about to happen, he almost wrecked everything by making a Lubbock girl pregnant. On my first visit to his hometown in late 1994, I talked to two of his close friends who are convinced the story is true. One of them prefers not to be named; the other was the Crickets' rhythm guitarist, and Buddy's third cousin, Niki Sullivan.

According to Niki, the young woman involved had been at Lubbock High School with Buddy and was dating him at around the time the Crickets got together and found their way to Norman Petty's studio. It was, says Niki, a casual and purely physical affair. 'Buddy and she were just two kids, hot for each other. They had nothing in common. There was no way they could have gotten along in a real relationship.' The second source claims to have dated the same person, and, like Buddy, to have 'gone all the way' with her. 'She was a flighty little thing ... as wild as a peach orchard boar!'

Niki Sullivan says he was there when the girl broke the news of her condition to Buddy. 'We were at the Hi-D-Ho drive-in in Lubbock. Buddy and this girl in the front of the car, I and a couple of others were in the back, drinking beer. Suddenly the girl started to throw up. Buddy was real pissed at her ... you know, like "How could you do that in my car!" And then she says, "I can't help it, I'm pregnant. And you're the father!" At that Buddy hit her. I mean, hit her real hard, so that she jerked forward and hit her head on the car windshield. I can still hear the smack it made against the glass.'

Such brutality might seem wildly out of character for Buddy, but the sad truth is that in the male-dominated late fifties – especially in a place like West Texas – even kindly and well-disposed young men saw nothing wrong in hitting their girl-friends. Having no special feelings for this particular young woman, possibly even rather disliking her, Buddy no doubt would have seen her pregnancy as a deliberate plot to ruin his life. And, indeed, it would have been the end of everything. In a community such as Lubbock, extra-marital pregnancy was the worst of all social disgraces. For someone raised in the Scriptures the way Buddy had been, abortion could not be an option, even if he knew how to procure one. The only way of saving his family and his church from public disgrace would have been to grit his teeth and marry the girl. Instead of soaring with the Crickets, he would be tied to Lubbock by diapers, mortgages and monthly repayments; instead of a rock 'n' roll star, he would have to turn into an adult.

'The situation in the car quickly quietened down,' Niki Sullivan remembers. 'Because behaving that way wasn't Buddy's style. That was the reaction of a man faced by something he did not need in his life at that point. He wanted to make it so bad ... God, he wanted it so bad! And when someone wants something that badly, and suddenly thinks he's going to be stopped from getting it, it's understandable that there's some kind of physical release.'

His usual confidant and saviour in times of trouble was his elder brother, Larry. But Larry Holley says now that he knew nothing about any of this. According to a close family friend, Buddy's mother was the one who found out after mistakenly opening a letter from the girl to him, repeating her accusation. His parents rallied to his support, visiting the girl's people and convincing them that a shotgun marriage to Buddy would create more problems than it solved. Between the two families a plan was hammered out to save them from public scandal, albeit one reeking of the sexual inequity of those times. The young woman would go away from Lubbock to have the baby, and afterwards put it out for adoption. Buddy would be absolved from responsibility, and could continue with his career as planned.

Niki Sullivan also claims to have been with Buddy at his one subsequent meeting with the young woman. 'It was later in the year when we were on tour. We came through Texas and passed near the unwed mothers' home where she'd been sent to have the baby. We stopped the car and Buddy got out by himself and walked over to the wire fence that ran around the place. The girl came along on the other side of the fence and the two of them stood there for a few minutes, talking through the wire. Then Buddy got back into the car and we drove away. He didn't talk about what had happened, and he never mentioned it afterwards.'

The story has just one flaw. The person named by several knowledgeable sources as the mother of Buddy's illegitimate child is adamant that she knew him only slightly and certainly never dated him. She got married in 1954, almost two years before Buddy allegedly made her pregnant, and her two children – by the same husband – were both girls. The trail stops here. But Niki Sullivan believes that a baby was born and that it was a boy. We are left with no more than a tantalizing thought: somewhere in America at this moment there may be a man in his early forties who has no idea that he's Buddy Holly's only son.

On 28 July, Buddy and the Crickets took the evening Trans World Airlines flight from Amarillo to New York, little suspecting how long it would be before they saw the West Texas plains again. The current week's *Billboard* listed 'That'll Be The Day' as a 'best buy', though it still had not broken into the magazine's Hot 100. Petty had had to go to Florida but was flying up to join them in New York the following day. Meantime, each had been provided with a sheet of detailed instructions.

Be at the Amarillo Air Terminal Sunday evening at least by
6.30 to check reservations and to check baggage. Take
enough cash along to pay for excess weight and meals
between flights. Take about $30–40 cash . . . the rest in
travelers' checks. Be sure to take all available identification
for each member of the group.

Sign only engagement contracts and nothing more.
Take extra sets of guitar strings and drum sticks, head etc.
Take out floater insurance for entire group with everyone's
name on the contract. Be sure pack records with clothes to
take on trip. Take all available clean underwear and other
articles for use on trip.

When you get to New York, take a cab directly to the
Edison hotel and check in there. We will see you about
noon of that day.

Get at least two dozen Dramamine tablets and take one
tablet at least 15 minutes before departure. Make out trip
insurance to your parents. Take at least 25 feet of extension
cord. Take small [shoe] shine kit for trip. Toilet articles of
your choice. Get telephone credit card and carry with you.
Take a small Bible with you and READ it. Get hotel credit
cards or at least make application for same. Be sure to get
and keep receipts for all money spent. Be sure to send
money back to Clovis for bank account.

On arrival at the Edison (where they had now risen to the
grandeur of a $27.70 per day suite) they found a telegram
awaiting them: 'Congratulations and welcome to the big city. See
you a little bit later. Papa Norman.'

The 'black tour', as it has come to be known among Holly
aficionados, passed off better than anyone had dared to hope.
Despite understandable bemusement at their presence, the Crickets' fellow performers showed them no hostility nor resentment;

on the contrary, Clyde McPhatter, the headliner, and most of the others went out of their way to be helpful and encouraging.

For opening night at Baltimore's Royal Theater, Papa Norman was on hand to support his 'boys' and, if necessary, arrange a rapid evacuation. There was admittedly a moment of stupefied silence from the audience when the MC announced 'The Crickets' and the curtain went up to reveal four white faces, two of them bespectacled, above four brand-new boxy pale grey suits. Then Buddy hit his Stratocaster and went straight into overdrive, as was his wont; by the first chorus, if it took even that long, the whole house was with the pick in the palm of his hand. The rest of the week went equally well, even though Buddy suffered an attack of laryngitis midway through and, on a couple of nights, was unable to sing at all. Niki Sullivan, who could mimic Buddy rather well, took over the lead vocals with no noticeable drop in applause-level.

Week two, at the Howard Theater, Washington DC, was equally successful. Word had spread by now that, although these Crickets might be white, they could give the black ones at least a run for their money. As an additional boost, the summit of Everest had come into sight at long last. On 12 August, 'That'll Be The Day' entered *Billboard*'s Hot 100 at number 65. Next to the chart, ironically, was a Chess-Checker record company display ad for the Ravens' competitive cover-version. Buddy's bill from the Ambassador Hotel shows how modest were his celebrations: 'Room, $5.31' ... 'LD phone $1.54' ... 'Phone, 20¢' ... 'Restaurant, $4.29' ... 'Restaurant, 16¢'.

The Apollo, New York, promised no such easy capitulation, however. Standing on 125th Street in the heart of Harlem, it had not presented a white performer on its stage since the 'mixed' orchestras of the jazz and swing era. Fortunately for them, the Texans had not been forewarned of the Apollo crowd's peculiar ruthlessness, expressed most forcefully in a weekly Talent Night

which reduced even performers from the immediate neighbourhood to palpitant wrecks. Still less did they appreciate that
Harlem was a place where white people should not walk, let
alone seek lodgings. Arriving for their week's engagement, they
cheerfully registered at the Hotel Theresa, right opposite the
Apollo, at 125th Street and Seventh Avenue, where a week's stay
for all four, including extras and taxes, cost $76.65.

A good luck telegram from Murray Deutch, 'Congratulations
and welcome back. I know you will knock them dead,' contained
more wishful thinking than certainty. Although everyone in the
Apollo's audience knew exactly who and what they were,
especially now 'That'll Be The Day' was in the Top 100, a frigid
silence greeted them at curtain-up. 'There was this big lady,
about 400 pounds, sitting right in front,' Niki Sullivan remembers. 'Before we could hit a note, she hollered out, "You better
sound like the record!"'

It was the last place on earth where Buddy's 'y'all' Texan
charm could be expected to work its usual magic. And, indeed,
the first couple of shows went as badly as they possibly could.
Apart from 'That'll Be The Day', the audience seemed indifferent
to the Crickets' original songs; apathetic silence changed to
spasmodic booing and the creative heckling for which the Apollo
was, and still is, famous. It might have ended catastrophically but
for Buddy's equal mastery of a far more acceptable type of
material. 'When we just couldn't get through with our own stuff,
Buddy turns round and says, "Ah, the hell with it, let's give 'em
'Bo Diddley'," ' Niki remembers. 'He started cutting up and
jumping around, giving it everything he'd got . . .' If the Apollo's
audience is pitilessly intolerant of failure, it also famously
respects courage and chutzpah. The Texans finished their set
amid wild applause and shouts for more, which were repeated at
every show for the rest of the week.

On 23 August, ever the punctilious correspondent, Buddy
wrote to his father, who was currently away on a building job in

Wichita Falls: 'We finished playing the Apollo last night, and it sure feels good to know that we can relax for a few days ... We are staying downtown now, at the Forrest hotel, so you can drop a card here if you have time ... There's not much else to tell except that we found out last night that we had sold half a million [of 'That'll Be The Day'] as of Wednesday night. Everyone says it should sell at least a million ...'

Big-time engagements were now coming thick and fast. On 23 August, Buddy and the Crickets travelled to Philadelphia to appear on a brand-new rock 'n' roll television show called *American Bandstand*. Fronted by a dapper young ex-sportscaster named Dick Clark, it was the first network show to reproduce the atmosphere of a teenage hop and the first to regard teenagers' opinions about the music as worth taking seriously. That simple formula would make it the longest running pop show on American television and Clark himself, unchangingly boyish and brush-topped, one of the most spectacular American triumphs over Anno Domini.

The most crucial factor in 'That'll Be The Day''s final chart-ascent, however, was the approval and endorsement of the great Alan Freed. On the strength of his claim to have invented the term 'rock 'n' roll', the one-time Cleveland disc jockey had become the most influential figure in American popular music. Aged thirty-five, with corrugated hair, bulbous eyes and a voice like congealing molasses, Freed sold himself with consummate skill to his youthful audience as the one and only adult in Creation who truly understood their music and them. As a deejay, he combined immaculate taste with unusual strength of mind: he always played the original records of black artists in preference to their bland white cover-versions. Later, he was to be fired from his own network rock 'n' roll show rather than yield to the sponsor's demand not to see black boys and white girls dancing together.

As well as coining 'rock 'n' roll', Freed also coined a fortune from it, appearing as himself in a succession of 'exploitation movies' like *Rock Around the Clock*, putting his name on innumerable songs as a quid pro quo for plugging them, and promoting live shows at Brooklyn's Paramount theatre which produced box-office grosses not seen since the Frank Sinatra mania of the late forties.

From 30 August to 5 September, the Crickets were added to Freed's *Holiday of Stars* spectacular at the Brooklyn Paramount, co-starring with Little Richard, Larry Williams, the Del Vikings, the Cleftones, Mickey and Sylvia and 'the Alan Freed Orchestra' (yet another nice little earner for Moondog), featuring black instrumental aces like Sam 'The Man' Taylor and saxophonist King Curtis. The pay was Musicians' Union 'scale' which, after deductions and Papa Norman's commission, worked out at just over $1,100 between four, for what the contract termed 'a minimum of 29 shows in any one week'.

The marathon Rock 'n' Roll shows put on in American theatres during the late fifties were closer to old-fashioned nonstop vaudeville than anything in the modern concept of a rock concert. At the Brooklyn Paramount there would be five, sometimes seven shows per day, the first at 11 am, the last at two the following morning. For a one-dollar ticket the rock 'n' roll fan got up to twenty acts, most of them with a record in the current Top 10, as well as a schlock Western or detective movie, the management's way of clearing the house between each live show. The waiting lines would stretch twice around the block, corralled by barricades and squads of mounted police dressed in the old-style flap-over tunics that made them look like Edwardian chauffeurs. Despite all these discomforts and provocations, trouble among the mixed-race crowd was virtually unknown.

With such a gigantic programme to get through, each act would be onstage for only a few minutes, enough to blast out their current hit, its B-side and, maybe, an upcoming new release.

The age of specialized sound-systems and dramatic light shows was not to dawn for another decade or so. Performers used the house microphones and lights, augmented by their own puny guitar-amplifiers. Vocalists and singing groups enjoyed the backing of the 'Alan Freed Orchestra', but a unique self-contained vocal/instrumental group like the Crickets had to fill the massive stage and dominate the huge, shrieking vault all on their own. They were thus compelled to develop a stage presence far more energetic and spontaneous than the synchronized swaying and finger-snapping of ensembles like the Diamonds and the Cleftones.

Buddy sang in a sidelong posture at the principal – often, only – stand-mike, his left leg planted firmly forward as if he were about to take a stride on a roller-skate. In the wilder rock 'n' roll numbers, he would start to 'cut up' – not with the self-conscious slinkiness of those who borrowed their body-language from Elvis, but in a cheerfully self-mocking way, swinging his Stratocaster around on its strap, snarling, whooping and Rebel-yelling, crouching double to sing a chorus into the low-level mike beside Joe B. Mauldin's bass fiddle, even slithering across the stage on his knees to the detriment of his new stone-grey slacks. If the stage were particularly wide, he always took care to visit each corner regularly for a few seconds' communion with the 'bad' seats.

Joe B., so unassuming elsewhere, matched Buddy in onstage mugging and clowning, at some moments keeling over so far with his bass that it and he would almost be lying on the ground. Niki Sullivan stood away to Buddy's left, compensating for his inaudible rhythm guitar by moving around a lot and conscientiously mouthing the backup 'Oohs' and 'Aahs'. J. I. Allison, who seemed to have grown several inches in height since leaving Lubbock as well as losing the worst of his teenage acne, belaboured his undersized drum-kit with his self-satisfied feline half-smile. Though none of the four could be called good-looking in the conventional (i.e., Presley) sense, they performed their three-song set amid a bedlam of feminine shrieks and squeals as mindless and undiscriminating as new born babies', as unrelenting as a Texan Blue Norther, as palpable and impenetrable as a brick wall.

They had all been excited at the prospect of a reunion with Little Richard, their old backstage crony at Lubbock's Cotton Club, now at the apogee of outrageousness and extravagance. But even knowing him as they did, the Texans were dumbfounded by the manner in which Richard said 'Hello again'.

'He called all four of us up to see him in his dressing-room at the Paramount,' Niki Sullivan remembers. 'When we walked in, Richard was there with his girlfriend, Angel, and Larry Williams [a Little Richard soundalike, soon to record the one-off classic "Bony Moronie"]. Richard was masturbating at the same time as licking Angel while Larry Williams made love to her from behind. None of them took any notice of Buddy, J.I., Joe B. and me, standing in the doorway. They just carried right on with what they were doing.

'Through the window we could see straight across the street, where there was some kind of hospital or institution for the elderly. When Richard had finished what he was doing with Angel, he fastened his robe, walked over to the window and looked over to this home or hospital or whatever it was. I mean, its windows were full of these elderly people in dressing-gowns, with doctors and nurses looking after them. "Oh, gee," Richard said, "I wonder if the folks over there would like me to go and witness [hold a religious meeting] with them."'

This is the origin of the scene in Richard's own memoirs where Buddy allegedly joins him in sex with Angel, then runs straight onstage to perform, still with a gaping-open fly.

In fact, during that début week at the Brooklyn Paramount,

Buddy had a more complex sexual agenda to pursue. For June Clark had given in to his pleas and flown up from Lubbock with her son Carley under the pretext of visiting her shoe-model sister Tuddie. Buddy and June were reunited under the camouflage of a party for Buddy Knox; after that, Tuddie lent them her apartment on West 10th Street. When Tuddie needed to be at home, they would meet to make love at a nearby apartment hotel.

Suspecting that J.I. Allison might still also be sweet on June, Buddy was careful to keep his liaison from his best friend. But Niki and Joe B. knew all about it. 'One afternoon, Buddy took the two of us with him when we went to meet June,' Niki says. 'We had to wait outside the apartment for him while the two of them got it on.'

The strained relations between Niki and Jerry had seemed to improve of late, especially since J.I.'s eighteenth birthday, on 31 August, when his fellow Crickets threw a surprise party for him at their hotel. A commemorative snapshot shows the four of them kneeling like schoolboys against one of two single beds in a tiny, chaotic room. Spread on the coverlet before them is a miniature birthday cake, ringed by an elaborate pattern of coloured candies. Below, more candies are arranged in neat capital letters to spell out the birthday boy's Cossacky middle name, IVAN.

But, a couple of nights after Buddy's assignation with June, trouble between Niki and J.I. broke out again. Niki admits that he was in a hyperactive and aggressive state, having been forced to give up smoking to please 'Papa Norman'. 'Jerry and I were shouting at each other and, to get back at him, I blurted out that Buddy had met June and what they'd done. It was dumb, I admit. Jerry got real mad and we had an all-out fist fight. I got him good above one eye, I mean it swelled up real big. Right after that, we had to go up on the Paramount's roof and have pictures done for out first album, *The Chirping Crickets*. They had to retouch the print to try to hide Jerry's swollen eye, but you could still see it. You can see it to this day.'

What even Niki did not know was that Buddy's infatuation with June had grown even more intense during the weeks they had been apart. 'He told me time after time that it wasn't just a crush – that he wanted to have a permanent relationship with me,' June says now. 'I seriously thought about it, because I did have feelings for him. But in the end, I realized I could never leave Carley.

'The last time we were due to be together, just before he left on that first big national tour, we ended up just talking on the phone. Buddy told me again that he wanted me to leave Nig and go away with him. I kept saying I couldn't because I had a little boy. It went on for about an hour, him begging, me saying no I just couldn't. In the end, there was nothing else to do but just hang up. I took Carley back to Lubbock, and I never saw Buddy or spoke to him again.'

The rollercoaster was picking up speed every second. From the Brooklyn Paramount, Buddy and the Crickets went straight into a nationwide multi-act tour put together by New York's most powerful rock 'n' roll agent, Irving Feld of the General Artists Corporation. Called 'The Biggest Show of Stars for 1957', it also featured Chuck Berry, Fats Domino, Paul Anka, the Everly Brothers, Frankie Lymon, the Drifters, LaVern Baker, Clyde McPhatter, Johnnie and Joe, the Spaniels and the Bobettes. The tour opened in Pittsburgh on 6 September, the day before Buddy's twenty-first birthday, and continued virtually without a break through September, October and November.

These so called 'package tours' were designed by hard-headed men like Irving Feld with a single objective: to carry hitmakers to the largest possible audience during the brief span of favour which they could be expected to enjoy. Even the hyperbole of the show's title reflected this hasty opportunism – i.e., it may be 'The Biggest Show of Stars for 1957' but don't expect too many of them to be still around in 1958. Wages were minimal: Buddy and the Crickets between them received $1,000 per week out of which they had to pay for their own subsistence on the road. Like everyone else, they did not do it for the money but for the prestige, the exposure and the additional record-sales they might generate by performing 'That'll Be The Day' and 'Peggy Sue' in approximately sixty cities throughout the U S and Canada.

Being on the road with a 1957 rock 'n' roll show was nothing like the movable feast of luxury and self-indulgence it would become during the sixties and seventies. The whole enormous troupe of artists were packed into a single bus, with a second one for the full orchestra which travelled with them. The itinerary consisted entirely of one-nighters, planned with a blithe disregard of all geographical logic. The opening ten-day stretch, for instance, took them from Pittsburgh south-east to Richmond, Virginia, then north-east to Annapolis, Maryland, south-east to Norfolk, Virginia, north-west to Cincinnati and Columbus, Ohio, east to Hershey, back in Pennsylvania, north (by air) over the Great Lakes to Toronto, Montreal and Quebec, Canada, south to Syracuse and Rochester, New York, then south to Baltimore, Maryland.

The hundreds, sometimes thousands, of miles between each night's venue seldom left enough time for the performers to go to an hotel after their show. As often as not, they would be herded straight back on to the bus in their stage clothes to drive through the night and most of the following day. 'If you're eighteen to twenty years old, the way most of us were, you can live that kind of life,' Joe B. Mauldin says. 'You'd climb up into the luggage-rack and go to sleep – and sleep like a baby, usually.

Those things mean nothing when you're on tour with Chuck Berry ... Fats Domino ... girls screaming for you and asking for autographs ... It's all one big adventure.'

Among this gaggle of hyped and hyperactive youngsters, vice and self-indulgence were notably absent. Drinking was minimal and drug-taking almost unknown, among the white performers at least: on one of the Canadian legs, Frankie Lymon's manager was busted for marijuana possession. The punishing schedule allowed few opportunities to take advantage of the girls who mobbed them after each performance. Among the different acts, big and small, black and white, there was an almost total lack of jealousy or competitiveness. On the marathon interstate journeys, if not playing cards on suitcase-tops, they would all jam together. 'We didn't need drink or drugs,' Niki Sullivan says. 'We were all on a natural high. The Drifters used to sit there at three in the morning and sing 'How Deep Is The Ocean' with beautiful a cappella harmony that still brings a lump to my throat when I think of it. Now, what makes guys sing for no money, at three in the morning?'

The black performers, being a little older and more experienced, tended to look after the white newcomers. LaVern Baker, the only female star on the bill, acted as den-mother, sewing on stage-suit buttons when they came adrift. Chuck Berry is not usually considered a generous or unselfish figure, but to the Crickets on that tour – especially to their diminutive bass-player – he was kindliness itself. 'Chuck was a super guy,' Joe B. remembers. 'If ever you asked his advice about something, he'd say, "Well, come on, let's sit down and talk this through ..." He and Fats Domino were following the bus in their own cars, and Chuck invited me to ride in the beautiful Cadillac he had, and did everything he could to set me straight on the music business.

'Fats Domino was a sweet guy, too, but if you ever went too deep with him, he'd just talk to you in the titles of his songs.

Like, after a show, he might say, "How are you fellers getting to the next town?" we'd say, "On the bus, Fats," hoping he might offer us a ride in his car. "So how are YOU getting there?" But Fats would just give a big smile and start clicking his fingers and singing, "I'm walkin' . . . yes, indeed, I'm walkin' . . ."'

Understandably, the most immediate rapport which Buddy and the Crickets struck among their fellow artists was with the Everly Brothers, Don and Phil. 'We were all from the South, we'd all started out in country music,' Phil Everly says. 'It was like belonging to a fraternity.'

Don Everly remembers first meeting the Texans backstage at the Forum in Montreal. 'They were really friendly, funny guys, and they all had on these grey suits which you could tell had been bought in Texas. Phil and I were maybe six months ahead of them career-wise, and were already into Ivy League clothes, like the jackets with buttons right up the front, the pants with the little belt in back. As soon as Buddy saw what we were wearing, he looked at the other three, gave his big grin and said, "Let's go shop!"'

The Everlys' music, strongly guitar-accented, clearly articulated and innocent of smut, had much in common with Buddy's. But whereas the Crickets provided their own accompaniment the Everlys had to hire musicians at each venue, who frequently proved indifferent if not downright inept. And while Buddy wrote his own songs, Don and Phil depended on outside writers, principally the husband-and-wife team of Boudleaux and Felice Bryant. 'Phil and I had never thought of going round with a self-contained group like that,' Don Everly says. 'It made them seem real independent and solid against the world. They even had a kind of private language they spoke, through having grown up together. Yeah, we were supposed to be the big-timers, but we envied them in a lot of ways, even though they were so brand-new to the business and had all kinds of rough edges. Like, at that time, the only publicity picture they had was of the four of them back in Lubbock, in T-shirts and Levis, setting tiles on a roof.'

Buddy became a close friend of both brothers, for all that each was very different within their perfect vocal harmony, the elder Don tractable and humorous, the younger Phil highly strung and fastidious. Don remembers Buddy's neat and methodical ways, in contrast to the general slovenliness. Emulating his brother Larry, as always, and unmindful what a curious accessory it was for a rock 'n' roll star, he had recently bought himself a meerschaum pipe. 'I remember him bringing out this crazy pipe, the kind you saw old men in leather shorts smoking in Bavaria or Switzerland,' Don Everly says. 'He showed us all the special way you had to hold it, so as not to spoil the finish of it. And he had a special little case to carry it in.'

Even with rock 'n' roll names as big as Chuck Berry and Fats Domino, the racial attitudes of the South remained inflexible. *En route* between Atlanta and New Orleans, police flagged down the two tour buses and segregated them, putting all the white performers on to one and all the black on to the other. For the performances in Columbus, Georgia, Chattanooga, Tennessee, and Birmingham, Alabama, the white performers had to drop off the bill because local ordinances forbade blacks and whites to appear on the same stage. 'Some other places where we played used to hang a big curtain down the middle of the auditorium,' Joe B. Mauldin remembers. 'The whites would be sitting on one side of it, the blacks on the other.'

Life held risks for white performers, too, especially the more good-looking ones. Local boys whose girlfriends had screamed too loudly for this or that onstage dreamboat would sometimes form themselves into impromptu revenge gangs. 'Security', that indispensable feature of modern rock star life, was virtually non-existent in 1957. 'I remember coming out of the theatre, just to cross the street to my hotel,' Don Everly says. 'This big group of guys came after me, got hold of me and picked me up bodily. They just carried me for three or four blocks like a sack of potatoes, with no idea what to do with me, until some of the people from the show caught up with us and rescued me. It was one of the most frightening experiences of my life.'

'Buddy and the Crickets never seemed to alienate the guys the way Donald and I did,' Phil Everly says. 'But if it ever came to a fight, Buddy was never one to duck out. One time down in Florida, we were all going along a street, and I somehow got separated from the others. Suddenly I realize there's this whole group of young guys closing in all around me. I turned round, looking for help, and saw Buddy running – I mean, really sprinting – along the sidewalk to help me. He faced up to this whole gang of guys ... and they backed off. Seriously, he was ready to take on the whole group.'

The life of a rock 'n' roll sensation like the Everlys may have looked enviable from outside, but on the inside it was a fakir's bed of insults and belittlements. 'Everyone used to say the same to us,' Phil remembers. '"Do you kids realize how lucky you are to have gotten this far?" And "What are you going to do when rock 'n' roll blows over?" Fear and guilt, that's what we were conditioned by.'

Don agrees: 'The thing always pressing on your mind was "Where's our next hit coming from? How in the world are we going to pull it off again? And again after that?" It used to make you real close and secretive about all your ideas. Buddy was under the same pressure as all the rest of us ... even more as time went on. But he never had that secretive, looking-over-your shoulder attitude. I remember him playing a new song of his called "Maybe Baby" and asking us what we thought of it. He'd suggest ideas that were right for Phil and me ... he even wrote a song especially for us. He was the most generous person with his music I've ever met in this business.'

On 23 September, four months after its release, 'That'll Be

The Day' stood at number 1 on both the pop and R & B charts, making it the top-selling single across the United States. On *Billboard*'s Hot 100 chart, which combined retail sales with radio and jukebox-play, its highest place was number 3. There, to his chagrin, Buddy did not after all beat Paul Anka's 'Diana'.

'Peggy Sue', coupled with 'Everyday', had come out under Buddy's name alone on Coral on 20 September, and was now 'breaking' nationwide at a speed usually reserved for Elvis Presley records. The main Decca label also hastened to cash in on the name it had spurned eight months previously, releasing Buddy's inferior Nashville version of 'That'll Be The Day' (on which he'd been forced to give up his royalty-entitlement) coupled with the Sonny Curtis song 'Rock Around With Ollie Vee'. This obvious attempt to dupe teenagers into buying the dud version of 'That'll Be The Day' rather than the good one made Buddy angry and unhappy, but he was powerless to do anything about it. Further releases from those unhappy sessions with Owen Bradley were to shadow his successes on Brunswick and Coral until the Bradley's Barn inventory was exhausted, early in 1958.

For a rock 'n' roll act with a hit single in 1957, the next step was to release a long-playing record, still not generally known as an 'album'. Like so much else, it symbolized the anxiety of record companies to make the most of success which could not be expected to last. An LP usually bore the name of the hit single that had preceded it and – far from any notion of showcasing the performer's range or versatility – was seen as a way of making teenagers buy the same song all over again, at three or four times the price. A contract had already been made with Bob Thiele for Brunswick to put out the Crickets' first LP before the year's end. The problem was that they had not sufficient suitable material stockpiled in Clovis to provide the dozen-odd tracks necessary, and they would be on tour until the end of November.

Norman Petty solved the difficulty in characteristic fashion.

It happened that Petty's trio also was on the road, playing a week-long engagement at the Tinker Air Force base, just outside Oklahoma City. When 'The Biggest Show of Stars for 1957' stopped off at Oklahoma City, Petty borrowed the lounge of the Tinker officers' club and set up his Ampex tape-equipment there. On the night of 29 September, after the Norman Petty Trio had finished their performance, Buddy and the Crickets turned up and a recording session took place in the empty club lounge. It produced four new tracks of releasable standard: 'You've Got Love', Roy Orbison's 'An Empty Cup', a new version of 'Maybe Baby', and 'Rock Me My Baby', a Buddy performance of typically innocent charm, its lyric combining two nursery rhymes, 'Hickory-Dickory Dock' and 'Rockabye Baby'.

Buddy and Niki Sullivan finally realized they were distant cousins when the 'Biggest Show of Stars' played the Heart of Texas fair in Waco on 2 October. 'There were only thirty-five people in the audience,' Niki remembers. 'Seventeen of them were Buddy's relations, who'd come over from the Lubbock area to root for him, and the other eighteen of them were relations of mine. That audience of thirty-five got one hell of a show – and there was one hell of a family reunion afterwards.'

Bob Thiele's decision to separate Buddy's name from the Crickets and give him a parallel solo career had originated as a pure marketing ploy. But in Buddy's orderly and logical mind, it created yet another working blueprint. Following the pattern set by 'Words Of Love', his own-name releases on Coral would tend towards the adventurous and experimental while his output with the Crickets on Brunswick would be straightforward rock 'n' roll crowd-pleasers.

On this basis, the Crickets' follow-up to 'That'll Be The Day' presented something of a problem. In 1957, one rule governed the follow-up to a million-selling hit: it must sound as identical to that hit as was humanly possible. And among all the tracks stockpiled by Norman Petty in Clovis and at Tinker USAF base there was no obvious 'That'll Be The Day 2'. The nearest in atmosphere was 'Oh Boy', by the two young Texan writers Sonny West and Bill Tilghman, which Buddy and the Crickets had recorded on the same scorching, sandstormy June weekend that produced 'Peggy Sue' and 'Everyday'. The problem was that in the distant days of early last summer no distinction had existed between 'Buddy Holly' tracks and 'Crickets' tracks. Punters who bought the Crickets' second release would naturally expect it to sound like the work of a vocal group once again.

It was, of course, the simplest matter to dub background vocals on to Buddy's solo track. Unfortunately, Gary and Ramona Tollett, the husband-and-wife duo who had done such a good job for 'That'll Be The Day', were no longer available. And although Buddy's three fellow Crickets all had voices of a sort, they were quite unable to reproduce the Tollett's moody harmonies. Petty solved the difficulty by recruiting an outside vocal group named the Picks, comprising his Clovis school-friends John and Bill Pickering and a mutual acquaintance, Bob Lapham. Between July and October, while Buddy and the Crickets were on the road, the Picks overdubbed backing vocals on 'Oh Boy' as well as four tracks for the impending LP, 'Maybe Baby', 'An Empty Cup', 'You've Got Love' and 'Rock Me My Baby'.

'Oh Boy' is the most brazen 'cut up' of all the Crickets' greatest hits, a turbo-charged rock 'n' roll racer which from its opening motor-roar of 'All my love, all my kissin' / You don't know what you been missin'' never slips from metal-pressing overdrive. Buddy's vocal is an innocently amorous war-cry, so full of excitement and *joie de vivre*, you feel he is not addressing any girl nor anticipating any tryst in particular but, rather, standing with his Stratocaster on some hilltop and, like a well-tailored young coyote, exhilaratedly baying at the moon:

Stars appear and the shadows are fawlin'
You can hear my heart (hic) cawlin'!
A little bit of lovin' make ever' thing right!
I'M GONNA SEE MY BABY TO-NIGH-HIGHT!

'The Biggest Show of Stars for 1957', meanwhile, had reached California prior to heading north through Oregon and the state of Washington and up into Canada once again. Reflecting the new state of the record-charts, major changes in the bill had been made by the pragmatic Irving Feld. Out went the Spaniels, the Bobettes and Johnnie and Joe; in came the Crickets' old Texan friends and rivals Buddy Knox and Jimmy Bowen, the Rhythm Orchids, and Eddie Cochran.

When Buddy and the Crickets performed 'Peggy Sue' at the Memorial Auditorium, Sacramento, on 18 October, the song's pertly pretty blonde inspiration was among their audience. Peggy Sue Gerron had left Lubbock High to finish her education at Sacramento's Bishop Armstrong Catholic Girls' School; with a punctiliousness unimaginable in modern rock stars, her beau, J. I. Allison, had written to her mother for permission to invite her to the show. Though Peggy Sue had heard the hit bearing her name many times over the radio, she still had to keep pinching herself as she heard Buddy perform it live for the first time.

Eddie Cochran, the major new addition to the bill, was fresh from *The Girl Can't Help It*, selling a million copies of 'Sitting In The Balcony' and touring Australia riotously with Little Richard and Gene Vincent. A husky eighteen-year-old, born in Minnesota but transplanted to California, he combined Presley-esque looks, backswept hair and plum-in-mouth mumble with talent on lead electric guitar which, many say, surpassed even Buddy's. He was a prodigious womanizer, a hard hard-drinker and a firearms nut, collecting historic Western guns like the Derringer and Buntline Special, and perfecting a fast draw that would have done credit to Wyatt Earp.

Cochran and Buddy had everything in common, bar the drinking and fast draw, and over the next year were to become more like brothers than friends. By the time 'The Biggest Show of Stars for 1957' had left Canada for Denver, Colorado, prior to moving north-east to Wichita, Kansas, and St Louis, they had turned their adjacent hotel-rooms into a communal hangout for themselves and their respective sidemen. Interviewing Cochran after the concert at Denver Auditorium, deejay Freeman Hover of station KCSR asked about 'the good guitar music coming' from the next room. 'That's Buddy Holly and the Crickets,' Cochran replied. 'They've just stolen my baritone ukelele . . .'

Hover then interviewed Buddy and J. I. Allison while Cochran sat nearby, flourishing a new pipe he'd bought that evening (another pipe-smoking rock 'n' roller!) and commenting with approval how 'sophisticated' it made him look. After thanking the denizens of Denver, in his huskily polite fashion, for buying 'That'll Be The Day', Buddy begged leave to put in a plug 'for Eddie Cochran, settin' over there, so contented-like. He's starrin' in a picture that'll be out soon . . . he said he might be able to arrange it for the Crickets to appear in that picture . . . And so we've been buddyin' up to him . . . gettin' in as good as we can!'

'The Biggest Show of Stars for 1957' wound up its three-month itinerary at the Mosque theatre, Richmond, Virginia, on 24 November. On 27 November, Brunswick released the Crickets' 'Oh Boy', coupled with the six-month-old 'Not Fade Away'. Four days later, Buddy, J.I., Niki and Joe B. were back in New York City for the ultimate acknowledgement of their arrival in the show-business first division. They had been booked by CBS television to appear on the *Ed Sullivan Show*.

Their appearance, on the Sunday evening of 1 December, went out live, coast to coast, but was also preserved on primitive black-and-white videotape. By comparison with Elvis Presley's appearance a year earlier – and with the Beatles' seven years later

– the occasion was decorous. Sullivan's main attraction, for once, were not rock 'n' rollers but the All-American football team. Arrayed in black shawl-collared tuxedos, Buddy and the Crickets had two spots, playing 'That'll Be The Day' in the show's first segment and 'Peggy Sue' in the second. Whereas they had merely lip-synched on *American Bandstand*, they were expected to give a bona fide performance here, albeit with their sound turned down to a paranoiacally low level.

The result, preserved for posterity in grainy, distorted grey-and-white, gives little idea of their true impact as a stage band. To compensate for the restricted volume, both numbers are played much faster than one is used to hearing them. Assailed by ritual shrieks from the studio audience, Buddy looks a more unlikely rock 'n' roll idol than ever with his rumpled hair, half-frame glasses and anaemic smile. Around his neck, like some priestly regalia, hangs the V-shape of a newfangled body-mike; for all that, the sound quality is atrocious, robbing his voice of all colour and expression, reducing his guitar breaks to a wiry scrabble. There are cutaway shots of rubicund, shiny-eyed little Joe B. on bass, working hard at looking as if he's working hard; of Niki Sullivan (whose guitar was not even plugged in) mouthing inaudible background vocals; of J. I. Allison on drums, nonchalantly sleek and self-satisfied. Each song is rounded off by an intrusive blast from the studio orchestra, to which Buddy synchronizes a still little bow from the waist.

Their host, the mighty Ed Sullivan, proved well up to form as the sworn enemy of rock 'n' roll and all who espoused it. Hunched of shoulder and heavy of jaw, and wearing a sharkskin suit which looked as if it had the coathanger left in it, Sullivan took his customary pains to make his young guests feel anything but at home. Under the conditions of live television at that time, Buddy and the Crickets had to play with the great man standing just off camera, only a couple of feet from his namesake Niki. At one point in mid-number, Niki heard him give a satirical hiss of 'Go, Tex!'

The moment when Buddy is called back for a brief front-of-curtain interview, as the others hastily remove their equipment, likewise reeks of metropolitan condescension: let's give this hick a break and see if he can string two words together. Buddy's charm and fluency are all the more impressive for his obvious surprise that Sullivan should pick this of all moments to start being sociable.

'. . . Where do you come from? Lubbock, Tecksuss?' Sullivan asks, managing to make it sound like the name of some remote North Atlantic atoll.

'Lubbock, Texas, yes, sir,' Buddy nods.

'Do you go to school down there?'

'Well, we did . . . till we got out of high school, finally.'

'And after high school you started playing together?'

'Yes, sir, that's right.'

'And were you a big hit from the start, or has it been sort of a long . . .?'

'Well, we've had some rough times, I guess you'd say,' Buddy admits with a grin. 'But we've been real lucky, gettin' it this quick.'

'Texas . . . nice to have you up here,' Sullivan concludes, accepting the unscheduled handshake Buddy offers him – little guessing how drastically he will revise that opinion within the space of a month.

If the Crickets had expected a heroes' return to Lubbock on 4 December, they were disappointed. Awaiting them at the airport were no screaming girls, no celebratory brass bands, no reporter and photographer from the Lubbock morning *Avalanche*, no local dignitaries to present them with the keys of the city. Buddy had planned a triumphal homecoming, arriving at his parents' home on 39th Street in a hired limo', resplendent in one of his new Alfred Norton tuxedos. But alas, he did not warn Ella and

L.O. of his coming in advance and when he arrived, both of them happened to be out. As many a star before him had learned, and many have since, nothing brings one to earth quite like returning to one's home town.

The day after their return to Lubbock, Niki Sullivan announced he was leaving the Crickets. His reason was total exhaustion after three months of nonstop touring, from which there was still to be virtually no let-up over the approaching Christmas holiday. But in truth, Niki's ninety days as a Cricket had almost all been unhappy and uncomfortable as well as musically null and void. Being at loggerheads with J. I. Allison made him out man out within the quartet, since Buddy invariably sided with J.I. and little Joe B. followed the majority in everything. By the end of the 'Biggest Show of Stars' tour, Niki had felt totally isolated by the others' hostility and teasing; so much so that on the final day, when he took the tour-bus microphone to bid farewell to his new friends the Drifters, he almost broke down in tears.

Nowadays, such a defection from a group at the peak of its success would be headline news. Back in 1957, however, the national media took no interest in such things; even the Crickets' most devoted fans knew none of their names but Buddy's. Inside the music business, however, Niki's prestige stood high enough to win him a recording contract with the Dot label. Over the next few years he was to release several records under his own name and also front a band called Soul Incorporated before gravitating from rock 'n' roll into the electronics industry.

Niki Sullivan's attempts to extract some kind of compensatory pay-off from Norman Petty ought to have forewarned Buddy about the process of getting down to any kind of financial brass tacks with Clovis Man. Supported by his father, Niki asked Petty for details of the Crickets' earnings thus far, optimistically anticipating the quarter share which Buddy had insisted each member of the group should receive. 'We asked to see the books

twenty-two times, but Norman always had some excuse ... "Oh,
they're not at the studio right now ..." "They're being audited
..." My dad was right in what he said the first time he ever met
Norman. "Son, NEVER trust a businessman who keeps a Bible
on his desk."'

Worn down by Petty's evasions, Niki settled for a payment
of $1,000, his quarter-share of the proceeds of 'That'll Be The
Day' and one-third writer's royalties from 'I'm Gonna Love You
Too'. Though a trickle of royalties was to reach him over the
years, he says it never came anywhere near a quarter what
'That'll Be The Day' was eventually worth. Nor did his church
receive a cent of the tithe it had been promised. 'As I always say,
Jesse James wasn't killed in the eighteen-eighties. He was still
alive in Clovis, New Mexico, until the nineteen-eighties.'

There was initially some talk of replacing Niki with Sonny
Curtis, that stalwart of Buddy's pre-Crickets line-up. But Sonny
now had a flourishing career of his own, and in any case the gap
was purely a cosmetic one since Buddy and J.I. between them
generated all the power and more necessary for stage appearances. Even so, their decision to carry on as a trio was an
adventurous one. A three-man vocal/instrumental line-up was
unknown in rock 'n' roll to that point, and in the decades since,
has cropped up only rarely; Cream, the Jimi Hendrix Experience
and Crosby, Stills and Nash in the sixties and the Police in the
post-Punk seventies are the only other notable examples.

No one could pretend that Niki was greatly missed when the
new slimline Crickets re-convened at Norman Petty's studio on
19 December to work on two further tracks for unspecified
future use. One was 'Baby, I Don't Care', a Leiber-Stoller song
performed by Elvis Presley in his film *Jailhouse Rock*, now given
a far quieter, subtler treatment with softly-revving rhythm
Stratocaster and a repeat of 'Not Fade Away''s cardboard-box
percussion technique. Buddy's vocal acknowledged his debt to
'the King', though it was now in a style completely his own that

he sang 'You're s'square' in a soft, sighing register, then plunged into the sub-basement for 'Baby, I don't care ...' The second track, 'Look At Me', was a gently hiccoughy ballad, credited to 'Buddy Holly/Norman Petty/Jerry Allison', and typically blending self-confidence with uncertainty. 'Say (hic) hey look at me and tell me/ 'Bout that twinkle in your eye/ Is the twinkle in your eye meant for me/ Or meant for some other guy? ...' Here once again Petty decided that a piano rather than guitar accompaniment was called for, and Vi was summoned from her boudoir to provide it. Standing at the Baldwin grand in her hair curlers and slippers, the fidgety, flighty woman as usual metamorphosed into a calmly intuitive musician. Her rolling bass solo, under Buddy's knowing yet wistful voice, is one of the most charming mixtures ever to emerge from Clovis Man's electronic melting-pot.

The main consequence of Niki Sullivan's departure – one that would come back to haunt Buddy in future months – was to change the Crickets from a homogeneous group, like the Diamonds or the Platters, to a group-plus-front man like Gene Vincent and the Blue Caps. Norman Petty had at least prevailed on Buddy to acknowledge that, as a hit-maker under his own name as well group-vocalist, lead instrumentalist and principal songwriter, he was worth more than the equal fourth share he'd taken up to now. Instead, from here on, he'd receive 50 per cent and J.I. and Joe B. would divide the other 50 per cent between them. From here on, too – to Buddy's present glory but future detriment – concert posters and advertising would increasingly refer to 'Buddy Holly and the Crickets'.

Who got what was purely academic, in any case, since their combined earnings went directly to Petty to be paid into the Buddy Holly and Crickets joint bank account. Though Buddy, J.I. and Joe B. all had personal checking accounts at Lubbock banks, almost nothing ever came into these, and even less went out. Every bill that incurred, collectively and personally, was sent directly to Petty – retailers and suppliers of the late fifties really were that trusting! – and settled by Petty, using his power of attorney on their funds at Clovis National Bank. The cashed cheques in Clovis Man's archive record, among other things, session-fees to the Picks vocal group, instalment-payments on Joe B.'s double bass, repair work on Buddy's car at the Petty family garage, and 'telephone calls' (another of those bizarre occasions where Petty's name is a barely convincing forgery by 'Ma Petty'). There are also regular payouts of pocket-money to each of the Crickets – for instance, $600 on 25 October, the cheque made out 'To: Mrs L. O. Holley. For: Buddy.'

How much he was earning or spending – or paying his manager in commission – was the last thing on Buddy's mind at this point. All that mattered was the excitement of seeing his music leap into the charts, and the intoxication of having ready cash in his pocket. Back in New York, his new friends Don and Phil Everly had taken his sartorial image in hand, introducing him to Phil's menswear shop on Third Avenue, where all the rock 'n' rollers went for Ivy League clothes. Buddy, Jerry and Joe B. were all now faultlessly collegiate in long, thin tweed jackets with vertical stripes, thin lapels and four buttons up the front; shirts with pin-fastening collars; cuffless, back-belted trousers; shoes with side buckles instead of laces; and rakish little narrow-brimmed hats. 'We taught 'em about going to dinner in restaurants, too, instead of just grabbing a hamburger,' Don Everly says. 'And going to night-clubs instead of just to a movie. They caught on to all of that real quick.'

The boy who'd grown up in near-poverty, and spent almost all his early life in Levis and T-shirts, turned into a voracious shopper, with a natural homing instinct for the best in everything. It did not take Buddy long to discover that the classiest menswear in New York was not to be found at Phil's but at Alfred Norton on West 50th St. Clovis Man's paper treasure-trove includes receipts for Buddy's spending sprees at Alfred

Norton – bills for $150 stage tuxedos, $8.95 cummerbunds, ties at $3.50 or $1.50 apiece, and the $45 dark blue blazer with anchor-emblazoned gilt buttons which – after the Strat' – was his proudest possession. His waist-measurement is given, unvaryingly, as twenty-nine inches. The salesman, always the same one, is named as 'Frank'.

Don and Phil Everly claim credit for planting the seeds of the biggest image-change of all. 'We both kept on at Buddy to do something about his glasses,' Phil says. 'Those things he had, with the half-frames, were the same ones he'd been wearing since high school. Donald and I both told him, "Hey, look, you've proved that a guy who wears glasses can make it in rock 'n' roll. So why be ashamed of the glasses? Why not make them a real upfront statement, like 'OK, I wear glasses, and here they are'?"'

Back home in Lubbock on that pre-Christmas visit, Buddy continued his determined metamorphosis from gawky provincial nerd into smooth and seamless star. At the Everly Brothers' prompting, he had also been to a smart men's hair stylist in Manhattan to have his unruly dark curls styled in a permanent wave. But the style did not look or feel right and, as soon as he got home, he went to Jake Goss, the no-frills Lubbock barber who had cut both his and his father's hair for many years. 'I took the wave out and gave him a more natural look,' Goss remembers. 'But he never did decide the way he wanted to have his hair fixed.' After hair in the self-improvement blueprint came those disfiguringly snaggled and fluoride-stained 'West Texas teeth'. On 14 December and again six days later Buddy visited Lubbock dentist Dr Clifford E. Fisher and had his front teeth encased in gleaming caps: subsequently, the Buddy Holly and Crickets account was debited by $596.

Also on 20 December, as a reward to himself for the hours of discomfort under Dr Fisher's drill, he called at the Stewart-Meadors Chevrolet dealership in Clovis to collect the 1958-

registered car he had picked out for himself two days earlier. It was a Impala V8 two-seat coupé in symbolic coral pink. Norman Petty subsequently made the $300 down-payment from the Buddy Holly and the Crickets account, negotiating a $721 discount on the car's $3,648.55 list-price and paying off the balance within the month. At first, the Impala's 'Powerglide' automatic transmission gave trouble, refusing to shift out of 'low'. The day after collecting the car, having already clocked up 188 miles, Buddy took it to a Lubbock Chevrolet dealer and had the fault rectified (at a cost of $2).

Only his family and a few close friends knew why Buddy was especially anxious to cut an impressive figure around Lubbock this Christmas. Echo McGuire would also be home for the holidays from her college in York, Nebraska. At some point out on the road these past three months, Buddy's infatuation with June Clark had faded and he'd realized he was as much in love with Echo as ever.

When 'The Biggest Show of Stars for 1957' had performed at the Civic Auditorium in Omaha, Nebraska, on 4 November, Buddy had tried to phone Echo at college and ask her to come and see him, but, to her distress, the message hadn't reached her. At a later stopover in the Black Hills of Dakota, he'd had a present specially made for Echo – a gold charm necklace spelling 'Buddy Holley' in tasteful italic script. His use of his real surname rather than its world-famous mutation was highly significant. He wanted to reassure Echo he was still the same person she'd met all those years ago at Roscoe Wilson Elementary School and gone skating and hiking and praying with; that whatever might have happened to each of them in the intervening months meant nothing, and they could go on from here together just as they'd always planned.

But it was not to be. At college in Nebraska, Echo had fallen in love with a fellow student, a lanky, humorous boy from the Ozark Mountains named Ron Griffiths whose studiousness and

Christian ideals matched her own. When she returned home to Lubbock that Christmas of 1957, Ron came with her.

'I intended to tell Buddy about it face-to-face,' Echo says now. 'But somehow we never did manage to get together.' Ron has a different memory, however. 'I'm sure he did come by your house one time. Seems like I waited there while you and Buddy went to get a Coke.' At all events, the moment when Echo had to break it to Buddy that her feelings for him had changed, and that Ron Griffith was now the person with whom she wanted to share her life, had to come while they were talking on the telephone.

Buddy's brother Larry, always the one best able to read his heart, thinks he carried a torch for Echo all the brief remainder of his life. Her mother, Pansie McGuire, is equally sure of it. 'Every song he wrote was for Echo before they parted and after, too. People might say, "Well, why didn't he ever mention her by name?" but to me that was just like Buddy. He thought that maybe the songs might be recorded by other people some day, and he didn't want Echo's name passed around among a lot of musicians as if she belonged to anyone.'

Echo married Ron Griffith in Lubbock on St Valentine's Day, 1958. After leaving college in Nebraska, she studied at the University of Montana, then both she and her husband became teachers. During the early years of their marriage, Ron says, he knew that Echo still loved Buddy. But she was destined never to see him or hear from him again.

He never did find an opportunity to give Echo that custom-made gold charm necklace spelling out 'Buddy Holley'. 'After they split up, Buddy sent it to Mother to look after,' Larry says. 'I guess he couldn't bear to look at it again.'

Over that Christmas season, 'Peggy Sue' under Buddy's name reached number 3 while 'Oh Boy' under the Crickets' climbed steadily towards its eventual peak of number 10. Buddy, J.I. and Joe B. had joined another of Alan Freed's mammoth stage spectaculars, the *Holiday of Stars*, this one at the more prestigious Paramount Theater in midtown Manhattan. Sharing the marquee with them were the Everly Brothers, Fats Domino, Paul Anka, Danny and the Juniors and a new piano-punishing sensation from darkest Louisiana named Jerry Lee Lewis. Their triple chart-success had sent the Texans' price soaring to $4,200 for the ten-day engagement.

On 28 December, they made the most bizarre of all their television appearances, performing 'Peggy Sue' on the *Arthur Murray Party*, a show hosted by the doyen of strict ballroom dancing and his wife, Katherine. Heaven knows what prompted the Murrays to add rock 'n' roll to their usual programme of old-fashioned formation waltzes and foxtrots, but spots on peak-time television shows were not so numerous that any could be lightly turned down; besides, the fee offered was a handsome $2,000. Buddy and the Crickets were introduced as 'rock 'n' roll specialists' by Katherine Murray, a gowned and bejewelled woman with the clipped pseudo-British voice of a Park Avenue socialite, but evidently quite amiable and tolerant for all that.

'Now, whatever you may think of rock 'n' roll,' she admonished strict-tempo zealots all over the nation, 'I think you have to keep a nice open mind about what the young people go for, otherwise the young ones will think you don't understand them.' Buddy, Jerry and Joe B. then did their stuff on a cleared section of dance-floor – Buddy darting the odd incredulous look at the others – while a line of girls in stiff ball dresses stood behind them, one or two daring to sway fractionally with the drum-beat.

On New Year's Day, 1957, Buddy had had nothing to look forward to but a torn-up Decca contract and a country and Western tour, playing back-up to Hank Locklin and Cowboy

Copas. Twelve months later to the day, he had three records in the charts; his name was known across America and beginning to reverberate around the world; everyone seemed to be talking about rock 'n' roll's latest 'overnight sensation'.

Tours stretched solidly ahead, to ever more distant and thrilling locations. From the Christmas *Holiday of Stars* at the New York Paramount, Buddy and the Crickets set off on another GAC roadshow ('America's Greatest Teenage Performing Stars'), with the Everly Brothers, Paul Anka and Danny and the Juniors on a seventeen-day swing through North Carolina, Virginia, Maryland, Pennsylvania and Ohio. On 27 January they were booked to join Anka and Jerry Lee Lewis for two shows in Honolulu, Hawaii, the whole package then flying on for a week-long tour of Australia. Buddy and the Crickets were to receive $6,000 and be guaranteed '100 per cent' billing – i.e. their names in the largest-size type in all advertisements.

On 25 January, in a few snatched hours between packing and unpacking, Buddy had his first-ever recording session in New York. For the first time, the moving spirit was not Norman Petty but Bob Thiele of Coral Records. 'Buddy had been saying how he'd like the two of us to work together. So I booked him a session at Bell Sound studios, and got Milton de Lugg, the orchestra leader, in as producer, with extra session men, like Al Caiola on guitar,' Thiele remembered. 'We had a vocal group, the Jivetones, in on it, too. Petty, I know, got really uptight, thinking I was moving in on his boy. To be diplomatic, we had to let him be there as back-up pianist. All the time, I could feel the vibrations of jealousy.'

The session was prompted mainly by a song Buddy couldn't wait to record. This was 'Rave On', a new composition by the writers of 'Oh Boy', Sonny West and Bill Tilghman. 'We'd sent it to Norman, as usual – and, as usual, when it came out in published form, it had his name added to it,' Sonny West remembers. 'His original idea was that a group called the Big Beats from Dallas should do it. But Buddy said no one was to have it but him.'

The Bell session showed Buddy's ability to turn out first-class work at top speed, despite the pressure and fatigue of non-stop touring. The first half of the six-hour session was used to record tracks by the vocal group, the Jivetones. Between around 10 pm and 2 am two Buddy songs were completed: 'That's My Desire', a ballad which Frankie Laine had recorded in the late forties, and 'Rave On'.

'Rave On' is for many the ultimate Buddy Holly vocal, combining as it does a mood of total rock 'n' roll abandon (its first word, 'Well . . .' is pulverized into six distinct syllables) with a delivery of relaxed economy and elegance. It is the first uptempo Buddy number not to feature a strong guitar motif, instead employing heavy bass, a descanting jazzy piano – played by Norman Petty – and back-up vocals with the threatening 'walla-walla' chant of comic-book redskins on the warpath. Despite the one-third writer's cut he had ritually appropriated, Petty had good reason to feel chagrin. For here was proof that Buddy did not need his studio, nor any special one, to work short-order magic.

On 26 January, the day before he and the Crickets flew to Honolulu to join the Paul Anka/ Jerry Lee Lewis Australian tour, there was another major TV engagement to fulfil. In recognition of 'Oh Boy''s growing chart success, they had been invited back for a second appearance on the *Ed Sullivan Show*. The original plan had been for the Picks to appear also, performing the record's overdubbed backing vocals. 'Norman never paid us a cent for doing that session,' Bill Pickering says. 'And we never got any credit on the record-label. But Buddy liked what we'd done so much that he sent us the money to fly up to New York for the Sullivan show. Then at the last minute we were told that the Musicians Union wouldn't let us go on.'

Despite a $500 hike in their fee (from $1,500 to $2,000), being Ed Sullivan's guest proved no pleasanter for the Texans in early 1958 than it had been in late 1957. First, their scheduled two numbers were cut to one, then Sullivan requested them not to play 'Oh Boy' as he considered its lyrics too 'raunchy'. Buddy, however, insisted it had to be 'Oh Boy' or nothing. Sullivan was compelled to give in, but took revenge in characteristic fashion, muffling his star guests' introduction with a spoken promo for Mercury automobiles, 'the performance champions of 1958', then deliberately mangling their name into 'Buddy Hollerd ... and the Cruckutts ...'

The staging this time was considerably more polished and dramatic; Buddy was shown under a bright spotlight, standing astride his guitar-spiky shadow, with only occasional side glimpses of J.I. and Joe B. America could thus see all the more plainly what change had come about in the shy out-of-towner who'd sir'd Ed Sullivan so gratefully a month earlier. In place of the conventionally cut dark tuxedo was a long, pale, high-buttoning Ivy League jacket; in place of rumpled curls was the neat wavy wedge that his hometown barber, Jake Goss, had devised; in place of discoloured and irregular teeth, a gleaming, symmetrical smile. Most transformingly of all, the high school nerd's half-frame glasses had been replaced by a pair of black horn-rims whose outsize square frames, far from seeking to minimize their existence, proclaimed it defiantly, even trium-phantly. On yet another shopping spree a couple of days earlier, Don and Phil Everly had carried their point at last.

And in place of wonderment was devilment. Ed Sullivan's secondary revenge had been to have the Crickets' sound turned right down. On the video-recording, Buddy's right hand keeps darting to the Stratocaster's volume-knob in a vain attempt to get more power. He retaliates by 'cutting up' in 'Oh Boy' as never before; making it even more frantically fast; stretching it out with an unscheduled second chorus; at the guitar-break, wheeling round to show his new sleekly-coiffed, high-buttoned and horn-rimmed profile, and giving a mischievous coyote howl at the spotlight-moon:

A little bit of lovin' makes ever'thing right!
I'M GONNA SEE MY BABY TO-NIGH-HIGHT!

The sequence ends with a cut back to Ed Sullivan, amid the audience's delighted applause, smiling with the conviction of a man whose toenails are being extracted with red-hot pliers.

Part Three

IT'S SO EASY

THE NINETEEN-FIFTIES in Britain are regarded as a golden age of full employment, low crime, social cohesion and steadily accumulating prosperity; an era like none before, and none since, when life for everyone seemed to be getting better every day. A world war had been won and a monstrous tyranny overthrown, chiefly (we were assured) by our collective fortitude and self-sacrifice. A brand-new, shyly smiling young Queen sat on the throne, and the whole nation seemed at one in striving to earn her good opinion. Public transport was clean and efficient, letters travelled swiftly, taxation was low and food cheap; no beggars could be seen nearer at hand than Spain or Italy. In the whole length and breadth of our aptly named United Kingdom it was hard to find a street which could not be walked in perfect safety at any hour of the day or night.

To the young, however, this did not feel like enviable security, but suffocating dullness. The chaos and cruelties of history might all have been eradicated, but so, apparently, had all its excitement, passion, colour and surprise. One felt one had been born at the very end of the line, with everything settled, tidied and squared away, and nothing whatsoever left to look forward to. The 'pre-war' eras, with their distinctive character and costume and unrationed plenty, lay far behind; the future, with its promise of rocket-ships and robots, had not yet begun to reveal itself. The present was humdrum, predictable Eternity.

A decade after Victory in Europe, the ethos of wartime still exerted an all-powerful grip. The stereotypical British hero was Jack Hawkins or John Mills in one of the period's numerous black-and-white war films, clean-cut, pipe-smoking, unshakeably modest and reserved, sinking U-boats in the Atlantic or outfoxing Rommel in North Africa. Wartime austerity and self-denial lived on in the disgusting food and the monochrome dreariness of the streets. Cars came in two colours, black or beige. Women's fashions were subdued enough; for a man to stand out even slightly from the clerical grey mass meant instant condemnation as a hoodlum or a homosexual. This was the era when a journalist from a national newspaper went to interview a cabinet minister but was turned away because the minister couldn't face conversing with someone who wore yellow socks.

America lay an inconceivable way off, a destination for none but the rich and famous, reached as commonly by ocean liner as by the scarcely less opulent Comet jets of the British Overseas Airways Corporation. It was a landscape familiar to all from twice- or thrice-weekly cinema visits, yet enduringly opaque and mysterious; a country about which we knew for certain only that it was in every way the opposite of ours – its cities of towering glass, not heaped bomb-rubble; its houses long and white, not narrow and dingy; its people warm, spontaneous and generous, not stand-offish and penny-pinching; its refrigerators immense; its steaks overlapping the plate; its nomenclature bizarre; its cars multi-finned; its footballers helmeted; its police side-armed; its suits shiny; its vegetation lush; its coffee black; its sunshine unquenchable.

Despite the cataclysmic disruption of the Second World War, mid-fifties Britain remained essentially a Victorian society, still founded on a rigid class system, a respect for authority and seniority, a consensus of self-discipline and self-control. Youth lived under much the same constraints as it had half a century earlier, obeying the Victorian nursery precept of being seen and not heard. The 'teenager', long recognized in America as a potent economic force, was still barely noticed in Britain, where the only ones permitted to enjoy their teenage years were the small minority granted university education. The majority went directly from childhood to adulthood at the age of about seventeen, metamorphosing overnight from school uniforms to frocks and twinsets like their mothers' or tweed jackets, grey flannel trousers and manly briar pipes like their fathers'.

Before 1955, Britain's older and younger generations derived their entertainment from broadly similar sources. There remained a few variety theatres, not yet quite annihilated by movies. The omnipotent medium of popular music, as well as drama and light entertainment, was radio, in those days totally non-commercial and the monopoly of the BBC, which voluntarily censored and diluted its own output in accordance with the Calvinistic prejudices of its founder, Lord Reith. Television had two channels only: one the BBC's, the other shared by brand-new commercial companies, all dedicated to emulating the BBC, both in quality and conservatism. The main haunts of youth were dance-halls, where forties-style big bands featured pale imitations of American crooners like Eddie Fisher and Dick Haymes. A tiny intellectual fringe disputed the merits of traditional over modern jazz; a still smaller one, usually in beards and sandals, followed American folk and blues.

The culture was an almost wholly passive one, based on watching, listening and impotently admiring. Britain's long and rich tradition of amateur music-making seemed to have reached a full stop somewhere around 1930. Music had come to be regarded as an obscure, elevated science, like mathematics or medicine, which none but professors and experts should attempt to create. The only musical instrument generally taught to children was the piano. At my own school, music lessons consisted of standing in a circle and mindlessly and joylessly beating on kiddy-sized tambourines and triangles. Singing was something one did only under the direst sufferance, in church or at end-of-term concerts. To the introverted, self-conscious British schoolboy of 1955, few torments were as purgatorial as being made to stand up before an audience and give any kind of performance.

For all the furore that rock 'n' roll created in America, everyone over there knew where it came from, spiritually as well as geographically. At the heart of the garish new sound was a long-lived American virtue; the all-out energy, attack and commitment which F. Scott Fitzgerald defined as 'willingness of the heart' and which had already produced Hollywood, jazz, the Broadway musical and, for that matter, American sport and American politics.

The one thing notably absent from every section of British society in 1955 was willingness of the heart. All that most adult Britons knew for certain about rock 'n' roll was that it outraged every modest and downbeat virtue that the British Empire had epitomized for 500 years. Only a very few on the intellectual fringe recognized the colliding elements of country, blues and R & B. The rest heard a cacophony so impenetrable it might just as well have been beamed down from some hostile planet. This is not mere hyperbolic hindsight: in that first devastating glare of noise, Elvis Presley and his fellow perpetrators really did seem not quite human. I remember seeing early film of a shock-haired, crazy-eyed Little Richard, and being surprised when, at the end of his song, he bowed and smiled at his audience in the conventional way.

In Britain, unlike America, the rock 'n' roll controversy did not originally focus on race. Steeped though we were in the racism of our dwindling Empire, a distinction had always been made between our own, growing West Indian immigrant population and black Americans who as jazzmen, entertainers or sports personalities, were generally viewed with fascinated respect. To be sure, the first rock 'n' roll scapegoat in Britain was a white man, Bill Haley, and what the resultant uproar brought into ghastly relief was not our racial attitudes but our still rigid and rampant class-system. Rock 'n' roll was seen as an aberration of the working class, like alcoholism or wife-beating, which it was the duty of their betters – politicians, clergymen, Fleet Street editors – to discourage at every possible opportunity. The riots which had accompanied screenings of *Rock Around the Clock* allowed the stigma of criminality and vandalism to be attached to anyone who admitted liking it. Its earliest and most visible devotees were the 'Teddy boys' – young artisans who defied the nation's rigid dress code by sporting drape jackets with velvet collars, string ties and 'drainpipe' trousers, and who were known to carry on sartorial discussions with the aid of razors, knuckle-dusters and bicycle-chains. The jive, a dance-step familiar throughout the war, now souped-up to rock 'n' roll's slap-bass beat, was outlawed by dance-halls throughout the country (including my father's on the end of Ryde Pier). Even the new juvenile taste for Italianate capuccino-bars was viewed with suspicion and dread. It was perhaps the ultimate achievement of British Establishment paranoia to have made even frothy coffee seem dangerous!

Teenagers in the several class-gradations above Teddy boys and Teddy girls – lower-middle, middle, upper-middle, lower-upper, etc. etc. – remained largely unmoved by the first wave of rock 'n' roll. I myself was one such, in the lower reaches of lower-middle. My friends and I accepted our parents' and teachers' judgement that it was nothing but an ear-affronting confidence-trick; that rock 'n' roll singers could not really sing and only pretended to play their guitars; that in six months from now, the whole ludicrous, dishonest, unhealthy fad would have blown over.

Between Bill Haley and Elvis Presley, Britain experienced a smaller but no less influential musical insurrection. Around 1954, the traditional jazz musicians Ken Colyer and Chris Barber introduced us to skiffle, the homespun American folk music of the Depression era, when people often could afford no better instruments than guitars, mouth organs and kazoos, and would beat out a primitive rhythm on jugs, kitchen washboards and one-string basses made from an empty crate and a broomstick. The Chris Barber band's banjo-player, Tony Donegan (renamed 'Lonnie' in honour of bluesman Lonnie Johnson), broke away to form his own 'skiffle group' and had a huge record-hit with 'Rock Island Line', a train song which, unprecedently, ricocheted back across the Atlantic to become an American number 1.

Skiffle was a socially acceptable version of rock 'n' roll, glamorous in its American accent and references, yet without rock's taint of lewdness and subversion. Best of all, its glamour could be recreated, more or less, by anyone with access to a kitchen cupboard. The chronic self-consciousness and lockjaw of British youths instantly melted away. All over the country, in middle-class grammar schools as well as proletarian youth clubs, amateur skiffle groups materialized under rough-hewn collective names (the Nomads, the Hobos, the Quarry Men) to patter out the work-song repertoire of Woody Guthrie and Jimmie Rodgers on acoustic guitars, tea-chest basses and washboards. After decades of anonymity in folk music and dance-bands, the guitar became an object of thrilling glamour, something every young British male, however previously unmusical, longed to wear around his neck like Lonnie Donegan – and, of course, Elvis. True to our national character, it wasn't long before the papers were announcing a country-wide guitar shortage.

Commercially, the skiffle craze lasted barely eighteen months. By late 1957, Lonnie Donegan, its only substantial talent, was already moving into the sphere of comedy and music-hall; the handful of other groups who had won recording contracts simply disappeared. Behind them they left thousands of amateur skifflers, equipped with guitars, basses and drums and with a newly awakened hunger for performance, but no idea what to do now. Then, out of nowhere, someone came along to show them.

In Britain, unlike America, 'That'll Be The Day' was an immediate success. Within a couple of weeks of its release, in mid-September, 1957, it was in the Top 20; by early October it had reached number 1, cleaving through rival US chart-toppers like Pat Boone's 'Remember You're Mine', Charlie Gracie's 'Fabulous', the Everly Brothers' 'Wake Up Little Susie', and domestic ones like Lonnie Donegan's 'Dixie Darlin'', Jim Dale's 'Be My Girl' and Johnny Duncan and the Bluegrass Boys' 'Last Train to San Fernando'.

American rock 'n' roll hits in those days came from so far away and were around so short a time that, with a few exceptions, British record-buyers paid minimal attention to the name on the label. Collective nouns tended to denote vocal-groups: 'the Crickets' therefore were initially thought to be of the same genre as the Inkspots and the Platters, presumably black, probably an amalgam of males and females in the prevailing style. An additional small stir of interest came from the special resonance of 'cricket' to English ears – not the nocturnal insect-buzz of warm climates but the white-clad summer game still in those days a synonym for gentlemanliness, restraint and fair play.

Today, any pop record that has reached number 1 assails the ears unavoidably from every quarter. But in the Britain of 1957, even a hit as big as 'That'll Be The Day' had to be searched for with some tenacity. The radio airwaves were the monopoly of the BBC, whose popular music service, the Light Programme, had banned American rock 'n' roll since the first Bill Haley riots.

Other than buying the record – at the price of 6s (30p) no light undertaking – there were only two ways of getting it in earshot. One could pay sixpence for a barely audible version on the jukebox at some frighteningly low-class espresso bar. Or one could wait until after 7pm and then tune to Radio Luxembourg, away in almost equally unimaginable Europe, which transmitted an evening programme of record shows hosted by English disc jockeys, with American-style station IDs and commercials. Reception was often patchy and bedevilled by strident voices speaking in French, Flemish, German and Dutch. Endlessly re-tuning the radio's faint-lit dial, ears pressed close to its woven loudspeaker fabric, rock 'n' roll fans were like a Resistance against hostile occupation, struggling to pick up forbidden messages of comfort and encouragement.

It was on Radio Luxembourg that most young Britons first heard the name Buddy Holly, early in December, 1957, when 'Peggy Sue' began rolling out of the multilingual static. Although nowhere near as bizarre a name as 'Elvis Presley', it still struck oddly on our ears with that ungainly double 'y'; the 'Buddy' as American as dungarees and drugstores, the 'Holly' so English Christmas-card. Mystery hung in the air from the very begin-ning: we learned that Buddy Holly was lead singer of the Crickets, but that he'd recorded 'Peggy Sue' as a solo performer, even though 'Oh Boy', the Crickets' follow-up to their great autumn hit, was also concurrently climbing the charts. So had he left the group and been replaced by another vocalist? Or had he left, then had second thoughts and rejoined the line-up?

Another oddity was hearing the Luxembourg announcer (Keith Fordyce? Or was it Freddie Mills?) describe him 'the songwriter Buddy Holly'. In 1957, the only songwriters British people knew about were middle-aged men who sat in Tin Pan Alley garrets, penning the umpteenth rhyme of 'June' with 'moon'. The voice, too, with its low pitch and air of control, suggested someone more mature than the usual scowling rock 'n' roll whelp, which in those days inevitably meant someone black. I myself remember thinking he might perhaps belong to the elder statesman class of disc jockey, like Alan Freed in America and our own Pete Murray and David Jacobs.

If hearing American rock 'n' roll was difficult, obtaining any data about its performers was next to impossible. National newspapers offered minuscule coverage of the pop music scene, and that in a tone of middle-aged facetiousness; there was virtually none on daytime domestic radio; television had but a single pop show, the BBC's *Six-Five Special*, presented in the spirit of a youth club social and featuring exclusively feeble home-grown talent. The two specialist music papers, *Melody Maker* and the *New Musical Express*, owed their first duty to mainstream pop and jazz – and, anyway, were not sold by the vast majority of newsagents throughout the country. As with all underground movements, information circulated chiefly by word of mouth. Especially if you lived outside London, rock 'n' roll was a series of brilliant rumours, some absurdly far-fetched, others even more absurdly true.

Around January of 1958, three rumours about Buddy Holly began circulating among Maquisard groups throughout Britain's rock 'n' roll Resistance. First, that he was not black like Fats Domino and Little Richard, as had been widely supposed, but as white as Elvis Presley, Charlie Gracie or Paul Anka; second, that, in defiance of all pop music (and most show-business) precedent, he wore glasses; third, that, as well as fronting the Crickets and being 'a songwriter', he also confounded our parents' allegations of poor to non-existent musicianship among rock 'n' roll stars by playing all his own electric guitar solos. The glasses added to the whiteness and unprecedented instrumental ability gave him the aura of some brainy sixth-form student, mastering each department of rock 'n' roll like so many honours passes in the General Certificate of Education.

What had chiefly made 'That'll Be The Day' such an instant

hit over here was an electric sound more ravishingly metallic than Britain's guitar-besotted teenage boys had even dreamed possible. Elsewhere, the guitar seemed to be fading from American rock 'n' roll. Elvis Presley had given up wearing one as an essential performance-accessory, and his records no longer featured those jaunty Sun-era solos by Scotty Moore. On more and more new transatlantic imports, the lead guitar was displaced by hammering piano or squealing chicken-sax. But Buddy Holly records always provided the clanging, jangling uproar which adolescent Britons now hungered for almost sexually; alone of all the rock 'n' roll aliens, he seemed to us consistent, reliable, concerned with giving us what we wanted.

Hero and icon though Elvis was, he had always been remote and unknowable. To the 10,000 learner guitarists and would-be vocalists throughout Britain, his records were as mysterious as they were sublime, the voice fused to its instrumental backing by a process which baffled the ear. All other American rock 'n' roll presented the same implacable mystery, tantalizingly hinted at by exotic label-names like Atlantic and Liberty; penned like a genie in glistening grooves of the new, small-size 45 rpm discs; unreachably locked away inside the pink perspex arc of the jukebox.

But with Buddy Holly, in and out of the Crickets, one could instantly see how it was done. All his songs were written in the keys of A, E or D, translating into simple three-finger guitar-chords, and following the four-chord twelve-bar blues sequence every skiffler could play. Only a few daring or foolhardy souls had ever dared to try to imitate the way Elvis sang. But everyone could, and did, copy Buddy. The straightforward key and lowered pitch of his voice allowed the most untuneful, and the most bashful, to sing along without looking or feeling like an idiot. Exotic as was the origin of that voice, wild and many-hued as it could be in certain moods, it seemed not so very different from our one-dimensionally reserved and cautious British ones.

Anyone could get an echo of 'That'll Be The Day', at least in his own head, by lowering the chin, gritting the teeth and murmuring from the gills through lips held as straight and rigid as a ventriloquist's.

Elvis lyrics, if not garbled beyond comprehension, could be blush-makingly coy: 'Treat me nice ...' 'Love me tender' ... 'Let me be your Teddy bear ...' But Buddy's were clear, simple, neat, self-controlled, and never too serious, consistent in every way with the precious dignity of the average British fifteen-year-old. For those unwilling to venture quite so far, there was always the background chorus of 'Oooh', 'Aaah' and 'Ba-ba-ba' which lost nothing if the tongue stayed firmly in the cheek. In Britain, his most influential early song was 'Maybe Baby', released under the Crickets' name in March 1958: a simpler-than-ever blueprint for singer, guitar and backing vocals, scanned and rapidly mastered in living-rooms, garages, youth clubs and Boy Scout huts from John O'Groats to Land's End. 'Maybe baby, I'll have you ... Maybe baby, you'll be true ...' At a plectrum-stroke, all those bereft and directionless skiffle groups turned into busy, ambitious rock 'n' roll bands.

Not even the hostility and apathy of Britain's domestic media had prevented the aliens from beaming into our midst. They came via the cinema, in black-and-white 'exploitation' films like *Rock Around the Clock, Rock, Rock, Rock* and *Disc Jockey Jamboree*, whose flimsy story-lines were an excuse for strings of cameo-appearances by Bill Haley and the Comets, Freddy Bell and the Bellboys, Fats Domino, Buddy Knox and Jerry Lee Lewis, all introduced by Alan Freed in his role as The One Adult in the World Who Understands. Elvis, of course, was everywhere – on magazine covers, cinema posters, bubblegum cards; there was even a spoken communiqué from the King ('Hi, this is Elvis Presley, speaking from Hollywood ...') counselling his subjects to remain steadfast in the face of persecution and ridicule.

Yet almost four months after 'That'll Be The Day' had

jangled its way into our minds, we still had no clear idea what Buddy Holly looked like. Advertisements for his records (the ones that I saw, anyway) appeared without photographs; there seemed to be no fan club to write to for information or autographs; by early 1958, the only picture of him I'd seen was the blurry group-shot on the cover of 'Oh Boy' in sheet-music form – still an important market then – pinned just too high for my myopic vision in the window of Ryde's only record-shop.

Then, at long last, the *Chirping Crickets* LP came along to open our eyes. Released in America in November 1957, it did not appear in Britain until the New Year, and didn't swim into my personal ken until some time early in March. At 30s (£1.50) an LP was a precious rarity, less for playing than for passing around a reverent group to be studied as an art object in its own right.

How we ogled – even reverently stroked – that garish one-dimensional sleeve! 'The Crickets' was written in white capitals with 'Chirping' interposed in jiggly yellow ones, between con-descending quotation-marks. Underneath, four figures in identi-cal, high-buttoning pale grey suits were outlined against a blue background more garish than any natural sky, smiling broadly (little did anyone suspect the fist-fight that had preceded their photo-session on the New York Paramount roof) and cradling the bodies of two brown guitars between them. Even then, identification was not immediate since two of the figures wore glasses. Some instinct told us that Buddy was the one second from left, in half-frames, not transparent rims; the tallest of the quartet, with the longest neck, the darkest hair, the widest smile, the neatest V-shape of thin grey lapels, red tie and white shirt.

On the back of the record were liner notes as sparse yet suggestive as Japanese haiku. Little was vouchsafed other than that the supporting Crickets, the makers of those plangent background harmonies, so we all devoutly believed, were named Jerry Allison, Niki Sullivan and Joe B. Mauldin (which I and my friends misread as 'Maudlin', the way the British pronounce the name of Magdalen College, Oxford) and that all four came from a place called Lubbock in Texas. To me, the name was almost onomatopoeic, evoking a picture – not inaccurate, as it would one day prove – of Western saddles, dusty with hard riding.

As much as anything he sang or played, Buddy's appearance on the *Chirping Crickets* cover was a revelation. It showed that to play rock 'n' roll you did not have to be a bespangled Technicolor freak – you could be turned out smartly and conservatively enough to satisfy the most exacting parents, vicar or teacher. You did not have to be a pouting dreamboat like Elvis or like our own troubled Elvis-clone, Terry Dene. You could be thin, hollow-faced, a little goofy; heavens above, you could even be a foureyes! By what he was no less than what he did, he put the music into everyone's reach.

Until then, rock 'n' roll had been aimed principally at girls. It was something that made girls scream while their boyfriends stood by, fuming with impotent jealousy. Buddy Holly may not have been the first rock 'n' roller that British boys liked, but he was the first they could admit that they liked. Even the few misguided souls in my class at school who professed not to like his records, and called his voice 'anaemic' or 'rare' (an Isle of Wight term for bizarre), found it hard to resist his clothes. 'Ivy League' was an incomprehensible term to us, merely creating a Christmas-carol juxtaposition with 'Holly'. What that high-fastening coat with its two slanted left-hand pockets suggested to us was Edwardian hacking-jackets, and the upper-class London 'Guardee' look that went with chukka boots, string-backed driving-gloves and Austin-Healy sports cars. All over Britain, tailors were deluged by orders for high-buttoning suits.

Schoolboys who could not afford that (like myself) made do by pinching our serge blazer-lapels together at around the level of the breastbone.

I cannot put this strongly enough. We had been born into a world utterly without style. Now, in the same moment, we had been told that it existed, and shown how to acquire it for ourselves. To our newly awakened senses, everything connected with Buddy Holly seemed stylish. The British Decca company, for inscrutable reasons, chose to release both the Crickets' and his own-name songs on a hybrid label called Vogue-Coral, thereby awakening unconscious echoes both of the famous glossy fashion magazine and of one of Britain's classier chocolate selections (Cadbury's Vogue). Even the recurrent trio of names in brackets under his best song-titles, 'Allison–Holly–Petty', belonged to the same casually elegant corporate identity.

To the nation of learner-guitarists, he was like a teacher and guide, moving them on kindly but firmly with each new song he released; endlessly producing new patterns for the few chords they knew; showing what different effects could be produced by the same chords played with more difficult shapes higher up the fretboard; opening their ears and guiding their fingers to the subtler emotional suggestion of minors and sevenths. The hundreds of ex-skiffle groups all over the country subsisted entirely on his repertoire, rushing to grab each fresh blueprint as it became available, following his specifications to the smallest hiccup. In Liverpool, two truant schoolboys named John Lennon and Paul McCartney sat for hours in each other's living-rooms, playing over his songs on their two guitars, then trying to write similar-sounding songs of their own. The myopic Lennon had always hated his own thick-rimmed glasses; now, like thousands of other British nerds – or, as we said, 'weeds' – he discovered a positive cachet in having things on your nose which got foggy over hot tea.

Not every Vogue-Coral secret was instantaneously shared. Among his huge guitar-class, very few could puzzle out how to play the intro to 'That'll Be The Day' – or, indeed, muster an amplifier powerful enough to come near reproducing it. One exception was a younger schoolfellow of Paul McCartney's named George Harrison, who had joined his and Lennon's group, the Quarry Men, on lead guitar early in 1958. Soon afterwards, they scraped up enough money to finance their first demo record at a studio in central Liverpool. The song they chose to perform as the A-side was 'That'll Be The Day', with John Lennon doing a more than passable job of copying Buddy's voice and George's tinny, low voltage electric guitar stumbling at his Stratocaster's heels.

He gave British boys something else, too; something we barely realized at the time and could only fully appreciate years later. Our late fifties vocabulary did not contain words like 'upbeat' or 'positive'. Yet it seemed to us that this vague, bespectacled, high-buttoned being understood, and sympathized with, the peculiar hell of being us, and from his distant hemisphere was sending messages of comfort and hope: 'Listen to me, hear what I say ... every day, it's getting closer ... Take your time ... Look at me ... It's so easy ...'

The handful of American rock 'n' roll stars whom British teenagers had seen in the flesh thus far had mostly been a severe disappointment. The first to be brought over – by sea rather than air – were Bill Haley and the Comets, in February 1957. After docking at Southampton, they were carried to London by special boat-train, with crowds lining the tracks in the manner normally reserved for State funerals. At Waterloo Station, they were greeted by 3,000 shrieking fans in what one newspaper dubbed 'the second Battle of Waterloo'. Alas for Haley, with his roguish kiss-curl, double chin and hideous plaid jacket he looked more like a kiddies' entertainer than a revolutionary leader in whose name a hundred provincial cinemas had been trashed.

Everyone assumed that Elvis Presley would soon follow in Haley's footsteps, to face the same probable moment of truth. But Elvis was never to perform in Britain, a fact which kept his legend untarnished here for more than two decades, and which was always put down to brilliant planning by his manager, Colonel Tom Parker. Not until after Elvis's death, in 1977, did a different explanation emerge. The downhome Southern Colonel was in fact a Dutchman named Dries van Kuijk, who had entered America illegally in the early thirties. He had refused to take Elvis abroad for fear that the US Immigration Service would discover his own real identity and refuse to readmit him to America.

The prospect of seeing Elvis on British soil receded even further early in 1958 when the King was drafted into the United States army. The military authorities had offered a soft billet as a forces entertainer, but Colonel Parker in his wisdom ordained otherwise: Elvis must go through the same punitive barbering and boot camp as any other unlucky young recruit. Convinced that rock 'n' roll could not last much longer, and that he had dredged all he possibly could out of it, the Colonel had decided to change the billing of his carnival freak, from rabble-rouser and scandal-maker to patriotically meek and submissive all-American boy. So rock 'n' roll was deprived of its first guiding light, and Elvis was launched on the downward path that would take him through tenth-rate movies and the Las Vegas cabaret circuit to drug-addiction, obesity, bulimia, glaucoma, incontinence and death.

The original importers of rock 'n' roll into Britain were kindred spirits of Colonel Parker, old-fashioned Variety agents whose personal revulsion and bafflement were outweighed by a primordial urge to supply what the public demanded. The only way rock 'n' roll could be staged was as a part of music-hall or vaudeville. An American teen-idol, accustomed to Alan Freed's twenty-act roadshows, would find himself in Britain playing plush old Victorian theatres throughout the foggy Midlands and North, in company with jugglers, trick-cyclists and performing dogs.

For a visiting rock 'n' roller, as any overseas star, the plum television booking was ATV's *Sunday Night at the London Palladium*, a variety show transmitted live from the legend-encrusted theatre of that name in Argyll Street, W1. Here, in addition to jugglers and performing dogs, the limelight had to be shared with an audience-participation game called 'Beat the Clock', so boisterous that its contestants had to wear protective overalls. The top of the bill then had roughly seven minutes before the programme's credits began to roll and the entire cast appeared on a revolving platform, interspersed among high-plumed showgirls and giant letters spelling SUNDAY NIGHT AT THE LONDON PALLADIUM.

Such was the unreal context in which Britain's 9 million-odd Sunday-night television-viewers were invited to compare rock 'n' roll's substance with its shadow. *Sunday Night at the London Palladium* had already brought us Johnny Ray (thumbs down), Pat Boone (qualified thumbs-up) and Charlie ('Fabulous') Gracie, who provoked a murmur of delighted approval by actually being able to pick out a rudimentary boogie-woogie figure on his huge, shiny 'cello guitar.

Britain's most famous impresarios during the late fifties were the brothers Leslie and Lew Grade, who between them ran a theatrical agency handling most of the top names in domestic film, theatre and television. Lew Grade was also head of the company which owned Associated Television and numerous variety theatres, including the London Palladium, hence ATV's audience-hogging Sunday-night spectacular. On 7 February 1958, Leslie Grade wrote to New York booking agent Mannie Greenfield:

Dear Mannie,

Thank you for your very nice letter of February 4 and I
am delighted to have such a good report from you on
Buddy Holly and the Crickets. You can rest assured that we
shall look after them and, of course, Norman Petty and his
wife, and make them feel at home here.

The modern rock concertgoer, accustomed to superstar sets of
two hours and more, will smile at Leslie Grade's anxious caveat:

I have a little bit of a problem about the time of the act, and
would definitely like them to do approximately 25 minutes
– would you please try and get them to do this. You know
how it is here, they [British audiences] expect the top of the
bill to do a long act and if they did less than 23, 24 or 25
minutes the public would be very disappointed, so please
do what you can . . .

'And of course Norman Petty and his wife'? Could this be
the same self-effacing backroom boy who had hesitated to
become Buddy and the Crickets' manager for fear he would be
unable to spare enough time from recording sessions to accompany them on the road? Now that they had become a world-
class attraction, and the road led to destinations more alluring
than Pittsburgh or Oklahoma City, things were rather different.
If trips to Hawaii, Australia and Europe were on offer, Petty
naturally had no intention of being left behind twiddling knobs
in Clovis.

His management-style would nowadays be described as
'hands-on' but back then was best summed-up in the phrase
'Hands off'. Petty and Petty alone, in his view, provided everything his 'boys' could possibly need: he was their A & R man,
producer and publisher; he received and banked their income,
settled all accounts on their behalf from their joint bank account

with his power of attorney, doled out their day-to-day living expenses and pocket-money.

Anyone who offered the least threat to this creative and administrative monopoly, especially where Buddy was concerned, received the full ice-cave treatment from Clovis Man. Bob Thiele of Coral-Brunswick and Murry Deutch of Peer-Southern Music, those two crucial figures in the success story thus far, were aware of Petty constantly breathing down their necks for fear they might get too close to his 'diamond in the rough'. 'Buddy used to come to Bob and me for advice about this and that,' Deutch remembers. 'We both liked the kid and wanted to do all we could to help him. But Norman hated that. Whatever was going on with Buddy, he always had to know all about it. He was like a cross between a headmaster and a traffic-cop.'

But even Petty, that consummate control-freak, realized the need to maintain good public relations with Buddy's record company and East Coast song-publishers. When sales of 'Peggy Sue' reached 1 million copies, Thiele and Deutch were invited to Clovis to present Buddy with his Gold Disc in a ceremony at the Petty studio. For their arrival at the city's tiny airport, Petty laid on an extravagant welcome ceremony including a full brass band, and ceremonially presented each of them with a ten-gallon cowboy hat.

The urbane New Yorkers considered the brouhaha put on for their benefit more than a little absurd, and found the ménage at the studio where the hits originated bizarre in the extreme. Like many others, they took Norma Jean Berry to be the butch lesbian she appeared, in her jeans and shapeless plaid shirt, and wondered if Vi Petty might not be of the same persuasion since she and Norma Jean were always around together. If that was not sufficient to make the visitors uncomfortable, Petty's expansive welcome quickly proved to have limits. 'At meal-times, you felt you had to struggle to get a glass of milk,' Murray Deutch remembers. For Deutch, however, the trip had one worthwhile result. When he returned East he took with him the demo of a song called 'Sugartime' by a young Texan named Charlie Phillips, featuring Buddy on lead guitar. Over the next year, despite its 'suggestive' title ('sugar'= sex) it became an international smash by the McGuire Sisters and Guy Mitchell in the US and Alma Cogan and Jim Dale in Britain.

On 27 January, the day after 'cutting up' on the *Ed Sullivan Show*, Buddy and the Crickets left New York by Trans World Airlines to join the 'Big Show' tour in Hawaii and travel on with Paul Anka and Jerry Lee Lewis to their week of concerts in Australia. With them went Papa Norman, garlanded with the cameras which, after recording equipment, were his consuming passion.

For most of the trip, indeed, Petty behaved less like a manager than a tourist, filming extensive sequences with a 16 mm colour cine-camera which survive to this day among the treasures of his New Mexico mausoleum. Here is Buddy on arrival at Honolulu International Airport, evidently tickled pink as a smiling hula girl drapes a flowered lei around his long neck. Here he is with J.I. and Joe B., splashing like schoolboys in their hotel pool, and smiling and waving from afar in three horribly travel-creased white linen jackets. Here is the first colour still shot of the new Buddy, on the balcony of his hotel-room, a wand-slim figure in dark slacks and open-necked white shirt, gazing unsmilingly through thick black horn-rims out over the Pacific as if some terribly sudden and sad premonition has struck him.

Both of that night's two concerts at Honolulu's Civic Auditorium drew capacity crowds of 5,000. Though Paul Anka was the hit of the night, Buddy wrote to his sister Pat that the Crickets had gone over 'better than I thought we would' after their express air-hop from nonstop concerts, recording and television in America. The next morning, an Air Force friend of

Petty's gave them a conducted tour of Pearl Harbor, where many buildings still bore the scars of Japan's surprise attack in 1941. Then it was straight aboard a Pan American Airlines Constellation for the 6,000-mile overnight journey to Sydney. The Constellation's first-class passengers enjoyed the luxury of Pullman-style sleeping-berths, but Buddy and Co. were travelling tourist-class. Modern rock stars on uncomfortable long-haul flights relieve their boredom by getting drunk, snorting cocaine, insulting fellow passengers and screwing compliant stewardesses in the toilets; among 'the Big Show's' cooped-up superstars, the only disturbance was sporadic pillow-fighting.

In those days of propeller-borne airliners, trans-Pacific flights had to stop for refuelling at the tiny island of Canton, midway between Hawaii and Fiji. As the flight neared Canton – in what, with hindsight, can only seem like a chilling augury – one of the Constellation's engines developed valve-trouble, the plane had to make a hurried landing and the flight was delayed for several hours while the fault was repaired. J. I. Allison wrote home to his parents that, even at midnight as they hung around the tiny island airstrip, it was 'hotter than the john down at Frankie's drive-in on a July day ... They have some fine Australian beer here,' Jerry continued, 'but since the [schoolboyish hieroglyphic for Petty] is with us, we can't drink any.'

Unnoticed on the far side of the world, Australia was also in the throes of internecine warfare between a brash, novelty-hungry young generation – harder-drinking even than Texan teenagers – and a conservative older one whose idea of good music was 'Waltzing Matilda'. Capitalizing on the huge Australian record-market, and the dearth of home-grown talent, several major American rock 'n' roll names had been there ahead of Buddy, notably his friends Little Richard and Eddie Cochran, whose tour with Gene Vincent had caused spectacular riots at Newcastle, New South Wales, the previous autumn.

The elements on this tour seemed even more combustible.

Jerry Lee Lewis had just seen his second single, 'Great Balls Of Fire', leap into the world charts and was established as the most balefully brilliant piano man that even rock 'n' roll had ever seen. A pasty Louisiana boy with corrugated blond hair and a permanent lopsided sneer, he combined the hammering energy of a First World War machine-gun nest with a remorseless one-note voice and an air of complete disdain for his audience. Jerry Lee did not play pianos so much as ravish them; pounding their keys with his heels as readily as his hands; kicking their innocent stools viciously across the stage to stand and pound in a palpitant heap of Jell-o-scarlet drape-suit; finally climbing atop them to take an overview of his ravening devotees while he passed a comb disdainfully through his uncoiling golden locks.

Only a tour-bill of the late fifties could have featured Jerry Lee Lewis alongside a puppy-love heart-throb like Paul Anka, at the time still riding a huge Bondi wave of popularity after 'Diana'. Like those of all-in wrestlers, their nicknames foreshadowed conflict to come: 'The Killer' versus 'The Boy Millionaire'.

With three Australian hits to their credit ('That'll Be The Day', 'Oh Boy' and 'Peggy Sue' had all reached number 2), Buddy and the Crickets could not be anything other than the tour's headline act – and, indeed, were guaranteed '100 per cent billing' in their contracts. The troupe had scarcely touched down in Sydney when the tour promoter, an expatriate American named Lee Gordon, came to Buddy and told him that Jerry Lee Lewis was demanding top billing on all the posters and programmes. Buddy would have been fully within his rights to demand that the billing stayed as per contract, or he'd pull out of the tour altogether. With a hard-nosed professional manager instead of the camera-laden Norman Petty behind him, he most certainly would have done one thing or the other. Instead, sympathizing with Gordon's plight, he came up with a genially pragmatic solution: Jerry Lee could be billed in the biggest type, but in return Buddy and the Crickets would get extra money. (In the event, most of the posters show Paul Anka's name towering over everyone else's.)

The troupe did shows in Sydney, Melbourne, Brisbane and Newcastle, and also gave a charity performance at Melbourne's Nurses Memorial Centre which later went out as a radio show, sponsored by the Colgate-Palmolive company. Newcastle's city fathers, in particular, breathed a thankful sigh when the expected repetition of the previous year's Little Richard riots failed to materialize, no matter how hard Jerry Lee Lewis strove to incite them. Despite massive competition from Jerry Lee and Paul Anka – not to mention Australian rock 'n' roll star Johnny O'Keefe – the *Melbourne Herald* spoke for all in calling Buddy 'the undoubted star of the show'. Chippy Australian journalists who interviewed him found him engaging and unpretentious; one described him afterwards as 'the perfect representation of the American parson – ascetic, serious, dignified . . .'

A taped interview survives between Buddy and Australian disc jockey Pat Barton, backstage at Newcastle Stadium while Jerry Lee Lewis murders yet another piano out front. Barton asks about Elvis Presley's imminent career as an army conscript – and, in passing, reveals what a very insignificant managerial figure Norman Petty continues to cut.

BARTON: Norman Petty . . . now where does Norman Petty fit into the picture?

BUDDY: He's our manager and our recording engineer and just about the whole works.

BARTON: How old a man is he? He's not in Australia with you, is he?

BUDDY: Yes, he's sitting right over there.

BARTON: Oh, is he? Well, it's just Norman is it?

BUDDY: (to Petty) He'd like to talk to you if you would. [A strange reversal! A star arranging an interview for his manager!]

BARTON: Um, what's the picture as regards rock 'n' roll, say with Presley in the army? Does that alter things, do you think?

BUDDY: Well, I don't think it alters anything real outstanding in the music business. Presley will probably be a little unpopular for a while but I think he'll come back into it, into his own after he gets out.

BARTON: You don't think somebody will step into his shoes, like from the ranks . . .

BUDDY: No, I don't think anybody . . .

BARTON: Like Buddy Holly or Jerry Lee Lewis?

BUDDY: No, I don't think so.

On the road, Buddy's humour and good nature did much to defuse the explosive incompatibility of his fellow headliners. He admired the precocious songwriting talent of Paul Anka, with his usual open-heartedness changing from bitterly envying Anka to suggesting they might write songs for one another. Though quiet and orderly himself, (and bound by Papa Norman's no-drinking/smoking/cussing rule) he was completely unshockable: the worst that Jerry Lee could do in the drinking and hellraising department was nothing Buddy hadn't seen a hundred times before at Lubbock's Glasserama or 16th and J Club. One evening, at minutes to showtime, the Killer was discovered in a local bar, in no condition to walk let alone injure a piano. Buddy was the one who took him back to the troupe's hotel, flung him into a shower and sobered him enough to go onstage.

February 2 was spent in transit from Sydney to Brisbane for the two shows at the city's Cloudland ballroom the following night. As Buddy gazed down past blurred propellers to the azure continent, how could he possibly have visualized driving snow on an Arctic Midwest midnight, or known that there was exactly one year left?

The journey home included another stop-off in Hawaii for a show at Honolulu's Kaiser hotel. Buddy and the Crickets arrived back in Lubbock, via Braniff Airlines, on 10 February. There was just time to squeeze in a recording session at Clovis before they left on a week-long tour of Florida with Jerry Lee Lewis, Bill Haley, the Everly Brothers and the Royalteens ('The Big Gold Record Stars') then went straight on to begin their month of concerts in Britain. Other young performers, faced by such a murderous schedule, would have told their manager where to stick his cameras – but not Buddy and the Crickets. They had no idea how long this amazing rollercoaster ride would last, and were determined to make the most of every dizzy second.

The sessions in Clovis, between 12 and 19 February, produced another fistful of finished diamonds: 'Fool's Paradise', 'Tell Me How', 'Take Your Time' and, another gift-wrapped blueprint to Britain's ex-skifflers, 'Think It Over'. Also present were a male vocal trio called the Roses, who had sung on Buddy's session with the Norman Petty Trio and now were to supply background vocals as if by the Crickets. Though the Roses rehearsed with Buddy, J.I. and Joe B., their vocals were dubbed in separately, just as the Picks' had been. For 'Take Your Time', Petty played Hammond organ and, on the strength of contributing a single line to Buddy's lyric (the Mantovani'ish 'heart-strings will sing like a string of twine . . .') was able to claim a 50 per cent writer's credit as opposed to the one-third he took on 'Think It Over', 'Tell Me How' and 'Fool's Paradise'.

One whole night, in addition, was given to developing Jerry Allison as a solo performer. Under his middle name, Ivan, J.I. recorded 'Real Wild Child', a song he had picked up from the Australian rock 'n' roller Johnny O'Keefe (and which was destined to be a hit for Iggy Pop almost a quarter of a century later). The 'Ivan' session featured Buddy and the Roses on backing vocals, a substitute drummer, Bo Clarke, taking J.I.'s place, and Petty playing a finely-tuned selection of water-filled wineglasses.

The *pièce de résistance*, put into the can on the very first day, owed its inspiration to Little Richard, who would whip audiences to further frenzy between numbers by self-congratulatory cries of 'Well . . . all right!' Buddy turned the phrase into a love song infused with all his special quality of patience and optimism and his developing ability to make personal sentiments into universal ones. 'Well . . . All Right' is a riposte to all the criticism and condescension that teenagers faced from their elders in the rock 'n' roll fifties – and have in every decade since. The setting is as adventurously simple as that of 'Everyday': Buddy plays flamenco-accented acoustic guitar, with only a plashing cymbal for company. The mood is not one of youthful anger and defiance but of maturity before its time: calm, stoical, steadfast in affirming its 'dreams and wishes'. The intimacy in the voice could equally be that of lover or elder brother; girl or boy, you can fancy you and he are alone together, gazing into the fire and seeing the brightest and most comforting of futures reflected there:

> *Well . . . all right, well . . . all right,*
> *We will live and love with all our might.*
> *Well . . . all right, well . . . all right*
> *Our lifetime love will be alright.*

On the 'Big Gold Record Stars' Florida tour, the Everly Brothers were top of the bill and closed the show, preceded by Buddy and the Crickets and Jerry Lee Lewis in that order. As was his wont, the Killer pulled out every foot-hammering, piano-mountaineering, comb-wielding stunt to throw Don and Phil's pretty-boy duet into total eclipse. The Everlys still had no permanent backing band and relied on the promoters to provide them with musicians, a different set at each gig. 'When we got to this one place in Florida, we found the promoters had hired us three high school kids who could hardly play a note,' Phil Everly says. 'We literally could not take them onstage with us. So there we were with Jerry Lee working the audience over before us, and no band.

'When Buddy heard about the problem, he and the Crickets volunteered to be our backing group. Jerry Lee did his worst, left the audience stomping and cheering like maniacs, but we had some guys behind us who could give them something every bit as powerful. I always say it was only by the Grace of God and Buddy Holly that Don and I managed to come through that night.'

Just how exhausted but indomitable Buddy was we can hear in a scrap of conversation caught on tape in Clovis, just after he'd tried for the umpteenth time to get his tongue around Petty's saccharine 'heartstrings will sing like a string of twine'. The husky Texan voice slurs almost to unintelligibility, but still doesn't snap.

'Boy ... I just cain't get on it, Norm ... page just blurs ... can't even see the words, lookin' right at 'em ... Been through it so many times it's ... you know, it's a circle ... tightens up and catches it up with itself, and another time comes 'fore it's time to sing this one.' The complaint is defused by an audible smile. 'That's what's gettin' me so bad ... it's the concentration ...'

'Take your time,' J. I. Allison says over his mike in mocking falsetto.

Buddy breaks into his familiar snuffly laughter and promises he'll 'beat the crap' out of the elusive lyric this time. His composure restored, still audibly smiling, he gives the signal for the right-on take to come:

'Let's go ...'

Thanks to Norman Petty's assiduous colour-cine record, we can share Buddy's first sight of London, on 27 February 1958 – a

low-lying, murky expanse, still undisturbed by a single sky-
scraper or tower block, with the Thames curling through it like
a faint bronze serpent. We can be with him, looking from seat
number C2, tourist class, as British Overseas Airways flight
number 582 taxis up to the single-storey terminal at what is still
called London Airport rather than London Heathrow: another
marathon trek through the clouds safely over.

The party which disembarked that morning, stiff and diso-
rientated after its overnight transatlantic flight, numbered five in
all. As well as Buddy, J.I., Joe B. Mauldin and Papa Norman, his
cine-camera permanently clamped to his eye, there was also Vi
Petty, still bemused by this almost unprecedented act of sharing
on her spouse's part. He had decided to bring Vi along without
consulting his 'boys', who were not best pleased to find her
added to their retinue, along with a plethora of fussy little
holdalls and vanity bags. Even the usually quiet and tractable Joe
B. Mauldin remembers wondering whether Petty or they would
be paying for this extra ticket and hotel accommodation. 'But we
didn't say anything. And Vi sure was thrilled to be there.'

They had arrived at the threshold of a typical British March,
bitingly cold, with frequent rain and an enveloping Stygian
gloom, often little lighter at midday than at dawn or dusk.
Buddy, J.I. and Joe B. felt the shock particularly, having just left
the secure warmth of wintertime Florida. The matching black
'shortie' raglan raincoats in which they disembarked from their
aircraft may have looked wonderfully stylish to British eyes but
would afford scant protection in the four dank, chilly weeks that
lay ahead.

Britain's pop charts, by contrast, provided the warmest of
welcomes. 'Maybe Baby' under the Crickets' name, coupled with
'Tell Me How', was climbing rapidly towards its eventual high
of number 4. 'Listen to Me' under Buddy's name, coupled with
'I'm Gonna Love You Too', was number 16. The *Chirping
Crickets* LP was cutting a swathe through the exiguous album-

chart, finally to peak at number 5. All this was in marked contrast with America, where 'Maybe Baby' had made only number 16 and 'Listen To Me' and *The Chirping Crickets* both failed to chart at all despite enthusiastic trade press reviews. In gigantic America, with its myriad radio stations, there was felt to be too much Holly and Crickets music in circulation already. But tiny Britain, with only one domestic radio service, plus a nocturnal interloper from the Grand Duchy of Luxembourg, clearly could not get enough of it.

The party had reservations at the Cumberland Hotel, Marble Arch, where a comfortable room cost just over £3 per night, plus an extra 9d (less than 5p) if, as Buddy did, you wanted the non-inclusive luxury of a bedside radio. The era of rock stars being trapped in their hotels by screaming girls was still far in the future. Buddy, Jerry and Joe B. could walk the wintry West End streets in perfect safety, recognized by almost no one. The only publicity arranged by the British Decca organization was a press reception at a Soho club, the Whisky A Go Go, where, in a small triumph of addle-brained PR, America's Crickets were ceremonially confronted with two English Test cricketers, Denis Compton and Godfrey Evans. The Crickets' bafflement was as nothing compared to that of the cricketers; nonetheless Compton and Evans posed for photographers, showing Buddy how to hold a bat and take up guard at the wicket while J.I. and Joe B., in their uniform V-neck sweaters, crouched together in the slips.

The roadshow which the Grade organization had put together around them could not have been more bizarrely different from the touring rock 'n' roll menageries they were used to back home in America. In the continuing dearth of native rock talent, British teenagers had to rely on conventional big bands and vocalists from the crooner era for most 'live' versions of current chart-hits. Buddy, J.I. and Joe B. thus found themselves the only rock 'n' roll act on a variety bill which could just as well have taken the road in the late forties. Its backbone was the thirteen-piece Ronnie Keene Orchestra, which combined Swing classics like 'In The Mood' and 'The Woodchoppers' Ball' with items 'for the kids' like 'When The Saints' and the '6-5 Special Jive'. There were also the Tanner Sisters, a bubble-haired, taffeta-gowned duo modelled on the Andrews Sisters, and ballad-eer Gary Miller, soon to enjoy his one and only chart success with 'The Story Of My Life'. The compère was a new young singer-comedian named Des O'Connor.

Buddy and the Crickets' headline status was proclaimed by a crudely-drawn cartoon cricket on the cover of the one-shilling (5p) 'souvenir' programme sold at each venue. To placate Leslie Grade, they had worked up a twenty-five minute performance from among ten possible numbers listed in the programme – both current chart-toppers and lesser-known tracks like 'Mail-man, Bring Me No More Blues' and 'Ollie Vee'. Mystifyingly (or perhaps not) this list also included the Norman Petty Trio's 1957 hit, 'Almost Paradise'.

The opening show was on Saturday 1 March, at the now-vanished Trocadero cinema, at the Elephant and Castle. 'The place was packed to the rafters,' bandleader Ronnie Keene remembers. 'It was obvious that no one had come to see us, or any of the other British acts. We were just the cannon-fodder. Still, we weren't booed: they listened to us and clapped politely. But when Buddy and the Crickets were announced, the whole place erupted. At that moment, I realized it was all over for musicians like me. This was the future.

'They had hardly any power – only the house-mikes and that one little amp, which Norman Petty carried onstage for them. The bass-player, I remember, wasn't even amplified. But they still managed to make as much noise as the whole of my thirteen-piece orchestra.'

For British teenagers, the wonder of the occasion was not merely seeing Buddy and the Crickets in person at long last but discovering that, unlike all previous such visitations from across the Atlantic, they were able to reproduce the sound of their records in live performance. 'They got a terrific reception,' Ronnie Keene remembers. 'But it wasn't crazy, jiving-in-the-aisles stuff, the way it had been when Bill Haley came over. You could tell that the kids were really listening.' The critics from the jazz-biased music press were equally impressed. Keith Goodwin in the *Melody Maker* summed up the general view: 'This is rock 'n' roll like we've never heard it before in Britain.'

Buddy's stage persona was the very opposite of what had been expected – not cool, serious and grown-up, but friendly, funny and unpretentious. He introduced each song with wise-cracks about how 'pathetic' the Crickets' playing was, and clowned and mugged and threw his lanky, high-buttoned body around the stage with an abandon none had dreamed of that horn-rimmed rock 'n' roll swot. It seemed to matter not at all that in live performance his songs were shorn of the plummy background vocals which Petty's hired-in trios, the Picks or the Roses, had overdubbed on to the records. Despite Jerry and Joe B.'s evident muteness, British fans stubbornly voted them number 1 in a poll for the year's top vocal groups.

'After the show, there must have been 300 kids waiting outside the stage door,' Ronnie Keene remembers. 'But it was all very orderly. The kids seemed to take their cue from Buddy and the Crickets. They were very nice and courteous, and the kids were the same in return.'

The next day, a Sunday, they moved from south to north London, giving two shows at the Gaumont State cinema, Kilburn, whose exterior is a scaled-down facsimile of New York's Empire State Building. A member of the audience, Philip Bergman, can visualize to this day how Buddy 'literally exploded on to the stage'. Into the same evening they also somehow crammed the appearance on Associated Television's *Sunday Night at the London Palladium* which was built into their contract with the Grades. They found themselves taking part in a special gala marking the show's 100th edition and co-starring Bob Hope, the ballerina Dame Alicia Markova and actor Robert Morley. There was also the ritual interlude of audience-participation games, as usual so maddeningly drawn-out that a confused Buddy later wrote to his parents that he'd just done 'a show called Beat The Clock'.

Waiting to see him that night was the whole of his nationwide guitar-class, crouched over the bluish sixteen-inch screens of Pye, Cossor or Ferguson television sets. Up in Liverpool, John Lennon and Paul McCartney both had their noses practically touching the screen. I myself watched in my father's pale blue Formica bar at the end of Ryde Pier, half a mile out at sea where television-reception suffered from the Morse-code signals of passing ocean-liners.

Cudgel my memory as I may, those intrusive 'dit-dit-da's' from the *Queen Mary* and the *Mauretania* still break up the black-and-white memory of seeing Buddy Holly in live perform-ance. All ATV supplied was a straight-on view of the Palladium stage, containing three rather lonely-looking figures in tuxedos, a double-bass, a drum-kit and an amplifier. One could hardly see Buddy's guitar, let alone what his fingers might be doing on its fretboard. The sound on all three numbers, 'That'll Be The Day', 'Peggy Sue' and 'Oh Boy', was atrocious: his spot barely seemed to have begun when the gold-tasselled curtains swept shut again amid a blare from Jack Parnell's pit-orchestra, and Robert Morley came waddling back to tell another plummy English joke. I also search my memory in vain for any picture of Buddy on the revolving platform, waving goodbye in company with Bob Hope, Markova and high-plumed Palladium showgirls.

Sunday Night at the London Palladium was not videotaped, as the *Ed Sullivan Show* and even the *Arthur Murray Dance Party* had been, nor even recorded in audio, except by fans on reel-to-reel machines in their twilit living-rooms. The sole mementoes of the occasion are the famous black-and-white photographs of Buddy in mid-song on the Palladium stage, one of which would be used as a poster for the world-hit musical he inspired thirty years later. Today, hoardings all over the London Underground reveal what one missed on that fugitive night of 2 March 1958 – the look of faint, wholly understandable anxiety on the big-spectacled face; the immaculate dinner-suit but slightly rumpled dark curly hair; the Stratocaster's narrow machine-head with its six tuning-pegs all in one row; the long, bony fingers shaping a D major.

Neither Lew nor Leslie Grade bothered to meet the young stars of their tour before it left London for the provinces. In later years, when the transmogrified Lord Grade was asked for reminiscences of Buddy Holly, he would remove his trademark Havana cigar from his mouth and blankly reply, 'Who?' Liaison with the Grades' office was handled by David Bryce, now a senior figure in Cliff Richard's organization. There was also a 'road manager' named Wally Stewart, an elderly, red-faced man in a flapping gabardine raincoat, whose roadie duties were confined to driving the tour-bus and taking care of the baggage.

The three weeks of one-nighters were as punishing, and haphazardly planned, as any all-American roadshow's: from London south-west to Southampton; due north to Sheffield, Stockton and Newcastle upon Tyne; south on an illogical zigzag through Wolverhampton, Nottingham, Bradford and Worcester; back to outer London for shows in Croydon and East Ham; eastward to Ipswich; north again to Leicester, Doncaster, Wigan, Hull and Liverpool; back to outer London again for a single night in Walthamstow, then south-west to Salisbury, Bristol and briefly over the Welsh border to Cardiff.

If the distances to be travelled between concerts were vastly smaller than in America, the incidental discomforts were far greater. Here were no dependable roadside motels with standard kingsize beds and gleaming Sanitized bathrooms; only English provincial 'grand' hotels, where *en suite* baths were still a rarity, bedrooms were often heated by shilling-in-slot electric meters, and restaurants stopped serving dinner at around 9 pm. The hotel receipts for Buddy's party record a spartan diet of melon, pork chops and fried plaice, invariably accompanied by Coca-Cola and – thanks to Papa Norman's presence – without the slightest mention of alcohol. The inclusive cost for Buddy, Jerry, Joe B. and the Pettys seldom exceeded £10 per night.

Although Buddy had a cold for most of the tour, his spirits remained unflaggingly high. 'I used to sit next to him on the bus,' Ronnie Keene remembers. 'He was a lovely lad ... lovely. There were no big star affectations about him at all. He used to talk to the boys in my band just as if he was one of them.' Des O'Connor, the show's compère, has equally fond memories, even though the audience had little time for his jokes or his singing. 'Buddy was a real sweet, fun guy. We'd sometimes have to share a hotel bedroom and I'd be responsible for getting him out of bed in the morning, because an early riser Buddy was not. I'd get hold of his feet and just pull. "Don't do that, Des," this Texan voice would say from under the blankets. "I'm tall enough already."

'He'd ask me for jokes to tell between his songs, and I'd give him a few of my less good ones. But in that accent of his, they still went down a storm. In Harrogate, he said he wanted to have real English afternoon tea, so we went to a posh hotel and had the whole thing with dainty little sandwiches, scones and sugar-tongs. One day he went out and bought an acoustic guitar for jamming on the bus, and tried out eighteen different ones before he found one he liked, a Hofner. At the end of the tour, he gave it to me.'

Joe B. Mauldin remembers how Buddy, J.I. and he would burrow under the bedclothes in their unheated rooms, and huddle in hotel lobbies, where there would usually be a coal fire.

The Texans were buoyed up against the cold, damp and fatigue by the ecstatic welcome they received everywhere they went, and the fascination of being in a country so comprehensively different from theirs. Jerry Allison still remembers the novelty of leaving his shoes outside his hotel-room at night and the next morning finding them, not stolen but polished to a high shine.

J.I. had special cause to feel buoyant: in Australia he had told the others he intended to marry the inspiration for Buddy's first solo hit, Peggy Sue Gerron. 'He used to ask me what it was like to be married,' David Bryce remembers. 'He was particularly worried about what to do if he woke up on his honeymoon with smelly breath.'

Norman Petty's tireless colour filming provides fascinating glimpses of Buddy Holly and the Crickets meeting Olde England. Here they are, with the Pettys, standing on a bridge over the River Cam having stopped off *en route* to or from Ipswich to look at Cambridge University. Another sequence records the stopover in Salisbury, Wiltshire, at the half-timbered Old George hotel ('Built around 1320', the letterhead of their bill announced) where, Vi Petty would recall, 'the ladies fixed us hot chocolate and we drank it in front of the fireplace'. Late as it was, Buddy sat down to dash off another letter to his parents: 'Norman and Jerry are sitting over by the fireplace (this is a neat, quaint old place). Norman was telling about a dream [in which] all his front teeth fell out . . .' In what must be the first anti-Des O'Connor joke ever recorded, he added that his onstage jokes seemed to be getting bigger laughs than O'Connor's.

Birmingham provided another sightseeing break. Discovering that it was the primary place where Britain's still prestigious and individual Morris and Austin cars were produced, the car-mad Buddy begged to be allowed to visit an automobile factory. On 10 March, his party received a conducted tour of what was then the British Motor Corporation's plant and showrooms at Long-bridge. Petty took the opportunity to order an Austin-Healy de luxe coupé to be shipped back to Clovis after him. In Clovis Man's documentary treasure trove – along with hotel bills, air tickets, baggage receipts and bright green BOAC boarding-passes – we find a list of the Austin-Healy's luxurious extras: overdrive, heater, hardtop, wire wheels, push-button radio. The total price, including shipping-charges, was £996 5s or $2,303.94.

Abetted by his squirrellish spouse, Petty shopped assiduously throughout the tour. On 18 March, while passing through Manchester, he visited the cloth mill of Donald Shearer & Co. in Lower Mosley Street and ordered suit-lengths of worsted wool to be dispatched to Clovis in five duty-saving 'unsolicited gift parcels', addressed to himself, Buddy, J.I., Joe B. and Vi (which possibly never reached their destination since Shearer's salesperson took down the address as 'Clovis, Quebec, Canada'). A memo also survives from a Grade employee, deputed to reconnoitre Piccadilly fine china dealers on the Pettys' behalf: 'Royal Crown Derby do not make their vine pattern in any smaller article than a five-inch fruit saucer ... which is sold at twenty shillings each ... I saw a very lovely floral design, in round or rectangular shapes, selling at about 12 shillings each for the smallest size ...'

If rock 'n' roll left a questionable impression on Denis Compton and Godfrey Evans, cricket had made a lasting one on Buddy. During one of the tour's London interludes, he asked a friendly journalist, Keith Goodwin of the *Melody Maker*, to teach him more about the English sporting ritual his group's name unintentionally suggested. March being still far too early to find a live cricket match, Buddy had to be content with seeing a cinema newsreel report on the England team's current winter tour of Australia. Despite his usual indifference to all team games, he was fascinated by what he saw, and told Goodwin he'd like to try the game for himself when – as he intended – he came back to Britain in sunnier weather.

But by the end of the tour's second week, with a second chilly northward foray looming ahead, even his spirits began to droop. 'We're getting a little bit tired of England,' he admitted in a postcard to his sister Pat. 'It's awfully cold over here. Seems like it could never get summer here ... Well, so long for now. Love, Buddy.'

March 18 found him in Wigan, the Lancashire industrial town whose name has inspired English music-hall jokes since far back into antiquity. Before the night's two concerts at the Ritz cinema (a last-minute substitution for the St George's Hall in nearby Blackburn) Buddy's party booked in to Wigan's mock-Tudor Grand Hotel. The duty-receptionists were two local girls, Barbara Bullough and Jo Burroughs. Both were lively and attractive, especially Barbara with her big dark eyes and rather Latin-looking cupid's-bow mouth. As might be imagined, both took especial pains to ensure that their VIP guests were comfortable. 'We got on really well with them,' Barbara remembers now. 'It helped that my parents had been to America a lot, so I knew to say "sidewalk" instead of "pavement". One thing I do recall, though, is that I didn't like Norman Petty.'

Buddy was instantly and obviously smitten with Barbara. 'He asked me if I was going to the concert that night, and I said I hadn't thought of it. He said "You MUST come," and went off and made all the arrangements. I had no idea about rock 'n' roll – I'd been brought up with classical music – but I thought the show was wonderful. I remember what a thrill went through the place when Buddy came onstage.

'I still lived with my parents, and had strict instructions not to be home too late. We lived a little way out of town and by about 11 o'clock my last bus had gone, so Buddy asked if he could see me home. He seemed such a sweet person that I said yes. Our house was at the end of an unmade lane, so the taxi had to stop on the main road and Buddy walked me to my front-gate. We talked ... and cuddled and kissed ... then he asked if I'd go on the rest of his tour with him. I liked him a lot, but I knew my father would never stand for something like that, so I had to say no. Then he asked me if I'd come and see him play again when he was in Liverpool, and we said goodnight.'

Savour the moment for another second: Buddy Holly in Wigan in his too-thin black raincoat and side-buckled shoes, walking the well-bred Lancashire lass down the unmade lane to her front gate, giving her a chaste goodnight kiss, then returning, alone in the ratty local taxi, past cobbled streets of dark factory-chimneys and back-to-back houses, still 'looking for someone to love'. The bill from the Grand Hotel, Wigan, is slightly different from others preserved among Clovis Man's relics: it has the names 'Barbara' and 'Jo' and a row of kisses handwritten on it. Next to each of the Crickets' names is typed an admiring 'Oh Boy!'

Barbara kept her promise to go to Liverpool and see Buddy when he appeared at the city's Philharmonic Hall, two nights later. 'He'd told me "Just say you're Barbara from Wigan and they'll let you in."' She talked to Buddy backstage, but wasn't able to catch his performance. Nor, to their chagrin, were two of his greatest Merseyside fans. Neither John Lennon nor Paul McCartney, impoverished art student and schoolboy respectively, could afford the price of a ticket, and so had to rely on more affluent friends for descriptions of Buddy's suit and guitar, and what chords his fingers might have been shaping. For both John and Paul, his presence in Liverpool was thrill enough; more importantly, it kick-started the band which they themselves had formed the previous summer. Deciding to emulate Buddy's group and name themselves after an insect, they came up with 'The Beetles', just as Buddy and J. I. Allison had a year earlier. Pun-loving Lennon changed it to 'Beatles', after what was then called 'beat' music, and stuck to it tenaciously despite mirthful protests from all sides (much the same as had assailed Buddy and Jerry) that no group with such an idiotic name could ever hope to be successful.

The last stop on the tour was the Gaumont cinema, Hammersmith, West London, on 25 March. As Buddy and J. I. Allison were resting between the evening's two shows, Joe B. Mauldin entered their dressing room in a mood of unwonted bragadoccio, flourishing a large cigar which he said he intended to smoke as a ceremonial farewell to Britain. Both his colleagues loudly vetoed this plan to fill the place with noxious smoke. What the Buddy Holly legend has always termed 'a friendly scuffle' but was in fact quite a serious Texan brawl erupted, with Buddy and J.I. both trying to pin Joe B. down and wrest the cigar from his grasp. As they were rolling and grappling on the floor, Joe B.'s forehead jerked up and smashed against Buddy's mouth, knocking the caps from his two upper front teeth. With minutes to curtain-up, the only way of camouflaging the naked stumps was to paste chewing-gum over them. When the three finally came offstage, amid the usual rapturous applause, Norman Petty told them he'd never seen them give a worse performance.

Earlier on that last day, they had fulfilled their only other British television commitment, performing 'Maybe Baby' on Jack Payne's *Off the Record* show for the BBC. Payne was a former dance band leader whose surname well summarized his character; nonetheless, as a showcase for rock 'n' roll, his show was a considerable improvement on *Sunday Night at the London Palladium*. I watched it at my grandmother's flat, a squalid place used mainly to store the sweets and rock she sold from her seafront kiosk. Buddy lip-synched his latest British hit without great animation against a madly contemporary backdrop vaguely resembling a line of outsize turnstiles. At least this time I could see the Stratocaster plainly, although the plainer I saw it, the more implausibly flat and body-hugging it became; less like a guitar than the attachment for some futuristic vacuum-cleaner by Hoover or Electrolux.

I didn't know then that *Off the Record* had been videotaped and he and the Crickets had actually left Britain three days earlier. Nor can I say I was very upset by his departure: after so many good reviews, he'd obviously be back again before long. All that mattered was rushing to my own guitar (a fourteen-guinea Hofner 'Congress'); trying to pick out the 'Maybe Baby' intro for myself and discovering that, yet again, he'd made it easy for me.

Only three days after the end of their British tour, Buddy and the Crickets were on the road in America yet again. This sightseeing opportunity, though, held no allure for Papa Norman, who returned to Clovis with his rolls of exposed film, his many kilos of excess baggage and his wife. Free now to drink, smoke and cuss as they pleased, Buddy, J.I. and Joe B. joined Alan Freed's 'Big Beat Show', a forty-four-day circuit of Eastern and Midwestern states, featuring Jerry Lee Lewis, Chuck Berry, Danny and the Juniors, Frankie Lymon, Screaming Jay Hawkins, the Diamonds, Larry Williams, Billie and Lillie, the Chantels, the Pastels, Jo Ann Campbell, Ed Townsend and the 'Alan Freed Orchestra', and destined to be more spectacularly chaotic than any rock 'n' roll excursion since the dawn of Haley and Presley.

On Freed's customary mixed-race menu, the battle for the fans' attention waxed fiercer than ever. Danny and the Juniors were a finger-snapping – but otherwise barely animate – white teenage vocal group whose 'At The Hop' was destined to be the top-selling single of 1958. Screaming Jay Hawkins was a stage extrovert more uproarious and outrageous even than Little Richard; a one-man *Rocky Horror Show* who greeted his audience by climbing out of a coffin, and performed his solitary hit, 'I Put A Spell On You' – and other goodies like the much-banned 'Constipation Blues' – with the harrowing vocal effects of a poorly soundproofed abattoir.

The tone of the 'Big Beat Show' tour was set on its opening night, 28 March, at the Brooklyn Paramount theatre. Chuck Berry and Jerry Lee Lewis each regarded himself as top of the bill and demanded to be recognized as such by closing the show. Called on to arbitrate between the two grappling Brontosaurus-egos, Alan Freed ruled that Chuck Berry had the greater seniority. Consigned to the penultimate spot, Jerry Lee was later to take revenge with a piece of performance-art that would have upstaged the Second Coming itself. In the midst of pounding out 'Great Balls Of Fire', he produced a petrol-filled Coca-Cola bottle, gave his piano a liberal dousing, set a match to it and continued hammering while his keyboard blazed around his forearms like a backyard bonfire. Finally sauntering offstage, amid pyromaniacal shrieks of ecstasy from the audience, he gave Chuck Berry a satiated smirk and murmured what has gone down in history as 'Follow that, nigga!' but was more likely 'Follow that, Killer!'

The tour was, at least, less fatiguing than those of the previous winter, many of the journeys between its one-nighters being by air rather than overcrowded bus. However, the aircraft provided were very different from Pan-American Constellations; usually ancient DC3s which took to the air as laboriously as flying elephants and bucked and rattled alarmingly in the frequent turbulence. Buddy did not mind flying – quite the contrary, he adored it, hanging on and grinning through the worst shake-ups like a schoolboy on a fairground ride while his seat companions blanched and reached for airsickness bags. Danny Rapp, the lead singer with Danny and the Juniors, remembered afterwards how much Buddy adored to shoot craps on these journeys, and how recklessly he threw his money around, betting as much as $500 on a single roll of the dice. At Cincinnati, Ohio, came a further unheeded reminder of mortality: on the day the 'Big Beat Show' arrived, a helicopter crashed to the north of the city and its pilot was killed.

In the nightly spotlight-snaffling contest between Chuck Berry's duck walk, Screaming Jay Hawkins's coffin and Jerry Lee Lewis's grievous bodily harm to grand pianos, Buddy, J.I. and Joe B. more than held their own. It did not even seriously break Buddy's stride when the tour-bus was broken into during a meal-stop in St Louis and his Fender Stratocaster was stolen, along with several of J. I. Allison's drums. He went on to Canada, using a substitute guitar while an SOS call was routed via Clovis to Manny's music stores in New York. An identical brown sunburst Strat was flown out to him, arriving in time for the concert in Waterloo, Iowa, a week later.

The May portion of the tour ended in mayhem for which Buddy and the Crickets bore no responsibility and during which they were relieved to take a back seat for once. When the 'Big Beat Show' performed at Boston's Arena on 6 May, the whole city seemed to have assumed the persona of Jerry Lee Lewis. Rioting erupted outside, a nineteen-year-old sailor was stabbed, fifteen other people were injured and there was widespread mugging, store-looting, arson and vandalism. Trouble also broke out inside the Arena, apparently instigated by conservative Boston-Irish youths who objected to seeing white and black performers using the same stage. When Chuck Berry came on, he was pelted with refuse from the gallery and had to take refuge behind his drummer. Police and security men waded in, clearing the hall and making dozens of heavy-handed arrests, mainly among those who had been innocently dancing in the aisles. The city's Mayor, John Hynes, banned all future such shows while District Attorney Garrett Byrne castigated Alan Freed as the organizer and compère for inciting what he called 'rock 'n' roll paganism.'

The Boston riots sent a wave of renewed anti-rock 'n' roll fervour coursing through America's Establishment. No less a figure than the Director of the FBI, J. Edgar Hoover (whose penchant for wearing ladies' frocks none then suspected), gave his opinion that, as well as being godless and lewd, rock 'n' roll was part of the Communist plot to undermine Western freedom and democracy. Boston's District Attorney Byrne indicted Alan Freed under an archaic statute for 'inciting a riot' and 'conspiring to overthrow the Government'. Though the charge was later dropped, it proved to be the first step in Freed's sad and undeserved decline. Three pending 'Big Beat' shows – in Troy, New York, New Haven, Connecticut, and Newark, New Jersey – were cancelled by fearful municipal authorities. While Freed was broadcasting his radio show on New York's WINS, his Newark co-promoter, enraged by the ticket-sales that had been lost, appeared at the station with a handgun, threatening to kill him.

The 'Big Beat Show' tour's cancelled dates included its final one, in Newark, New Jersey, and Buddy and the Crickets flew home a couple of days earlier than expected. It was a journey which saw their first mild but decisive act of rebellion against Norman Petty. Each of the three had always wanted a Harley-Davidson motorcycle; since they had with them a substantial part of their tour-earnings, several thousand dollars in cash, Buddy suggested stopping off in Dallas, buying a Harley each and riding the 300 miles west to Lubbock like Marlon Brando's Hell's Angel gang (the 'Beetles') in *The Wild One*. The insurrection did not lie in buying these costly new toys, which Petty doubtless would readily have done for them, using his power of attorney over their collective bank account. It lay in acting on their own initiative rather than, as usual, letting Petty get them what they wanted via one of his many Clovis business friends with a cat's cradle of concessions and discounts. It lay in holding on to money rather than meekly handing it over; in rejecting, however mildly, Papa Norman's 100 per cent control.

In the event, it was not Harleys they bought, but English

motorcycles, at that time considered among the world's best. 'At
the Harley-Davidson place, the salesmen were real unfriendly,'
Joe B. remembers. 'They didn't believe we really had the money
to buy bikes that expensive.' Furious, the Texans hopped a cab
and went straight to Ray Miller's Triumph dealership, where
within a very few minutes Buddy had blown $3,000 in cash,
buying an Ariel Cyclone (registration: CNLF4510) for himself,
a Triumph Trophy for J.I. and a Thunderbird for Joe B., plus
denim jeans and jackets and jockey-caps emblazoned with
Triumph's winged emblem. Thus mounted and equipped, they
set off westward for Lubbock like a prophecy of *Easy Rider*,
happily unaware that a wave of ferocious rainstorms and mini-
tornados was currently battering West Texas. 'None of us had
ever ridden bikes that powerful before,' Joe B. says. 'And on the
journey it came on to rain real hard. We got soaked through, and
had to stop and buy ourselves more new sets of Levis.'

When Jerry Lee Lewis returned home to Ferriday, Louisiana,
that same week, he was given a civic welcome by the Mayor and
the Chamber of Commerce, driven through the streets in an
open Cadillac and presented with the keys to the city. Lubbock,
by contrast, remained seemingly quite unmoved by Buddy's
world-wide triumphs and the fact that he had made its name as
well as his own familiar to record-buyers from Sydney to Stoke-
on-Trent. Lubbock City Council announced no 'Buddy Holly
Day' to match the 'Jerry Lee Lewis Day' being celebrated almost
concurrently on the Killer's home turf. Even Buddy's old high
school offered no gesture of pride or approbation to its world-
famous graduate, while both the city's daily papers, the morning
Avalanche and the evening *Journal*, maintained an almost eerie
silence about his achievements.

Puzzled and hurt though Buddy was by Lubbock's indifference, it had its undoubted advantages. When he came home, as
now, exhausted by constant travel and performance, he could
escape completely from the pressures of rock 'n' roll stardom, go

hunting and fishing with his elder brothers, play with his nephews and nieces and hang out with old friends like Bob Montgomery and Jerry Coleman at old haunts like station KSEL and the Hi-D-Ho without being mobbed and pestered for autographs. He might have turned records into gold and trodden the boards of the London Palladium, but at the Holley family's modest home at 1305 37th Street he was still just 'Buddy', the baby of the family, expected to show the same respect as ever to his father, L. O. Holley, do whatever his tiny, feisty mother, Ella, considered to be for the best, keep his packs of Salem well hidden, and worship with his family in their pew at the Tabernacle Baptist Church.

One of his first acts after 'That'll Be The Day' became a hit had been to repay his brother Larry that whopping 1,000 dollar loan for his first Stratocaster and stage wardrobe. Anyone else who'd ever lent him money or given him credit was paid back, often in double measure. Now that Buddy was rich, or thought he was, his extravagant generosity became a byword among his family and around town. 'Whenever a group of us from the family would go on a fishing trip, Buddy would buy us all brand-new equipment,' Larry remembers. One day as he sat in a shoeshine parlour, the young man who was buffing his boots happened to admire the expensive wristwatch he wore. Buddy slipped off the watch and held it out, saying, 'If you like it that much take it . . .'

The one Lubbock authority which did show an interest in Buddy was his local draft board. On 28 May he received a letter summoning him to a medical examination to determine his fitness for military service. There was, however, not the remotest likelihood of Buddy's following Elvis Presley into the army. His appalling vision automatically disqualified him, with strong support from the nervous stomach condition which from here on would be formally referred to as his 'ulcer'.

Barely two weeks after riding into town incognito on his

Ariel motorcycle, he was back at Norman Petty's studio to cut three new tracks with the Crickets, augmented by the Roses vocal trio and an additional lead guitarist named Tommy Allsup. A twenty-six-year-old Western Swing musician from Lawton, Oklahoma, tall, swarthy and slow-spoken, Allsup had originally come to Clovis to back a singing group. Though his agile single-string technique seemed the very opposite of Buddy's chordal rhythm lead, it had the same freshness and directness, and Petty had asked him to stick around and try his hand on the Crickets' next session.

The first two songs featuring Tommy Allsup might have been consciously chosen to represent Buddy's own emotional state at this point: one was called 'Lonesome Tears', the other 'It's So Easy (to Fall in Love)'. And, as in his nature, brightness and optimism outweighed introspection and self-pity. While 'Lonesome Tears' is just a routine B-side, 'It's So Easy' stands among the best things he ever recorded; perhaps the nearest rock 'n' roll has ever come to pure aural sunshine. As in the blues call-and-response style, two-line verses alternate with a sinuous treble riff, the guitar jaunty and confident, the voice ruefully – and, it would seem, prophetically – owning up:

> People tell me love's for fools,
> So here I go, breakin' all o' the rules . . .

The second pearl of the batch was 'Heartbeat', written by Buddy's old friend Bob Montgomery, a Latin-accented ballad made to sound almost Hawaiian by Tommy Allsup's swooping steely riff and tearful tremolo. The lyric contained another of Norman Petty's Mantovani-ish lines ('Why does a love kiss stay in my memory?'), for which he claimed the same 50 per cent writing share he had on 'It's So Easy', though, for some reason, he allowed Buddy sole credit for 'Lonesome Tears'.

At Petty's, too, Buddy came down to earth – and appeared

happy to do so. The international star reverted to working musician, a 'pro' for whom the good of the music itself was more important than personal pride or vanity. Tommy Allsup was a fine guitarist whose playing gave the Crickets' sound an extra dimension; therefore Buddy was delighted to have him, and ceded him the lead spot without jealousy.

Remarkably for a twenty-one-year-old, especially in that era of throat-ripping competitiveness, he was keen to spot and encourage new talent, and unselfish in using his time, energy – and, later, his money – to help struggling musicians for all that they might well become his future rivals in the charts. He was still pushing J. I. Allison as a solo performer, under J.I.'s alter-ego of 'Ivan', and was proud beyond measure, Peggy Sue remembers, when Ivan's first release, 'Real Wild Child', made the outer reaches of the charts. On 6 June in Clovis, the big-time star once more reverted to session-man, playing back-up guitar for a young folk singer named Carolyn Hester, whom Petty had recently sold to the Coral label and whom Buddy himself had dated, platonically, in New York. With bass-player George Atwood, they recorded Buddy's song 'Take Your Time', Hester's own 'A Little While Ago', and two with real holly and berries attached, 'Christmas In Killarney' and 'Hurry, Santa, Hurry.'

He also spent a lot of time with Bob Montgomery, that wonderfully envy-free figure from his Country music days who had stood aside so selflessly when Destiny seemed to beckon from Nashville. Driving around Lubbock together, they revived the Buddy and Bob partnership by co-writing two songs, 'Love's Made A Fool Of You' and 'Wishing', which Buddy with his usual creative generosity decided were far better suited to the Everly Brothers than to himself. Instead of the usual rough demo, he made finished studio versions of the songs to sell them to Don and Phil, backed by Tommy Allsup on lead guitar, bassist George Atwood and drummer Bo Clarke, and with his vocal double-tracked to underline how perfectly custom-made each was for the brothers' seamless harmony. Don and Phil Everly loved both tracks, especially 'Wishing', but were prevented from recording them by political difficulties with their regular songwriters, Boudleaux and Felice Bryant. The net result was two more future Buddy Holly evergreens which, despite his best intentions, no one else could have sung quite that way.

Otherwise on this extended spring furlough, he spent his time mainly with J.I. and Joe B., riding, tinkering with and posing beside their new English motorcycles. A colour ciné-film, taken by J.I.'s brother James, shows them skylarking like truant schoolboys on the grass verge outside the Allison house. Buddy, in an unlikely outfit of striped matelot sweater, dark glasses and Hell's Angel peaked cap, parodies a biker's duel with J.I., brandishing a miniature penknife.

Even Buddy's huge appetite for performing and perpetual motion had been more than sated by the past year. When the offer of yet another tour came in, which would have meant cutting short their time off in Lubbock, he had no hesitation in refusing it. The normally easygoing and undriven J.I. was cast in the unfamiliar role of sergeant-major, protesting that such offers might not be around for ever and that they should soak up every dollar they could, while they could. Buddy said that they owed it to themselves to take a rest, have fun and ride their new motorbikes. If J.I. wanted money for a new Cadillac, he added grandiosely, then *he'd* buy him the new Cadillac. Enjoying their health and youth was more important than just piling up money, he argued, and J.I. has never forgotten the words with which he carried his point: 'What if you died tomorrow . . .?'

Their run of success in the American charts was now definitely over, though in Britain it continued at full throttle. The glorious 'Rave On', released under Buddy's name on 20 May, made only number 37 in America but spent fourteen weeks in the British Top 20, peaking at number 5. 'Think It Over', under the Crickets' name, failed to make the US Top 20 but reached number 7 in Britain. The pattern was repeated by Buddy's first own-name LP for Coral, *Buddy Holly*, which failed to chart in America but reached number 8 in Britain, notwithstanding the widespread puzzlement created by its cover. This was a head-and-shoulders portrait of Buddy, wonderfully smart in claret-collared jacket and pin-fastened shirt, but minus his black horn-rims and revealing a decided squint. So did this performer wear glasses or didn't he? To compound the mystery even further, some copies of both *Buddy Holly* and *The Chirping Crickets* misprinted the name of his home city, informing data-hungry British boys that 'Buddy Holly was born in Bullock, Texas...'

For any other performer in that time, the response to falling-off record-sales would have been a hurried return to well-tried earlier formulae. But Buddy knew no way but forward. On 19 June, he was back in New York for his second recording session there. This time, the venue was Decca's studio at the Pythian Temple building on West 50th Street. The producer was Dick Jacobs, whose lush string orchestra recorded for Coral and who had recently replaced Bob Thiele as Coral-Brunswick's director of A & R. Instead of J.I. and Joe B., Buddy's backing musicians were high-powered Eastern session-men, including Sam 'The Man' Taylor from Alan Freed's stage-band. Also in attendance was a female gospel group, the Helen Way singers.

The session was ostensibly to record two cover-versions. Another up-and-coming singer-songwriter, Bobby Darin, had been about to defect to Brunswick from the Atco label, and under Dick Jacobs's supervision had already recorded two of his own songs, 'Early In The Morning' and 'Now We're One', as his début single. Unfortunately, Darin's last Atco release, 'Splish-Splash' (a novelty number mentioning those two rock 'n' roll heroines Miss Molly and Peggy Sue) had turned out to be a huge hit. Atco now understandably refused to let him defect to another label, and the two tracks he had cut for Brunswick were unusable.

Buddy's version of 'Early In The Morning' is less rock 'n' roll than spiritual and, as everyone involved must have known full well, stood no earthly chance in the pop charts of mid-1958. What it proved – most significantly to the hard-nosed Dick Jacobs – was that Buddy could perform grown-up gospel and soul as brilliantly as he could adolescent rock and pop; that if rock 'n' roll were to disappear tomorrow, here was a real singer, fit to rank in his own fidgety, hiccupy way with Frank Sinatra, Tony Bennett or Johnny Mathis.

The lyrics of 'Early In The Morning' contain an unwitting reference to Buddy's most fervent British standard-bearers in the following decade. It's like a moment of clairvoyance when he sings, and the gospel choir echoes, 'Oh, a rollin' stone ... don't gather no moss ...'

Whenever Buddy and the Crickets were in New York, they always made a point of calling on Murray Deutch, the tersely affable executive vice-president of Peer-Southern Music, who had originally coerced Coral-Brunswick into taking a chance on 'That'll Be The Day'. Outside Deutch's office was a small reception area where visitors emerging from the elevator were greeted by a petite young woman with coiled-up dark hair, a heart-shaped face and an alluring Hispanic accent. The young woman's name, one destined to be inextricably linked with Buddy's from here on and ever after, was Maria Elena Santiago.

Maria Elena was born near San Juan, Puerto Rico, on 7 January 1933, the daughter of a detective in the San Juan police department. Her mother, a nurse, died when she was seven and, with her father out on police business at all hours, Maria Elena had to learn to look after herself and her brother, Miguel. After her father had remarried and been widowed a second time, he decided the best future he could give her was to send her to finish her education in America.

Puerto Rican immigrants to America in the late forties and early fifties generally faced racial prejudice and ghettoization little better than that endured by black people. But Maria Elena was luckier than most of her compatriots in New York. After lodging initially and not very happily with a sister of her father's, she moved in with her mother's unmarried sister, Provi Garcia, a high-powered woman who ran the Latin-American division at Peer-Southern Music and had an apartment on 10th Street in Greenwich Village.

Provi's job involved frequent trips abroad, and Maria Elena became a kind of secretary/companion, packing her aunt's suitcases, buying her clothes, occasionally acting as hostess at cocktail parties for Peer-Southern writers and performers at the apartment. Towards the end of her schooldays, she also took a job as a translator for Spanish-speaking patients at St Vincent's Catholic hospital, and ended up in charge of a clinic there. Though she lived a busy social life, frequenting smart restaurants and mingling with creative, cosmopolitan people, it was always with her strict spinster aunt as chaperone. Indeed, by the age of twenty-five, Maria Elena now insists, she had never had a date with a young man, let alone been kissed by one. She was highly attractive, accustomed to organizing other people, chic, worldly and sophisticated, but also conventional, self-contained and rather lonely.

She had originally wanted to be a dancer, but that ambition fell by the wayside as she became more and more involved in Aunt Provi's world. When a vacancy for a temporary Spanish-speaking receptionist occurred at Peer-Southern, she joined the company and, before long, had graduated to the vestibule outside Murray Deutch's office. It was here that she first met Buddy, one morning in June 1958.

'He came in with Jerry and Joe B. and said they had an

appointment with Murray. I said, "Have a seat, he'll be with you in a moment," and they sat down beside my desk. While they were waiting, Buddy tried to get me into a conversation and, of course, I tried to be polite. I didn't even know who he was at that time. And then the three of them started kidding around. Jerry wanted to ask me out, and then Joe B. said, "No, *I'm* going to be the one taking her out." But of the three, the one I really hit it off with right away was Buddy. The first moment we looked at each other, it was like "Boom". He asked me out to lunch, too. But I had to say No. At Peer-Southern we were strictly forbidden to go on dates with people who came into the office.'

Nothing further might have happened but for Murray Deutch's secretary, Jo Harper, who had previously run Norman Petty's New York office. 'At lunch, the two of us would usually go downstairs to Jack Dempsey's,' Maria Elena says. 'But on this day Jo said, "Why don't we go to Howard Johnson's for a change?" I said, "Oh God, that place is always full, you have to wait in line and we only have one hour for lunch." Jo said, "I assure you you won't have to wait in line." When we got to Howard Johnson's Buddy was waiting in a booth with the two Crickets – and Norman Petty came later, too. Buddy had spoken with Jo beforehand and made her promise to bring me there.

'They put me in the middle with Buddy on one side of me and Joe B. on the other. Joe B. was trying to grab my hand under the table. But Buddy made it very clear to both him and Jerry, "Whoa, wait a minute, she's not going out with either of you guys. Don't waste your time. She's going to go out with me. And I'm going to marry her." I thought that was just part of their kidding around.'

By the end of lunch, Buddy had asked Maria Elena to have dinner with him tête-à-tête that same night. 'I told him I'd have to convince my aunt and that it would be tough because I wasn't allowed to go on dates and – though I didn't say this – because

Above: J. I., Joe B., Niki Sullivan and Buddy, the 'real gangly' quartet who first recorded with Petty (*Jerry Fisher*)

Right: The Pettys and their bookkeeper, Norma Jean Berry, in the guest suite at their West Seventh Street studio compound (*Jerry Fisher*)

Buddy and J. I. Allison interviewed by deejay Freeman Hover in their hotel room on the road with Biggest Show of Stars for 1957. One of the rare occasions when Buddy allowed himself to be seen smoking (*Freeman Hover*)

Left: Buddy and Canadian deejay Red Robinson (*Red Robinson*)

Below: Barbara Bullough (right) the receptionist at the Wigan Grand Hotel, who allowed Buddy to see her home. 'He was the perfect gentleman' (*Barbara O'Nions*)

Buddy with Maria Elena on tour, 1958 (*Griggs Collection*)

Buddy in Decorah, Iowa, during the bumpy Summer Dance Party tour, July 1958 (*Linda Roed*)

December 1958: despite pressing financial worries, Buddy keeps up a cheerful
front with his friend Phil Everly in Phil's room at the Park-Sheraton hotel,
New York (*Griggs Collection*)

Above left: J. P. Richardson, 'the Big Bopper', at the Kato Ballroom, Mankato,
Minnesota, on 25 January 1959, nine days before the fatal charter-flight
(*Dianne Cory*)

Above right: Ritchie Valens at the Kato Ballroom. Buddy intended to take his
career in hand when they returned to New York (*Dianne Cory*)

Buddy and his protégé Waylon Jennings find something to laugh about in a
photo-booth during the nightmare Winter Dance Party tour (*Griggs Collection*)

Right: Poster for Buddy's last appearance (*Elwin Musser – Mason City Globe Gazette*)

Below: Investigators probe the wreckage of N3794N (*Musser – Globe Gazette*)

she wouldn't like the thought of me going out with someone who was a musician. She worked with musicians and liked them, but she knew the kind of lives they led. And, of course, rock 'n' roll musicians were worst of all in the eyes of older people like her. The only person I had ever been allowed to go out with, other than her, was her secretary, Margie. But I kept on pleading all afternoon, and Provi was ringing around the company, to Murray Deutch and all kind of other people, checking on Buddy. Eventually, she said, "OK, you can go, but you have to be back by midnight. Don't drink anything, come straight back to the house and be careful because these musicians are all crazy."

'Buddy called me about three or four times during the afternoon to see how it was going with my aunt. He had told me he was staying at the Edison Hotel on 42nd Street and the last time he called, I said I could meet him but I didn't get off work until 5.30 so it couldn't be until around 6.30. He said, "Please make it before then" because he had to go to a radio station in the early part of the evening to do some live interview-jingles. I couldn't even go home to change or anything. I went out to a store and bought a new sweater and cardigan to wear, and I refreshed myself in my aunt's office, which had its own powder-room and shower. I had never rushed so much in my life! I started to walk from the Fifties to 42nd Street, then I managed to grab a taxi. As I came up to the hotel, Buddy's limo' was just pulling away. But, luckily, he saw me. So he stopped the limo', jumped out and came over and paid off the taxi and put me in the limo'.'

After recording his radio jingles, Buddy got rid of J.I. and Joe B. and took Maria Elena to dinner at P. J. Clarke's saloon. P.J.'s cosy wood-panelled interior – famously displayed in a film-noir classic, *The Lost Weekend* – has always been a hangout for Manhattan's show-business and media élite. Over steak (for Buddy) and veal (for Maria Elena) they discovered a rapport that transcended their different ethnic origins, their hugely dissimilar upbringings on opposite sides of the continent, even the four-year gap in their ages. 'It's hard to know why you hit it off with someone and feel as comfortable with them after a few minutes as if you've known them all your lives,' Maria Elena says, 'But that's the way I felt – like it all had happened before, like I knew him for years already. And Buddy told me he felt the same, which was more unusual for him. Sure he liked people, but he never was one to be out there with somebody right away. It always took him a while to warm up to people.

'In a way we were both similar types, both a lot older than our years. I had had to grow up quickly because of having to look after my brother first, then my aunt. And Buddy was the same way, a young man of twenty-one but going on fifty, the way he thought, the way his mind worked. I always say he was an old soul.

'He told me all about Lubbock and his father and his mother, all the personal things in his life and his family. He was very funny and light-hearted in the way he talked, but when he told me about his music and what his intentions were in his career he was completely serious. He told me that he didn't write music just for himself, but that he wanted everyone to be able to enjoy it, and that he intended to go right to the top in show business, and nothing was going to stop him.

'While we were having dinner, Buddy got up from the table and said "I'll be right back." I thought he just gone to the boys' room, but when he came back he had both his hands behind him. He brought out a red rose and said, "This is for you. And I have something to ask you. Would you marry me?" I though, "Oh my God! My aunt was right. These people are insane!" Of course I thought he was joking or just handing me a line to make me feel nice, but deep inside of me I was hoping that it was true, because I fell in love with that man right away.

'But I pretended to take it very lightly. I said, "When do you want to get married? Now? Or when we finish dinner?" He said, "You think I'm kidding, don't you? But I'm very serious. As a matter of fact tomorrow before I leave New York I want to talk to your aunt." I said, "Oh you do? Then you be there at our apartment at nine in the morning!" Again, here I go, saying these things, thinking, "He'll never show up. When he gets to his hotel, he'll forget all about it."

'But nine o'clock next morning, the concierge in our building calls up and says, "There's a young man called Buddy Holly here to see you and your aunt." It was a Saturday, and Provi was still in bed. The night before when I got home, I hadn't mentioned anything about what had gone on to her, only that I had a nice evening. At first Provi thought Buddy had just wanted to pay a social call on her after taking me out. But he was very straightforward about the whole thing. He told my aunt, "I'm here because Maria Elena and I, we want to get married. I asked her last night. Didn't she tell you?"'

No one who knew Buddy would have been much surprised by any of this. The same impetuous nature was at work which, six months earlier, had been ready to break up the Crickets if June Clark would leave her husband and run away with him. His chaste brief encounter with Barbara Bullough, the Wigan hotel receptionist, had further underlined how desperate was his search for someone – anyone – to assuage the heartbreak of losing Echo McGuire.

And Maria Elena was a bewitchingly attractive young woman, especially to one of Buddy's peculiar susceptibilities; a mixture of big city sophistication and almost quaintly old-fashioned decorum, of doll-like femininity and evident strong-mindedness, humour and resilience. She was also very nearly as tiny in stature as Echo – and as his mother. Like L. O. Holley before him, gangly Buddy was irresistibly drawn to a small woman of large character whom he might appear to shelter and protect but who in effect would manage and motivate him as well as guarding him (and his name, after he had gone) with the ferocity of a terrier.

But even for Buddy, never inclined to wait for anything or anyone, this was an all-fire hurry. Undoubtedly it weighed with his competitive nature that his best friend, J. I. Allison, even though two years his junior, was already engaged to Peggy Sue Gerron and planning a midsummer wedding. In a few months he himself would be twenty-two, an age when most young men of his era and background expected to be married and starting a family. It's almost as if he sensed in some way that the sands were already running out, and he had only weeks, hours and minutes to enact his urgent destiny. Maria Elena has never forgotten his answer when a bewildered Aunt Provi asked if it wouldn't be wiser to wait a little before rushing into marriage. 'I don't have time,' Buddy told her.

Amazingly, the stern Spanish-American lady capitulated at once, agreeing to give them her blessing. 'I still don't understand how it happened, after she'd always been so strict with me and not wanted me to go out with musicians,' Maria Elena says. 'If she'd been against it, I would have to listen to her. But she just asked me, "Is this really what you want?" I said, "Yes," and she said, "OK. I think you people ought to wait and get to know one another better. But if that's what you want, go ahead." She figured that if she tried to stop us, we'd just go ahead and do it anyway.'

A jubilant Buddy then went to the phone and broke the news to his family in Lubbock. Knowing their youngest son as they did, L.O. and Ella Holley were not totally astounded to hear that he'd found himself a wife in New York. 'He was just lookin' to get married, any way, anyhow,' his brother Larry says. 'Jerry was about to do it, and Buddy didn't want to be left behind. And I knew he'd been real heartsick since it all ended with Echo. He was lonesome, he needed someone ... and Joe B. wasn't going to fill the bill.'

For all that, the Holleys' blessing was even less a foregone conclusion than Aunt Provi's had been. Even West Texans as decent and good-hearted as L.O. and Ella found two reasons for deep disquiet in Buddy's news. First, Maria Elena was Puerto Rican and so of the same ethnic origin as Lubbock's despised Mexican underclass. Second, and even more explosively, being of Hispanic origin must mean she was a Roman Catholic. To the Holley's Tabernacle Baptist Church it had been heresy enough when Larry briefly dated a girl from the Church of Christ. What Buddy was now proposing could bring Heaven literally crashing down around their ears.

L.O. and Ella Holley flew up to New York immediately and in evident consternation. At the sight of Buddy's new fiancée, however, all their misgivings melted away. 'Buddy's father and I hit it off, boom, right from the beginning,' Maria Elena says. 'He was a very sweet, easygoing kind of man. His mother was different – she was the one who directed traffic in that family. But they both made me feel welcome right away. They said Buddy had found a gorgeous girl. They thought I was a little doll with my clothes ... my accent. They made me feel like I was something breakable.'

Buddy's two fellow Crickets also knew by now that the Peer-Southern receptionist whose hand they had competed to grab under the table at Howard Johnson's four days earlier was to become Mrs Charles Hardin Holly. Despite the obvious implications for their Three Musketeer brotherhood, J. I. Allison and Joe B. Mauldin closed ranks around Buddy as loyally as would the Beatles, a decade later, when John Lennon introduced Yoko Ono into their midst. J.I. could sympathize with the probable religious difficulty, since Peggy Sue's parents also were Roman Catholics and were putting him under pressure to convert to Catholicism before they'd agree to her marriage. Accustomed to doing everything together, Buddy and J.I. began planning a double wedding ceremony. And Joe B., as usual, went along with the majority. 'I was pretty surprised by the suddenness of it,' he says now. 'But it was going to make Buddy happy, I was for it one hundred per cent.'

The sole opponent of Buddy's marriage plans was the one that might have been predicted – his manager/record-producer. Norman Petty had been present at the fateful Howard Johnson's lunch, and even then had shown spinsterly unease at Buddy's flirtation with Maria Elena. Perhaps naïvely, Buddy had hoped for Papa Norman's felicitations along with the rest. Instead, with quite uncommon forthrightness, Petty told him he was making the worst mistake of his life, and one which could have only disastrous consequences for his career. Rock 'n' roll stars of 1958 simply did not get married, nor even have visible female companions. The teenage girls who bought their records did so largely in the belief that they were unattached, fancy-free and so, at least theoretically, available to each and every one of their fans. With Maria Elena's demure silhouette, Petty saw Buddy's world-wide sales almost visibly start to evaporate. He saw, too, the end of his master-jeweller's control over that globally profitable 'diamond in the rough'. 'Norman never liked me from the very beginning,' Maria Elena says. 'He saw the danger in me. He knew the problems I was going to cause him. He knew I was going to take over. In his mind, Buddy was his and nobody else's.'

In fact, Buddy had started to rebel against Papa Norman's rule a good while before he met Maria Elena. On that first dinner date at P. J. Clarke's, she remembers, he talked at length about his various dissatisfactions with Petty's management. He complained about how little publicity he seemed to get in comparison with other rock 'n' roll chart-toppers, the dual result of Petty's stinginess and failure to appreciate the growing importance of image and PR. Despite knowing how much Buddy wanted to follow his friend Eddie Cochran into the movies, Petty had made no effort to push him that way. Indeed, Clovis Man had turned down an offer for the Crickets to appear with Cochran in *Go, Johnny, Go*, deciding in typically oracular fashion that 'it wasn't right' and 'better things would come later'. 'The only photographs they had were the ones taken by Norma Jean [the Petty studio bookkeeper],' Maria Elena says. 'Buddy had always trusted Norman and believed in his judgement. But when he got to New York and started talking to people there, he realized how backward Norman was.'

He was also beginning to chafe against Petty's total control of his and the Crickets' income, and the necessity of going to Clovis, cap in hand, for everything he needed to live the life of a rock 'n' roll star. At the beginning, when they had been on the road for months at a time, it had seemed only sensible to let Petty be the conduit for their earnings from performing, recording and publishing, banking the money in their collective account and settling all their bills with his power of attorney to write cheques on their behalf. But ten months on, what had been a system to spare them anxiety and boredom increasingly looked like a means of keeping them from the money they had worked like galley-slaves to earn.

Admittedly, Petty had never been tight with the funds he administered on their behalf and would generally sign a cheque (or let Ma Petty forge his signature) for anything Buddy or J.I. or Joe B. asked, even though it frequently made Norma Jean raise her masculine eyebrows in despair. Soon tiring of his '58 Impala two-tone coupé, Buddy exchanged it that summer for a powder-blue Lincoln with a rear window that could be automatically raised and lowered. To his growing guitar collection had lately been added a luxurious Guild F 50 acoustic model ($275.00, plus $67.50 de luxe plush-lined carrying-case). He and Joe B. also had gone shares in a motorboat to use in their waterskiing sessions on Buffalo Springs lake, a few miles outside Lubbock. 'We'd been to see a movie that had people using jet-skis,' Joe B. remembers. 'The next day, we went out to look for some jet-skis of our own, but wound up buying a ski-boat complete with skis, harness, lifejackets, everything. That was the kind of impulsive thing Buddy would do.'

Yet Petty, while allowing these liberal, even reckless inroads into the Buddy Holly and the Crickets account, was mysteriously reluctant to discuss precisely how much it had accumulated to date, beyond assuring Buddy, J.I. and Joe B. earnestly that the sum was far smaller than they might imagine. This was surprising news to a group which had already had two million-selling singles and roughly calculated that, at a two-cent royalty, Brunswick-Coral alone must owe them $20,000 between them ($200,000 by today's values), never mind the hits in Britain and Australia, never mind the earnings from their tours and television appearances and via BMI (Broadcast Music International), the agency which collected fees for radio-airplay on their behalf.

While unable to deny that they were due sizeable sums, Petty kept on stressing the slowness with which record-companies, in particular, paid out artists' royalties. All these months after 'That'll Be The Day' and 'Peggy Sue' had 'gone gold', the money from Brunswick Coral still had not come through, so he said or implied or otherwise led them to believe. As for the $1,000 per week they had so religiously sent home from hugely drawn-out tours like 'The Biggest Show of Stars for 1957', it had almost all been swallowed up by travelling expenses, clothes-buying sprees at Alfred Norton, session-fees for the Picks and the Roses, musicians' union dues, car-repayments and long-distance phone-calls.

By mid-1958, even unassertive Joe B. Mauldin had begun to ask about his share of the money and to tire of Papa Norman's equivocations. 'I'd go to him on a Friday and say, "I'm going in to Lubbock and I need some money for a new set of car-tyres."

Norman would say, "I'll get you the tyres, but go get 'em at Montgomery-Ward, not at Sears or Firestone." "I need some cash in my pocket, too," I'd tell him. But there was always some excuse, like Norma Jean's already gone home or there are no more spare cheques left in the chequebook.'

At P. J. Clarke's, that first night, Buddy had also told Maria Elena how it irked him to go to Petty for everything, and about the accumulated royalties which Petty must now be sitting on. Since her Aunt Provi was a senior executive at Peer-Southern Music, Maria Elena had no difficulty in finding out for herself how Buddy and the Crickets' publishing royalties were paid over. Aunt Provi confirmed that everything was channelled via Petty and his company, NOR VA JAK. 'I could tell from the beginning that something wasn't right,' Maria Elena says. 'I made it a condition of my marrying Buddy that he got this whole situation resolved. I told him, "I don't want to sit around all the time, waiting for handouts from Norman Petty. If you want us to be married, you have to get your finances in order."'

Unaware how much the tide was running against him, Petty fought to keep Buddy all his with tactics that revealed an entirely new side of normally discreet, subtle and underhand Clovis Man. 'He tried to break us up,' Maria Elena says. 'He told Buddy not to marry me because I was a whoreish kind of woman, that I'd slept with all kinds of other men who'd come in to Peer-Southern. Buddy knew that wasn't true, of course. He got so mad, he wanted to leave Norman right there and then.'

Angry and defiant though Buddy might be, Petty's financial coils still bound him hand and foot. His own personal bank account in Lubbock did not have enough in it even to buy Maria Elena an engagement ring. He therefore had to suffer the humiliation of asking Petty for the money with the slurs against his fiancée still ringing in his ears. Petty, to his equal chagrin, could not refuse – though, Maria Elena remembers, he tried to talk Buddy into buying something cheap. The cheque drawn on the Buddy Holly and the Crickets account that 19 June and signed by Petty, reads, 'To: Gift Mart Jlrs Inc. $515 For: Ring – engagement.'

With no royalty-payout in prospect, the quickest way of raising money for the new commitments Buddy now faced was to forget what he'd preached to J. I. Allison about taking it easy and enjoying themselves, and go out on the road again. Fortuitously, just before he'd met Maria Elena, the General Artists Corporation had offered a ten-day tour through the 'upper' Midwestern states of Illinois, Michigan, Wisconsin, Indiana, Minnesota and Iowa.

Billed as 'The Summer Dance Party', and set to begin on 4 July in Angola, Indiana, this was an excursion very different from GAC's normal multi-star spectaculars. Many of the gigs were not theatres or arenas but ballrooms; Buddy and the Crickets were the only big name involved, and took with them their own support-act, a four-man, sax-blowing Western Swing band recruited and fronted by Buddy's stand-in lead guitarist Tommy Allsup. The remainder of each night's show was to be filled by local singers and groups. Instead of the usual bus, the seven-man troupe provided their own transport, Buddy, J.I. and Joe B. travelling in Buddy's new Lincoln, Tommy and the three Western Swing bandsmen in a yellow deSoto station wagon representing a further major disbursement ($3,981) from the Buddy Holly and the Crickets account.

Buddy had wanted Maria Elena to accompany him on the tour, but here at least Aunt Provi insisted that old-fashioned propriety be observed. So, while Provi flew off on business to Argentina, Maria Elena remained in New York to shop for her wedding trousseau with some money Buddy had left behind for her.

That the 'Summer Dance Party' got off to a shaky start we know from subsequent correspondence between GAC's Chicago office and Harry K. Smythe, owner of Buck Lake Ranch, Angola,

Indiana. As the cartoon drawings around its rustic letterhead indicate, Buck Lake Ranch was a family resort with a boating lake, a picnic-area, horse-riding and a children's amusement park as well as live music and dancing for teenagers. Two weeks on, Harry Smythe is still fuming about the disruption which the 'Summer Dance Party' caused his Fourth of July programme.

> . . . In answer to your letter of July 14 regarding the CRICKETS and BUDDY HOLLY. We are very sorry but at no time have we ever lied to you. We gave you the facts in our previous letter and again we repeat that if the seven-piece orchestra was here, why was it necessary for Buddy Holly and two members of his band to borrow instruments and drums from an Act we had booked on the Show that day? Truthfully, Buddy Holly was going nuts, wondering where in hell the other four men were, because they had all left Texas together and this was their first date, and they hadn't rehearsed together . . .
>   . . . I don't give a dam what Buddy Holly or New York or George Petty [sic] says, or anyone else, we were charged for seven men and only three appeared for the three shows, and at no time were they prepared to present the seven men on the Stage during the entire day or evening. To me, this is the case that has been quite evident throughout our season this year. THE CUSTOMER IS NEVER RIGHT, IT'S ALWAYS THE ARTIST WHO'S RIGHT. Frankly, I'm dam sick of it and it will be a long time before I'll ever buy a GAC act again.
>   Best wishes

Buddy, J.I. and Joe B. tried to dress as for a summer ball, in dark blazers and white slacks. Joe B. no longer played his stand-up bass, having switched to one of the new Fender electric bass guitars. Buddy gave such valuable endorsement to the Fender company that they had donated two new Stratocasters and two amplifiers, one for him, the other for Tommy Allsup. A couple of days into the tour, their station-wagon trailer was burgled and one of the Strats and an amp disappeared. 'That meant that, until we could get a replacement, Buddy and I couldn't play in the same group,' Tommy Allsup says. 'I'd open with the Western Swing guys and then pass over the Strat to Buddy for his set with the Crickets.'

The seven-man, two-act line-up proved an awkward one all along the line. Some promoters were only interested in putting Buddy and the Crickets onstage, and refused to pay the Swing Band's fee despite having signed a contract for them. And it felt strange to a group which had appeared at the London Palladium only five months earlier to find themselves now playing for glorified teenage hops at holiday camp venues like Buck Lake Ranch.

This was the part of America where Buddy was to travel to his death, under horribly similar festive billing, just a little over six months from now. Free of its winter snow and biting cold as the Midwest was in early July, placid and safe as the woodlands and lakes must have appeared to him, there were times when one might almost have thought they were trying to warn him off. After a waterskiing-session on Cedar River near Waterloo in his nemesis state of Iowa, J.I., Joe B. and he tried to balance on some half-submerged logs and all three slipped off into the water. While swimming alone in a lake at Wausau, Wisconsin, on 13 July, Buddy was overcome by fatigue and had a struggle to reach the shore. He played that night's show at Rhinelander's Crystal Rock Ballroom in a state of obvious exhaustion, only perking up when the audience shouted for 'Rave On'. During the intermission, a group of fans went to look at his car in the parking-lot and found him asleep in the back seat.

On this tour, in open defiance of Norman Petty, the performance-money was not sent back to Clovis, but shared out among

Buddy, J.I., and Joe B. on the spot. 'Buddy collected the money from the promoters each night and kept it in the glove-compartment of his car,' Tommy Allsup remembers. 'We'd be going down the road and Jerry Allison would say "Hey, I need some money." Buddy would open up the glove-compartment, get out a handful of bills and pass 'em back.' Neat and methodical as ever, he kept a scrupulous record of their daily petrol consumption and casual expenses, backed up by receipts for even the most microscopic amount. (July 9: Standard Service, Waterloo, Iowa, gas $4.90, 1 pair sunglasses, $1.00, tax 2c, total $5.92. July 11: Ruckdashel Co., Duluth, Minnesota, check and adjust power brakes $5.00, Jerry Schmedt mechanic; Duluth and Superior Bridge Co. 50c.)

Carrying around such a large sum in cash held obvious risks, even in the law-abiding Midwest, and to a Texan raised as Buddy had been there was only one possible source of security. With the wad of large-denomination bills in the Lincoln's glove-compartment lay a German-made .22 calibre pistol which he'd recently bought second-hand from Tommy Allsup. Buddy knew very well how to handle the .22 and, as Joe B. remembers, was not at all averse to demonstrating his quickness on the draw. 'Right after we'd gotten paid one night, there was a problem in the parking-lot. Some headlights came up behind us real close and wouldn't let us back out of our space. Buddy reached into the glove-compartment, buzzed down the Lincoln's automatic rear window, turned round and pointed his gun through it. Those headlights just disappeared!'

Part Four

LEARNING THE GAME

ON 22 JULY 1958, tiring of the difficulties being put in the way of their engagement, J. I. Allison and Peggy Sue Gerron eloped from Lubbock to Honey Grove, East Texas (where Buddy's father had been born and raised), and were married by J.I.'s Uncle Raymond who, conveniently, happened to be the local minister.

Buddy knew nothing of the plot beforehand and was a little put out when J.I. triumphantly called him up the next morning. For the past month he'd been counting on his friends to go to the altar in company with Maria Elena and himself. To make amends, J.I. and Peggy Sue offered to delay their honeymoon until after Buddy's wedding and make a foursome of that instead. 'Buddy asked me where I wanted to go,' Peggy Sue remembers. 'I said, "Somewhere warm, with white sand. How about Acapulco?" He laughed and said, "I'll take care of it."'

At the beginning of August, Maria Elena Santiago flew from New York to Lubbock to become Mrs Charles Hardin Holly. The original plan had been for her Aunt Provi, or another aunt, to go with her as a chaperone, but in the event she made the journey by herself. Buddy met her at the airport and drove her to the Holley home, where she was to spend the week prior to the wedding. L.O. and Ella gave her the warmest of welcomes, insisting that she call them 'Dad' and 'Mother' and showing her off proudly to their family, friends and neighbours. 'I found I didn't need a chaperone,' she remembers. 'I had my own room, completely separate from Buddy's. It was all very proper.'

The expected religious tug-of-war did not materialize after all. Although Maria Elena had been brought up a Roman Catholic, she was not especially religious and Buddy escaped the usual stringent demands made by the Catholic Church of Protestant marriage partners. He did not have to be married by a Catholic priest nor promise his children would be raised in their mother's faith. And the Holleys' Tabernacle Baptist Church, though liking Catholicism least of almost anything in the doctrinal spectrum, waived its objections in view of Buddy's celebrity and the generous donations it received from him. Indeed, in an impressive charm offensive, he even managed to talk his pastor, Ben D. Johnson, into performing the ceremony.

This took place at the Holley home on 15 August, a day when Lubbock was gripped by heat in the high nineties. Maria Elena wore a white sheath dress and a veil; Buddy wore a dark suit, a broadly striped tie and sunglasses. Only close family members, Buddy's fellow Crickets and the new Mrs J. I. Allison were present. With most top rock 'n' roll stars, a manager who doubled as record-producer might be expected to count as 'close family'. But Norman and Vi Petty were conspicuous by their absence.

The solemnities over, J. I. Allison went to a gramophone in the next room and put on Buddy's latest B-side, 'Now We're One'. The newlyweds posed for photographs in front of the family television set, Buddy now grinning at the camera in his wildly out-of-character mafioso shades, now leaning down to his tiny, unveiled bride to steal a kiss. As a gesture of appreciation to his church for making things so easy, he then wrote Pastor Ben D. Johnson a cheque for $100 from his personal bank account.

The double honeymoon in Acapulco, which had sounded

such a fun idea in theory, turned out to be hard going for everyone concerned. Despite their absorption in their respective brides, Buddy and J.I. could not resist a sneaking desire to 'hang out' together in the way they had for years around Lubbock and on tour. And while they might be soul-mates, their brides, all too clearly, were anything but. To twenty-five-year-old Maria Elena, eighteen-year-old Peggy Sue seemed gawky and provincial and given to embarrassing displays of high spirits. To Peggy Sue, Maria Elena seemed forbiddingly adult, formal and self-contained. 'She was sophisticated, worked in New York and wore smart clothes. I'd only just hung up my can-can petticoats.'

They had booked rooms at the luxurious Las Brisas hotel, but were disappointed to find it didn't overlook the breathtaking bay which is Acapulco's principal attraction. The Las Brisas also proved excessively formal and disapproving of Texan high jinks in its pool, so after a couple of nights the party transferred to a friendlier, ocean-front establishment, the El Cano. Among the water-sports on offer was Buddy's favourite, water-skiing, and he instantly gambolled off to rent a high-speed motor-boat. 'But Maria Elena didn't want to try,' Peggy Sue remembers. 'And Jerry had trouble with his ears, and couldn't go under water. So Buddy ended up teaching me to water-ski.' That cannot have helped an atmosphere which even happy-go-lucky J.I. was later to describe as 'uncomfortable' and 'weird'.

For much of the time, Buddy's high spirits kept the party going. 'One night at a club we watched a man demonstrating matador passes,' Peggy Sue remembers. 'Later, when Buddy got up to put some music on the jukebox, he did a perfect imitation of this man. He was so deft and graceful in the way he moved, he could have been a matador himself.'

But towards the end, even Buddy seemed downcast by the tense atmosphere and the realization that Maria Elena wasn't enjoying herself as much as he'd intended. 'He and Jerry and I were in the hotel restaurant one evening, waiting for Maria Elena to come down and join us for dinner,' Peggy Sue remembers. 'Time passed, she still didn't show, and Buddy got more and more agitated. Eventually he went off to the house phone to call her up in their room. After a while, he came back and said, "She's not coming down for dinner after all. She's going to have it up in the room." He looked tense and stressed in a way I'd never seen him before.'

To prevent a boycott of Buddy's records by grief-stricken female fans, the marriage was not publicized in any way, and everyone present at the wedding was solemnly sworn to secrecy. Keeping such a secret in 1958 was admittedly not very difficult; newspapers as yet took little interest in the private lives of celebrities apart from a few jet-set figures like Aly Khan and Porfirio Rubirosa, and a handful of Hollywood stars like Elizabeth Taylor and Marlon Brando. Even so, there were scandal-sheets which might have made unpleasant capital about a rock 'n' roll big name entering on a 'mixed' marriage, as Brando had done not long previously. Hence Buddy's world-wide public would know nothing of Maria Elena's existence until after she had become a widow.

Married or single, he had always intended to keep Lubbock as his base, and had gone so far as to draw up plans for a house he intended to build there, using his family's manifold constructional resources. But with Maria Elena's advent, the blueprint changed; the Lubbock house would be for his parents, and his occasional use. His new wife's home, New York City, was the only possible place to settle down.

Fortunately, he could embark on married life with some real money in his pocket at last. Early in August, Peer-Southern Music disgorged $28,338-worth of publishing royalties in five separate cheques. Clovis Man's bank records show a substantial payment to each Cricket on 11 August from the Buddy Holly and the Crickets account: $3,887.93 to Buddy, $1,453.82 to J. I. Allison, $4,877.48 to Joe B. Mauldin. On 26 August, Buddy received a further cheque, for $14,467, bearing the notation 'From record royalties. To Church', but made out in his name. Since that sum vastly exceeds any tithe he could have pledged to his church, it's possible some tax-avoidance was going on here.

In seeking their first home in Manhattan, it was natural for the new Mr and Mrs Holly to gravitate to the downtown area where Maria Elena had lived since her schooldays. At 9th Street and Fifth Avenue, just round the corner from Aunt Provi's apartment, they found the Brevoort, a smart, new residential block, built on the site of a house once occupied by Mark Twain. An apartment was available on the fourth floor and in a premium corner position – one bedroom, living-room, dining-room, and 'wraparound' outside terrace. Though the monthly rent was more than $1,000 ($10,000 by today's values) Buddy took it without hesitation.

Two or three blocks from the Brevoort, Greenwich Village was in full late-fifties flower with its jazz joints, coffee cellars and antique shops: a colony where the artless 'beat' of rock 'n' roll had come to define all manner of complex, intellectual things; where the 'beat' novelist Jack Kerouac and the 'beat' poet Allen Ginsberg nightly declaimed their edgy, free-form works to saxophone accompaniment; where the fashionable young of both sexes wore shapeless black clothes and dark glasses and styled themselves 'beatniks'; and where age-old jazzmen's terms like 'dig', 'jive' and 'hip' now punctuated earnest espresso-fuelled discussions about Camus and Sartre. October's surprise hit single, 'Tom Dooley' by the Kingston Trio, had given folk music the same brief hour of high fashion in America that skiffle previously enjoyed in Britain. Every hip bar and club in the Village now had its own resident folk singer-guitarist, male or female, seated on a high stool and strumming to a circle of rapt, deathly white faces.

To Maria Elena the sights and sounds of Greenwich Village were familiar enough. But Buddy's experience of New York until now had been mainly confined to uptown hotel suites. He found it endlessly fascinating to explore this brownstone and tree-lined quarter, below the Stonehenge rim of silver sky-scrapers, where everything was low-rise, jumbled and heterogeneous, manners were free and easy and the wildest eccentricity – even of that of being a transplanted West Texan rock 'n' roller – was absorbed into the scene without question.

All that marred the excitement of setting up home with Maria Elena and exploring his new neighbourhood was continual disappointing news from the charts. 'Early In The Morning', released as a solo Buddy Holly single in July, had not reached the Top 20 in America and had only just scraped in in Britain. 'It's So Easy', released under the Crickets' name in early September, ironically proved too complex for its intended audience, failing even to make the US Top 100 and becoming the first Holly production not to enter the British Top 20, although in Australia it reached number 8.

Buddy was not alone in feeling his fortunes start to slip. Over the previous six months, one after another supernova in the rock 'n' roll firmament had come crashing to earth. Elvis Presley, shorn of his kingly sideburns, was bulling his army boots at Fort Hood, Texas, about to be shipped to West Germany as part of NATO's armoured bulwark against the expected Soviet onslaught. The ever-unpredictable Little Richard had forsaken rock 'n' roll without warning half-way through his 1957 Australian tour. Seeing the Russian Sputnik satellite shoot through the night sky, he interpreted it as a summons from God, threw the largest of his diamond rings ceremonially into Sydney Harbour and went off to train as a minister. Jerry Lee Lewis's first British tour had disintegrated in chaos after journalists discovered that his wife, Myra Gale, was only thirteen years old, and his first cousin to boot, and that he'd had two wives before her. So much for the more wholesome impression of American rock 'n' rollers that Buddy and the Crickets had left behind them.

For someone with Buddy's canny eye on the market, future prospects did not look very bright either. Rock 'n' roll in 1958 was, if anything, even more of a social outcast than it had been in 1956. In the wake of the Boston riots and a highly publicized jeremiad from the evangelist Billy Graham, more and more radio stations throughout middle America were deciding it wasn't worth the trouble and sanctimoniously cutting their rock 'n' roll output. Those who had accused the music of cynically duping and manipulating its young audience were starting to find hard evidence to back up their claims. Late 1958 saw the first faint media rumblings about a practice which had always been rife in the music industry but which during the rock 'n' roll era had become even more shameless and blatant: the bribing of radio disc jockeys to push one new release in preference to others. It was a Heaven-sent opportunity for the Establishment to take vengeance on figures like Alan Freed and Dick Clark who had so long and defiantly encouraged the nation's children to behave like yahoos. The so-called Payola Scandal would grow into the Watergate of its day, culminating in a Senate Committee of Inquiry and the satisfying public disgrace of several prominent deejays, Freed among them.

Rock 'n' roll, in any case, had been around for three years, a prodigious run for an American fad. Now it seemed to be suffering the fate of hula hoops, dance-marathons, and pogo-sticks before it: people wanted something new. Among recent hit singles, only a handful still had the authentic rock 'n' roll voice, undiluted by subtlety or self-consciousness. The majority were ballads, like the Platters 'Twilight Time' and the Everly Brothers' 'Dream', or hymns to teenage self-pity like Jody Reynolds's 'Endless Sleep', the Four Preps' 'Big Man' and Ricky Nelson's 'Poor Little Fool'. There had been a brief craze for Latin-flavoured instrumentals, like Perez Prado's 'Patricia' and the Champs' 'Tequila', and a summer-long spate of comedy records, Bobby Darin's 'Splish-Splash', the Coasters' 'Yakety-Yak', Sheb Woolley's 'Purple People-Eater' and David Seville's 'Witch Doctor', prefiguring the ghastly Chipmunks.

Most crucially, the definition of glamour and sex-appeal in pop singers had begun to change. A new breed of teenage heart-throb was emerging, no longer greasily coiffed in the Elvis style, but neatly brush-topped and trim about the ears; no longer lip-curlingly subversive, but soft-centred, simpering and ingratiating. Whereas Elvis had been a superb vocalist with coincidentally devastating looks, these newcomers often were young men who'd won recording deals on the strength of their prettiness alone, and whose vocal efforts would not have been releasable without artful enhancement by studio engineers. The chart-sensations of the hour were Frankie Avalon, a seventeen-year-old Italian-American like a sawn-off Sinatra, whose 'De-De-Dinah' had lately sold a million, and Dion and the Belmonts, a New York vocal quartet named after an avenue in their native Bronx, who purveyed a saccharine teenage version of the street-corner 'doowop' style. The Top 10's flavour changed from raw spirit to warm milk. As if anticipating investigative tribunals of the future, record companies now cast around for product which suggested the polite, the respectful and the law-abiding.

Buddy naturally was disappointed by his run of misses, but he did not allow it to depress him. As always, half a dozen new songs and a hundred new ideas were germinating inside his tousled head. Sooner or later, he had no doubt, he'd come up with the right blueprint to take him back to the top. Other rock 'n' roll originals poured scorn on teenage crooners like Frankie Avalon, but not Buddy: he bought all the new hit records and listened to them in his usual analytical way to see what he could learn from them. The normal reaction for a performer in eclipse is to grow secretive, introverted, and misanthropic as he struggles to plot his way back to the limelight. But Buddy remained as open-heartedly generous with his music as ever (witness the trouble he took over his two demo's for Don and Phil Everly) and as unselfishly energetic in fostering new talent that he considered promising.

In 1958, few pop singers even dreamed of turning themselves into businessmen and impresarios, but by the time he settled among the Greenwich Village beatniks Buddy was well on the way to becoming both. That autumn, he set up a recording and publishing company called Prism and intended to be the focus of his developing parallel career as a talent-spotter and producer.

Moving to New York did not mean he had cast off West Texas and forgotten his boyhood roots in country and rockabilly music. Quite the opposite; Prism's chief objective was to tap the huge reservoir of West Texan musical talent and give a helping hand to some of the numerous young singers he had heard and admired on his trips home. Buddy Holly might not figure significantly in Lubbock's scheme of things, but he was planning to put his home city on the musical map as firmly as Nashville or Memphis. The original plans he had made for a house in Lubbock developed into a recording studio and office complex which would serve both as a command-centre for Prism and a new home for his parents.

The studio was to be on much the same lines as Norman Petty's, with the very latest in equipment and stay-over accommodation for musicians. Under the original plan, indeed, Petty was to run it in tandem with his Clovis establishment. And, ever conscious how L. O. Holley had worked a back-breaking lifetime without ever having owned a business, Buddy took care that the blueprint should include a record-store 'for Daddy to take care of'. This blueprint for a multi-faceted music company, not controlled by the usual soulless middle-aged money men but fired by youthful energy and idealism, has more than a whisper of the Beatles' Apple organization, ten years in the future.

Lubbock's top radio station was no longer KDAV nor KSEL,

but KLLL, situated on the top floor of the Great Plains Life insurance building, the city's highest high-rise, and operated by three ebullient brothers, Larry, Sky and Slim Corbin. With an output designated as 'hillbilly-rock', the station had stolen thousands of listeners from KDAV and KSEL, and now fielded the area's top team of disc jockeys, among them Slim and Sky Corbin, a 'gospel-jock' called Mr Sunshine and Buddy's old mentor and manager, Hi Pockets Duncan. By the autumn of 1958, 'K triple L' had hubris enough to advertise in *Cash Box* magazine, boasting of the West Texas recording stars who were its supporters and regular visitors, like Terry Noland (Brunswick) the Four Teens (Challenge) Sonny Curtis and Niki Sullivan (Dot). To Buddy, in particular, KLLL became almost the home-from-home KDAV had once been; when in Lubbock, he was always stopping by to chat to the Corbins or Hi Pockets on air or give a spontaneous live solo performance. He even recorded a set of promotional jingles to the tune of some better-known Holly songs, including:

> *Everyday,*
> *It's a gettin' better,*
> *Gettin' more cards and gettin' more letters.*
> *Ev'ry-body*
> *Wants to tune our way.*

The newest recruit to the KLLL airways was a snakily handsome young man of twenty-one named Waylon Jennings from Littlefield, thirty miles north-west of Lubbock. Despite his huge local popularity as a disc jockey, Waylon had ambitions to turn his preternaturally deep voice from announcing to singing. Buddy had been his idol since KDAV *Sunday Party* days and now, in 'bull' sessions around the KLLL mike, the two struck up a firm friendship. At Hi Pockets Duncan's suggestion, Buddy became Waylon's sponsor, advising him on the wardrobe and hairstyle an aspiring music star should have, and promising him help in getting his musical career off the ground.

Despite the rift with Norman Petty over his marriage, and the growing pull of New York, Buddy continued to regard Petty's studio in Clovis as his main creative home, hoping with his perennial optimism that the difficulty and bad feeling would blow over eventually. Petty remained a co-director of the nascent Prism organization, along with Ray Rush of the Roses vocal group, and had agreed to sell Buddy one of his treasured Ampex tape-recorders and a microphone as Prism's start-up equipment.

On 6 September, Buddy was back at Petty's studio, playing guitar for a singer named Jerry Engler in a late-night session which ran into the first hours of his twenty-second birthday. Three days later, he was there again with J.I., Joe B. concocting yet another audacious new sound-effect. He had been an admirer of the R & B saxophonist 'King' Curtis since they'd traversed the US together on Alan Freed's 'Biggest Show of Stars for 1957'. The father of the braying 'chicken-sax' style, Curtis had since contributed memorably manic solos to several rock 'n' roll classics, notably the Coasters' 'Yakety Yak'. Ignoring the convention that white and black musicians did not usually record together, Buddy persuaded him to come down from New York to Clovis in exchange for his air-fare, accommodation and a $100 studio-fee.

On 10 September, Buddy, the Crickets and King Curtis – prefiguring the 'two-tone' group line-ups of the 1980s – recorded two tracks, 'Come Back Baby' and 'Reminiscing'. The latter, an ambling bluesy ballad, featured Buddy's voice alone and exposed in the way it had been on 'Mailman, Bring Me No More Blues'; stretching, hovering and swooping to the point of self-parody; at times not singing so much as mimicking the breathy, nonchalant tenor riffs that shadowed it.

Curtis then joined Petty's two house musicians and the Roses on Waylon Jennings's first recording session, financed by Buddy

and his first essay as a producer for his Prism organization. The
resulting two tracks, on which he also found time to play guitar,
were Waylon's composition 'When Sin Stops' and 'Jole Blon', a
song in Louisiana's pidgin-French Cajun dialect (i.e., *jolie
blonde*) first popularized by Harry Choates in the mid-forties.
No one having any idea how to pronounce the Cajun lyrics, let
alone what they meant, Waylon had to bluff his way through a
rough phonetic version. Though 'Jole Blon' would not take him
anywhere near the late fifties charts, it was the first vital step in
the evolution of a future country music giant. Buddy's taste as
an A & R man would eventually be vindicated when the song
became a hit for Gary 'US' Bonds in 1980.

The clock-cheating drive from Lubbock to Clovis was now
no longer made, at 100 mph-plus, by three carefree young
bachelors, laughing, singing and hurling empty Falstaff beer-
bottles at mailboxes along the way. Buddy naturally wanted to
have Maria Elena with him while he cut his records. Like the
Beatles when John Lennon brought Yoko Ono to their *White
Album* session, J. I. Allison and Joe B. Mauldin pretended this
was 'no problem'. But, like Paul, George and Ringo, they were
privately hurt and mystified that an outsider – and a woman –
should thus disfigure their creative brotherhood.

As Maria Elena sat in the control-room, she could feel
freezing hostility from all sides. Clovis Man, of course, could not
object to her presence, but he made his disapproval plain with
the subtlety of a scalpel. Even the normally good-natured and
timid Vi joined in, making fun of Maria Elena's Hispanic accent
with Norma Jean Berry. 'Whenever I said anything, both of
them would laugh and imitate the way I spoke. Vi said it was all
in good fun, they thought my accent was cute. But I didn't find
it funny. I said to them, "At least I can speak your language. You
can't speak mine."' Despite herself, she could not repress a
twinge of sisterly compassion for Vi. 'Norman paid no attention

to her. She had no say-so. She was not asked anything – she was just told. The poor woman was just kind of existing in that weird atmosphere.'

To fastidious Maria Elena, the studio itself was a strange and uninviting place, even though Pa and Pa Petty's garage had now been replaced by a frontal façade displaying their son's NOR VA JAK logo. 'That place where Buddy recorded was old ... dilapidated ... ooh, it was horrible!' To her dismay, as Buddy's session ran late, she realized she was expected to stay overnight in the communal bedsitting-room behind the studio. Even more ominously, Norma Jean, the Pettys' bookkeeper, now seemed to be showing interest in something more about her than her accent. 'This woman who looked just like a man kind of took a fancy to me. She kept saying, "Oh, you're so nice ... you're so petite" and trying to paw me. I wouldn't go to sleep in that back room. I just sat there. In the end, Buddy and I went out and got some sleep in the car.'

In New York Buddy acquired a second young protégé, a singer named Lou Giordano whom he'd met through Joey Villa of the Royalteens. Convinced of Giordano's potential, Buddy helped get him a contract with Brunswick and also gave him a newly-written song, 'Stay Close To Me'. Giordano's début session took place at Beltone studios on 30 September. Buddy and Phil Everly co-produced, also playing back-up guitars on 'Stay Close To Me' and contributing a falsetto chorus to the B-side, 'Don't Cha Know'.

Two days later, Buddy appeared with the Crickets on Alan Freed's *Dance Party* television show to lip-synch his imminent own-name single, 'Heartbeat'/'Well ... All Right'. He and the Moondog then had a brief conversation which has survived in audio. It's poignant to listen in on their warm, civilized exchange – so very different from modern pop interviews – and realize how desperately close each now was to the edge of the abyss:

FREED: ... What have you been doing and where have you
          been?
BUDDY: Well, we haven't been working all summer, Alan. [He
          had, of course] We've been kinda loafing and taking it
          easy and running around some. Enjoying what we hadn't
          enjoyed for the whole year previous with all the work.
FREED: Boy, you worked hard that year, Buddy.
BUDDY: So, uh we're getting ready to start in with some new
          work now.
FREED: You're going on tour again?
BUDDY: I think so, uh-huh.
FREED: Buddy, we had a lot of fun, we did a lot of flying.
BUDDY: Yeah, we sure did ... We just got into town the other
          day in Cincinnati, you remember when we landed there
          and, uh, the helicopter had crashed that day we got in
          there?
FREED: I think we rode every kind of airplane imaginable.
BUDDY: (laughing) Uh-huh, we sure did.
FREED: Those DC3s were really something.
BUDDY: [mimics racketing motion] With the oomp-oomp!
FREED: Oh boy, without the seatbelts we'd have been right
          through the top, that's for sure.
BUDDY: We sure would.
FREED: Buddy, we've had a lot of fun together, and I hope we're
          going to have a lot of fun together in the future ...

The huge mixed-race rock 'n' roll roadshows of the past two
years were similarly on the decline, and those that survived
reflected the shrinking market and the prissy shape of things to
come. The tour Buddy mentioned to Alan Freed was a GAC
presentation lasting only sixteen days instead of the customary
three months, and billed with overt revisionism as 'The Biggest
Show of Stars for 1958 – Fall Edition'. With Buddy and the

Crickets in the 'white' section of the programme were Frankie Avalon, Dion and the Belmonts, Bobby Darin, Jimmy Clanton and Jack Scott, a bland and lightweight crew to be pitted against seasoned black performers like Clyde McPhatter, Bobby Freeman and the Coasters. After rehearsals at New York's Nola Studios, the show opened on 3 October in Worcester, Massachusetts, moving on, with the tour-planner's usual illogicality, to one-nighters in Connecticut; Ontario and Quebec, Canada; Indiana; Ohio; Pennsylvania; New York state; Virginia and North Carolina.

Gone, never to return, was the Crickets' simple, self-sufficient stage line-up of Joe B. Mauldin on bass fiddle, J. I. Allison on drums and Buddy on vocals and rhythm-lead guitar. To match the competition of Frankie Avalon and Co., a more ambitious presentation was felt to be needed. So big, genial Tommy Allsup, the new lead guitar voice of 'Heartbeat' and 'It's So Easy', was invited to make his second tour as an extra Cricket. Into the live line-up, too, came the Roses, the male vocal trio whose churchy 'Ba-ba-ba's' and 'Fa la la la's' Norman Petty had overdubbed on tracks like 'Think It Over' and 'It's So Easy'. The Roses' leader, Robert Linville, remembers the lavishness and care with which Buddy chose stage outfits at Alfred Norton for him and his two colleagues, David Bigham and Ray Rush: light grey blazers, black slacks, black velour waistcoats, grey and black striped ties.

The final unprecedented addition was that of a wife. Buddy would not think of making the tour without Maria Elena and, tenaciously pursuing the double honeymoon idea, urged J.I. to bring Peggy Sue along also. But Peggy Sue – wisely as it turned out – preferred to stay in Lubbock, flying up to join them when they returned to New York. Clearly it was impracticable for Maria Elena to travel on the bus, so she and Buddy followed behind in Buddy's third new car of that year, a taupe (grey-brown) Cadillac 60 Special sedan. J.I., Joe B., and Tommy also travelled separately in their communally owned DeSoto station-wagon.

To preserve the illusion of Buddy's bachelorhood, Maria Elena was introduced to people as the Crickets' 'secretary'. If she had ever cherished any illusions about the glamour of rock 'n' roll tours, these were quickly shattered. 'There were no roadies to do the work in those days. We had to carry all the luggage ourselves, set up and dismantle the equipment. I had to wash shirts ... underwear. The food was terrible. Buddy had told me about his gastric problem, that a doctor in Lubbock had told him his stomach-lining was prone to ulceration. I'm sure a lot of that came from the awful greasy food he had to eat on those tours.'

As usual on a tour of one-nighters, the acts were paid individually by the promoter at each venue. Maria Elena took over the job of collecting the money, a role for which her forthright, businesslike nature well suited her. The one or two occasions when a local showman tried to short-change Buddy revealed his doll-like Puerto Rican bride to be a woman of formidable temper. Following now standard procedure, the earnings were not sent back to Clovis but kept – by Maria Elena – in a plaid holdall known as the 'Scotch bag' and doled out to the others in regular instalments. The discovery that the bag also contained a .22 pistol did not disconcert Maria Elena. 'With all money in cash, it was necessary for security. A lot of the performers in those days used to carry guns.'

One awkward consequence of her sheltered Manhattan upbringing was that Maria Elena had never learned to drive. Buddy therefore had to pilot their Cadillac the hundreds of miles that frequently lay between engagements as well as performing to the limit every night. Towards the end of the tour, even his usual rock-like steadiness behind the wheel began to falter. Traversing New Jersey on 20 October, he was flagged down by a police patrol and accused of speeding. 'Buddy was tired and on edge,' Maria Elena remembers. 'He didn't think he had been speeding and he got mad, so the police took him off to the station . . . just left me in the car at the side of the road. When they realized who he was, they brought him straight back again.

'One time when we were on our way to a concert, he was so exhausted that he could hardly keep his eyes open. But we couldn't stop, we *had* to be there at a certain time, so Buddy told me I'd have to drive, even though I'd never driven a car in my life before. He said, "It's real easy, you just point the car down the highway and hold the wheel steady . . ." To make it even more scary it was at night . . . there were huge trucks coming up behind us all the time. Buddy told me, "If the trucks honk their horns, don't worry, if they want to pass you, let them pass you." He let me do it for a few minutes to be sure I was all right, and showed me on the map where we had to make a turn-off, so that I'd know in time to wake him up. Then the poor soul went to sleep in the back, and I kept that car straight on . . . straight on. I found out very quickly that when you have to do something, you do it.'

Travelling separately in the Cadillac with his wife isolated Buddy from J.I. and Joe B. and heightened their feeling that Maria Elena was all he cared about now, and they had been relegated from blood brothers to mere subordinates. Although also now a married man, J.I. was still only eighteen, and primarily interested in having fun, if not with Buddy then with his willing follower Joe B. Since groupies and drugs still were almost non-existent pleasures of 'the road', having fun meant one thing only. 'We'd sometimes be drunk in the morning,' J.I. has since admitted, 'and stay drunk all day.' This slackness and unpro-fessionalism infuriated Buddy; there was an angry scene and the two miscreants, genuinely sorry, promised to 'tighten up a little bit'.

In New York they were joined by Peggy Sue, fresh from

Lubbock, full of the thrill of seeing Carnegie Hall for the first time, and convinced that Buddy and the Crickets would appear on its hallowed stage before long. With the masculine condescension of that era, a day's shopping was arranged for the two Cricket wives. Peggy Sue remembers that Maria Elena spent much of it complaining to her about J.I.'s behaviour on the tour. That evening the Hollys and the Allisons were to have dinner at Mama Leone's Italian restaurant, one of Buddy's favourites, and then attend a movie première. The outing went badly for Peggy Sue: at Mama Leone's she broke the clasp of a new evening purse she'd bought only that day. Then, as they walked to the movie theatre, she caught one of her stiletto heels in a subway grating and snapped it off. 'I was terribly embarrassed – I wanted to run straight back to our hotel. Jerry and Maria Elena were both really irritated with me for making such a fool of myself, but Buddy just laughed and said it didn't matter and I certainly wasn't going to miss the première. So I walked into the theatre in my stockinged feet. I can't remember now which movie we saw, except that it had an elephant in it.'

Back in the autumn of 1957, when rock 'n' roll still swept all before it, a Canadian disc jockey named Red Robinson had put a prophetic question to the jukebox sensation of the hour. 'Buddy, if trends change, would you hop on the trend ... or would you just give up?'

'I'd hop on the trend,' Buddy replied without a second's hesitation.

'You would?'

'Uh huh. Because I'd prefer singing something a little bit more quieter, anyhow.'

Now, a year later, one could say he was about to 'hop on the trend' for softer music if that would restore him to the charts. But Buddy, being Buddy, still could not help staying streets ahead of the pack.

The idea had originally come from Norman Petty, almost four months earlier. Long anticipating the decline of rock 'n' roll, Elvis Presley, Pat Boone and many others had hedged their bets by recording slow ballads that verged on the mainstream. But even Elvis had never dared to mix his technique with the archetypal 'easy listening' sound of a string orchestra. When Petty suggested that Buddy might be the first to make this radical leap into convention, he refused to entertain the idea at first, but came round to it during the summer, especially after hearing that, in common with other major record labels, Decca was cutting down on rock 'n' roll output. One day just before their relationship began to nosedive, as they sat together in an airport lounge, Buddy turned to Petty with a grin and said, 'Norm . . . when are you going to arrange my string-session?'

Dick Jacobs, Coral-Brunswick's new head of A & R – and a successful orchestra-leader in his own right – had proved only too willing to try Buddy in this new medium. The session finally took place on 21 October at Decca's Pythian Temple studios with Jacobs presiding as both producer and conductor. As a consolation prize to Norman Petty for being thus comprehensively supplanted, one of the three songs to be recorded was his composition 'Moondreams', which Buddy had demo'd with the Petty Trio in Clovis a year and a half earlier. The other two were 'Raining In My Heart' by the Everly Brothers' songwriters Boudleaux and Felice Bryant, and yet another so-called Buddy Holly–Norman Petty joint effort, 'True Love Ways'.

A couple of hours before the session was due to start Buddy burst into Dick Jacobs's office carrying his guitar-case and waving a piece of paper. 'He told me it was a new song that Paul Anka had just written specially for him, called "It Doesn't Matter Anymore", and it had to be in the session,' Jacobs recalled afterwards. 'I said, "OK," and called my copyist in and we wrote the lead sheets from Buddy's version of the song on his guitar. Because time was so short, we could only do the very simplest arrangement, with pizzicato parts for the violins.'

When Buddy walked on to the studio floor promptly at 7.30 that evening, he found Jacobs and Coral had done him proud. Awaiting him was an eighteen-piece orchestra including eight violins, two violas, two 'cellos and a harp. As well as string players recruited from the New York Symphony Orchestra and the NBC Television's house orchestra, there were top session-men like guitarist Al Caiola and Abraham 'Boomie' Richmond, formerly of the Benny Goodman band, on tenor saxophone. It was also to be the first time Buddy had ever been recorded in the new, high-status medium of 'stereo'.

Watching the proceedings, their mutual antagonisms temporarily on hold, were Maria Elena Holly, J.I. and Peggy Sue Allison, Joe B. Mauldin, Norman and Vi Petty and Jo Harper, from Peer-Southern Music. At the last moment Paul Anka joined them, curious to see what would happen to the song which had been snatched out of his hands so unceremoniously earlier that day.

Having never met a rock 'n' roller before, let alone been asked to perform with one, the string-players from the New York Symphony were more than a little cynical and supercilious about the task in hand. Dick Jacobs remembered afterwards that Buddy faced them at a stand-microphone, like the vocalist with some old-time swing orchestra, but Peggy Sue is sure that he sang with headphones on inside an isolation booth. 'I was sitting right beside it. I could see Buddy's face through the glass. He seemed tense at first. But after a moment, I saw him smile at me.'

The superciliousness of the orchestra vanished when the rock 'n' roller performed 'It Doesn't Matter Anymore' perfectly in his very first take. Although from the same bravura pen that had written 'Diana', it turned out to be pure Buddy; a lament for lost summer love, mixing anguish and playfulness in its exclamations of 'Buy-bee!', 'Golly-gee!' and 'Whoops-a-daisy!', its bridge ending with a long downhill 'ou' vowel that cried out to be hiccuped in half. Buddy adjusted his wide-awake Texan voice to the medium of written notes and gliding bows as if he'd worked in it all his life, instinctively toning down his vocal acrobatics to meld with the Straussy lilt of the plucked violins and the tiffling snare-drum. As the last notes died away, there was very nearly a burst of applause. Jacobs remarked that if they went on like this, the session could wrap inside an hour.

In the event, it took only three and a half hours to complete the three remaining tracks, 'Raining In My Heart', 'Moondreams' and 'True Love Ways'. All were slow, reflective ballads, without a hint of beat, and Buddy sang them completely 'straight', banishing all clicks and hiccups from his voice, drawing only on its warmth, its conviction, its gentleness, its ability to address the listener personally and privately.

Everyone at Pythian Temple that day agreed Buddy's treatment of Boudleaux and Felice Bryant's 'Raining In My Heart' to be the high-spot of the session. Only his mother, Ella, picked 'True Love Ways' as the stand-out track, though even she did not dream what an imperishable standard it would become. Written ostensibly for and about Maria Elena, its stupendous charm lies in its mixture of intimacy and universality. While speaking directly and uniquely to Buddy's young wife, and looking forward to the life ahead of them both, it is also a message to 'all those who really care', as ever counselling patience, hope and trust in the benignity of Fate.

On 28 October, Buddy appeared on Dick Clark's *American Bandstand* television show, lip-synching his new 'own-name' single, 'Heartbeat'. J. I. Allison and Joe B. Mauldin then joined him to mime the Crickets' current single, 'It's So Easy'. Although they did not know it at the time, this was to be their last performance together.

Even the patient and ever-optimistic Buddy had finally reached the end of his tether with Norman Petty. He was tired of Petty's failures as a manager – revealed in ever starker detail by living in New York and seeing how the careers of rival artistes were run. He was tired of Petty's excuses for not paying him the money he had coming in royalties from Coral-Brunswick. Above all, he was tired of Petty's calculated snubs to Maria Elena, and the whispering campaign that went on behind her back. By the time of the 'string-session' – ironically a time when Clovis Man must have felt his prestige once more in the ascendant – Buddy's mind was made up. He would fire Petty as his manager and producer, and demand the release of the royalities (he still had no idea how much) which had supposedly been accumulating for more than a year in the Buddy Holly and the Crickets bank account.

Having that sizeable lump sum of cash behind him was essential to the detailed game-plan Buddy had worked out. It would allow him to stop dissipating his time and energy on concert tours and instead stay put in New York with Maria Elena, exploring new directions in his music with Dick Jacobs, establishing his profile with the press and media, finding and developing talent for his Prism organization and using the Big Apple's matchless creative resources to get himself back into the charts.

This did not mean the end of the Crickets, however. When Buddy first revealed his intentions to J.I. and Joe B., he made it clear that he wanted the three of them to continue recording and performing together. J.I. and Joe B. by now fully shared his resentment at the withholding of their royalties and were in just as rebellious a mood with 'Papa Norman'. They enthusiastically accepted Buddy's proposal that they should confront Petty as a group, force him to release their money, then fire him by unanimous vote and take off for New York together.

The undoing of this strategy was foreshadowed in a jokey exchange with Dick Clark on *American Bandstand*:

CLARK: Are you going back to Lubbock, Texas or where's home...?

JOE B: Well, home is Lubbock, Texas and I'll be going back just as soon as I can get a plane out of New York.

CLARK: Does that hold true of everybody, Buddy?

BUDDY: No, I've got my car up here, Dick, and I'm gonna have to take about a three-day journey getting there...

As things turned out, both J.I. and Joe B. made the journey back to Lubbock by air, arriving several days in advance of Buddy. From long habit the two drifted over to Clovis and, during conversation with Petty, news of the impending show-down leaked out. No doubt they had felt some misgivings about the role they would play in Buddy's new life, and the familiar sights and scents of Clovis Man's West Seventh Street cavern – Vi in her flower garden with Speedy the chihuahua, Norma Jean at her reception desk, the almost hypnotic fragrance of their producer's British Sterling aftershave lotion – must have eroded their resolution still further.

At all events it took Petty only a very short time to talk them out of their pact with Buddy and convince them they should remain with him. He told them they'd hate New York; that hometown boys like themselves would never 'fit in' to the music scene there; that, in weeks rather than months, they'd come running home with their tails between their legs. If they continued to be guided by Papa Norman, on the other hand, they could still have a career as the Crickets without Buddy, as good or even better than before. As J. I. Allison remembered afterwards, he spiked these inducements with a subtle threat, reminding them that he still controlled their money and that, if they insisted on following Buddy, 'there was no telling what might happen'.

When Buddy arrived at his parents' home with Maria Elena on 2 November, after their three-day car journey, he was greeted by the news that J.I. and Joe B. had gone to Clovis without him and were now safely in Norman Petty's pocket. His mother later told his brother Larry of his furious reaction. 'She said Buddy stormed out of the house, got into his car and went straight over to have it out with Norman then and there. She said he was mad enough to fight.'

Maria Elena went along, too, determined this time not to tolerate Petty's silky condescension towards her. 'Buddy walked into the office and told Norman they had to talk. Norman said, "OK, we'll talk," then he looked at me and said, "You go out and visit with Vi while Buddy and I talk business." I told him, "Whatever you have to say to Buddy, you say in front of me." And Buddy said the same thing.'

Petty's agreement to manage Buddy and the Crickets, in late 1957, had been a purely verbal one and, more than a year on – thanks to Clovis Man's lackadaisical business methods – remained still unratified by any kind of formal contract. Buddy thus was spared the experience of young pop stars in later eras, for whom the price of freeing themselves from their managers would often be an arm and a leg. He could simply say, 'You're fired,' and walk away. Petty, indeed, offered surprisingly little resistance to losing his 'diamond in the rough', merely shrugging and saying that if that was what Buddy really wanted, so be it.

Other than recording agreements, all that existed on paper was Buddy's writer's contract with Petty's publishing company, NOR VA JAK, which had grown wealthy both from publishing Buddy Holly songs and from Petty's continuous appropriation of writers' credits. 'Peggy Sue', Buddy's great solo *tour de force*, did not even have his name on it as joint composer, but had ended up credited to Petty and J. I. Allison. When Petty refused to change the billing, Buddy had been forced to lodge a formal claim with Broadcast Music International, the agency which collected airplay royalties on songwriters' behalf. According to Larry Holley, the long-agreed trade-off for allowing Petty's name to go on so many songs was that Buddy would receive a half-share in NOR VA JAK. When Petty was reminded about this at their confrontation on 3 November, he pretended total amnesia on the subject. But – apparently content with his piece of 'That'll Be The Day', 'Oh Boy', 'Not Fade Away', 'True Love Ways' and all the others – he agreed to cancel Buddy's writer's contract.

What he flatly refused to do was pay over the accumulated royalties from the Buddy Holly and the Crickets bank account which Buddy was depending on to finance his solo career in New York. As always Petty claimed to have scrupulous fairness and correctness on his side. He said that no money could be released to Buddy until a full accounting had been carried out and J.I.'s and Joe B.'s proportionate share of the recording and publishing income had been calculated. Even when Petty's desk-top Bible obliquely entered the argument, he remained implacable. 'Buddy needed money to tithe our church, too, and he told Norman that,' Larry Holley says. 'But Norman told him, "Don't worry, I'll tithe *my* church instead."'

By the end of the meeting, Buddy was extremely angry and even usually composed and ice-cool Clovis Man had begun to show signs of passion. His parting-shot, allegedly, was words to the effect: 'You'll starve to death before you see a penny of those royalties!' Petty himself, to the end of his days, vehemently denied ever having said such a thing. Possibly he did not mean it as the vindictive threat it appears, but as a warning that Buddy's new solo career would end in disaster. At all events, both Maria Elena Holly, who was there, and Buddy's brother Larry, who saw him immediately afterwards, corroborate the phrasing.

Buddy returned from Clovis more upset and depressed than

his wife, even his family, had ever seen him. He still couldn't believe that, despite the strategy they'd agreed so carefully together, J.I. and Joe B. could have let themselves be suborned, so giving Petty a cast-iron excuse to continue withholding the money. He was convinced that once he got hold of J.I. and Joe B. and talked to them himself, the whole thing might still turn out to be a ghastly misunderstanding.

'Buddy went straight to Jerry and said, "What is this?"' Maria Elena remembers. 'Jerry said that he and Joe B. didn't want to come to New York because they wouldn't fit in there. But the real reason was that Norman had told them if they went with Buddy I would be the one deciding everything, and they'd have no say-so. Norman convinced them that they didn't need Buddy … that they were the real nitty-gritty of the Crickets. He'd bamboozled those two boys into doing what they did. Buddy tried to convince Jerry that Norman wasn't looking out for their interests, only his own. But, of course, they didn't listen. Norman was a good talker. He filled their heads with so many ugly things that the boys got scared.

'Buddy was devastated. He could not believe Jerry would let himself be talked into something like that. The two of them had been like brothers. And he knew that Norman was lying to these kids – that on their own they weren't going to do anything out there, and they were just being used to try to harm Buddy. When we came back to the house that night, Buddy cried. He really cried his eyes out.'

He made one last attempt with J.I. a couple of days later when they bumped into each other at a café on Main Street, Clovis. Peggy Sue, who was sitting with her husband, well remembers the painful encounter. 'Buddy asked Jerry if he was really sure about what he was doing. Jerry said that, as far as he could tell at that moment, he was. Buddy said, "The person I really worry about in all this is Joe B." "Don't worry," Jerry told him. "I'll take care of Joe B."'

With typical magnanimity, Buddy agreed to let J.I. and Joe B. continue to perform and record on Brunswick as the Crickets while he worked under his own name only on Coral. 'He came to me and said, "They want to go on with the name, what do you think?" Maria Elena remembers. 'I told him, "Sure, let them have it. You don't need it. You can make it on your own."'

Personal appeals to Petty having failed, Buddy's only recourse was to see a lawyer. Back in New York, his new aunt-in-law, Provi Garcia, arranged a consultation with Peer-Southern Music's legal advisers, but as Peer-Southern royalties figured in the dispute, their lawyers could not represent Buddy. It so happened that his great friends the Everly Brothers were already involved in legal proceedings, for not dissimilar grievances, against their manager, Wesley Rose. Don and Phil recommended Buddy to their attorney, Harold Orenstein, a specialist in the often tortuous business and personal affairs of famous musicians, whose client-roster also included Pat Boone, Ray Charles, Benny Goodman and Errol Garner (and who, in later years, would engineer a costly 'divorce' between the Rolling Stones and that ultimate manager of the next generation, Allen Klein).

On 5 November, Coral released what Buddy intended to be his last 'own-name' product from the Norman Petty studios, 'Heartbeat' coupled with the acoustic, future-gazing 'Well ... All Right'. For this magnificent double A-side, as we should nowadays call it, the reception was only marginally warmer than it had been for the last Crickets release, 'It's So Easy'. 'Heartbeat'/'Well ... All Right' did at least make the US Top 100, but thereafter could manage only a laborious ascent to number 83. In Britain, where Top 20 placing was all that counted, it stayed firmly shut out in the cold at number 30.

To make matters worse, Buddy's three closest friends in the business seemed to be doing as well as before, or even better, in the post-rock 'n' roll charts. The Everly Brothers' hits had continued through the summer with 'Bird Dog' and 'Devoted

To You'; that December they were to have a US number 2 with the inaptly-titled 'Problems'. Eddie Cochran had ceased copying Elvis and hit on the mixture of wry social comment and Buddy-simple acoustic chord sequences that produced his September million-seller, 'Summertime Blues'. Just what was it that Eddie, Don and Phil knew but he didn't?

On 24 November Buddy's lawyer, Harold Orenstein, wrote to Norman Petty, very clearly under instruction from his new young client not to strike too hostile or combative an opening note:

Re: Buddy Holly

Dear Mr Petty
As Mr Holly has undoubtedly told you, he has retained me generally to act as his counsel in all matters affecting his activities as a musician and composer.

So that I may properly advise Mr Holly, I will need all agreements, books, records and tax returns affecting his business. I understand that you have this material and will appreciate your sending it to me.

Mr Holly has further asked me to advise you that he wishes immediately to cancel the power of attorney which he has given to you.

I would particularly appreciate your sending me all copyright registration certificates, publication agreements, mechanical licenses, agreements between Mr Holly and any co-author of any song in the writing of which he collaborated, agreements relating to Mr Holly's personal appearances and agreements, if any, between Mr Holly and the other members of 'The Crickets' or yourself. We should also like at the earliest possible moment a complete statement of account with respect to any moneys which you have received on behalf of Mr Holly and a check to Mr

Holly's order for the full balance of any moneys due to him.
Mr Holly is about to engage in certain business enterprises
in which he will need any available funds.

Since we are now nearing the end of the year, you will
understand that there is some urgency in connection with
my request.

Mr Holly asked me to send you his personal regards
when I wrote to you and I add my own.

Petty replied on November 28:

Dear Mr Orenstein:
Congratulations to you as you take over the affairs of
BUDDY HOLLY. He is an outstanding talent and since he is
so confident in your abilities . . . the two of you should
enjoy great success.

Please be advised that books and tax records are being
prepared now for BUDDY HOLLY & THE CRICKETS and
as soon as the audit is complete . . . as I informed Buddy
when he was in Lubbock . . . the complete information
concerning all money and all monies due Buddy will be
forwarded to you.

As to other agreements . . . there were no written ones
between Buddy and me nor between Buddy and the
Crickets . . . only verbal agreements in which all of the boys
came to a mutual understanding. Bookings . . . you will find
a complete list of such bookings at General Artists
Corporation there in New York. Buddy has some of the
contracts and some of their TV contracts which I have never
seen . . . so complete information you request can be
obtained only from GAC. Buddy received all money due
him and the boys and made disbursement of same. He sent
some checks here for deposit and we will send you a list of
them. He paid out the remainder of their earnings and

should have knowledge of how the money was spent. I
received some record royalty checks for them and
statements of these royalties will be sent to you at your
expense of duplication and upon your request. However,
you may obtain this information directly from Decca
Records in New York and Buddy can then find out all the
information as to the codes and rates of payment. All
checks which I have received for them have been placed in
an agency account . . . upon advice from the Treasury
Department and our accounting firm. Buddy will be paid
his share just as soon as the above-mentioned audit is
complete. As to agreements with Buddy as a writer . . . all
such agreements are in New York, retained by MELODY
LANE PUBLICATIONS in our behalf. You may obtain this
information directly from them since they keep all contracts
and records for our firm.

I trust this information will be to your satisfaction. If I
can be of further assistance, just let me know.

One can imagine Buddy's shock when his lawyer showed
him this letter. For months he had supposed, and been led to
believe, that his and the Cricket's income had been flowing into
an account under their name; that Petty's hold over their money
was simply by power of attorney and that termination of that
power would make the funds accessible to them. But here was
the truth at long, long last, if not yet fully spelt out: their
recording royalties had not been banked under their name but
under Petty's. The 'agency account', alluded to with such delight-
ful vagueness, was in fact one of Clovis Man's warren of one-man
corporations, the Norman Petty Agency Inc. Even without the
excuse of conducting a full audit of Buddy and the Crickets'
earnings, Petty could sit on the money for as long as he liked.

To Maria Elena, when Buddy showed it to her, the letter
bore out everything she had suspected both about Petty's

financial duplicity and the shambolic, semi-detached way he had managed the second hottest act in rock 'n' roll. Yet Buddy, the ever optimistic, continued to hope that the dispute would be resolved quickly and amicably, that his back-royalties would come through by Christmas – even that, once these financial arguments were disposed of, he and Petty would be able to resume some kind of limited artistic partnership. Petty was still a codirector of Buddy's Prism Record Company, along with Ray Rush of the Roses. On December 3, Rush dropped out of the company and was repaid his $3,500 stake. But Buddy still regarded Petty as future general manager of the studio complex he planned to build for Prism in Lubbock.

All his hopes were now concentrated on the first release from his 21 October orchestral session, 'It Doesn't Matter Anymore' and 'Raining In My Heart'. With 'Heartbeat'/'Well ... All Right' still getting radio airplay, a new Buddy Holly solo single clearly could not be launched until early in the new year, 1959. Meanwhile, as his lawyer locked horns with Clovis Man, he settled down with Maria Elena to their new life among the Greenwich Village beatniks.

Like that of a rock 'n' roll star, life in the Village went on around the clock. Five minutes' walk from their apartment at the Brevoort took Buddy and Maria Elena into its raffish, restless heart. The two would spend hours wandering streets that remained crowded long after midnight, then sit over espresso coffee into the small hours at intellectual hangouts like the Bitter End and Café Bizarre. 'Buddy loved those places ... the strange clothes the people wore, the poetry-readings, the way they talked to one another,' Maria Elena remembers. 'And he loved the freedom, the way everyone was allowed to do their thing. Late at night, if we couldn't sleep, we'd get up and go out in our pyjamas. We'd roll them up so that no one could see them under our coats.'

Most of all he loved the music that drifted enticingly from

every other doorway – not only blues and folk joints but 'serious' jazz venues like the Village Gate and the Blue Note where modern colossi such as Thelonious Monk, John Coltrane and Cannonball Adderley wove their complex tapestries with ferocious cool, buttoned into the sternest of Ivy League suits. The Hollys' favourite haunts were the Village Vanguard, Johnny Johnson's and Café Madrid, where there was live flamenco guitar music. 'Buddy was curious about everything,' Maria Elena says. 'He'd sit up there with the musicians, asking them, "How do you do that?" After that he decided he wanted to learn to play finger-style flamenco guitar, so we found a neighbour of my aunt's who could give him lessons.'

Despite the smallness of their $1,000-per-month apartment, the newlyweds found they could co-exist happily and comfortably. In the centre of the living-room Buddy had set up the Ampex tape-recorder he'd bought second-hand from Norman Petty. Pending the establishment of his Prism company, he was using the Ampex to tape rough versions of the several new songs he'd written in New York. Maria Elena got used to hearing him jump out of bed, rush into the living-room and pick up his guitar to try out the further brand-new ideas which had galvanized him into wakefulness. Aunt Provi, who lived on 10th Street, only a block away, had a piano at her apartment and Buddy would often go round and use it during the hours when she was out at work.

The list of things he planned to do, when his money finally came from Petty, grew longer and still longer. In common with a prescient few, he recognized that the future of pop music lay as much with albums as with singles, and was determined to be out there in the 33 rpm vanguard. As soon as he'd become proficient on flamenco guitar, he wanted to make an album of Latin-American songs, symbolizing his love for Maria Elena and commitment to her culture. At various times that winter, he talked of making a jazz album, a Cajun album, even an album of classical pieces.

After the happy experience of the King Curtis sessions, he was on fire with eagerness to build more such bridges between white rock 'n' roll and black soul. His dream was to make an album with Ray Charles, the only black singer equally at home in blues, rock 'n' roll, ballads or country. The concept of such a 'duet' album – let alone one co-starring a white and a black performer – was unheard of at that time. In the eighties and nineties, when Paul McCartney recorded 'The Girl Is Mine' with Michael Jackson, Elton John duetted with Dionne Warwick and Stevie Wonder played harmonica behind the Eurythmics, Maria Elena was ruefully to remember Buddy's idea all those years before. 'While we were in LA, we even went round to Ray Charles's house to try to see him, but his people told us he was away on tour. Buddy never got another chance to see him.'

For all this sophisticated big city life, Buddy kept to the simple and absolute religious beliefs with which he had been raised. Indeed, dwelling among the Village's modish atheists, existentialists and nihilists brought a powerful resurgence in his spiritual motivation. It troubled him that two years as a rock 'n' roll headliner had not enabled him to 'do God's work' in accordance with his boyhood promise to the Tabernacle Baptist Church. High on his list of pressing projects was one intended to reaffirm his personal faith as well as carry him into yet another sphere from which white musicians were traditionally excluded. He planned an album of gospel music, on to which he hoped to inveigle the greatest of all female gospel singers, Mahalia Jackson.

Maria Elena was the sounding-board for all his ideas, and an invariably positive force. To her, Buddy confessed his long-cherished dream of following Elvis Presley and Eddie Cochran into the movies – but 'real' movies with real acting, not just Alan Freed-style rock exploitation flicks. Long hours in coffee-house candlelight were spent discussing his two great screen idols, James Dean and the (occasionally bespectacled) Anthony Perkins. 'Buddy talked a lot about writing music-scores for movies, too,' Maria Elena remembers. 'And he told me how much he admired Anthony Perkins and wanted to be like him. I said "You want to be like Anthony Perkins, then get out there, get involved..."'

So, with her encouragement, Buddy registered for classes at Lee Strasberg's Actors' Studio, where Dean and Marlon Brando had studied the Method technique. In preparation for possible TV 'specials' in the future, he also decided to take formal dancing lessons. Maria Elena, who'd once hoped to be a professional dancer, offered to teach him and choreograph some movements for him to use onstage. 'We thought we could begin, just the two of us, in the apartment. I said, "I'm going to teach you how to dance Latino music." Buddy said, "I want to learn how to do the rumba."'

His most pressing need was for a new manager to guide him not only through an uncertain new year but also into the uncharted waters of a fast-approaching new decade. At different times, he thought of Don Costa, who'd masterminded Paul Anka's huge success; of Irving Feld, who'd staged those mammoth touring roadshows for the General Artists Corporation; even of Murray Deutch of Peer-Southern Music, a staunch friend and adviser to him and the Crickets from the very beginning. Flattered though Deutch was by Buddy's offer, he declined it. 'I couldn't think of a better way to spoil our good relationship. I told him, "Buddy, I don't want to be your mother, your father, your banker, your rabbi..."'

Meantime, he and Maria Elena did the job between them, the best way they were able. One great consolation for the fall-off in record sales was the sizeable fan-mail he still received, forwarded to the Brevoort from Clovis or Coral Records. His converts in Europe had learned about his 'going solo' from the Crickets, and many now wrote with evident dismay to ask if the parting was permanent. Buddy replied to all the letters personally, saying he hoped to get back with the Crickets at some future date, writing a neat 'Ans' on each envelope as he dealt with it. Another pressing task on his list was the organization of a fan-club to establish proper relations with these thousands of intimate strangers.

In the absence of professional advice, he continued to work on his image with only his own instinctive good taste as a guide. He had recently acquired a new pair of glasses, with modishly blunt-cut black plastic Faiosa frames, found for him in Mexico by his ever-attentive Lubbock optician, Dr J. D. Armistead. Dr Armistead also brought him back a second pair, of identical design but in dark brown tortoiseshell. Buddy had lenses fitted to the black pair by New York opticians Courmetts & Gaul and asked his oculist there, Dr Stanger, to keep the tortoiseshell pair on file for him.

The new glasses were ready in time for his first publicity photographs as a solo performer. Appalled by the cheapness and low standard of his pictures with the Crickets, Maria Elena sent him to Bruno, then New York's top show-business photographer. Bruno's flattering lens – helped by an unaccustomed layer of make-up – softened the angularity of Buddy's face, removed all taint of myopia from the eyes inside the ultra-contemporary squared black frames and toned down his usual happy grin to a pensive, almost enigmatic smile. For some shots, he exchanged his pin-collar shirt and herringbone jacket for a chunky ribbed sweater after the style of Greenwich Village cognoscenti. The session went so well that he arranged with Bruno to return for a second one: another eager appointment destined never to be kept.

Perhaps the most sadly ironic feature of these final months was the interest which Buddy suddenly developed in light aircraft. His brother Larry had been taking flying lessons down in Lubbock and was about to qualify as a pilot. As always, anything Larry did was an irresistible spur to Buddy. On 5 November, just before returning to New York, he'd had his first (and, it would prove, last) flying lesson with the Champs Aviation Service at Lubbock airport. The aircraft used was a Cessna 175, wing-registration N9274B. Larry sat in on the lesson, during which Buddy's instructor deliberately stalled the Cessna's engine and let it drop sickeningly to earth for a few seconds before calmly levelling it out again. 'Afterwards, I told Buddy he'd had a thirty-minute lesson,' Larry remembers. '"Man," he said, "That stall seemed to last for thirty minutes!"'

Another of Buddy's schemes – once he had his money – was to buy his own aircraft and pilot himself across country from one concert appearance to the next. But this was something he did not mention to his wife. Maria Elena had been terrified of small planes since her childhood, when a family friend had flown her mother and herself in one from San Juan, Puerto Rico, to St Thomas in the Virgin Islands. On a later flight over the same route, the plane had crashed and its pilot and some friends of Maria Elena's parents had all died.

Grounded for the present in Apartment 4H at the Brevoort building, Buddy kept himself as busy as always, drawing, painting and refining blueprints he'd made for the house and recording studio that were to be Prism's Lubbock headquarters. He also designed furniture for the apartment, notably a cabinet for his stereo equipment which was then made up in highly modish white Formica.

Maria Elena, by her own admission, was not much of a cook, but fortunately cheap restaurants abounded in their neighbourhood. Buddy enjoyed cooking – simple southern-style things like fried chicken, steaks and potatoes – and, to show him how much she loved him, Maria Elena took an occasional stab at it. 'One of Buddy's favourite things to eat was fried okra. I'd never even seen fried okra before I met him, but I thought I'd make some for dinner. I bought the okra, but I went ahead and boiled it first, and it came out horrible. I told Buddy, "I made fried okra for you but it didn't come into pieces, it just came into a big lump. I don't know what I did wrong." The minute he saw it he laughed and said, "I know what you did wrong."'

With his new taupe Cadillac sedan and immaculate Alfred Norton clothes, his neighbours at the Brevoort took him to be as affluent as anyone in the building. And, indeed, Buddy continued to spend money as if all accounts could still be forwarded directly to Papa Norman. Early in December, little dreaming how fast time was now running out, he treated himself to a new wristwatch, an Omega set with diamonds and engraved with his name and the date. One evening, as he and Maria Elena were leaving a club with Phil Everly, he handed Phil a $100 bill to pay a check of about $8. Mistaking the bill for a $10 one in the Stygian gloom, Phil airily told the waiter to keep the change. 'But when Buddy realized what had happened, he just laughed,' Phil remembers.

In fact, his financial situation was growing desperate. Petty continued to withhold his record-royalties, claiming that J. I. Allison's and Joe B. Mauldin's share of the payout still had not been calculated. The lump sum in publishing royalties he had received at the time of his wedding had long since evaporated, as had his earnings from the October tour. With neither savings nor income for the foreseeable future, and $1,000 per month to find in rent alone, he had been forced to accept financial help from Maria Elena's Aunt Provi. 'We didn't have a red cent,' Maria Elena admits. 'My aunt was paying for everything. Buddy felt bad about taking money from her, but she told him, "Look on it as a loan. You can pay me back when you get your money from Norman."'

As Christmas loomed, and still no cheque materialized from Clovis, Buddy decided there was only one sure, quick way to put some cash into his pocket. He must forget his resolve to stay in New York until he'd cracked the problem of getting a hit record; he must go out on tour again.

His first call was to GAC, the agency which had booked

almost all his domestic tours with the Crickets. Despite his fear that they would be less interested in him as a solo act, GAC quickly came back with what seemed a providential offer. Early in the new year they had scheduled a three-week tour of the same Midwestern territory covered by Buddy and the Crickets' 'Summer Dance Party' the previous July. Although slightly more ambitious than its warm weather namesake had been, this 'Winter Dance Party' still reflected the shrinking scale of rock 'n' roll roadshows. Opening on 23 January 1959, it featured just four other acts: Ritchie Valens, the Big Bopper, Dion and the Belmonts and Frankie Sardo. Still, it was work, and Buddy instantly agreed to join up, agreeing to provide his own backing musicians to replace the Crickets.

Maria Elena says she disliked the sound of the 'Winter Dance Party' from the beginning. 'It was not the right thing for someone like Buddy to be on ... it was a tour for beginners. I pleaded with him not to go. I said, "You don't need to ... this is not a tour for you." He said, "Yes I do, I need to bring some money in. I'm not going to continue to ask your aunt to lend us money. It's time for me to go to work, no matter what it is." We had some kind of argument about that. He said, "It's only a short tour ... and I'll bring some money back." With Buddy, once he made up his mind, that was it.'

Everything was arranged by 14 December when he wrote to his old Lubbock friend Terry Noland, full of plans for writing and recording together: 'I'm leaving on tour January 23rd, so I hope you'll be here before then as I would like to be at your next session. However that tour doesn't last but three weeks and I'll be back in New York by the middle of February.'

As December drew on, an old friend came in to town. Eddie Cochran was appearing in the New York Paramount's Christmas show (from which Buddy this year was a conspicuous absentee) and staying at the Park-Sheraton hotel directly opposite the theatre. Also there was a dark-haired, forceful seventeen-year-old named Sharon Sheeley who'd become a part of the Everly Brothers' West Coast circle during the 'Biggest Show of Stars for 1957' tour, the previous winter. She had gone on to write a hit single, 'Poor Little Fool', for Ricky Nelson and transfer her affections from the married Don Everly to the determinedly unattached Cochran. This coming Christmas season, after almost a year of trying, she would finally win his heart.

Buddy spent an afternoon with Don and Phil Everly and his protégé Lou Giordano 'hanging out' in Cochran's room at the Park-Sheraton. 'From Eddie's room, you could hear the sound of the show going on in the Paramount across the street,' Sharon Sheeley remembers. 'Eddie would stay up there until the end of the act that was on right before him. He had it so perfectly timed, he could walk over to the Paramount, put on his guitar and step out onstage at the exact moment the emcee announced him.'

To both Cochran and Phil Everly, Buddy confided his frustration at the drawn-out wrangle with Norman Petty over his money, and his mystification that neither 'It's So Easy' nor 'Heartbeat' had made the charts. 'He wasn't suicidal about it,' Phil remembers. 'I guess you can say his pride was a little hurt, but he was determined to get back up there again. That's why I was surprised when he told me he was going out on the road again. The last I heard he'd decided to stay in New York and work on his records until one of them went Top 10.'

For a time it looked as if Eddie Cochran might co-star with Buddy on the 'Winter Dance Party'. 'Buddy asked him to go,' Sharon Sheeley remembers. 'And those two always found it hard to say "No" to each other. But then Eddie got an offer to be on the Ed Sullivan show early in February, and Buddy said "Yeah, sure man, that's much more important."'

Most unusually for him, with his nervous stomach, Buddy had a couple of drinks that December afternoon in Eddie

Cochran's hotel-room. Between Phil Everly and him there was a long-standing agreement that if one got 'snockered', the other would make sure he reached home safely. So it was Phil who, later on, found a cab, pushed Buddy's long limbs into it and delivered him back downtown to the Brevoort and Maria Elena. 'He had a professional tape-recorder set up in the middle of his living-room,' Phil remembers. 'He played me about six new cuts that he'd put down, just as demo's, accompanying himself on acoustic guitar. They all sounded great to me.'

These last recordings Buddy would ever make were called simply 'Songs' on the Scotch tape-box that housed them, but are known to posterity as 'the Apartment tapes'. Any other young songwriter set down in the heart of Greenwich Village might well have been carried away by its intellectual pretensions, its cosmopolitanism, its sheer wackiness. But Buddy, wherever he was, knew only how to be Buddy. Sitting alone with his Gibson J200, four floors above the coffee houses and jazz clubs, he created songs that were as simple, open and honest as the West Texas plains had nurtured him. Worried and uncertain as he was about his personal situation, he could still be humorous, philosophical and optimistic in his old familiar way; still adopt the role of adviser, comforter and sympathetic friend when those were the very things which he himself needed the most. Never did he speak more plainly, honestly and intimately than when he believed his audience to be slipping away.

On 3 December he had recorded 'That's What They Say', a song about waiting for love in his usual hopeful, wistful mode, and 'What To Do', a plea for advice 'what to do ... now she doesn't want me. That's what haunts me ...' One of the ideas running through his mind was to make the high school heroine of his biggest solo hit a recurrent character like 'Annie' in the Hank Ballard songs. So, on 5 December, he'd taped 'Peggy Sue Got Married', a sequel as light-hearted as the original had been darkly serious, turning the Allisons' brazen nuptials into a 'rumour from a friend' that the singer is almost too thunder-struck to repeat.

On 8 December, he had recorded 'That Makes It Tough', a lament poised between wailing country and growling blues, whose seeming despair, as ever, yields to irrepressible stoicism. On 14 December he had recorded 'Crying, Waiting, Hoping', another simple but flawless blueprint, instantly comprehensible to all those boys clutching their fourteen-guinea Hofners against their school blazers somewhere beyond the Atlantic. On 17 December he had recorded 'Learning the Game', a fragile ballad that seems to distill the sad experience of a lifetime far longer than twenty-two years:

> *Hearts that are broken and love that's untrue,*
> *These go with learning the game . . .*

The slow, measured strum of his guitar has a quality that is almost hymn-like. His voice sounds far-away and lonely, as if 9th Street and the Village have vanished, and obliterating snow and ice already stretch all around.

'I tell my blues they mustn't show,' he had sung on the B-side of his new orchestral single. And when he took Maria Elena home for Christmas – the last time he would ever see his mother and father or Lubbock – Buddy put on a determinedly upbeat and confident front. As far as his family knew, he was still a star at the pinnacle of success, and with money to burn.

'They brought back a whole mess of Christmas presents with them,' Larry Holley remembers. 'Buddy looked like some kind of New York playboy, 'stead of the little knucklehead we remembered, running round in his jeans.' It seemed to Larry that he now spoke more slowly and carefully, as if to sound less like a Texan, more like a native-born New Yorker. 'His speech seemed like he was taking on the tone of a foreigner just a little bit. Trying to be more of a gentleman type 'stead of a rogue. He was spreadin' it all on a little thick. I think he blew just about all the money he had on coming here to impress us.'

A colour home-move silently commemorates that Christmas Day family gathering in L.O. and Ella's living-room. Children play with their new toys on the carpet; in the foreground, Larry turns round, smiling, with his pipe. Maria Elena, small and vivacious in a dark cocktail dress, hands out expensively wrapped gifts from the pile which Buddy and she have brought from New York. Buddy himself sits away to the left, almost painfully smart in his yellow shirt, black waistcoat and Slim Jim tie, delving into the wrappings on his knees with small-boyish eagerness.

Many of his old Lubbock cronies still found it hard to believe that he was married and that everywhere he went, Maria Elena now had to go too. The more urbane of Buddy's brother musicians, like Sonny Curtis and Terry Noland, had no problems with the new Mrs Holly, nor she with them. But simpler good ol' boys' who had known Buddy since their schooldays were at a loss to understand how he could have fallen for a Puerto Rican four years his senior, and a New Yorker to boot, instead of some nice West Texan girl.

Blissfully happy in his marriage as Buddy declared himself, there were some who felt that Maria Elena's powerful personality somewhat overwhelmed his; that she organized his life altogether too efficiently, damping down his high spirits and spontaneity, forcing him to concentrate on business matters, lawyers' meetings and paperwork. During a trip over to Clovis, the Hollys had lunch with Jimmy Self, who'd been at the Petty studio when Buddy first auditioned there. Remembering the ebullient, impulsive young Texan of those days, Self was disconcerted to see how Buddy even allowed his new wife to choose his food for him, rejecting his favourite Mexican dishes for salad, 'because of his ulcer'. L.O. Holley declared that, on the contrary, Maria Elena had made Buddy his own man instead of the overgrown baby of the Holley family, eternally tied to his mother's apron strings. But there were others who doubted whether, a few months from now, he would find this kind of highly organized domesticity quite so charming.

One of the few old friends who saw Buddy tête-à-tête on that final visit was Jack Neal, his original playing partner on Radio KDAV and the first to whom he'd confided that he wanted the world to remember his name. Jack remembers sitting with Buddy in the Cadillac outside their old teenage haunt, the Nite Owl restaurant, and hearing about his Prism organization and his plan to build a recording-studio in Lubbock. To prove this was more than just a pipe-dream, he had already bought the land where the studio was to be built and contracted with his father for the erection of a 'six-room brick veneer house with four bathrooms'. He also planned to have his own record label – named Taupe after his Cadillac's grey-brown designer shade – for the string of younger protégés he planned to develop along with Lou Giordano. 'He said "Jack, there's a real mess of talent here in West Texas, if only it could get a start. I want to do something to help them along." Then he laughed and said "Maybe I can make YOU a star, too!"'

Despite the continuing deadlock with Norman Petty over his royalties, Buddy also drove to Clovis and called at the Petty studios. His old friend Bob Montgomery was now working there as an engineer, and Buddy wanted Bob to be involved with Prism, possibly running the company's publishing division in New York. An encounter with Petty himself was unavoidable, but – according to Jimmy Self – the two conversed together quite amiably. However, Buddy made no attempt to see J. I. Allison and Joe B. Mauldin, who were both by that time living in Clovis. Mulling over their defection at a distance, his initial forbearing sadness had turned to anger. 'He was mad with J.I. and Joe B. for what they'd done,' a friend remembers. 'He wanted to kick their asses.'

A condition of joining GAC's 'Winter Dance Party' was that Buddy must recruit – and pay – backing musicians to take J.I.'s and Joe B.'s place. As a symbolic break with the recent past, he had decided on a four-man line-up – himself, lead guitar, bass guitar and drums. A lead guitarist, at any rate, was easily found. Tommy Allsup, now working with a band in Odessa, Texas, jumped at the chance to tour with Buddy again. In another Odessa club, playing with Ronnie Smith and the Poor Boys, he found Carl Bunch, a young drummer with a faint look of J. I. Allison as well as almost comparable energy and style. Though Bunch had regular employment with Ronnie Smith's group, Buddy was allowed to borrow him for the three weeks of the tour.

To play bass guitar, he wanted Waylon Jennings, the wolfish young KLLL deejay whose recording début he had sponsored the previous autumn. In vain did Waylon protest that his instrument was guitar and that he didn't own a bass nor have the faintest idea how to play one. Buddy swept all his objections aside, promising to buy a bass guitar for him and tutor him, somehow or other, before 23 January when the 'Winter Dance Party' hit the road.

As on the previous trips home, Buddy's most carefree hours were spent hanging out at KLLL with Waylon, the Corbin Brothers and the other jocks. On one visit, he wrote a new song, 'You're The One', dashing it off in fifteen minutes, then recording it on the station's acetate machine with Waylon and Slim Corbin providing handclaps. Another day, he appeared on a KLLL outside broadcast from the Morris Fruit & Vegetable Store. It was his first live show in Lubbock since becoming famous and he was uncharacteristically nervous about it; he felt guilty about losing touch with the audience that had nurtured him, and remembered only too well the special impatience and hyper-criticality of West Texan music fans. He need not have worried; Lubbock flocked to see him along with the pumpkin and cranberry specials at Morris's, and cheered him as if he'd never been away. Buddy enjoyed the occasion so much that he agreed to let Slim Corbin organize a formal 'homecoming' concert for him the following summer.

Even Larry, who could usually read him like a book, received no inkling of the worries gnawing at him. One afternoon, he came over to Larry's house, the one he'd help to build in the early summer of 1957, while 'That'll Be The Day' was still footslogging up the charts. Seated on the sofa, he played and sang 'Raining In My Heart', which even hard-boiled Larry thought 'one of the purtiest tunes I ever heard.' The show of heedless affluence was kept up to the very end. Before leaving his parents' home on New Year's Eve, never to return, Buddy produced his chequebook and grandly wrote the Tabernacle Baptist Church a cheque for $800.

On 5 January, Coral released 'It Doesn't Matter Anymore' and 'Raining In My Heart'. That same week, Buddy received some New Year tidings which all but wiped his anxiety over his new single from his mind: Maria Elena told him she was pregnant.

So certain was she that she felt it unnecessary to consult a doctor for confirmation. 'If you're a woman and you're pregnant, you *know*! We hadn't been trying to have a baby. It was an accident; it just happened. I didn't want to have a child because it was going to interfere with all the projects we had starting out. But Buddy was elated about it. I told him, "If I have a baby, that means I won't be able to travel around with you like you want me to." But he said, "No, that'll be fine. The baby can come with us."'

They agreed to delay breaking the news to their respective families until Buddy's return from the 'Winter Dance Party' tour. 'He said, "When I get back, we'll go to Lubbock together and tell Mother," Maria Elena remembers. 'I knew already it was going to be a boy. Buddy told me "It'll be just as nice if it's a girl," but I told him, "I know it's a boy."'

The pregnancy promised not to be an easy one; Maria Elena already felt unwell for most of the time, and was suffering extreme bouts of morning sickness. For that reason, allied to shortage of money, they did little to celebrate her twenty-sixth birthday on 7 January. Knowing how much she loved flowers, Buddy brought her an extravagant bouquet. They also opened some champagne, and Maria Elena persuaded him to take a few sips, even though it usually disagreed with his nervous stomach. To her distress, he felt ill afterwards; these days his stomach had more reason than ever to be nervous.

On 8 January, he sat down at his typewriter and wrote Norman Petty the politest and most tactful of reminders about the still unfinished business between them:

> Dear Norman,
> I will appreciate it if at your earliest convenience you will send me the writer's contract that I had with you and the cancellation of same as per our agreement during the month of November.
> I have been waiting for you to send it but as I have not received it yet, no doubt you have forgotten to mail it.
> My lawyer has informed me that he has already gotten in touch with you urging settlement of the matter pertaining to my money. I am sure that you will do your utmost to bring this matter to a satisfactory climax.
> Thanking you in advance, I remain
> Yours truly
> Buddy Holly

But the temperature of the dispute was already rising. True to his promise, Petty had very quickly found 'a new guy' to front the Crickets in Buddy's place. The new discovery was Earl

Sinks, a curly-haired eighteen-year-old from Levelland, Texas, with a faint look of James Cagney and a voice superficially like Buddy's, though with little of its acrobatic variety and none of its inner warmth. Papa Norman was quite satisfied, however, and already had Sinks recording with J. I. Allison and Joe B. Mauldin as if no disruption had ever taken place. On 9 January, he wrote to Isabelle Marks, an executive at Coral Records:

> Dear Miss Marks
> Please be advised that Buddy Holly is no longer a Cricket, as of the first of the year.
> All new recordings by The Crickets will feature the new lead voice. Buddy will be heard only on his Coral recordings.
> Best regards for the new year.

Between Buddy's legal advisers and Petty, letters had been flowing at regular intervals since late November, yet still without unlocking the lump sum in royalties which, as a father-to-be, Buddy would need more urgently than ever. Harold Orenstein had by now handed over the case to one of his associates, George Schiffer, who on 12 January wrote patiently yet again:

> Dear Mr Petty
> Thank you for your letter of January 3, 1959.
> We are somewhat concerned by its contents since we had thought that as Buddy's personal manager you had substantially complete books concerning his income and expenses.
> With respect to his income from personal appearances, Buddy tells me that since last August the bulk of the money received was disposed of. We cannot, of course, evaluate that accounting since we have received no written records concerning it.

With respect to record income, Buddy indicated that his understanding of the division differs substantially from that set forth in your letter. He understands that you are to retain 10 percent as full compensation for your services and that he is to receive 77 and a half percent of the remainder (from which he makes his contribution to his church). It may be, of course, that I misread your letter; I think that this point should in any event be clarified.

We would appreciate if it you would supply us with all of the facts, figures and statements which you may have available, even if they are not complete, as quickly as possible. We particularly want to know what funds you are presently holding for Buddy and what arrangements have been made with respect to his tax liability for 1958 and 1957 if any.

With respect to Buddy's music writing, we still do not have the list of compositions which we requested or the accounting from NOR VA JAK which will also be essential. We also require copies of Buddy's contracts with NOR VA JAK.

In view of Buddy's manifold activities and the many problems which have to be resolved, it might be convenient if we could discuss the situation. Will you be in New York at any time in the near future? If so, I will be very glad to meet you at your convenience.

That same day, Schiffer learned of Petty's announcement to Coral that 'Buddy Holly is no longer a Cricket as of the first of the year'. Buddy, it is true, had told J.I. and Joe B. that they could continue working as the Crickets without him. But his lawyers were not about to let him give away the name on two of his three biggest hits. And Petty's high-handed tone was one calculated to make any self-respecting attorney see red. George

Schiffer immediately fired off an indignant rebuke by Western Union telegram:

STRONGLY OBJECT TO YOUR LETTER OF JANUARY 9 TO CORAL RECORDS. BUDDY HOLLY HAS FULL RIGHT TO USE THE NAME 'THE CRICKETS' AND WILL CONTINUE TO USE THAT NAME. STRONGLY OBJECT TO MISLEADING USE OF THE NAME IN CONJUNCTION WITH SINGER OTHER THAN HIMSELF. LETTER FOLLOWS. PLEASE BE ADVISED THAT IN VIEW OF THE FACT THAT YOU NO LONGER REPRESENT MR HOLLY YOUR ATTEMPT TO GIVE INSTRUCTIONS TO CORAL RECORDS REGARDING HIS FUTURE RECORDING IS UNWARRANTED AND UNAUTHORIZED.

The next day, 13 January, Isabelle Marks gave Petty equally short shrift on behalf of Coral:

Dear Mr Petty:
We are in receipt of your letter of January 9 in which you advise us that Buddy Holly is no longer a Cricket.

Our contract covering the performance of the Crickets is with Buddy Holly, Jerry Allison and Joe Mauldin. We must insist that the performances by the Crickets be with the individuals who are parties of the contract and we cannot accept any substitutions.

Petty replied on to George Schiffer on 14 January:

We acknowledge receipt of your telegram dated January 13, 1959, and naturally immediately conclude that there is a misunderstanding by Buddy Holly if he is of the opinion that he is 'The Crickets'. The original 'Crickets' consisted of Niki Sullivan, Joe Mauldin and Jerry Allison.

By an instrument dated December 14, 1957, Niki Sullivan relinquished all his interest in 'The Crickets' and in all previous recordings designated or labelled 'Buddy Holly' or 'The Crickets' in consideration of the assignment of him of ten percent of all monies received for one recording on Brunswick Records of 'That'll By The Day' by 'The Crickets'.

It would seem obvious that Buddy Holly was never actually a member of 'The Crickets'. All personal appearances, all recordings and any other artistic presentations by Buddy Holly with 'The Crickets' were usually billed and shown to be two separate entities, that is 'Buddy Holly and The Crickets'.

We feel constrained to advise therefore, in behalf of 'The Crickets', who now consist of Joe Mauldin, Jerry Allison and a new member, that Mr Holly is definitely not at liberty to use the name 'The Crickets' in any artistic presentation without their express written consent.

Brunswick's original agreement with the Crickets for 'That'll Be The Day' had indeed borne only the names of J. I. Allison, Joe B. Mauldin and Niki Sullivan. But that had been merely subterfuge, to conceal Buddy's presence in the group from Brunswick's parent company, Decca. Subsequently, his contractual difficulties with Decca had been sorted out and his name had been appearing on all the Crickets' Brunswick contracts since October. The wording on this or that concert-poster was quite irrelevant: what had happened, as Clovis Man well knew, was that Buddy had developed two parallel careers, one as lead singer with the Crickets, the other as a solo singer backed by them. J.I. and Joe B. had not been 'two separate entities' but a single entity under two names. Remembering the cohesion and cameraderie that had taken them round the world together, it's hard to understand how the other two could have been parties to such a breathtaking misrepresentation.

Petty's letter crossed with one from Schiffer, following up his telegram:

> It is quite clear that Buddy has as much right, and probably more, to the use of the name 'The Crickets' as the other two boys. He has no intention of surrendering his rights. It would not be proper for the boys to use another singer with the group under the name 'The Crickets' because the name and reputation were built primarily on Buddy Holly. It is he who was responsible for the bulk of their success and he who obtained the bulk of the rewards.
>
> From my limited knowledge of the commercial situation, I believe that Buddy can continue to use the name to some good effect, but that no reputable record company and no reputable booking organization would accept the subterfuge of substituting another singer for Buddy in a group to be called 'The Crickets'. Even if such arrangements could be made, it would seem to me not desirable for either group that there be another group with the same name concurrently working.
>
> So as to avoid further complications and any possible loss of income either to the boys or Buddy, I think that we should resolve the above mentioned matter and the accounting as quickly as possible, if necessary by meeting.
>
> Please let me hear from you concerning these matters at your earliest convenience.

That same day, Schiffer wrote to Isabelle Marks at Coral:

> As you know, Buddy Holly has an interest in funds which become payable to 'The Crickets' pursuant to the agreement

between them and Coral even though he is not a party to
that agreement.

Accordingly, the notification which we previously sent
you was intended to apply to royalties becoming due on
account of 'The Crickets'' records on which Mr Holly
performed. It will be satisfactory to us if the entire royalty
for such records is held by you for the time being. In no
event should any part of it be paid to Mr Petty instead of to
Mr Holly since, as you know, Mr Petty no longer represents
Mr Holly.

George Schiffer's patience with Clovis Man was starting to
wear thin. On 16 January he wrote:

Re: Buddy Holly and 'The Crickets'.

Dear Mr Petty
In view of your failure to respond satisfactorily to our
numerous letters requesting an accounting and payment of
the sums due to Mr Holly, demand is hereby again made
for the immediate payment of all sums presently held by
you which belong to Mr Holly, together with a full
accounting and copies of all contracts between Mr Holly
and the other members of The Crickets, between Mr Holly
and you and between Mr Holly and NOR VA JAK.

Also on 16 January, Schiffer wrote the Clovis National Bank:

Gentlemen:
Norman Petty, formerly manager of Buddy Holly, received
substantial sums of money in his fiduciary capacity, which
sums beneficially belong to Mr Holly. As attorneys for Mr
Petty, we learned that some or all of these funds may be
deposited in your bank.

Please be advised that all of Mr Petty's powers to deal
with the property of Mr Holly or to represent him have
been terminated and that Mr Petty is not empowered to
make deposits or withdrawals of funds belonging to Mr
Holly or otherwise to deal with any matter with or to enter
into any transaction concerning Mr Holly or his property.

The bank's reply, on 19 January, showed predictable solidar-
ity with a valued local customer:

We are in receipt of your letter of January 16 concerning Mr
Buddy Holly and Mr Norman Petty his personal manager.
    We do not have an account in our bank for Mr Holly.
Money that has been deposited here is under the heading of
Norman Petty Agency Inc. and we cannot honor any
signature other than Mr Petty's.
    We have been unable to contact Mr Petty personally,
but his office manager says that all royalty checks that came
in were made payable to Mr Petty or the agency.
    You realize we are acting only as a depository and
know nothing further about any fund belonging to Mr
Holly.

That same day, Petty's secretary, Norma Jean Berry, wrote
to George Schiffer:

Dear Mr Schiffer
We acknowledge receipt of your letters of Jan 12, 1959 . . .
Jan 14, 1959 . . . and Jan 19, 1959, the last arriving today
containing contracts for the signatures of Jerry Allison and
Joe Mauldin [for their last appearance on Dick Clark's
American Bandstand].
    Please be advised that Mr Norman Petty has not seen
any of these letters as he has been out of town since last

Thursday, Jan 15th, the day on which the first of the above mentioned letters arrived.

Mr Allison and Mr Mauldin are also out of town this week and will not be available to examine the contracts you sent until this coming weekend, at which time Mr Petty will also return to Clovis.

Thus was more time allowed to run out.

Buddy had arranged for his new band to spend a week rehearsing with him in New York before the start of the Winter Dance Party tour on January 23. Tommy Allsup and the drummer Carl Bunch checked in to a local hotel but Waylon Jennings, as Buddy's special protégé, was invited to stay at his apartment. All three of the Texans were deeply impressed by Buddy's Manhattan lifestyle, Tommy in particular by the Brevoort's valet parking service.

These few days were all Waylon had to pick up the rudiments of the brand-new Fender bass guitar Buddy had bought for him. He remembered later that when he arrived in New York, Buddy simply handed him copies of the *Chirping Crickets* and *Buddy Holly* albums with a grin and told him, 'Here's my songs. Learn 'em.' Kind-hearted Tommy came to his aid, teaching him enough basic rhythm-patterns to get by. Not a word was said to any of the band about Maria Elena being pregnant.

Two weeks had now passed since the release of 'It Doesn't Matter Anymore'. Though widely played and praised by radio deejays and admired by Buddy's fellow musicians, it still had not appeared in the *Billboard* Hot 100. 'That was really worrying Buddy while we were rehearsing for the tour,' Tommy Allsup remembers. 'He couldn't figure out why, whatever he did, the hits seemed to have dried up for him.'

Along with the consoling blueprints for Prism and the Taupe

record label, another new plan took shape in Buddy's mind. If America didn't want him, then he'd return to the country which had given him so unexpected a hero's welcome the previous March. 'He'd talked to GAC about going back to England,' Tommy says. 'That was another reason for doing this "Winter Dance Party" deal for GAC. Afterwards, he was coming back to New York for two weeks, then going off on a six-week European tour.'

Maria Elena concurs: 'He was always talking about how much he liked England, what a welcome the people had given him over there. After his recording studio in Lubbock was established, he wanted to open studios in other cities – either LA or London. The LA smog hurt his throat, so he decided on London. He said there was so much talent in England that no one seemed to be interested in developing. "You'll love it over there," he kept telling me. "You'll love it."'

Ever conscious of Buddy's precarious finances, hospitable Aunt Provi had the whole band to dinner at her apartment. Another night, for economy's sake and to please Buddy, Maria Elena volunteered to cook for the four of them. 'I had a book that had Spanish recipes. I decided to fix steaks with rice and red beans and a salad. I went ahead and did the rice, and that didn't come out too bad. But I forgot I'd put the red beans on the stove, and they all burned and got stuck to the bottom of the pan. As we were eating, I could see the look on Waylon's face when he tasted these horrible burned beans. But Buddy was kind of kicking him under the table and saying, "Mm, isn't this wonderful?" He wouldn't hurt my feelings for anything.'

Between rehearsals, Buddy continued to tape songs on the Ampex in his living-room, accompanying himself on acoustic or electric guitar, sometimes with Waylon or Tommy Allsup sitting in. The society of fellow pickers from his home state seems to have lifted his spirits, for the second phase of Apartment Tapes are noticeably less melancholy and introspective than the first.

They include Little Richard's 'Slippin' and Slidin'', the Coasters' 'Smokey Joe's Café', even an old vaudeville song, a favourite of his mother's, 'Wait Till The Sun Shines Nellie'. One version of 'Slippin' and Slidin'' was recorded at half-speed, suggesting that Buddy intended it to be a chipmunk-voiced comedy number. Another day he recorded his version of 'Love Is Strange', the Mickey and Sylvia song which had inspired his double-track masterpiece 'Words Of Love'. An unintended prelude is the sound of Tommy Allsup knocking at the apartment's front door.

There were also frequent trips uptown to West 57th Street to confer with George Schiffer, not only about the continuing non-appearance of his record-royalties but now, too, about Petty's stupefying claim that Buddy had 'never been a Cricket'. Schiffer's advice was that a lawsuit against Petty now seemed inevitable, but on 20 January he made one last try to resolve the dispute informally:

Re: Buddy Holly and 'The Crickets'

Dear Mr Petty,
I am most surprised by the content of your letter of January 14, 1959. Not only have numerous recordings been made with 'The Crickets featuring Buddy Holly' but Buddy has always been treated by the public as one of The Crickets. I might add that he, in terms of his share of receipts, owns a good deal more than half of that name.

In any event, and without regard to possible technicalities, there can be no question but that Buddy has rights in the name at least equal to those of the other boys. The position which you take is, to my mind, not only unwarranted in law or fact, but unfair. Coupled with your failure to account for the large sum of money which you are now holding on behalf of Mr Holly, your taking this position represents, to my mind, the first step in what may prove to be a long and unnecessary disagreement.

I understand that you will be coming to New York very soon. Since we would still like at least to try to adjust this whole matter amicably, I would appreciate your calling me for an appointment as soon as you arrive in New York. Should you fail to do so, you will leave us no alternative but to take steps to enforce such legal remedies as Mr Holly may have available.

Don and Phil Everly were still using the same law firm in their battle with their ex-manager, Wesley Rose. One afternoon as Don and Phil arrived at the firm's office for a conference, they met Buddy coming out. The brothers asked whether the dispute with Petty was anywhere near a resolution and Buddy replied gloomily in the negative. They agreed to meet as soon as possible after the Everlys' forthcoming Australian tour.

Despite its cosy suggestion of fur-wrapped sleigh-rides and hot chocolate, Maria Elena still had dire misgivings about the 'Winter Dance Party', and was determined to travel with Buddy and watch over him as she had on his October tour. The prospect of the Midwest in midwinter did not daunt her; as a New Yorker, she was well used to blizzards and below-zero temperatures and, indeed, positively relished cold weather. But Buddy would not hear of it. She was still suffering daily bouts of nausea which two weeks on the road could only aggravate. 'He said I had to take things easy,' she remembers. 'I needed to find a doctor to take care of me through the pregnancy. And there were lots of things for me to do in New York.'

The arrangements Buddy made to cover his three-week absence were as meticulous as always. While Maria Elena continued organizing his fan-club and personal PR, Aunt Provi was to find material for his projected album of Latin-American music. One song that he definitely planned to use, for obvious reasons, was 'Maria Elena', a breeze-soft ballad destined to be an instrumental hit for Los Indios Tabajaros in 1963. He also got in touch with Niki Sullivan, the original fourth Cricket whose past conflicts with J. I. Allison were now, perhaps, a little easier to understand. Having heard nothing from Buddy since December 1957, Niki was amazed to be phoned by him and asked to join a three-way song writing partnership with Paul Anka. According to Tommy Allsup, Buddy also asked GAC for an advance on his tour-earnings to leave behind as a contingency fund for his pregnant wife. But Maria Elena herself says they remained totally reliant on Aunt Provi, both for day-to-day necessities and for money in the bank to pay the whacking monthly rental for their apartment.

Despite the veiled threats now coming from Papa Norman, there was no question in Buddy's mind about the billing of his new band. On 22 January he recorded a spoken promo to be sent to radio stations along the 'Winter Dance Party''s route: 'Hi, this is Buddy Holly. The Crickets and I are really happy to be coming your way on the "Winter Dance Party". We certainly hope to see all our old friends and to be making some new ones, too. Also, I hope you like my latest Coral release, "Heartbeat". See you soon.'

He tried to reassure Maria Elena that the three weeks would soon pass, that before she knew it they'd be back together again, strolling the Village streets with pyjamas under their raincoats or having dinner at their favourite table at Café Madrid. But she remained deeply unhappy and uneasy about letting him go off without her. 'I got so that I couldn't even listen when Buddy and the others were discussing the tour,' she remembers. 'Waylon said to me later, "It's amazing how strongly you were against the whole thing."'

On the night before Buddy's departure, as she lay beside him for the very last time, Maria Elena had a singularly vivid and upsetting nightmare. 'It was like I was standing by myself in a big, vast, barren area, like a farm. I didn't know where I was or how I got there. And then all of a sudden I could hear noises, like shouting, and it got closer and closer. In the distance I could see all these people, running, running, running, and shouting, "They're coming! Hide! They're coming!" These people were desperately trying to run away from something. They were coming towards me like cattle in a stampede and I knew I would be trampled, but I couldn't move. I was standing there like I was glued there. But they all ran past me and one person, I remember, said to me as they went past, "Run! Run!"

'Then I can hear this terrible noise, "Woosh", really loud, like a storm coming in, and then a rumble, and then I look and I see this big ball of fire coming out of the sky like a comet, headed straight for me. I try to move but I still can't and I think, "Oh my God, this thing's going to kill me." Then, for some reason, I start running, but I know it's too late and this thing's going to crush me. Then I hear this horrible noise on top of me and then passing me, and ahead of me I hear a crash and see a huge explosion. I can see a hole with black smoke coming out of it and I go up to it and tried to look in, but all I can see is just blackness and smoke . . .

'That's when I woke up, and Buddy woke up and told me he'd had a dream, too. He dreamed he was flying in a plane with me and his brother Larry, and they'd landed on top of a building. Larry had wanted to leave me there. He said, "On our way back we'll pick her up." Buddy said, "No, wherever I go, she goes." But Larry convinced him that it was not going to be too long and I should just wait there. So Buddy had to leave me, but he said to me, "Wait right here and I'll be back to pick you up." When he woke, he was upset that he'd left me. He held me and he was crying, really crying.

'We were both dreaming the same dream at the same time. And there was so much that came true if you put two and two together ... Buddy leaving me ... an airplane crash ... in a farm ... It was like someone saying something to me, but I didn't listen. I still feel bad at times that I didn't listen.'

They were both in a state of deep distress the next morning as Buddy finished his packing. His wardrobe, immaculate as always, showed what a deep impression English tailoring had made on him during his brief visit to London. Rather than a tie he now preferred an ascot, or dress cravat, knotted inside the fur shawl-collar of a pale brown leather 'shortie' overcoat, styled after the smoking jackets of Pall Mall clubmen. Maria Elena had recently bought him a set of polka-dot ascots in various dark colours with matching breast-pocket handkerchieves. He carried his toilet articles in a smart brown leather bag with a zip-up side-compartment where he kept his .22 pistol. To make the bag more comfortable to carry, he'd bound its handle with white adhesive tape.

When it was time to leave, he found that Maria Elena had also packed a suitcase and had it waiting by the front door. 'I told him that I was feeling fine, that the morning sickness had gone away, but he knew that wasn't true and he wouldn't let me go with him. He was as upset about saying goodbye as I was. But he was determined to get that money.

'I kept saying to him, "I don't want you to go. I don't want you to go." One thing I always have in my mind, and that I'll always regret, is that I wasn't more determined, that I didn't insist more. Because I know that if I would have gone with him, Buddy would never have taken that plane.'

The 'Winter Dance Party''s two other headline acts were new-comers to the pop business, each illustrating how unpredictable was the formula for chart-success on the cusp of 1958–9.

In Ritchie Valens, aka Richard Valenzuela, a teen-idol had at last emerged from America's vast and varied Hispanic culture. A seventeen-year-old Californian of Mexican-Indian ancestry, Valens was a prolific songwriter and a talented guitarist, singing in a flamenco-high voice that belied his stocky build and rather loutish looks. His début single, 'Come On, Let's Go', had been a minor US hit the previous autumn and reached the British Top 10 in a cover version by Tommy Steele. In December, he had seen both sides of his second single leap simultaneously into the American charts: one, a puppy-love ballad called 'Donna', the other a fiesta-happy torrent of pidgin Spanish called 'La Bamba'.

As great a contrast with Ritchie Valens as Hardy with Laurel was twenty-eight-year-old J. P. Richardson, the 'Big Bopper', a bulkily built radio deejay-turned vocalist from Beaumont, Texas. In September, Richardson had made the US Top 10 with 'Chantilly Lace', a telephone monologue to a prospective date, picturing her decked out in that whipped-cream style of French lace 'with a purty face and a pony-tail, hangin' down ...' Rock 'n' roll thus far had not produced a purely comic performer – at least not one consciously so – and the Bopper more than filled the bill with his outsize Stetson hat and ankle-length fur coat, his expression of pop-eyed lasciviousness, his growly-bass catch-phrases 'Hell-o Bay-bee!' and 'You know what I like!'

The other two acts on the bill had been chosen to supplement what otherwise would have been a rather meagre diet of sex-appeal. Fourth in prominence were Dion and the Belmonts, the New York vocal quartet whose peach-fluff doo-wop harmonies belied their evolution from Italian street gangs in the Bronx. Bottom of the bill was Frankie Sardo, another Italian-American, short on vocal ability but long on attractiveness to females under eighteen.

After a brief rehearsal period in Chicago, the tour opened on 23 January at George Devine's Million Dollar Ballroom, Milwaukee. Most of the subsequent gigs were to be at ballrooms of the type that Buddy and Tommy Allsup had played on the 'Summer Dance Party', in the same small towns bordering on scenic lakes or forests. But now the lakes were frozen solid and the forests in the grip of a winter that made even New York's seem mild by comparison. The states of Minnesota, Wisconsin and Iowa were bound into one immense, featureless tundra, bombarded by incessant blizzards, littered with abandoned cars and struggling snowploughs, swept by wicked winds like voices moaning out of some vast echo-chamber. Temperatures as low as those of deepest Siberia, 30 degrees below zero, were by no means uncommon.

On the 'Winter Dance Party's' famous – one should say, infamous – black and yellow tour poster, 'Buddy Holly and the Crickets' appear at the top with a small inset picture of Buddy, flanked by Ritchie Valens on the left and the Big Bopper on the right. Since none of the other acts had backing bands, Tommy Allsup, Waylon Jennings and drummer Carl Bunch acted as musicians for the whole show. The three were uniformed with Buddy's usual fastidiousness in black jackets and grey slacks, with ascots instead of ties. Performing in a line, with their clerkly dress and solid guitars, Buddy, Tommy and Waylon provided the first inkling of how every guitar 'beat group' would look in the first half of the next decade.

Buddy's nightly set mixed his own songs with rock 'n' roll classics like 'Be Bop A-Lula' and 'Whole Lotta Shaking', and country songs from his teenage years like 'Salty Dog Blues'. He seemed more concerned with having fun than pushing 'Heartbeat' and 'It Doesn't Matter Anymore', even though both were included. He began each performance alone on the stage, an immaculately-coiffed and tailored figure, strumming his guitar and singing another big hit of the hour, Billy Grammer's 'Gotta Travel On'. For Buddy, doubtless, the lyric echoed his feeling that his long fallow period was nearing an end and he'd soon be up and running again; with hindsight it has a sadly different resonance:

I've laid around and played around
This old town too long.
Summer's almost gone, yeah
Winter's coming on.
I've laid around and played around
This old town too long
And I feel like I've gotta travel on . . .

GAC had drawn up the itinerary in customary haphazard fashion, scheduling appearances in the order in which they were booked and with blithe disregard of geographical logic. The result was a continual criss-crossing zigzag in and out of three states, with each one-night stand separated by distances of up to 400 miles. This would have been fatiguing enough in summer; in the Midwest's sub-Arctic January, it was purgatorial. As often as not, after their show there would be no time for the 'Winter Dance Party' troupe to check into an hotel; instead, they would be herded straight back on to their bus for a non-stop journey lasting through the night and most of the following day to reach their next gig on schedule.

The transportation provided on earlier GAC tours, while never the lap of luxury, had at least always been reliable. But in these days of shrinking margins, rock 'n' roll promoters were out to save every penny. The contract for bussing the 'Winter Dance Party' through the Siberian Midwest had gone to a charter company offering cut-price rates and a fleet to match. The bus in which they started their journey lasted only a few hours on the frozen highways before grinding and sputtering to a stop. The fault proved beyond any local mechanic to repair, and the whole troupe had to disembark, unload their equipment themselves and huddle in what warmth they could find while their road manager, Sam Geller, contacted the charter company and a substitute vehicle was found.

The second bus proved little better than the first and, likewise, had to be replaced after barely a day's travel. A third was rustled up but it, too, quickly fell by the wayside – as did a fourth, a fifth and, unbelievably, a sixth and a seventh. They were, indeed, a sorry load of clapped-out junk, with engines unequal to the appalling road conditions and heaters which barely mitigated the ferocious cold which seeped through their ice-encrusted windows. Each long wait for yet another replacement in the middle of snow-drifted nowhere put additional strain on an already murderous itinerary, cutting the musicians' rest-periods, condemning them to longer and longer spells on the move as their driver, murmuring prayers for the health of his latest carburettor, struggled to make up lost time. After the fifth or sixth breakdown, the only replacement that could be found was a school bus, yellow and rangy – then as now – with hard metal seats. But its heater was, at least, noisily efficient.

Rock stars of today would not put up with such conditions for five minutes. But rock stars of 1959 were an infinitely hardier, more philosophical breed. With amazing good grace, the 'Winter Dance Party' troupe allowed themselves to be decanted into one rattletrap vehicle after another; resignedly hunkering down in their thin coats for another six or seven hours with poor or non-existent heat; keeping up their spirits with card games and jam-sessions even when fingers grew almost too numb to deal the next hand or shape a guitar chord. However bad the weather and chaotic the schedule, no one even thought of 'blowing out' the tour. They considered themselves to be in show business as much as in rock 'n' roll and, as everyone knew, the show must go on.

At each night-time oasis of coloured neon and polished dance floor they were greeted by an audience numbering between 1,000 and 1,500, many of whom had driven almost as far, through weather just as atrocious. To these Wisconsin, Minnesota and Iowa teenagers, locked up in their hibernating communities for months on end, live entertainment of any kind was a boon little short of miraculous. As cold and exhausted as the musicians felt, it was hard not to respond to the wild welcome they received each night by playing to the limit.

Common adversity bonded the five acts together; despite the difference in their styles, all soon became friends. Five of the 10 performers – Buddy, Tommy Allsup, Waylon Jennings, Carl Bunch and the Big Bopper – were country boys from the South-west, which made for unanimity in humour and outlook. Only Dion and the Belmonts, with the natural cliquiness of New York Italians, held themselves slightly aloof. 'They seemed a little bit like foreigners to the rest of us,' Tommy Alsupp remembers.

The Big Bopper kept everyone feeling 'real loose, like a long-necked goose' with his constant stream of jokes and deejay wordplay. 'J. P.' or 'Jape' as the others called him, overflowed the stage each night in his big Stetson hat and a tent-like leopardskin jacket he called 'Melvin'. As well as an hilarious performer, he was a talented songwriter, having written 'Running Bear' for Johnny Preston as well as 'Chantilly Lace' and its follow up, 'Big Bopper's Wedding'. The previous April, on his home station, KTRM in Beaumont, he had set a new world record for being continuously on the air, playing discs and wisecracking for 122 hours, 8 minutes – an achievement proudly engraved on the back of his wrist-watch. For all his outrageous flirting, he was a devoted family man and, like Buddy, soon to become a father.

The Bopper had been booked to do cabaret in Las Vegas straight after the 'Winter Dance Party', and was racking his brains for visual gimmicks to grab his audience's attention like the huge 'Hel-lo Bay-be!' at the start of 'Chantilly Lace'. Over needlessly cold beers in a wayside bar one night, Tommy Allsup and Waylon Jennings came up with a suggestion. 'We knew a midget in Hobbs, New Mexico, who played the bass and sang real well,' Tommy remembers. 'So we called him up from where we were and fixed for him to be in the Bopper's Vegas act. The idea was for the MC to announce "The Big Bopper" and then for this little guy to come running out on to the stage.'

Even though the Bopper was six years his senior, Buddy seemed the elder statesmen of the party in his chunky new Faiosa spectacle-frames and fur-collared coat. To his teenage co-stars, he was a self-controlled, abstemious figure who preferred to be alone in his hotel-room – when there was an hotel-room – rather than joining the others to 'shoot the bull' down in the bar or coffee-shop. Because of his stomach condition, he now ate little and cautiously and drank no alcohol, not even beer. Since his marriage, he had also given up smoking, although that resolution proved impossible to maintain on the endless bus-journeys when everyone around him lit up all the time and the scrape of a book-match provided significant extra warmth. A set of snapshots taken in a wayside photographic booth show him with Waylon Jennings, flourishing a cigarette and sticking out his tongue like a defiant schoolboy.

He was obviously missing Maria Elena, about whom he talked continually to Waylon and Tommy Allsup. But he was exhilarated, too, by the reception he got onstage every night and the realization that he could still pull out a first-class performance without the safety-blanket of J. I. Allison and Joe B. Mauldin wrapped around him. 'He wasn't uptight, the way he'd been on the "Summer Dance Party",' Tommy remembers. 'He felt really good about being free of Norman Petty. He was always talking about the plans he had ... the new studio ... his European tour. He just seemed like he was about to explode.'

He had been mildly apprehensive about working with seventeen-year-old Ritchie Valens, a chart-topper as precocious in early 1959 as Paul Anka had been in late 1957. Ritchie certainly looked the consummate young punk in his frilly turquoise satin shirt and silver-studded black bolero and vaquero pants. But he showed none of the abrasive arrogance which the 'Boy Millionaire' had at his age. 'He was a great kid,' Tommy Allsup says.

'He'd grown up being like a father to the younger kids in his neighbourhood, playing guitar for 'em, singing to 'em, telling 'em stories. He wasn't one of those who know it all. He asked questions all the time. He wanted to learn about everything.'

Ritchie looked up to Buddy in much the way Buddy had once looked up to Elvis. He played a sunburst Fender Stratocaster exactly like Buddy's, and had included yet another passing homage to 'Peggy Sue' in his song 'Ooh, My Head'. Such hero-worship is not always gratifying, especially if one's fan and disciple happens to be doing better in the charts than one is oneself. But Buddy was as incapable as ever of resenting another musician's success. He admired the chunky teenager's multi-faceted talent and warmed to his high spirits and appetite for life. From their long chats on icy-windowed buses evolved yet another plan for the golden age that was to begin directly this slushy, shivery tour had ended. Ritchie would join Waylon Jennings and Lou Giordano on Prism Records and Buddy would produce his sessions personally.

Although Buddy had mentioned his dispute with Norman Petty to Waylon and Tommy, neither guessed the anxiety it was causing him, especially since he still had not said a word about Maria Elena's pregnancy. Twice a day, at least, he would struggle to a payphone and place a long-distance call to her in New York, hoping there might be further news about his back royalties from George Schiffer at Harold Orenstein's office. 'He'd call me at around noon from the road, then at night from the place where they were playing,' Maria Elena remembers. 'That was how I met Ritchie Valens; Buddy introduced us over the phone and said he was going to produce him and that Ritchie would be coming to stay with us in New York. When Buddy went onstage, he'd get Ritchie to hold the phone, so that I could hear him singing "True Love Ways". I always knew he was singing that one just for me.'

The news from George Schiffer, relayed by Maria Elena, was

of further delay and further complication. Back in the distant days of late 1957 when the Crickets first became a hot attraction, they had hired a New York agent named Mannie Greenfield to work for them in the several managerial areas where Norman Petty had neither experience nor the inclination to acquire it. Greenfield had proved a valuable ally, getting them their first exposure on national television and fixing their tour of Britain through his good friends Lew and Leslie Grade. The agreement had been a verbal one only, and in the autumn of 1958, just before Buddy's parting from J.I. and Joe B., a dispute had arisen over the rate of commission they had promised Greenfield. They said it was 5 percent of all fees he negotiated on their behalf. Greenfield claimed the figure was 5 percent of all their perform-ance earnings during the period he represented them.

Though Buddy had made the original deal with Greenfield, Petty had always worked in friendly co-operation with him and it was to Petty, as the Crickets' manager, that Greenfield addressed his complaint. In January 1959, having obtained no satisfaction after almost four months, Greenfield began legal action against Petty, claiming $10,000 in unpaid commissions. New York law provided that, when one party in a lawsuit resided outside the state, all monies in contention could be attached, or frozen, pending resolution of the case. On 23 January, the day that the 'Winter Dance Party' kicked off in Milwaukee, Greenfield's lawyers served a writ of attachment on Coral-Brunswick records, suspending payment of further royal-ties to Buddy Holly and the Crickets. The same was done to Peer-Southern Music and its sister company Southern Music in respect of publishing royalties.

Coral-Brunswick had in fact already suspended payment of all Crickets and Buddy record-royalties at the request of Buddy's lawyer, George Schiffer. On 26 January, as Buddy sat in yet another frozen, fainthearted bus, *en route* for Fournier's Ballroom in Eau Clair, Wisconsin, Petty dictated a plaintive letter to Coral-Brunswick's Isabelle Marks about the company's decision to co-operate with Schiffer. He contended it was wrong to withhold royalties due the Crickets in a legal dispute involving Buddy since, by failing to sign the group's original Brunswick contract, Buddy had legally 'never been a Cricket'.

He was also anxious to correct what he called 'the misapprehension' that the Crickets' royalties from Brunswick and Buddy's from Coral were merely channelled through him to their collective bank account and administered by him under power of attorney. And indeed, when Isabelle Marks checked Coral-Brunswick's files, she found it was a misapprehension. The crucial piece of paperwork relating to Buddy and the Crickets' royalties was not any of the recording agreements which they'd signed as a group or which Buddy had signed as a solo performer. The contract that mattered was the one covering the sale of the finished master records by Petty's studio to the Decca organization, an agreement which Petty had negotiated on his own account and which he alone had signed. This master purchase agreement, dated March 1957 – a document which it is doubtful whether Buddy and the Crickets ever saw, let alone studied in detail – stipulated that all royalties they earned from Coral-Brunswick were to be 'paid to the order of Norman Petty and statements rendered to him'.

Thus, the hiving-off of the bulk of Buddy's earnings into an account under his manager's name, for his manager to disgorge as and when inclined, proved to have been perfectly legal and correct. Nor could Petty be said to have told a lie – at least not an outright one. Buddy and The Crickets had, indeed, had a collective bank account all these months, administered by Petty on their behalf. The trouble was that only the smallest residue of their earnings had ended up there. As so often, the pious effrontery of Clovis Man almost takes the breath away. For Petty now to complain to Isabelle Marks that his own secretiveness, economy with the truth and oily sleight of hand had created 'a misapprehension' is rich indeed!

On the following day, 27 January, as Buddy was *en route* to the Fiesta Ballroom in Montevideo, Minnesota, George Schiffer finally managed to get Petty on the telephone. Petty tape-recorded their conversation and had the recording transcribed by Norma Jean; its eight closely typed pages are among the relics in Clovis Man's cave. After elaborate opening pleasantries, Schiffer renews his efforts to set up a face-to-face meeting with Petty, inquiring whether he has plans to visit New York in the near future. Petty replies that he doesn't, but invites the lawyer to come and see him and the 'beautiful country' in New Mexico. He insists that he doesn't want to be 'hard to get along with' and agrees to give Schiffer what facts and figures he can over the telephone. His tone when referring to Buddy is that of a long-suffering adult, discussing some illogical, over-demanding child. He says that Buddy 'while an outstanding talent does have a tendency to want to make contracts and then get out of them', citing the contractual problems with Decca and Cedarwood publishing which he, Petty, had to sort out before Buddy could begin recording with him.

About the money owing to Buddy he is surprisingly forthcoming and precise. He tells Schiffer that the Coral-Brunswick royalties now held for Buddy by the Norman Petty Agency are in the region of $70,000. Groping for the relevant papers on his desk, he is more specific still: the cheques from the Buddy Holly and the Crickets account he has signed on Buddy's behalf total $33,215.53, leaving a balance to be paid of $35,926. He claims that Buddy still owes J.I. and Joe B. a total of $10,000 in performance-fees and that a further $10,000 has been put aside, with Buddy's consent, in case they should have to pay out in the Mannie Greenfield case.

Speaking to Schiffer as one man of the world to another, he portrays Buddy as a feckless, chaotic and even dishonest character who kept back all the Crickets' performance money instead of paying it into their account, spending lavishly on himself, gambling intemperately and wilfully refusing to garner a single receipt to be offset against income tax (a lie refuted by the bulging folders of receipts which probably lie directly in his sightline). He continues aggrievedly that Buddy isn't the only one to be owed money; he himself hasn't yet been paid the $2,000 for the Ampex tape-recorder and microphone he sold Buddy second-hand the previous autumn, even though he's holding some $7,000 for Buddy as start-up funds for the Prism organization. 'Technically [Buddy] has stolen equipment as far as my insurance company is concerned, if we wanted to get nasty . . .' (If?) He then rather pointedly asks Schiffer where Buddy is at this moment:

SCHIFFER: He's out of town and he's moving around a bit. I can get in touch with his wife. She's . . .

PETTY: Well, I would appreciate you finding out because I would like to dispose of this immediately.

SCHIFFER: Yes, but it may be . . . as I say . . . you might probably . . . I mean this is a relatively small matter.

PETTY: Now let me ask you this . . . Our lawyer here is contending like you that the boys are entitled to the name . . . the Crickets. Now we have instructed *Billboard* and the other magazines not to accept the name the Crickets until this thing is settled . . . I don't believe it is fair on your behalf to assume you already have the name The Crickets when neither one of us knows for sure. Probably we'll have to take it to court to decide, which is all right with us.

SCHIFFER: Well, you see, that's something else again which I think we should discuss in person because I'm not sure of anything at the moment except what Buddy has told me and what I can see from the sharing arrangements

and what I know of the history of the Crickets. Buddy
was the most important man in there.

PETTY: According to Buddy.
SCHIFFER: Beg pardon?
PETTY: According to Buddy.

Schiffer complains that, despite repeated requests, he still has
not received a full list of Buddy's compositions published
through NOR VA JAK. Petty promises to forward a copy of
every relevant contract. He then tries to persuade Schiffer not to
insist on the freezing of the royalties from Coral-Brunswick. But
Schiffer affably stands firm. Petty's only weapon of reprisal is
the mild, polite little note which Buddy sent him on 8 December:

PETTY: Oh, Buddy was asking about his writer's contract, so
you can tell him ... You know the personal writer's
contract with us.
SCHIFFER: Yes.
PETTY: Well, I prefer to leave that status quo, too, until we get
some of these matters solved.

On Friday, 30 January, the 'Winter Dance Party' chasséed
down the frozen highway to play the Laramar Ballroom in Fort
Dodge, Iowa. When Buddy called Maria Elena that lunchtime,
she had to break it to him that, after almost four weeks, there
still was no sign of 'It Doesn't Matter Anymore' in *Billboard*'s
Hot 100. Buddy made a brave show of not being worried, telling
her it would probably turn out to be another 'sleeper' like
'That'll Be The Day'. But inwardly he resigned himself to having
missed yet again. That night, close to despair, he called his friend
Eddie Cochran, who was recording in the enviable warmth of
California. 'Eddie came back from the phone really concerned,'
Cochran's girlfriend, Sharon Sheeley, remembers. 'He said "Bud-
dy's so down, he thinks it's all over in the charts for him. I told

him, don't be a fool. You're the best there is. You'll be back up there again soon."'

The following night, the 'Winter Dance Party' played the National Guard Armory in Duluth, Minnesota. Among the 2,000 fans who had paid $2 each to be there was a scrawny teenager named Bobby Zimmerman from the nearby town of Hibbing. In a few months from now, he would change his surname to Dylan in homage to Dylan Thomas, sign with Columbia Records and begin his turbulent metamorphosis into rock's greatest poet, preacher and satirist. Between the young Bob Dylan and the young Buddy Holly there is almost uncanny similarity: both started out as unprepossessing country boys, both had unstoppable energy and self-belief, both had girlfriends named Echo (in Dylan's case, Echo Helstrom). The American critic Greil Marcus has noted how indebted was Dylan's raucous, malleable phrasing to Buddy's, especially on rock 'n' roll numbers like 'Midnight Shift'. As for Dylan himself, through the eras of his perpetual self-reinvention, almost the only memory he has ever admitted to is seeing Buddy onstage that snowy night at Duluth Armory. 'Buddy was great,' he told a *Rolling Stone* interviewer in 1980. 'Buddy was fantastic.'

It seemed that conditions could get no worse, but still they did. In the early hours of Sunday, 1 February, the 'Winter Dance Party' were travelling from Duluth to Appleton, Wisconsin, a journey of 300 miles, in their eighth bus since leaving Milwaukee. As it toiled up a hill on Route 51, in the midst of the 'Great North Woods' mentioned in Bob Dylan's 'Tangled Up In Blue', the vehicle stopped dead. A piston had gone through the engine block. The troupe were marooned for several hours in pitch darkness with no heat, an outside temperature of 30 below and a real danger of being attacked by bears. The only warmth that could be obtained came from hipflasks and setting light to newspapers in the aisle.

Yet, somehow or other, they remained cheerful. Buddy and

the stand-offish Dion formed a friendship by huddling under the same blanket and swapping stories of their respective boyhoods in West Texas and the Bronx. Dion has since said that Buddy was one of the very few musicians he ever looked up to. The streetwise New Yorker was also impressed to learn that the smart leather toilet-bag in the rack above their heads had a .22 calibre pistol concealed in its zip-up side pocket.

When a truck finally came to their rescue, Carl Bunch, the drummer in Buddy's band, was found to have severely frostbitten feet and removed to the Grand View Hospital in Ironwood, Michigan. The others were ferried by car to the nearby town of Hurley, where the only place they could find a hot meal, the Club Carnival, refused service to their black bus-driver. The afternoon's matinée performance at the Cinderella Ballroom in Appleton was cancelled; while their bus was fitted with a new engine, Buddy and some of the others went on to the next stop, Green Bay, Wisconsin, by the Chicago-Northwestern Railroad.

Even the hospitalization of the troupe's only professional drummer did not stop the 'Winter Dance Party' that evening at Green Bay's Riverside Ballroom. Several of the other musicians, Buddy included, were more than passable drummers, and the various acts were already well used to mixing and matching. Among the backstage crowd was a local photographer named Larry Matti whose portfolio records the cheery scene in all too living colour. Here is Ritchie, in flamenco turquoise, silver and black, caught in a nest of piled-up chairs. Here is the Bopper, crewcut and leopardskin-clad, with a maidenly Green Bay girl on each arm, still clowning indefatigibly despite an obvious heavy head cold. Here is Buddy, looking less like a rock 'n' roller than some classical violinist with his fur-collared coat and red polka-dot ascot. Another stage-door paparazzo caught him ready to travel on yet again, cradling his brown leather toilet bag with the white adhesive tape around its handle.

The whole company was at the lowest possible ebb, riddled

with coughs and sniffles and, by now, dirty and scruffy as well as exhausted. Eight days of virtually nonstop road travel had left no time to have their stage outfits dry-cleaned and their shirts and underwear laundered. The day after Green Bay, 2 February, had originally been blank on the schedule, allowing a few hours to get thoroughly warm, have their laundry done and catch up on some sleep. That respite had now vanished, thanks to a late booking by the Surf Ballroom in Clear Lake, Iowa. Clear Lake lay only about 100 miles north of Fort Dodge, where they had performed three nights earlier: arranging the dates in logical sequence would have given them an easy journey, punctuated by a night's rest. Instead they were now faced with a 350-mile journey along hazardous roads from the top edge of Wisconsin, across eastern Minnesota, into northern Iowa. And still there was to be no let-up. On the following night, 3 February, they were booked to appear at the National Guard Armory in Moorhead, Minnesota, 400 miles north-west of Clear Lake. To be in Moorhead by the early evening of 3 February meant setting off directly after their Surf Ballroom show – in other words, yet another through-the-night journey on an underheated, unreliable bus.

The journey from Green Bay, Wisconsin, to Clear Lake, Iowa, took most of the daylight hours of Monday 2 February. There was time only for a brief stop at an army surplus where – fearing a repetition of the North Woods incident – the Big Bopper bought himself a well-padded ex-military sleeping-bag. Buddy, as usual, seized the chance to phone long-distance to New York. 'When he got back on board the bus, he was really upset,' Tommy Allsup remembers. 'He'd thought there was about $50,000 in his and the Crickets' bank account, but he'd just been told there was only a couple of thousand. He said, "When this tour's over, I'm going back to Clovis and I'm going to kick Norman Petty's ass. I'm going to get my money out of that studio, one way or the other." Usually he never came out with anything as strong as that. "And if J.I. and Joe B. are there," he said, "I'll kick them, too."'

There was yet more bus-trouble *en route*, and the 'Winter Dance Party' did not reach Clear Lake until around 7 pm, less than an hour before the first of the two shows they were scheduled to give that evening. Clear Lake proved to be the smallest and remotest venue on the tour yet, a wooden hamlet scattered along the shores of the 3,600-acre lake for which it was named. During summer, the lake made the town a popular holiday resort, swelling its minuscule population six- or seven-fold. In the premature darkness of Monday, 2 February, it revealed little but an expanse of pack-ice ringed by shut-up holiday chalets half-buried in snow. Almost the only lights in the town emanated from the Surf Ballroom, a one-storey building in the usual hangar-like style, looking across the highway to the icebound lake.

According to Tommy Allsup, the idea of chartering a plane occurred to Buddy on the way to Clear Lake. The 400-mile onward journey to Moorhead, a night and a day's hard grind by road, would take a light aircraft only about two and a half hours. Fastidious about his clothes and grooming as Buddy was, he hated having to recycle his shirts and go onstage with trousers not faultlessly pressed. He also needed to continue the long-distance conference about his financial situation, curtailed by a revving bus-engine earlier that afternoon. Flying to Moorhead ahead of the troupe would give him a whole clear day before the night's show at the Armory. There would be ample time to sleep, have his laundry and dry-cleaning done at an express establishment, and get back on the phone with George Schiffer and Maria Elena.

It was not such a tremendous brainwave for Buddy to have had. On previous tours, he'd flown thousands of miles in every kind of plane from super-luxury Pan-American Constellations to rackety DC3s. The past week's Antarctic odyssey had shown that Midwesterners routinely used aircraft to avoid the frightful conditions on the ground. At the 'Winter Dance Party''s gig in Kenosha, Wisconsin, for example, the compère, Jim Lounsbury, had come in from Chicago by small plane, a Beechcraft Bonanza. The idea had special appeal now that Buddy had caught the flying bug and intended to qualify as a pilot and criss-cross the country in his own Cessna. Admittedly, the snowy night sky over Clear Lake did not look promising for air-travel. But once he got an idea in his head, he did not easily let it go.

The glacial expanse of Clear Lake might be heart-shiveringly bleak. But inside the Surf ballroom, the welcome was even more fervent than usual. Something like 1,300 rock 'n' roll fans had gathered for the 'Winter Dance Party', driving on well-chained tyres from all over Iowa and points far afield in the neighbouring states of South Dakota, Nebraska and Illinois. As its name suggested, the Surf had little to do with north Iowan scenery: the interior was designed to suggest a Florida beach club, with green-upholstered booths fringing the enormous maple dance floor, and a vaulted ceiling of tropical sky-blue on which a projector threw illusions of lazily drifting clouds. Nor was the foot-stomping, petticoat-whirling throng an exclusively teenage one. The Surf's manager, an affable thirty-nine-year-old named Carroll Anderson, liked to promote a family atmosphere, and encouraged parents to accompany their children by letting them in for nothing.

The night's compère was Bob Hale, a disc jockey on radio KRIB in nearby Mason City. Hale was struck by the high spirits and good humour of the 'Winter Dance Party', despite the punishing all-day journey they'd just endured and the even more punishing all-night journey which awaited them. Ritchie Valens was euphoric, having just been notified that his song 'Donna', written for his high school sweetheart Donna Ludwig, had qualified for a Gold Disc by selling a million copies. Dion and the Belmonts were humming and do-wopping their next release

– and first big hit – 'A Teenager In Love'. Playful arm-wrestling took place for the benefit of a reporter from the *Clear Lake Mirror*. Autographs were signed with customary patience and friendliness; fans who had forgotten to bring autograph books went away with 'Ritchie Valens', 'The Big Bopper' or 'Buddy Holly' written on their hands. Bob Hale thought the three stars to be all 'warm, classy young men'.

As soon as he arrived at the Surf, Buddy asked Carroll Anderson what were the chances of chartering a plane to Fargo later that night. It transpired that there was an airport at nearby Mason City and that its facilities included a charter and air-taxi company, Dwyer's Flying Service. Anderson knew the pro-prietor, Jerry Dwyer, personally, and offered to phone him and try to book his services on Buddy's behalf.

Dwyer proved not to be available, however, and Anderson was referred to another pilot with Dwyer's Flying Service, Roger Peterson. Peterson had been at work all day and was supposed to be taking the next day off, but in that era, especially in the Midwest, 'flying service' meant what it said. He agreed to accept the charter, despite at that stage not knowing the identity of his passenger or passengers. Buddy's destination, Moorhead, Min-nesota, had no airport, but there was one at Fargo, North Dakota, only about ten miles to the west. It was arranged that Buddy would report to Mason City airport straight after his second performance at the Surf, some time around midnight.

The aircraft which Peterson would be using had space for three passengers. To defray the charter-fee of $108, Buddy looked among the 'Winter Dance Party' for fellow travellers. Dion DiMucci has since said he was one of the first to be offered a seat on the plane for a third of the cost, $36. But he balked at parting with what seemed an enormous sum, the amount his whole family back in New York spent on rent each month. The logical arrangement, quickly reached, was that Buddy should be accompanied by his two remaining band members, Tommy

Allsup and Waylon Jennings. The plane would also carry the entire troupe's backlog of dirty laundry, which could then be dealt with in time for the following night's show. The plan also suited the hard-pressed tour-manager, Sam Geller, who had had to deal with inefficient promoters as well as unreliable buses. In addition to Buddy's various personal errands during his day's grace in Moorhead, he would be able to look in at the National Guard Armory and make sure the arrangements for the evening's show were in order.

A few minutes before going onstage for the first of his two sets at the Surf ballroom, he called Maria Elena from a payphone in the lobby. She remembers him telling her how relieved he was she hadn't come with him on the tour, that it was cold and miserable and chaotic, and conditions seemed to be getting worse all the time. 'He mentioned that they were having problems with the bus, that whenever they arrived any place, there was a big mess-up, and so the man who was in charge of the tour had asked if he would go on ahead and check things out. I said, "That's not your place, why do you have to do that?" But knowing Buddy as I did, he just couldn't stand to see things not done properly. He wanted to fix things right away. And besides people on the bus were getting sick and he was afraid he might get sick, too.'

Maria Elena remembers that he hinted he might fly but, knowing her fear of small planes, did not say it was to be by charter. 'He said, "I'm going to see if I can get another method of transportation." I said, "Well, get a commercial flight and get up there."'

One of the more poignant of the legends clustering around Buddy's final hours concerns the two estranged Crickets, J. I. Allison and Joe B. Mauldin. During the previous week, while the 'Winter Dance Party' were trekking through the Midwestern snows, J.I. and Joe B. had been back in Clovis, working at Norman Petty's studio with the 'new guy', Earl Sinks, taking

Buddy's place on vocals; both of them seemingly content for Petty to lay claim to the Crickets' name on their behalf by saying that Buddy had never legally belonged to the group. As legend has it, J.I. and Joe B. were themselves now growing suspicious of Petty and bitterly regretting taking his part rather than Buddy's. Both have since said, in any case, that the break-up was amicable and that Buddy had left the door open for a reunion at any time. 'That's what he used to tell us,' Joe B. Mauldin says. '"It only takes a phone-call."'

According to legend, it was this very last night of Buddy's life that his two old friends chose to make that phone-call, anxious to bury the hatchet and recreate their old world-beating line-up. Early in the evening of 2 February, they telephoned Maria Elena in New York and asked her where Buddy was. 'They thought I was unhappy with them for going with Norman instead of with Buddy. But I was the first to say how delighted I was that they wanted to get back together. Jerry told me later that they phoned the Surf ballroom, but it was very noisy and the person who answered couldn't get hold of Buddy, or he'd already left. So they phoned ahead to the next place and left a message for him to call them back. But, of course, he never got the message.'

It's certainly possible that J.I. and Joe B. were attempting to reach Buddy simply in the name of friendship, nostalgia and regret. But the principal message from Clovis that Buddy never received was an impersonal and threatening one, arising from legal dispute over a trademark. Petty's correspondence a few days hence would make mention of 'letters and cablegrams which were sent on Monday, February 2, after we learned that Holly was on tour with a group he called The Crickets.'

Backstage at the Surf, meanwhile, Tommy Allsup and Waylon Jennings both were under pressure to give up their places on the Fargo flight. The Big Bopper went to work on Waylon with all the pop-eyed pathos at his command. For someone of his bulk, the bus-journeys had been especially uncomfortable and, despite his new sleeping-bag, he was dreading that night's twelve- or fourteen-hour ride back up half the length of Minnesota. To add to his discomfort, the head cold he'd been nursing over the past few days was developing into full-blown influenza. Getting to Moorhead early would allow him to see a doctor and get a shot of antibiotics that might keep the symptoms at bay for the tour's remaining week. Waylon good-heartedly agreed that the Bopper's need was greater than his. Young and strong as he was, and still intoxicated by being on tour for the very first time, he could face another night on the road with equanimity.

Ritchie Valens angled for Tommy Allsup's seat, pleading that he'd never flown in a small aircraft before. This was true – but entirely of Ritchie's own choosing. Two years earlier, while he was attending Pacoima Junior High School in the San Fernando Valley, two aircraft had collided directly above the school, crashing down on to its premises and killing two students. Ritchie himself, by chance, had been away from school that day, attending his grandfather's funeral. He'd since had recurrent nightmares about the incident, and vowed never to go up in anything less than a commercial airliner. Tonight at Clear Lake, for some reason, that nagging phobia evaporated. He, too, had a cold, and would have suffered on another all-night bus-journey. He needed the spare hour or two in Moorhead to get his hair cut. And anything planned by Buddy and 'Jape' could hardly be other than a great adventure.

Tommy, however, refused to give up his seat on the plane, having an urgent need of his own to be in Fargo ahead of schedule. A registered letter from his mother was at Fargo post office, awaiting his collection. Flying up would give him ample time the next day to collect his letter as well as get his dry-cleaning done. But Ritchie refused to take 'no' for an answer, and throughout the evening kept riding Tommy with the same question: 'Are you gonna let me fly, guy?'

Above the murky ice-floes of Clear Lake that night, one thing at least was crystal-clear. Ritchie Valens might have the nation's hottest single; the Big Bopper might have created the number one catchphrase of the hour; Dion DiMucci might be the new, foxy face of rock 'n' roll. But was not any of them who had brought 1,300 people here through the snowdrifts of three states. Bob Hale, the deejay-compère, was always to remember what an electric thrill ran through the huge ballroom when he announced 'Buddy Holly'. 'The reaction was fantastic ... just one big surge.'

Buddy opened his set, as usual, alone on the stage, slenderly immaculate in his space-age black frames and red polka-dot ascot, strumming the brown Strat that seemed like an extra limb and singing the Billy Grammer hit he liked so much: 'I've laid around and played around this old town too long ... now I feel like I've gotta travel on ...' There was, to be sure, a restless, even impatient air about him that night, as several onlookers would later testify. At the beginning, he made little attempt to woo or amuse the big semicircle of upturned faces before him, bounding from one song to the next with only a husky 'Thank you' in between.

Most of his greatest hits were there, the titles now deleted from jukebox menus and radio play-lists; milestones that had come almost too quickly on the short, blinding highway of his fame. Each one had its special memories ... the cold February night in Clovis, with Larry Welborn and the Tolletts, when they'd got 'That'll Be The Day' right at long last ... The sound of Norman Petty's voice and the smell of his British Sterling aftershave ... Vi working in her flower garden, watched by Squeaky the chihuahua ... the 'Peggy Sue' session, with dust-storms raging outside and J. I. Allison playing paradiddles in the lobby alongside the red-and-white Coke machine ... the real cricket chirping in the echo-chamber on 'I'm Gonna Love You Too' ... the Harlem Apollo ... the New York Paramount ... Little Richard wanting to 'witness' with the old folks ... Eddie Cochran and his pipe ... 'Oh Boy' and Ed Sullivan ... the *Arthur Murray Dance Party* ... 'Maybe Baby' and England, half-timbered hotels, shilling-in-slot gas-meters and kissing a girl in Wigan ... Who knows what visions may have passed before those outside glasses, glinting under the placid summer sky of the Surf's light-show? It would later seem to more than one of his companions that he played and sang with special intensity, almost as if sensing this was a farewell performance.

Good humour and joie-de-vivre could not long be kept at bay, however. For the finale of Buddy's set, Ritchie and the Big Bopper joined him onstage – an *ad hoc* trio fated never to dissolve – and the three joined in an hilarious, none-too-expert version of 'La Bamba'. It's hard to see how Buddy's last number on earth could have been more in character: unenviously singing someone else's song, with a big smile on his face.

The show ended just before midnight, leaving only a few minutes for the three fortunate plane-passengers to extricate themselves from autograph-hungry fans, change from their stage suits into everyday clothes and get out to Mason City airport. Rather than waste time calling a taxi, Carroll Anderson, the Surf's ever-helpful manager, had offered to drive them there himself. It was only now that Waylon Jennings told Buddy he'd given up his seat on the flight to the Big Bopper. 'Well, I hope your old bus freezes up,' Buddy joked, prompting a riposte which Waylon was to spend almost four decades wishing he could unsay.,

'Well, I hope your ol' plane crashes,' he grinned back.

Buddy and the Bopper took their seats in Anderson's station wagon, which was backed up to the Surf's stage-door, a few yards from the communal band-room. Also in the vehicle were Anderson's wife Lucille and eleven-year-old son Tom, who had asked to go along for the ride. Emcee Bob Hale and his wife were there, too, despite the freezing conditions and flurrying snow, to wave the party off.

The third person on the flight, Tommy Allsup, was still somewhere inside, attending to details which, in later eras, would be left to half a dozen roadies. The plane was too small to carry his and Buddy's Stratocasters, so they had to be put on to the bus, where Waylon had promised to keep a special eye on them. 'I came out and put my satchel full of dirty shirts in the back of the station wagon,' Allsup remembers. 'Buddy was in front and the Bopper was in the second one. Then Buddy asked me to go back the dressing-room and check we hadn't left anything behind. Because a couple of days before, Carl Bunch, our drummer, had left his clothes-bag hanging somewhere. And I needed to double-check that our amps had gotten safely on to the bus.

'When I went back inside, Ritchie was still there, signing autographs. He said, "Are you going to let me fly, guy," and I said, "No." "Come on," he said, "let's flip a coin for it." I don't know why, because I'd been telling him no all evening, but I pulled a half-dollar piece out of my pocket. I've never understood what made me. It was like the solo on "It's So Easy"; it just happened. I flipped the 50-cent piece and said, "Call it." Ritchie said, "Heads," and it came down heads.'

According to other bystanders, the silver face of Benjamin Franklin that foreshadowed his death was greeted by Ritchie as the first real stroke of luck in his seventeen-year-old life. 'Hey!' he exulted. 'That's the first thing I ever won!'

Tommy returned to the station-wagon and laconically pulled his bag of dirty laundry off the back seat. 'I said, "Ritchie'll be here in a minute, he's going to go," and Buddy said, "What are you talking about?" I said, "We just flipped a coin, I lost and he's going to fly in my place." Then I asked Buddy if, when he got in to Fargo he'd pick up the registered letter from my Mom that was waiting for me at the post office there. "It's got a cheque in it," I said, "and if I go up on the bus, I may not have time to collect it."

'Buddy said, "Yeah, I'll pick it up, but they won't let me have it unless I show them your ID. Give me your driver's licence." They were needing to be away to make the flight, so, rather than waste time hunting through my wallet for my driver's licence, I said, "Here ... take my wallet." I held it out to Buddy and he stuck it inside his coat.'

Mason City's municipal airport in those days was a stark, windswept place comprising a scatter of hangars, a rudimentary passenger terminal and a control tower of strictly limited technological competence. In air-traffic terms, Mason City ranked only as an 'omni station', meaning that it did not possess radar, but put out an omnidirectional beam, which incoming aircraft had to locate and lock on to by themselves.

Such life as could be found at Mason City airport in early 1959 derived largely from Dwyer's Flying Service and its proprietor, Hubert J. ('Jerry') Dwyer. Dwyer's fleet of six charter planes generated most of the airport's employment; he also bought and sold aircraft ('Your friendly Cessna dealer') and held the licence for the tower's fixed-base ground-to-air radio. A rugged, short-spoken individual, Jerry Dwyer already had little cause to bless the Iowa weather. A freak tornado in the district some years earlier had all but wiped out his business. By the beginning of 1959, he'd just about built it back up to where it was before.

Dwyer had spent that Monday evening of 3 February at a Chamber of Commerce meeting in Mason City. Arriving home at about 9.30, he learned from his children's babysitter that Carroll Anderson of the Surf ballroom had been trying to reach him to book a flight for three 'entertainers' after their night's show. As the babysitter had not known how to reach Dwyer, the inquiry had been referred to his employee, Roger Peterson. Peterson was out when Dwyer called his home, but his wife confirmed that he'd accepted the charter to Fargo. Dwyer left word that Peterson should call him if he needed help with getting the chosen aircraft out of its hangar as there was another one parked in front of it.

Folks in northern Iowa are no less devout than those in West Texas. Dwyer drove over to collect his wife from a church meeting and, at 10.10 pm. retired to bed. At about 11.30 he got a phone-call from Peterson, who did need help in getting out the plane. Conscientiously Dwyer rose, dressed and drove to the lonely little airport complex a few miles east of Clear Lake. Here, at about 11.45, he rendezvoused with his pilot, a young man with the Midwest's archetypal Scandinavian looks, fair-haired, rubicund and just twenty-one years old.

Since receiving the Surf's call, Peterson been in regular touch with the control tower, checking weather conditions there and at Fargo and the forecasts for the rest of the night. Though hardly good, the weather was not severe enough to curtail flying, especially not in this resourceful part of the world. The temperature was 18 degrees with light snow flurries, winds gusting at 38 m.p.h., a cloud ceiling of 4,000 feet and visibility between six and ten miles. At Fargo, 400 miles to the north, conditions were about the same; however, Mason City's duty controller had just received warning of a weather front expected to move into the Fargo area at around 3 am, the flight's estimated time of arrival. After delivering his passengers, Peterson had planned to fly straight back to Mason City. But, with deteriorating weather conditions in prospect, Dwyer told him he should be prepared to stay at Fargo overnight.

Having given the chosen aircraft a thorough inspection, Dwyer and Peterson rolled it out of its hangar on to the snowy forecourt. It was a single-engine Beechcraft Bonanza – the same make and type as had delivered the 'Winter Dance Party''s

compère to their Kenosha gig – jauntily striped in red and white
with a V-shaped tail and the wing registration N3794N. It was a
long way from brand-new, having been manufactured in 1947
and acquired fifth- or sixth-hand by Dwyer in July of 1958 after
eleven years' continuous service, with something like 1,200 flying
hours to its credit. However, Dwyer's team maintained it well: it
had received a major overhaul on 2 January and, since then, had
logged only about forty hours in the air. Three days previously,
a local sheriff's deputy had taken it up for a spin and pronounced
it to be in first-class mechanical order.

The Bonanza was fuelled from Dwyer's private gas-pump,
and Roger Peterson climbed into the cockpit and started the
propeller to warm it up. Despite his youth, Peterson seemed
more than equal to the task ahead. He had been flying since the
age of seventeen and had qualified as a private pilot in October
1955, as a commercial one in April 1958, and as an instructor
only a week before tonight. He had logged a total of 710.45
flying hours, 318 as an air-taxi-driver and 37.35 night-flying as
pilot in command. Two hundred of these flying hours had been
logged in the past ninety days, without mishap or incident. Of
all Dwyer's charter-planes, he knew the red-and-white Beechcraft Bonanza best; it had been bought specifically for him to use
and he had so far logged something over 130 hours in it. He was
an easygoing, personable and – as we can already deduce –
obliging young man, frequently praised by passengers for his
care and consideration. Jerry Dwyer considered him 'experienced
and very competent'.

But there were things about Roger Peterson that would have
caused his passengers extreme disquiet had they known of them.
He suffered from 'a hearing disability' in his right ear – or, in
plain speech, was partially deaf. Such a handicap obviously had
serious implications for a flyer's co-ordination and sense of
balance. Yet the civil aviation authorities of the day had seemed
curiously unperturbed about it, allowing Peterson to ascend the

ladder from private pilot through commercial pilot to instructor with no sanction worse than a 'waiver', or official acknowledgement that his senses were partly impaired, in the margin of his licence. Whether any of those whom he ferried across Iowa or taught to fly in the skies above Clear Lake would have endorsed that waiver is highly debatable.

There was another disability, even more worrying. Flying by day in clear weather, with the Iowan wheatfields stretching to infinity all around, Peterson was a skilled, careful, cool and confident pilot. But when he flew by night or was enveloped suddenly by cloud or fog, an alarmingly different personality revealed itself. On the tests in flying by instruments alone which had punctuated Peterson's career, his instructors had rated him 'below average'. The tests by their nature simulated emergency in the cockpit; a sudden blank-out of all visibility, demanding instant change from reliance on one's senses to total cool-headed accuracy in reading and correlating half a dozen different gauges and dials. At such moments of controlled crisis, Peterson invariably reacted badly, suffering attacks of panic and disorientation, muddling and misreading his instruments, failing to tune and use his radio properly and follow air-traffic control procedures, even on occasion letting the aircraft slip out of his control and go into 'diving spirals to the right'.

Vertigo, the nauseous, tingling horror of finding oneself in a high place, is the very last malady from which any pilot should suffer. But it was a term frequently used in connection with Roger Peterson. Just the previous month, he'd taken yet another instrument test and failed: his instructor then had been worried by his 'false courage', proneness to vertigo, susceptibility to distraction and tendency to become 'upset and confused' and to 'let the plane get away from him'. Along with the hearing disability waiver his licence bore a notation that in instrument-reading 'holder does not meet night-time requirements'.

Thirty-seven years ago, the regulations governing pilots' rest-periods were far less stringent than they are today: in rural Iowa, they barely existed at all. On the evening that Roger Peterson was approached to make an after-midnight flight, he had already been up for between seventeen and eighteen hours. He had spent a strenuous working day, from 8 am to 5 pm, on aircraft maintenance inside Dwyer's hangar, eaten dinner at home, then gone to Mason City for a 'Jaycee' (Junior Chamber of Commerce) meeting, which was where Carroll Anderson contacted him. Dwyer's chief mechanic, Charles E. McGlothlen, had been with Peterson at the meeting and had lent him his car to go to the airport and check the meteorological reports. At about 9.30, McGlothlen and his wife had got together with Peterson and his wife of four months, De Ann, for coffee and pie at the Petersons' home. McGlothlen would later testify that when they parted at around 10 pm Peterson did not seem tired and that he'd been 'in a very good mood all the time'.

The night's weather condition *en route* to Fargo certainly would have presented no problem to any pilot of all-round competence, like Jerry Dwyer himself. But to one of Roger Peterson's peculiar handicaps, they were ominous in the extreme. The weather front moving in on North Dakota might bring with it blizzards, fog or extensive cloud. To avoid flying by instruments alone, which he was unqualified as well as deeply reluctant to do, Peterson would in effect be racing the front to Fargo. Even the relatively good weather around Mason City offered warning and hazard, or should have, to him. The cloud ceiling had by now lifted to 6,000 feet, but for most of its journey the Bonanza would need to maintain an altitude of at least 7,000 feet. Peterson thus faced the options of climbing through the cloud-ceiling, which again would mean flying by instruments, or remaining dangerously below it. Any one of these considerations should have been sufficient for Jerry Dwyer to send Peterson home to his young wife and take over the charter himself. But it didn't happen.

At about 12.40 am, Carroll Anderson's crowded station-wagon crunched to a stop outside Dwyer's Flying Service. Not until the 'three entertainers' walked into Jerry Dwyer's office did he realize his clients weren't middle-aged musicians from the dance bands which the Surf usually presented, but nationally famous rock 'n' roll stars. The gruff charter-boss had no love of teenage music, and expected rock 'n' rollers to be as the media portrayed them – unruly, disrespectful louts who, at this late hour, could be expected to be blind drunk into the bargain. Instead, he found himself greeting 'three real nice kids', good-humoured and high-spirited but polite, full of gratitude for his firm's exertion on their behalf and without the smallest taint of booze on their breath. Young Roger Peterson, for his part, was elated. A devout rock 'n' roll fan, he particularly admired Buddy, but was equally thrilled to shake hands with Ritchie Valens and the Big Bopper and to contemplate having all three to himself up in the air for the next couple of hours.

There was almost a party atmosphere in Dwyer's office as each passenger paid his $36 fare and tickets and receipts were written out. Buddy was in especially good spirits and looking forward to the flight even more than was the triumphant Ritchie. He spent some minutes discussing small planes with Dwyer, mentioning that his brother Larry had qualified as a pilot three weeks previously and that he himself intended to do the same and buy himself a Cessna. On the wall hung a map of the United States with a pencil attached to it by string. In the remaining couple of minutes before their flight was called, each star in turn traced the distance from Mason City to his home turf, Ritchie's in the San Fernando Valley, the Bopper's in Beaumont, Texas, Buddy's in Lubbock. Alas, they were closer than they knew.

The dirty laundry they were taking to Fargo on their bus-bound colleagues' behalf, added to their own briefcases and holdalls, made an unusually large amount of baggage for a three-passenger flight, 42 lb in all. Though his night's obligations were already more than discharged, Carroll Anderson lingered behind to give a hand in loading the luggage compartment, situated midway in the belly of the plane. The overflow, including J. P. Richardson's acoustic guitar, was packed into the cockpit. Halfway through the loading process, Buddy realized that he'd left his leather toilet-bag in Anderson's station-wagon and had to run back to retrieve it. The passengers were on the point of boarding when a car drew up; it was full of fans, female and male, who'd been among the Surf's audience and wanted to say, 'Thanks for the show.' Many rock 'n' rollers, buttonholed in sub-zero temperatures at almost 1 am, would have found it difficult to respond with any grace. But these three cheerily waved back and shouted, 'You're welcome.'

Jerry Dwyer, too, had come out of his office to watch the party board. In common with all light aircraft, the Bonanza's cockpit had a single access door, on the right-hand side. Dwyer was later to remember that Ritchie and the Big Bopper climbed in first, taking the double rear passenger seat. By mutual tacit agreement, the privilege of riding beside the pilot, in the front right-hand seat, went to Buddy. It stuck in Dwyer's mind that, palpably eager to be off, Buddy got into the plane too early and had to get out again to allow Peterson to climb across to his left-hand seat at the controls.

When everyone was settled, Dwyer slammed the door shut, then got into his car and drove to the control-tower to watch their take-off. He found the duty controller, Mr Bryan, was already talking to Peterson over the radio. Dwyer's standing instruction to all his pilots was that they must file a flight-plan with the tower before leaving the ground. Peterson had not followed this instruction, the controller told Dwyer, but had promised that he'd attend to it as soon as he was airborne.

The tower's open-air observation platform afforded Dwyer a

good view of runway 17, where the Bonanza had been directed to take off. He remembered later that it sat at the end of the runway for a few minutes, then made a normal southward departure, breaking ground about a third of the way down the runway, levelling off at about 800 feet, then making a textbook 180 degree turn and heading north-west for Fargo.

Dwyer went back into the control-room and asked Mr Bryan if Peterson had yet filed his flight-plan. But Peterson had not. The charter boss's later deposition clearly indicated that he was annoyed with his employee for this lapse, no doubt the result of Peterson's fascination with his famous passengers and desire to cut a dash in front of them. Dwyer asked Mr Bryan to tell Peterson over the radio to file a flight-plan for both his outward and return journeys without further delay. The controller tried several times, but was unable to get Peterson on the frequency on which they had previously spoken. After a few minutes, he ceased calling, but left his transmitter open in case for some reason Peterson had decided to change frequencies.

Dwyer went outside on to the platform again and watched the plane's white tail-light dwindle away to the north-west. It disappeared as the Bonanza apparently flew through a patch of cloud or fog, but after a moment or two Dwyer picked it up again. The runway's northerly edge was marked by two towers, each with a red light at the top. In relation to the two towers the Bonanza's tail-light did not seem to be climbing but, in Dwyer's words, 'drifting gradually downward'. At the time, he thought this must be an optical illusion; that the light was not descending, just getting further and further away.

Beyond the runway-end lay infinities of Iowa farmland, its rich earth frozen rock-solid under the packed-down snow of months. The nearest house belonged to a farmer named Reeve Eldridge, who always left a light on in his front hall as an extra marker for departing planes. What farmer Eldridge heard at around 1 am that morning he would later tell in an official deposition whose halting words evoke the wind-torn darkness and the impending catastrophe with peculiar vividness:

> Woke out of a sound sleep by motor roar. Sounded smooth, but pulling as though climbing. Couldn't see nothing because of darkness, but was low from sound. Strong wind blowing with a south-easterly direction. Woke my wife succenly [sic] & scared her & child.

Likewise the testimony of Eldridge's neighbour, farm-worker Delbert Juhl:

> We got home about 10.15. The weather was pretty good, it was snow a little bit now and then. We went to bed, then between 12 and 1 we heard a plane go over. To me the motor was working good and he had it going pretty good and that was the last we heard of it. To me I think the plane went somewhere near our place. It was pretty low and it keep [sic] right on going. The wind was blowing from the south-west.

Back in the control-tower, Jerry Dwyer stood by as Mr Bryan, the controller, continued his efforts to raise Roger Peterson on the radio. But there still was no response from Peterson. Now definitely uneasy, Dwyer asked Mr Bryan to send a teletype message to Fargo airport, requesting to be notified the moment Peterson made contact with the tower there. Mr Bryan also sent messages to the three other airports along the Bonanza's probable route. Alexandria, Minneapolis and Redwood Falls, asking whether Peterson had contacted any of them. It was all that could be done for the moment, and at 1.30 Dwyer returned home, although not to sleep.

He telephoned Mr Bryan at 2 am, but was told there still had been no word from Roger Peterson. Of the three airports connected by teletype, only one had responded and it had not heard from Peterson either. At 3.30, half an hour past the Bonanza's estimated time of arrival in Fargo, the message was the same. Dwyer himself then placed a call to the Fargo control-tower. The controller there said he'd had no contact with an incoming flight N3794N and did not expect one since the expected weather front had just hit and a heavy snowstorm was in progress.

Dwyer hung on the telephone until 4 a.m., interrogating his chief mechanic, Charles McGlothlen, 'to see if he could give me any information as to where Roger might have gone'; briefly clinging to the hope that the Minneapolis city airport, with its vastly superior technology, might pick up the Bonanza where intermediate 'omni stations' could not. But Minneapolis could find no trace of it either. At 4.10, Dwyer had no alternative but to ask Mr Bryan to post the flight officially missing and tell Minneapolis air-traffic control to issue a general alert.

By 8 am, a bleary-eyed Dwyer was back in his office at Mason City airport, staring at the wall-map on which, a few hours earlier, three excited rock 'n' roll stars had traced how far they were from home. Finding N3794N was now the responsibility of the 10th Air Force Search and Rescue Coordination Center. But, rather than just sit and wait, Dwyer decided to roll out another aircraft from his hangar and follow Peterson's route to Fargo in the hope of finding some clue. He had barely cleared the runway when he spotted wreckage in the snow, four or five miles to the north-west. He radioed back to the control-tower for the police and two ambulance but did not land, thinking it more important to remain in the air and mark the spot for the emergency services.

The Bonanza had come down in a snow-covered stubble field, tearing off its right wing, then ploughing 540 feet across the unobstructed terrain to finish, tail-up, against a wire boundary fence. The impact, at full speed – 170 mph – had torn the red-and-white fuselage apart like paper, killing all four occupants instantly and flinging three of them into the air with the horrendous velocity of human cannonballs. J. P. Richardson's body lay forty feet away from the wreckage, on the far side of the boundary fence. Those of Buddy and Ritchie Valens each lay about thirteen feet away, to the south and south-west respectively. Roger Peterson's was still inside the tangled remains of the cockpit. It could have happened no more than five minutes after take-off.

In 1959, as now, few types of disaster were more exhaustively investigated than those involving civil aircraft. But, despite a prompt and lengthy inquest by the United States Civil Aeronautics Board, the cause of the crash was not established, and has not been to this day. Thirty-seven years on, it remains surrounded by a fog of rumours and theories, most far-fetched and illogical, all affording thousands throughout the Holly subculture much the same gloomy relish as picking endlessly at a scab that can never heal.

The one party that can be totally exculpated is the aircraft itself. Tests by a battery of CAB inspectors (including one with a surname of special poignancy to Buddy, Leo C. McGuire) confirmed the Bonanza to have been in perfect structural and mechanical order. The dashboard instruments had all been functioning normally, diligently clocking up their terrible readings in the final seconds until the impact stopped them dead: airspeed 165–170 mph, rate of descent 3,000 feet per minute, attitude indicator stuck at 90 degree right bank and nose-down position. The Lear auto-pilot was switched off and the radio still tuned to Mason City's control-tower.

The enduring mystery is why, just four or five minutes after his faultlessly executed take-off, a pilot should have flown a well-maintained and mechanically sound aircraft at top speed straight into the ground. Most of the legends and rumours revolve around some or other alleged incident in the Bonanza's cockpit which fatally distracted Peterson's attention or even did him violence. One story has it that there were drugs on board; another that the Big Bopper was trying to change seats and toppled on to the pilot or upset the trim of the plane; another that four passengers and 42 lb of luggage were too heavy a payload; another that the .22 calibre pistol Buddy carried in his toilet bag somehow went off, killing or wounding Peterson.

All this can safely be dismissed as nonsense. None of the plane's passengers used drugs, nor were they in any mood for self-destructive rock-star horseplay. All three were exhausted, thankful to be liberated from their purgatorial tour-bus, thinking only of reaching their destination, having a hot bath and tumbling in between clean sheets. Though certainly heavily loaded, the Bonanza was within its weight-limit. The idea that Buddy might have taken out his handgun and gratuitously waved it around contradicts everything we know of him. Getting four people into the Bonanza's small cockpit meant packing them together as tightly as sardines. Crossing or uncrossing one's legs was difficult enough: moving from the back seat to the front would have been impossible.

The only possible causes of the crash were weather or pilot-error, or a combination of both. Though the weather was not bad and visibility was generally clear for the Bonanza's take-off, Jerry Dwyer on the tower-platform remembered seeing its tail-light disappear into 'a patch of fog or cloud'. Either would have been well below freezing, and it's possible that even that short immersion made the Bonanza's wings ice up. A small plane can ice up within seconds and the result is always the same – to obstruct the flow of air over the wings that gives it its lift. The plane heard by farm-worker Delbert Juhl had sounded 'pretty low', i.e., lower than it should have when well clear of the runway. The 'motor roar ... pulling as though climbing' which awoke Reeves Eldridge and scared his wife and child could well have been the Bonanza, with both wings perilously ice-crusted, unsuccessfully struggling to maintain height.

In light of what the CAB investigators subsequently discovered about Roger Peterson's flying-record, pilot-error would seem to have been, at very least, a strong contributory factor. Over-excited by the company of his three musical heroes, chattering to Buddy on his right and Ritchie and the Bopper over his shoulder, Peterson probably was taken completely by surprise by the fog-cloud, and in his confusion misread his instrument-panel as he was so prone to do. Unfortunately, the instrument most easy to misread on that particular aircraft was the altitude-indicator, showing the angle of its nose. The Bonanza was fitted with a Sperry gyroscope, which registered the nose-angle in inverted form, descending when the plane was ascending and vice versa. The only explanation for Peterson's steadfast plunge to earth was that, habitually careless over instruments, he totally forgot the peculiarity of the Sperry gyroscope – that he believed he was climbing when in fact he was diving. This would explain the descending tail-light which Jerry Dwyer mistook for an optical illusion. When a snowy stubble field suddenly rushed up out of the darkness, panic and vertigo overwhelmed Peterson, his sensory imbalance allowed his right wing to dip down, and the plane 'got away from him'.

Over the years, in common with many others, I've imagined the horror of those last few seconds inside the plunging cockpit. Now at last, in November 1995, I find myself sitting opposite the person who must have thought about it more than anyone: Buddy's widow, Maria Elena.

She admits that scarcely a day passes without a picture of that bleak Iowa night returning to her mind, along with the memory of the bad dream she and Buddy had together just before he left her. 'I think how terrible it would have been, him going down, although I hear it was very fast ... him thinking of the condition that I was in that he wouldn't see his child, that I'd be by myself . . . I still think about it, and it bothers me.'

The night on the bus to which Tommy Allsup's good sportsmanship had condemned him turned out a far less trying one than he'd expected. Snuggled in the Big Bopper's new sleeping-bag, stretched along the wide back seat, he slept soundly for most of the 400-mile journey to Moorhead. 'When we got to our hotel, I was the first one off the bus,' he remembers. 'Right in the lobby there was a TV set with a picture of the Bopper on the screen. I thought it must be some kind of advertisement for the show at the Armory that night.

'So I go bouncing straight up to the guy at the front desk and say, "Do you have reservations for the Crickets?" He says, "Yeah, we got all you guys here." I says, "What room's Buddy in?" He says, "Haven't you heard? Buddy Holly's been killed in a plane crash. It's on the news right now."'

Dazed, Tommy went back out to the bus, where the rest of the 'Winter Dance Party' troupe were returning to consciousness, yawning, rubbing their frozen hands and stretching their cramped limbs. Always a man of very few words, the big Oklahoman did not lose his taciturnity even now. 'Fellas . . .' he said. 'They didn't make it . . .'

The story had broken with unusual speed thanks to a local ham radio enthusiast, who intercepted Jerry Dwyer's message to the emergency services, then tipped off the Mason City media. By no means all of the radio and wire-service reports now chattering across the continent rated Buddy first in importance among the 'three top rock 'n' roll stars' who had perished. 'In order of bigness,' one bulletin said, 'that would probably be Ritchie Valens, then Buddy Holly . . .'

Initially there were reported to be five victims: Buddy, Ritchie, the Bopper, Roger Peterson – and Tommy Allsup. For

Buddy had been carrying Tommy's wallet as the ID needed to pick up his registered letter from Fargo post office. The first sifters of the plane wreckage calculated the death-toll by the number of personal identifications they found, not the number of bodies. Still unaware of this, Tommy rushed to a phone to call his mother, tell her the dreadful news about Buddy and reassure her that he was safe. 'My Mom hadn't heard a thing about it yet,' he remembers. 'But all the time I was talking to her on the phone, a neighbour of hers from down the street was trying to get through to tell her I'd been named as one of the dead.'

Buddy's old friend and partner Bob Montgomery, now also a married man, had been away on a trip to central Texas with his new wife. On Tuesday, 3 February, the Montgomerys were driving home to Lubbock, taking turns behind the wheel. 'When my wife took over, I told her, "Really be careful how you drive because I've got this bad feeling in the pit of my stomach, like we could be going to have some kind of an accident,"' Bob remembers. 'I had that same weird feeling all the way back to Lubbock, that something just wasn't right right. When we got home, I called Echo McGuire and the first thing she said was, "Isn't it awful? . . ."'

A thousand miles westward in snow-free Los Angeles, the news devastated Buddy's close friends Eddie Cochran and Phil Everly, and Cochran's fiancée, the songwriter Sharon Sheeley. Sharon heard it over her car-radio. 'The shock hit me so badly, I had to stop the car and throw up. When I got back to my house, the phone started ringing. It was Phil Everly, just back from his Australian tour and full of life and fun. I'll never forget the awful silence down the phone-line when I told him Buddy had gone.'

For Eddie Cochran, Buddy's death was a blow from which he would never recover. 'The two of them had been like brothers,' Sharon Sheeley says. 'And Eddie couldn't get it out of his mind that he'd almost gone on that tour with Buddy, but had dropped out to do the *Ed Sullivan Show*, which was supposed to be happening that very week. All the Sullivan people were at the airport waiting for Eddie – but he didn't get off the plane. He'd taken his station-wagon and gone off into the desert by himself, to mourn.'

After their unsuccessful attempt to reach Buddy at the Surf ballroom, for whatever reason, J. I. Allison and Joe B. Mauldin had gone on working with Norman Petty until the small hours, then both had driven back from Clovis to Lubbock. Joe B. was awoken by a telephone-call from his sister. He later recalled how he refused to believe what she told him until he'd dressed and gone out for a newspaper, even though he could have confirmed it by simply turning on the radio. Some early bulletins in the Lubbock area said Buddy's two fellow-victims been 'his group, the Crickets', and assumed that to mean J.I. and Joe B. For several hours, until the true facts emerged via national radio, the families of both were deluged by anxious calls from relatives and friends.

Petty himself had been told the news by a contact at a radio station in Indiana. First to clock in at the Seventh Street studio compound that morning was Robert Linville of the Roses vocal trio. Linville found Petty and Vi up in their apartment, both sitting on the floor weeping among their parchment-and-gilt lamps, Murano glass vases and long-necked ceramic cats. Every few seconds, the telephone would ring and yet another grief-stricken voice would plead, 'Say it isn't true.'

Larry Holley, that morning, was in Lubbock, working on a tile-job with the same absorption and perfectionism his kid brother had always brought to music. Stopping for lunch around midday, Larry drove over to the site where Travis, the gentle, quiet middle Holley brother, was supposed to be working. But the only sign of Travis was a scatter of tools, lying on the ground as if they'd been hurriedly dropped. Larry drove home, but could find no trace of his wife, Maxine, either, so in pique he decided to eat alone at a nearby café. 'As soon as I walked in, the

lady said, "Isn't it terrible about those three boys getting killed!" '
I ran straight out and drove over to Daddy and Mother's place. I
can still feel the sick feeling in my stomach when I saw all the
cars parked outside.'

L.O. and Ella Holley had begun the day alone and in usual
harmony at their spotless house on 36th Street. Unsure quite
where Buddy would be at this point, but confident he would call
or write soon, they were loyally listening to his favourite radio
station, KLLL. For them, the news did not burst like a bombshell
but emerged by slow degrees, in the agonized tact of a telephone-
caller uncertain whether they'd heard it yet. 'We got this call
from a friend of ours ... Niki Sullivan's mother,' Ella recalled in
an interview with Dutch television in 1988. Framed in pitiless
close-up, she is by now a frail as well as tiny figure. Her quiet,
steady voice, with its old-fashioned far-western pronunciation,
seems to belong to another century. But the indomitable strength
and spirit that lifted her baby boy to the first rung of the ladder
still shine out of her.

'[Niki's mother] wanted to know if we were listening to the
radio. I told her we were, and she said, "Well, have you heard
anything?" I said, "I don't know what you mean. We're listening
to music." She said, "There's been some news. Have you heard
it?" I said, "Why, no, I haven't. What are you talking about?"
She said, "Well, maybe I'd better find out some more about this,
and then I'll talk to you later."

'Then I told my husband and said, "Turn the radio on and
see if there's some news." And immediately we heard: "There's
been a small plane crash in Iow-ee." And, just the minute I heard
that, I knew what they were going to tell.' After almost thirty
years, her voice still breaks on the words; she looks down to
hide her tear-filled eyes. 'That's what came, just the minute we
turned the radio on. "There's been a small plane crash ... up in
Iow-ee ..."'

In New York City, what snow there had been was already

piled in sooty banks along the Greenwich Village sidewalks. Four storeys above the junction of Fifth Avenue and 9th Street, Maria Elena was still in bed, racked with another bout of morning sickness. For her, too, finding out was made all the worse by someone's efforts to break it gently. 'I got a phone-call from Lou Giordano, the young singer Buddy had been produc- ing. He said, "What are you doing?" and I said, "I just woke up. As a matter of fact, I'm still in bed." He said, "Well stay in bed, don't get up. I'm on my way right over. But do me a favour. Don't turn the TV on." Well, of course, as soon as someone tells you not to do something like that, you do it right away. And at that precise moment, my aunt was on her way over to the apartment.'

By early afternoon, disc jockeys across the nation were broadcasting tributes to the three fallen stars. Alan Freed's first act on stepping before the television cameras was to call for a minute's silence. One of the deejays quickest off the mark was 'Snuff' Garrett, a friend of Buddy's at KLLL, Lubbock, now working for KSYD in Wichita Falls. Garrett followed up his regular show with a special Buddy Holly memorial programme, interspersing his records with telephone hook-ups to J. I. Allison and Joe B. Mauldin and Norman Petty. Both J.I. and Joe B. were audibly struggling to hold back the tears. But, whatever Clovis Man's anguish earlier that day, he had completely recovered by the time he spoke to Snuff Garrett. His tone was as politely philosophical as if he'd merely been informed of some regrettable but unavoidable disaster continents away, an Indian famine or African *coup d'état*:

GARRETT: ... I'm certainly sorry about it and I'm very sorry to bother you.
PETTY: Well, Snuff, things like this happen and there is nothing we can do to control them.
GARRETT: That's true.

PETTY: We often wonder why things like this happen but, of course, there is always bound to be a reason somewhere.

GARRETT: Uh, Norm, does Buddy have any more records in the can?

PETTY: He had two more, uh, that we did in New York. Do you know this last new one of Buddy's?

GARRETT: Paul Anka's? The Paul Anka tune?

PETTY: Right. We have two others that were done at the same time, and then I probably have some here in Clovis.

GARRETT: I see.

PETTY: He was supposed to go out for another session just next week.

GARRETT: Oh.

PETTY: However, the ones he did there and the ones I have here are the only ones we have left.

GARRETT: I see. I guess . . . uh, will you put most of these out? I hope you will, those last ones of Buddy's.

PETTY: It depends. There's bound to be some legal action [!] which we are not going to comment on. But I'm sure these last two from New York will be out.

Thanks to the five-hour time-difference (six if you were in Iowa), Britain did not learn of the crash until early in the evening of 3 February. There was, even so, ample time to make the two national television news bulletins, on BBC and ITV, and the sole national radio news bulletin on the BBC Home Service. But to none of these august organizations did even the highest rock 'n' roll tragedy rank as broadcastable matter. Fleet Street, the following morning did rather better. The *Daily Mirror*, brashest of the country's two tabloid dailies, ran the story as its front-page lead, though still unable to avoid patronizing quotation-marks: TOP 'ROCK' STARS DIE IN CRASH. The main picture was of the Big Bopper in his big Stetson hat, spreading his arms the width of the page. Buddy appeared as just a mug-shot in the body of the text. I myself did not find out until early that evening, when I arrived at Ryde Pier Pavilion to play in a band at my father's draughty and lacklustre thrice-weekly rock 'n' roll dance. I can still see the stricken face of my fellow guitarist, Alan Packer, as he showed me the *Mirror*'s front page.

Despite the loss of its three headline attractions, and the traumatized grief of its surviving personnel, the 'Winter Dance Party' had performed at Moorhead National Guard Armory on 3 February as advertised. Into the breach that night stepped a young Fargo group called the Shadows whose vocalist, Robert Velline, was a better-than-average Buddy-mimic. It was the beginning of big things for Velline who, renamed Bobby Vee – and directed by Buddy's friend Snuff Garrett – would lead the next generation of mimsy heart throbs with Buddy-inflected, double-tracked songs like 'Rubber Ball', 'Take Good Care Of My Baby', 'Run To Him', and 'The Night Has A Thousand Eyes'. The Moorhead promoter ran true to type, first begging the depleted tour-troupe not to disappoint the fans, but after-wards trying to pay them less than the agreed fee because their main performers had not appeared as per contract.

GAC showed the same hard-nosed attitude, informing them that they must play all twelve of the dates remaining on the tour's wild interstate zigzag – Sioux City, Des Moines and Cedar Rapids, Iowa; Spring Valley and Chicago, Illinois; Waterloo and Dubuque, Iowa; Louisville, Kentucky (the craziest detour yet); Canton and Youngstown, Ohio; Peoria and Springfield, Illinois. To replace Buddy in front of his band, GAC flew in Ronnie Smith, from Odessa, Texas, whose group had originally supplied drummer Carl Bunch – still languishing in hospital with frostbite back in Michigan. Tommy Allsup and Waylon Jennings were promised that if they overcame their shock and grief, and backed Ronnie Smith for the rest of the tour, they could share the unpaid balance of Buddy's salary between them. For the remaining week and a half, Waylon played Buddy's Stratocaster, hugging it to him like a talisman that might summon its owner back from the snows.

The job of travelling to Iowa, formally identifying Buddy and bringing him home for burial could only rightfully be done by the eldest brother who had always watched over him like a second father. Chartering a plane from the West Texas Aircraft company, Larry Holley left Lubbock on his heartbreaking mission on 4 February, accompanied by his sister Pat's husband, J. E. Weir. But when they reached the Wilcox Funeral Home in Clear Lake, the tough ex-Marine who'd witnessed death wholesale in World War II, 'chickened out', as he self-deprecatingly puts it, and his brother-in-law made the identification in his place. 'When J. E. came out, he said, "I'm glad you didn't see Buddy that way, Larry. 'Cause he was pretty beaten up."'

They also drove out to the crash-site, where the Bonanza's tangled wreckage was by now covered by several inches of snow. Nearby lay what was perhaps the saddest part of the debris, the stage-suits and shirts that had belonged to Buddy, Ritchie and the Bopper and those they'd been carrying for their tour-companions to be drycleaned in Moorhead. 'There were beautiful, colourful clothes all piled up in a heap,' Larry remembers. 'I was asked if I wanted to take Buddy's things, but I said, "No, get rid of them all. Burn them." Then I spotted his little leather ditty-bag, the one he carried his shaving-kit in. I said, "I'll take this. Just this."'

The bag was missing the zip-up side compartment where Buddy carried his on-the-road earnings and his .22 pistol. He had been paid in cash after the Surf Ballroom show and so must have had something like $1,000 in the bag when the Bonanza took off. But no money was reported found apart from what he, Ritchie and the Bopper had in their wallets. Among the pathetic tally of personal effects – Buddy's black Faiosa glasses, a pair of poker-dice, the Bopper's watch, engraved on the back with details of his record-breaking disc-a-thon – there was no .22 pistol either. That would not turn up until the winter's snows had thawed and the farmer who owned the field, one Albert Juhl, was ploughing it up prior to spring planting.

When the pistol was handed in to the local sheriff's office, one of its five chambers was found to be empty. So was born the enduring legend of the crash's having been caused by horseplay or even violence in the Bonanza's cockpit. The truth proved rather more prosaic: Farmer Juhl later confessed that it was he who'd fired the .22, to see whether it was still working after its weeks in the frozen earth.

Having all but ignored Buddy in his lifetime, the Lubbock papers now could not honour him enough. LUBBOCK ROCK 'N' ROLL STAR KILLED was the evening *Journal*'s strident but oddly impersonal front-page banner on 3 February. An adjacent story described how the Midwest's icy talons had reached down even as far as the Texas plains with a 'killer storm' of snow and freezing sleet which had shut down schools and caused traffic chaos in the Odessa–Kermit area. SERVICES PENDING FOR BUDDY HOLLY, VICTIM OF IOWA PLANE CRASH, said the next day's headline; SINGING STAR'S BODY DUE HERE TODAY. A long inside feature proudly detailed some of the plans Buddy had been making – his album of 'devotional music', his homecoming concert in Lubbock the following summer, and the European tour from which, it was said, he'd wanted to return by ocean liner, 'just for fun'.

By a horrible irony, the aircraft bringing Buddy's temporary coffin from Mason City ran into bad weather soon after take-off and had to put down for an extended delay at Des Moines. Much as he wanted to stand watch over his brother on this last trip home, Larry Holley had to travel separately. 'All the way back, I was praying,' he remembers. 'But not for myself. I was saying,

"Please Lord, let Daddy and Mother find the strength to live through this."'

In New York, meanwhile, the shock and anguish which Maria Elena had suffered at the news of her husband's death brought a second bereavement. Two days after losing Buddy, she also lost the baby which he was so sure would be a boy. By coincidence, the emergency room to which she was rushed happened to be at St Vincent's, the Catholic hospital where she'd once worked as a translator. The Puerto Rican doctor who treated her ('I can see his face now') was a colleague from those days.

Barely five weeks pregnant as she had been, Maria Elena was in no danger herself, and could return home after a few hours' observation. Weak and distraught though she was, she then caught a plane to Lubbock for Buddy's funeral. The Holley family, of course, did not even know she had been pregnant, and in the coming days of mourning – for reasons known only to her proud, defensive heart – Maria Elena did not mention her miscarriage. Consequently, there would later be wagging tongues, (mainly from the Clovis area) which cast doubt on whether it had ever really happened.

The 'killer storm' had melted away and normal Lubbock winter weather in the mid-forties had returned by Saturday, 7 February, when Buddy's funeral took place at the Lubbock Tabernacle Baptist Church. The service drew a congregation of 1,500, the largest the church had ever seen, and too many even for its cavernous premises to accommodate. A number of the mourners had to be content to pay their respects from the vestibule, some even from outside in the parking-lot. In some Southern Baptist funerals, the coffin is left open, allowing a formal farewell to be paid to the deceased. But the terrible injuries which Buddy had suffered made that impossible. His family were still palpably in shock but, as ever, took strength from his mother, who remained composed and dignified throughout.

The pallbearers were Buddy's original fellow Crickets J. I. Allison, Joe B. Mauldin and Niki Sullivan, his teenage country music cronies Bob Montgomery and Sonny Curtis, and his close friend Phil Everly. Phil's elder brother Don, always considered to be the less serious of the two, had found himself more affected by Buddy's death than anything in his life before. 'I couldn't go to the funeral,' he says now, 'I couldn't go anywhere. I just took to my bed.' Another notable absentee was Waylon Jennings, the musician who owed most to Buddy's generosity and unselfishness. As a further inducement to finish the 'Winter Dance Party' tour, GAC had guaranteed Waylon time off to attend Buddy's funeral, even promising to pay his air-fare back to Lubbock. That promise had now been conveniently forgotten, however, and Waylon was stuck on an icy bus somewhere between Iowa and Illinois, still wishing he could unsay his very last words to his mentor and friend.

The service was conducted by Ben D. Johnson, the same pastor who had performed Buddy's wedding on that sweltering, impatient day just five months earlier. The service included surprisingly little music for one who had lived and breathed it. Nor were any of Buddy's records deemed fit, as yet, to be heard in his own church, even though he had created rock 'n' roll as purely joyful as any hymns. Instead, Bill Pickering of the Picks vocal trio sang a spiritual called 'Beyond The Sunset'. The congregation also listened to one of Buddy's favourite gospel records, 'I'll Be All Right' by The Angelic Gospel Singers.

The casket was then carried to its resting place, just a mile or so from the simple wooden house where Buddy had been born and in the lee of the huge grain elevator which in the coming decades would mark his whereabouts like a Texas Taj Mahal. Sick with grief and still in pain from her miscarriage, Maria Elena did not feel equal to attending the funeral nor visiting Buddy's grave. She has not seen it to this day.

Epilogue

CRYING, WAITING, HOPING

NORMAN PETTY wasted no time in returning to practicalities. On the day after Buddy's death, Petty wrote to Dick Jacobs at Coral Records:

Dear Dick,
The Crickets, Mr Jerry Allison and Mr Joe Mauldin,
have asked me to authorize you to ask Brunswick Records
to issue a new contract to the group known as
THE CRICKETS. The boys will be able to use a new
vocalist whenever they choose . . . with your permission
of course. The new contract should be made payable to
the Norman Petty Agency Inc., Box 926, Clovis, New
Mexico.

This agency will receive all royalties due the Crickets
consisting of Mr Jerry Allison and Mr Joe Mauldin, and will
make payments to them when received.

This is your authorization by power of attorney
invested in me to issue the new recordings of the above-
named Crickets. The selections are 'Someone Someone' and
'Love'll Make A Fool Of You [sic]' the selections you are
now holding on tape from us.

We are anxious to hear of your prompt action in this
matter.
Best regards

> The Crickets
> Norman Petty
> manager and power of attorney.

While all around him registered only desolation and disbelief,
Clovis Man calmly proceeded with the business of getting his
own way, untroubled by any sense of timing or appropriateness.
With the Brunswick label compliant, and no one else around to
stand in his way, Petty was now free to register the Crickets'
name as a business trademark, encompassing two people only, J.
I. Allison and Joe B. Mauldin, and managed and administered
solely by himself. In a further stroke of magnificent insensitivity,
the date on which he sent off the completed copyright registration papers was Saturday, 7 February, the day of Buddy's funeral.

With copyright documents filed, it was a simple matter to see
off the second-edition Crickets, Tommy Allsup, Waylon Jennings and Carl Bunch, whom Buddy had recruited to back him
on the 'Winter Dance Party' and who naturally, if naïvely, hoped
to continue working under that name. For a time there was talk
of turning Allsup, Jennings and Bunch into another group, the
Jitters, fronted by Ronnie Smith, the singer whom GAC had
flown in to take Buddy's place for the rest of the tour. But that
idea came to nothing, and four redundant Crickets were left to
make their own dispirited way back from New York through
the ice and slush to West Texas. The others remember letting
Waylon Jennings out of the car on a windswept corner in St
Louis, Missouri, all blissfully unconscious that a future country
music giant was walking away from them.

The sense of Buddy being deeply and sincerely mourned was
palpable. In schools throughout both America and Britain, whole
classes turned up for their lessons wearing black armbands. Yet

the grief was curiously unfocused. Among his huge world-wide constituency, only an infinitesimal number had ever seen him perform or gained any but the vaguest impression of his character. Grief was tinged with guilt, for not making more of him while he was around. Why hadn't one learned more of his words, bought more of his records, ferreted out his curriculum vitae, fought one's way to a live concert of his by hook or by crook? The most specific shock came from belatedly finding out that this being who had encouraged, soothed and reassured us had himself been only twenty-two. Even to a fifteen-year-old, accustomed to regard people in their early twenties as crusty adults, that seemed a horribly unfair moment at which to have to go.

The most hardened music industry opportunist did not dream at that point how Buddy's death would be the means of lifting his fame – and sales – into the stratosphere. It had never happened before. Previous famous casualties of popular music, the jazz cornettist Bix Beiderbecke, the bluesman Robert Johnson, the singer Billie Holiday, Buddy's own great country hero Hank Williams, all had been elevated to mythological status by early and unlucky death. All, too, had ceased to be regarded as commercial propositions from the moment they were lowered into the earth. Until Buddy, the accepted wisdom among record companies was that 'stiffs don't sell'.

But this was no longer old-time jazz or blues with their familiar adult themes of pain and mortality. This was rock 'n' roll, the all-excluding *raison d'être* of every worthwhile teenage life; a constantly unfolding social as well as musical melodrama whose players – like its audience – had hitherto been regarded as indestructible.

Buddy was the first white rock 'n' roll star to die in any circumstances whatever. That alone, in teenage eyes, was sufficient to bestow a glorious martyrdom. How or why he had died initially seemed less important than that the grim and grey real world had succeeded at last in plucking one of the music's foremost jewels from its gaudy crown. Strangers to pain, certain of their own immortality, young people have always been fascinated by the idea of sudden death, never more so than when it claims one of their own. By pulverizing his Porsche sports car and himself, for no discernible reason, three years earlier, James Dean had become the first true icon of rock 'n' roll culture. But here was an end even more sudden, dramatic and – one truly thought – glamorous. In the late fifties, in Britain at least, few young people had any direct experience of flying, and the news media did not report tragedy in the voyeuristic detail they do today. Few of those who grieved for Buddy could begin to imagine the terror he must have felt in his final moments, the sickening squalor of the wreckage strewn about that snowy cornfield or the horrific long, grieving twilight now faced by his family. It seemed an instantaneous and painless transition from life into a legend already enshrined by Tommy Dee's 'tribute' record – 'a new star . . . up towards the north'.

The immediate commercial lift-off did not come from any belated appreciation of Buddy's talents, merely the piquant fact that the last single he'd released before his death had been called 'It Doesn't Matter Anymore'. With morbid hindsight, that seemed almost a comment from beyond the grave on his late unsuccessful struggle to get back into the charts. The record had been available, and selling poorly since early January. But now the shadow of the Grim Reaper seemed to add an irresistible extra something to the pizzicato violins and lighter-than-air voice. Within days of Buddy's death, 'It Doesn't Matter Anymore' leapt into the *Billboard* Hot 100, eventually peaking at number 13. In Britain, it spent twenty-one weeks in the *New Musical Express* Top 20, reaching number 1 on 6 May.

Nowadays, the deaths of three major rock stars in such a plane crash would bring lawsuits against the charter company by the stars' respective spouses or families, calculated on potential future earnings which could now never be realized, and so probably running into billions rather than millions of dollars. Thirty-seven years ago, even in America, such litigation was still in its infancy. The suits faced by Dwyer's Flying Service for that ill-fated midnight charter totalled just $3.5 million – $1 million each from Buddy's and J. P. Richardson's families and $1.5 million from Ritchie Valens's. A judgement in their favour would still have been more than enough to wipe out the business which Jerry Dwyer had already seen wrecked once by the vagaries of the Iowa weather. Fortunately for him, Iowan state law in those days put a ceiling of $50,000 on legal damages payable to any individual plaintiff. The Holley, Richardson and Valenzuela family each had no choice but to settle for that amount, and the $150,000 was paid by Dwyer's insurance company.

Although Dwyer's business survived the tragedy, his life was to be plagued by it for ever afterwards. The official report into the crash made no criticism of his personal conduct, which indeed had been thoroughly conscientious. What, clearly, would have been questioned if the lawsuits had reached court was his judgement in allowing Roger Peterson to take off that night with weather conditions as they were. In the following weeks, grief-stricken fans of all three dead stars reached their own intemperate verdict: Dwyer received a deluge of hate mail, including several death threats.

As the years passed, and Clear Lake and the crash site became places of pilgrimage, the unlucky charter-boss found himself an object of pitying or resentful fascination, endlessly pointed out as The Man Who Sent Buddy to his Death. Unable physically to hide, Dwyer was to take refuge in a gruff taciturnity, refusing to discuss the events of 3 February 1959, or to speculate on what might have ailed Roger Peterson beyond a single, cryptic sentence: 'My pilot was indisposed.'

The doomed aircraft itself, that once jaunty red-and-white-striped Beechcraft Bonanza, was to suffer a similarly strange and tortuous fate. After the teams from the Civil Aeronautics Board had finished sifting through it, there was nothing to be done with its remains – now no longer the property of Dwyer's Flying Service – but to sell them off as scrap metal. The purchaser, in some weird approximation of nostalgia, was none other than Jerry Dwyer. For decades, the rumour among Clear Lake pilgrims was that Dwyer had the plane's carcase locked in a hangar at Mason City airport, and intended one day to have it broken into small pieces which he could then sell to Buddy fans as key-ring charms. Only recently has he disclosed that he had the remains of N3794N transported to a secret location in the Iowan wilderness and given decent burial.

Buddy had not filed a will, though his lawyer, Harold Orenstein, remembers that one had certainly been drawn up for him – indeed, it happened to be among the papers on Orenstein's desk on the morning after the crash. New York law at that time prescribed that when a person died intestate, the first $50,000 of the estate went to the surviving spouse and the remainder was to be divided between the spouse and the parents of the deceased. Apart from Buddy's personal possessions and the $50,000 in damages from Dwyer's Flying Service, the main assets of his estate as it stood were the record royalties still being held back by the Norman Petty Agency. Even with Buddy dead, however, Petty continued to find reasons not to pay over the money. Maria Elena was obliged to leave the gentlemanly Orenstein and seek more aggressive legal representation, whereupon Petty finally disgorged what his books said he owed Buddy and what Maria Elena now describes as 'a paltry sum', just over $35,000. Paltry or not, it would have made the difference between struggling through the Midwest on a second-rate tour or staying safe and warm in the Brevoort building, among the hippies and coffee-houses. It was enough, in every sense, to have kept Buddy alive.

Petty's victory in disinheriting Buddy from the Crickets and cleaving them unto himself alone was, ironically, to bring him small satisfaction or profit. The group which he had reconstituted with vocalist Earl Sinks released only one single on Brunswick, 'Love's Made A Fool Of You' coupled with 'Someone, Someone'. In April 1959, J. I. Allison and Joe B. Mauldin followed Buddy's example in leaving Clovis Man – though, unlike their late friend, they took with them their share of record royalties from the Holly heyday. In Joe B.'s case, the payment was $10,000. 'I was sure it ought to have been more than that,' he says now. 'But my accountant told me, "Norman's books are in such a mess, you'd better take what you can."'

The Buddy-less Crickets were to have a long if fitful history. J. I and Joe B. had latterly been joined by Sonny Curtis, who had just missed being one of the original Crickets – and who'd come back into the group chiefly in the expectation that they were about to be reunited with Buddy. Sonny had himself developed into a talented songwriter, and was to be mainly responsible for tracks on the Crickets' first post-Buddy album that made Buddy seem almost still there – 'When You Ask About Love'; 'I Fought The Law' (subsequently a hit for the Bobby Fuller Four); 'More Than I Can Say', co-written with J. I. Allison, which was to launch the career of Buddy's Fargo stand-in, Bobby Vee. As if in a gesture of condolence and support, the Crickets were then booked on an Australian tour as backing musicians to their old friends the Everly Brothers. Times had changed, indeed, since Don and Phil Everly first met Buddy, J.I., Joe B. and Niki, way back in 1957 – when what had impressed the Kentucky brothers about the West Texans was their self-containment and independence as a performing unit.

Though J.I., Joe B. and Sonny would keep the Crickets going for an impressive numbers of years, and enjoy one or two minor Buddy-accented hits ('My Little Girl'; 'Please Don't Ever Change'), they were never to find 'another guy' to fill the shoes of the one they had lost. Among the several replacement lead singers who would come and go during the next decade, only one could be seriously compared with Buddy – but not, alas, in vocal or instrumental ability. His name was David Box and in 1964 he, too, would die in a plane crash.

Coral-Brunswick were not slow to exploit the gusher they had tapped. *The Buddy Holly Story*, a compilation of Buddy's major tracks from the previous eighteen months, presented almost in the form of a movie biopic, its cover adorned by the gentle face of the Bruno photographic session, went straight on to *Billboard*'s album-chart, whither it would return intermittently over the next three and a half years. Maria Elena, meanwhile, had given Dick Jacobs the dozen or so new songs which Buddy had put on tape in their Greenwich Village apartment during the last weeks of his life. It being unthinkable to release any of these in their original form, with only Buddy's acoustic guitar accompaniment, Jacob's assistant, Jack Hanson, was given the job of dubbing instrumental backing on to them. Hanson's 'sweetened' versions of 'Peggy Sue Got Married' and 'Crying, Waiting, Hoping' were later to be reviled by Buddy purists, but at the time they pleased and comforted his fans as much as had anything released during his lifetime.

Within the year, responsibility for producing and releasing all posthumous Buddy Holly material had been assumed by Norman Petty. It was an inevitable decision since dozens of Buddy tracks still lay in the Clovis vaults, dating right back to the breezy version of Chuck Berry's 'Brown-eyed Handsome Man' which he'd played for Petty by way of audition in late 1956. Though the Holley family were well aware of Buddy's battle with Petty at the end, they felt they had no choice but to cede him this absolute control. Innocents in the recording world that they were, it seemed preferable to deal with someone they knew personally. In any case, Petty had showed them consideration in the aftermath of Buddy's death, advising them on outstanding matters concerning his taxes and insurance.

Petty could now take sweet revenge on the Crickets by

refusing to let them overdub the instrumentation on to archive Buddy tracks as he issued them. Instead, he brought in a young West Texan group called the Fireballs, giving their lead guitarist George Tomsco the awesome task of augmenting – sometimes even obliterating – Buddy's original Stratocaster riffs. For that arch-manipulator Clovis Man, it must have been the perfect consummation: a band of obedient boys out there in the studio and Buddy's voice to do with as he pleased, unhampered by Buddy's teeming ideas or Buddy's iron will.

The prayer Larry Holley had murmured to himself on the journey back from identifying Buddy's body seemed to have been answered. His parents not only survived their horrendous loss but were able to confront it with a fortitude which, to their good Baptist eldest son, appeared to come from a source outside themselves. Within a couple of weeks of Buddy's death, both L.O. and Ella could talk about him without breaking down, even play his records with equanimity. Among many personal keepsakes they kept at their house was the Ariel motorcycle on which Buddy had blown $1,000 cash in Dallas, that tornadoey spring of '58. L. O. Holley took a pride in maintaining the bike and, despite his advancing years, even took it out for the occasional spin. There also were two dozen-odd pairs of high-fashion rockstar shoes, too big to fit anyone in the family, so L.O. gave them to Jake Goss, the only barber who'd ever been able to sculpt Buddy's springy curls into a style which pleased him.

As more and more 'posthumous' releases came out in Britain, fans would write to the music papers expressing doubts that his unquenchably alive and effervescent voice could really be Buddy's. One issue of the *New Musical Express* carried a letter from L.O. and Ella in Lubbock, thanking Buddy's British following for their loyalty and assuring them that they had not been deceived.

Larry himself received no divine help in coping with the loss of the kid brother he'd regarded as more like a son. For a good ten years after Buddy's death, Larry could not listen to any rock 'n' roll music nor bear even to turn on a radio. Nor did he ever look under his bed, where he kept the brown leather overnight bag of Buddy's that he'd retrieved from the crash site.

Professionally, Buddy could be said not to have left a single enemy behind. 'He never knocked anybody down in his life,' runs a testimonial lyric by Sonny Curtis, one of countless friends in and out of the music business who were to mourn him as deeply, and for as long, as did his family. Joe B. Mauldin refused to accept that he was gone 'for about the next two years ... I kept thinking it might all have been just a publicity stunt ... and one day he'd come walking down the street, and I'd see him ...' To Waylon Jennings's grief were added torments of guilt for having let the Big Bopper fly off with Buddy that night instead of himself. Don Everly refused to travel by plane for years afterwards, and would not attend a funeral until the early 1990s, when his own father died.

Worst stricken of all was Eddie Cochran, the closest to an equal Buddy had as a guitarist or songwriter, and the only person to whom he'd confided his despair at the very end. At Cochran's next recording session, he had intended to record the newly-written 'tribute' song 'Three Stars'. But the lyrics proved too emotionally charged. As Cochran spoke the line 'Buddy Holly, I'll always remember you with tears in my eyes', his usually tough, blasé voice choked with distress. 'When Eddie came back into the control-room, he was in a terrible way,' his fiancée, Sharon Sheeley, remembers. 'He told his producer, "If you ever release that song, I swear I'll never make another record again."' So Tommy Dee's version of 'Three Stars' was released instead.

Far from assuaging his grief, the passage of time seemed to make Cochran still more deflated and morose. When he returned to Britain on tour with Gene Vincent in early 1960, he was taking tranquillizers for what today would be diagnosed as clinical depression. He also had became convinced that he was fated to die as prematurely, suddenly and as violently as had Buddy. While appearing in north-west England, he even visited a gypsy clairvoyant on Blackpool promenade, hoping to discover when and where he would meet his nemesis. 'We were staying in Manchester or somewhere and Eddie woke up screaming in bed beside me,' Sharon Sheeley remembers. '"My God!" he said. "I'm going to die and there's nothing anyone can do to stop it!"

'From the day Buddy was killed, Eddie hadn't been able to bear to listen to his music. But while we were in England, he sent me out to buy all of Buddy's records and he'd sit and listen to them over and over. I asked him, "Doesn't it upset you, hearing Buddy this way?" "Oh, no," Eddie said. "'Cause I'll be seeing him soon."'

On Easter Sunday, 1960, Cochran, his fiancée and Gene Vincent were returning from the West Country by hire car to catch their return flight to America from Heathrow Airport. Near Chippenham, Wiltshire, the car skidded out of control and hit a roadside lamp-post. Its three passengers were rushed to hospital with multiple injuries, Sharon's including a broken back and pelvis. When she regained consciousness and asked the doctors how Eddie was, they broke it to her that he was dead. In a further eerie replay of the Buddy Holly Story, he, too, had left behind a new single whose title suddenly seemed all too grimly appropriate. It was called 'Three Steps To Heaven'.

To the brand-new decade, with its thin-lapelled suits and goody-goody sounds, fifties rock 'n' roll appeared no more than a demented interlude whose flashy exuberance already seemed a hundred years out of date and whose principal exponents, one way and another, seemed to have come to the bad end so long prophesied for them.

Alan Freed, the movement's mellow-toned Pied Piper, had

been broken both in fortune and in health by the Payola scandals. Jerry Lee Lewis's career had never recovered from the furore over his marriage to his thirteen-year-old cousin. Little Richard, now ostensibly studying for the ministry, had been beaten up by police after being caught loitering in a public toilet. Chuck Berry had received a two-year prison sentence for illegally transporting an under-age girl across a state line. Even the angelic Everly Brothers had been brought low, cancelling a tour of Britain after a failed suicide attempt by Don in his suite at the Savoy Hotel.

They survived only who renounced the faith – Elvis Presley with his conveyor-belt Hollywood movie musicals, Roy Orbison with his sobbing sub-operatic arias, Bobby Darin with his Sinatra-style revamp of Kurt Weill's 'Mack the Knife'. To be a teenage idol, you had to be called Bobby (if not Darin, then Vee, Vinton or Rydell), sport a button-down shirt and bog-brush haircut, and look as though you wouldn't hurt a flybutton. In all the world, the only place a rock 'n' roll song could still make the charts was Britain, and the only person who could put it there was Buddy Holly.

One remnant of nineteen-fifties music, at least, seemed to have no difficulty in adjusting to the new decade. In parallel to his doctoring and regular release of years-old Buddy Holly tracks, the career of Norman Petty as a manipulator of sounds and people continued to prosper. Petty's production of his own instrumental composition 'Wheels', played by a group called the String-a-Longs, became an instant hit in 1961, reaching number 3 in America and number 12 in Britain. Two years later, he welded his Buddy 'ghost' backing group the Fireballs together with vocalist Jimmy Gilmer on a seemingly uncharismatic little song called 'Sugar Shack'. After the Fireballs had left the studio, thinking the track complete, Petty overdubbed a piping Solovox organ riff that horrified them to the depth of their manly Texan souls. 'Sugar Shack' went to number 1 and became the biggest-selling American single of 1963.

'Sugar Shack' was Clovis Man's triumphant reply to the many – among his friends no less than his enemies – who had doubted he could ever again score a coup to compare with Buddy Holly. But his second wave of success with the Fireballs and other groups through the middle and late sixties tempted Petty into fatal hubris. In 1969, he closed down the little studio complex on West Seventh Street where so many Gold Discs had been mined, exchanging his clumpy Altec board for a state-of-the-art control-room in the auditorium of the old Mesa theatre on Main Street. The key to the old studio's efficacy – not to mention its profitability – had been simplicity and improvisation. But at the Mesa, lavish ostentation prevailed. The stage, for instance, was fitted with steel curtains whose hundreds of individual strands had been dipped in fourteen-carat gold.

Thereafter, Petty's once acute, single-minded business sense became increasingly clouded by vanity, self-indulgence and misjudgement. Nostalgic for his early years as a disc jockey, he started two radio stations, one AM, one FM. He opened a diamond store in downtown Clovis and acquired numerous other properties around the city including a warehouse and part of an old church called the Citadel at West Seventh and Main. The Citadel was converted into living-quarters for Petty, his wife Vi, their animals and their vast collection of brass and coloured glass gewgaws. However, he kept the chapel area intact, and even spoke of making it available for weddings, to be conducted by himself. A further lavish sum was spent in endowing his own place of frequent and ardent worship, Clovis's Central Baptist Church, with a magnificent pipe organ – though some whispered that it was not his money, but Buddy Holly's, which paid for the instrument.

By the early seventies, Clovis Man was in serious financial difficulties. The new studio at the Mesa theatre, for all its twenty-four-track board and fourteen-carat gold curtains, had not succeeded in turning out a single hit record. Both the new radio stations had too weak a signal to carry Petty's middle-of-the-road shows to any but the most limited audience. The only unquestionably desirable asset that remained in his hands was the Buddy Holly song-catalogue, administered by his NOR VA JAK company and containing evergreen songs in which he had so far-sightedly appropriated half or one-third of the writers' credit all those years ago. Hence the 1975 sale of 'That'll Be The Day', 'Peggy Sue' and virtually every other worthwhile Buddy song to Paul McCartney's MPL company.

Hollywood's ludicrous 1979 version of Buddy's life and career felt it unnecessary to mention that he had ever met a man named Norman Petty or recorded in a place named Clovis, New Mexico. As well might one leave Colonel Tom Parker out of the Elvis Presley Story or Brian Epstein out of the Beatles'. Petty affected not to care about having been disinvented. But thereafter his claim on the credit for Buddy's success became noticeably more grandiose. Thanks to his habit of taping all his telephone-calls, we can eavesdrop on him, around 1980, assuring a journal-ist, in that mellow, almost ministerly voice, that he and Buddy used to write songs as 'a 50–50 partnership ... I worked on lyrics, Buddy worked on melodies. He didn't like to write bridges to songs, so on something like "True Love Ways", I'd do that ...'

In the early eighties, Petty was stricken with leukaemia, the same disease that had killed his elder brother Billy back in the thirties. Pinpointing the causes of leukaemia is difficult as a rule. But in Petty's case, the disease may have been engendered by years of inhaling toxic fumes from the carbon tetrachloride he used to clean his studio equipment. His decline was swift and pitiable, the slim, stooping figure shrinking to bones inside its beige safari-suit, the once blandly good-looking face ageing far beyond its fifty-seven years. His last months were consumed with bitter regret for having ever left the original studio on West Seventh. His friend Jerry Fisher remembers him saying time and again how unique had been the atmosphere he had created there and how he'd never been able to recapture it.

His final music project was a ironic one, considering with what determination he had blanked Buddy out of his life and memory in 1959. He was arranging and recording synthesizer versions of 'That'll Be The Day', 'Peggy Sue' and other tracks from their '50–50 partnership' for a projected album to be called *Electric Buddy Holly*.

Norman Petty died on 15 August 1984 – the twenty-sixth anniversary of Buddy's wedding. He predeceased his mother, the redoubtable Ma Petty who had been pumping gas in front of the studio on the first day Buddy arrived there, and who had never ceased to dote on and coddle her 'Normie'. For the short remainder of her own life, Ma refused to believe he was gone; she would sit at the window, waiting for him to come home, cuddling a child's plastic doll as his surrogate.

His business affairs were found to be in spectacular chaos. The proceeds from selling Buddy's song-catalogue to Paul McCartney had been frittered away, with little or nothing to show for them. Secretive to the last, Petty had taken no one into his confidence concerning the network of small corporations he had created over the years, the bank accounts he had set up in their name, and the numerous offices and bolt-holes all over Clovis to which he would periodically retreat to transact their mysterious business. His bewildered widow, Vi, now found herself in possession of an immense bunch of keys, with not the first idea how to find the locks they fitted.

Knowing Vi's inability to deal with the simplest business transaction, Petty did not bequeath his estate directly to her. Instead, it was handed over to the two other people he come to rely on the most during those painful final months. One was his financial adviser, Lyle Walker, the other was a former minister from Portales named Kenneth Broad. Walker and Broad were appointed joint administrators of Petty's studio and publishing interests, and entrusted with responsibility for Vi's welfare.

During Petty's illness, the old studio compound on West Seventh had sunken into squalor. Norma Jean Berry, the Petty's bookkeeper, herself now in poor health, occupied the old guest suite at the rear; the echo-chamber became silted up with empty boxes and broken furniture while Clovis Man's once spotless and orderly control-room was reduced to a malodorous home for Vi's collection of thirty-six stray cats. Before the BBC *Arena* documentary team came to Clovis in 1984, Petty's former associate Jerry Fisher volunteered to put the studio back into order. Fisher spent weeks of loving altruism on the job, restoring the single-track Altec board, which had soaked up Buddy's greatest musical moments, to its old pride of place on the veined work-surface; stripping down and reassembling Ampex tape equipment corroded almost beyond recognition by cats' urine.

The chief consolation of Vi's widowhood was the annual Clovis Music Festival, when friends from the old days, like Jimmy Self and the Roses, would foregather to perform and reminisce. In 1991, Vi died of a gastric complaint, compounded by years of self-neglect. The Petty estate then passed to Lyle Walker and Kenneth Broad. Some of those who worked with or for Petty in the glory days of the old studio are less than happy that it should now belong to two such comparative outsiders. But, to their credit, Walker and Broad have preserved the place as a museum, accessible free of charge to groups of Holly pilgrims by appointment.

Even death was not to give Vi her husband's undivided company nor silence the persistent rumours about that strange triumvirate which ruled so many years at 1313 West Seventh Street. With them under their headstone at Clovis city cemetery lies their ever-faithful bookkeeper and amanuensis, Norma Jean.

*

For two decades after Buddy's death, Lubbock maintained the seeming indifference it had shown him during his lifetime. The ever-increasing stream of fans who arrived to pay their respects were astounded by how little and grudgingly his home city commemorated him. In a land where civic honours and testimonial plaques are easily bestowed, Lubbock might have been expected to inaugurate a Buddy Holly Stadium, a Buddy Holly Freeway, at the very least a Buddy Holly Street. But what was given so readily in other places to individuals of far less moment failed to materialize in the 'City of Churches' for its one and only modern hero. The single amenity which bore his name was the 'Buddy Holly Recreation Area', a small landscaped plot reclaimed from common land where, in former days, Buddy would park with his dates or write songs alfresco with Bob Montgomery.

As the years passed, Lubbock's City Council could not but recognize what an asset Buddy represented, both in international prestige and in potential tourism and conference business. Various ideas were mooted for some more permanent memorial, such as a statue, but all fell by the wayside for one reason or another. Finally – as if exasperated by all this council-chamber dickering – the elements took a hand. In 1970, the worst tornado West Texas had seen in living memory tore through the centre of Lubbock, completely demolishing the whole north side of Avenue Q. The subsequent extensive redevelopment included a new Civic Center plaza where, in 1980, a eight-foot-six bronze statue of Buddy was at last unveiled.

The work of Texan sculptor Grant Speed, it shows Buddy with his Stratocaster, in the sidelong striding posture recognizable to anyone who ever saw him perform. Apart from innumerable classic photographs, the sculptor's main reference-point was Travis Holley, the quiet, introverted elder brother whom Buddy most resembled facially. Set about by beds of orange marigolds, framed at certain angles by an intrusive satellite-dish, the statue may not be a particularly artistic or lifelike piece of work. But to the pilgrims who congregate around it with their cameras during the course of each year, Michelangelo's David could hardly be more beautiful or fulfilling. Below is a 'Walk of Fame', since augmented to honour other historic names in West Texas music, J. I. Allison, Joe B. Mauldin, Niki Sullivan, Roy Orbison and Waylon Jennings. 'Buddy Holly contributed to the musical heritage of not only Texas but the entire world,' runs his city's overdue encomium. 'It is significant that this first plaque in the Walk of Fame bears his name. The citizens of Lubbock pay tribute to "their native son".'

The dearth of generally available background information about Buddy was to continue, mystifyingly, long after magazines like Jann Wenner's *Rolling Stone* had made rock journalism respectable – even fleetingly literate – and the rock 'n' roll era had become a legitimate subject of academic study. In the absence of illuminating books, films or even articles, Buddy's fans had no option but to become researchers and investigators in their own right, expending what for many were capital sums on travelling to Lubbock and Clovis to meet his family and former associates; in several cases starting magazines or newsletters to share their findings with hundreds of eager subscribers. Hardcore Buddy Holly enthusiasts as a result tend to be more competitively knowledgeable and fiercely proprietorial than any other species of rock fan, with the possible single exception of Beatles ones. For the still unconstituted Chair in Buddy Holly Studies, numerous worthy contenders exist, both in Britain and America. But none has shown more selfless dedication to the subject than Bill Griggs.

The son of two professional musicians, Griggs was born in 1941 and brought up in Hartford, Connecticut. As a rock 'n' roll-obsessed teenager in the late fifties, he saw every package show that ever played at Hartford's 4,000-seat State theatre, eventually becoming such a fixture that the theatre took him on as an usher. It was there that he first saw Buddy Holly and the Crickets on 'The Biggest Show of Stars for 1957'. He remembers vividly the several things about them that struck his soul awake with delight – the way they could reproduce the sound of their records onstage; the contrast of their dapper dark suits to usual gaudy rock 'n' roll threads; above all, Buddy's stage presence and energy, and the good-natured way he devoted a few moments of his set to the 'bad' seats at either end of the seventy-foot stage.

There was much more to Bill Griggs than just rock 'n' roll: he had intended to train as an astronomer, and had been a national drag-racing champion. But fifties music, especially that of Buddy Holly, inexorably took over his life. In 1976, realizing to his amazement that his idol had no American fan-club, he founded one himself, naming it the Buddy Holly Memorial Society. Four years later, he moved his family from Connecticut to Lubbock, by chance settling just a couple of blocks from Buddy's parents' house. He has devoted the past sixteen years to compiling a week-by-week – even day-by-day – dossier on Buddy's twenty-two years, accumulating documents and memorabilia against the hoped-for day when Lubbock will open a museum devoted to his life and career.

The place where Buddy died has been rather more assiduous in commemorating him than has the place where he was born. On the twentieth anniversary of his death, 3 February 1979, a memorial convention took place at the Surf Ballroom in Clear Lake, Iowa, his final port of call on the 'Winter Dance Party'. Despite Iowa's unmitigatedly inhospitable winter weather, the Clear Lake convention was to grow into an annual event, attended by delegates from all over America and Europe, with personal appearances by Buddy's family and close friends, and performances by musicians who owed their careers to him – the Crickets, Bobby Vee, Mike Berry and many more. The lake-bordering highway outside, from which an ever-optimistic young man took his last look back at coloured lights and icebound water, has been renamed Buddy Holly Avenue.

The cornfield where the plane came down is still there – as is the same wire boundary fence which brought it finally to a stop. A couple of feet inside the fence stands a simple metal memorial, the silhouettes of a guitar and three discs, one for each of the recording stars who perished. At convention-time, the memorial is usually buried under snow: in summer, it must be hunted for among corn almost as high as an elephant's eye. The field's present owner does not mind who treks across his land to visit it so long as they do no damage to his crops.

The cause of the crash continues to be argued over as hotly as ever. In recent years, a new voice has entered the controversy – that of an Iowa clergyman, the Revd Jerry Miller, who claims that he alone knows the true reason why N3794N crashed so soon after take-off, and that he has irrefutable proof in the briefcase he carries everywhere. Latterly, too, the charter-boss Jerry Dwyer has begun to drop tantalizing hints which seem to link the sudden 'indisposition' of his young pilot, Roger Peterson, with the .22 pistol Buddy carried on the flight. According to Bill Griggs, Dwyer has told a third party that Civil Aeronatics Board investigators discovered a bullet-hole through the back of Peterson's seat but that, for some reason, officialdom decreed that the matter be covered up. However, as Griggs drily remarks, 'If you're three young guys just taking off at midnight in bad weather, who in their right mind is going to shoot the pilot in the back?'

The last days of L.O. and Ella Holley were clouded with anxiety, to add to their ineradicable grief. L.O. suffered a stroke which left his speech and mobility impaired – though he took a pride in still having his hair cut by Buddy's old barber, Jake Goss. Handling their share of Buddy's increasingly valuable estate put the Holleys into a tax-bracket that gave them as much worry as benefit. In 1982, they found themselves facing a hefty demand from the Internal Revenue Service, but with no reserves to meet it. As a result they were forced to sell Paul McCartney's MPL company the 'mechanical' (airplay) rights they held in 'That'll Be The Day', 'Peggy Sue', 'Everyday' and a clutch of Buddy's other songs. L. O. Holley died on 8 July 1985; the unfailingly courageous and dignified Ella followed him on 20 May 1990. Their equally modest tablets lie in the grass next to Buddy's at Lubbock municipal cemetery.

Maria Elena was never fully to recover from Buddy's death either. In the sixties she met and married Joe Diaz, a Dallas toy-manufacturer, also of Puerto Rican background, and bore him three children, two sons and a daughter. The elder boy was named Carlos, the Hispanic equivalent of Buddy's real Christian name, Charles. The marriage to Diaz did not last, and Maria Elena spent some years in Florida, indulging her unexpected passion for deep-sea fishing. Now sixty-three, she lives alone with two pedigree cats in a suburb of Dallas and devotes her whole existence to guardianship of the inheritance she wishes had never come her way. If people exploited Buddy during his lifetime, Maria Elena is fiercely determined it shall not happen now he is dead: she personally approves and licenses all commercial uses of his name and likeness, and has prevailed on the Texas legislature to pass the so-called 'Buddy Holly Law', protecting him as a trademark as sacrosanct as that of Disney or Coca-Cola in his home state.

Like Norman Petty all those years ago, many who have fallen foul of Maria Elena, or failed to bend her to their will, consider her demanding and unreasonable, but I have to say she did not seem so to me. Under an admittedly tough, uncompromising exterior, I found a genuine eccentric, warm and humorous, admirably courageous and self-sufficient, though clearly rather lonely and still prone to clutches of grief for the young bride-groom she lost thirty-seven years ago. As we drove through the countryside near her house, Maria Elena gestured out of the window. 'Look . . . a farm,' she said with a wry grimace. 'Buddy's plane came down on a farm. And where do I end up living? Close to a farm!'

If rock 'n' roll stars were once regarded as pagan gods, they seem to our modern age more like palpitant and preening patron saints whose smallest possessions are as eagerly sought after and jealously cherished as the holiest relics of medieval times. In the boom market for rock 'n' roll memorabilia, Buddy has posthumously earned the price of his survival a hundred times over. Sotheby's famous rock 'n' roll auction of 1991 saw his grey wool stage-jacket and French-cuff shirt go for $5,225, his high school diploma for $3,300 and his birth certificate (on which the Registrar prophetically filled in his surname as 'Holly' not 'Holley') for $1,000. His Gibson acoustic guitar, in the blue-and-black leather jacket he made for it, went to Gary Busey, the actor who had portrayed him on screen, for $242,000 – a price-tag which did not include the guitar's shoulder-strap. The City of Lubbock recently spent $200,000 on acquiring his last Fender Stratocaster, stage-clothes, shoes and childhood mementoes including school exercise books, his slingshot and Cub Scout badge. The wallet that Tommy Allsup lent him to show as ID at Fargo post office now has pride of place on the walls of the Dallas Hard Rock Café. Tucked inside is one of the business cards Buddy had already had printed for his new Prism recording company.

His principal fan and archivist-in-chief, Bill Griggs, has amassed a remarkable personal collection of Buddy memorabilia, as the basis of a possible future Holly Museum. It includes Buddy's sunglasses, his movie camera, his fedora, the dice he loved to roll with Chuck Berry, a red polka-dot cravat from the set which Maria Elena bought him to wear on the 'Winter Dance Party'. A few years ago, Griggs visited Buddy's New York opticians, Courmetts & Gaul, to see if his records were still on file and, if so, whether they contained any letters or documents signed by him. It turned out that Dr Stanger, the oculist who had treated Buddy, still worked for Courmetts & Gaul and that he had more on file than mere paperwork. Put away in a drawer was a second pair of Mexican Faiosa spectacle-frames – these not black but tortoiseshell – which Buddy had left with Dr Stanger as spares in the autumn of 1958. Griggs was able to buy them at face-value, $72.

There is one memento, however, which even the tireless Griggs has been unable to track down. The simple wooden house on 6th Street where Buddy was born ought by rights to be preserved as a shrine to a quintessential American hero. Instead, we are confronted by that mysterious empty grass plot between its former next-door neighbours. After the Holley family left it, the house gradually declined in fortune and, during the late seventies, was condemned as unfit for human habitation. It was scheduled to be demolished on 3 February 1978, the nineteenth anniversary of Buddy's death. Before the order could be carried out, an unknown party bought the condemned structure and had it lifted from its foundations and towed away, to be resited outside the jurisdiction of the public health authorities. It may well be still there to this day, somewhere just beyond Lubbock city limits. Bill Griggs has mobilized search-parties of up to fifty fans, armed with photo-references of that covered front-end porch ... those distinctive window shutters with playing-card club-shapes cut into them. But, despite all his efforts, the house continues to elude him.

When I last visited Lubbock, in January 1996, Griggs took me to see another remarkable Buddy Holly relic which had lately turned up just a stone's throw from his grave. Separated from Lubbock cemetery by a traffic fly-over is a steel-fenced lot where hundreds of late fifties Chevrolet automobiles stand row on row, gaudy-coloured and befinned, in the rattlesnake-haunted grass. The owner of the lot, a Chevy nut named Bill Clement, believes he has acquired the '58 Impala coupé which was Buddy's

Christmas gift to himself in the euphoric December of 1957. It stands in Clement's yard, a crouching, eviscerated shell, its coral-pink body and white roof bleached almost colourless and eaten away by rust. But the serial number matches that of the vehicle whose 'Powerglide' briefly gave trouble but was rectified for a $2 charge. And Buddy's brother Larry has confirmed it to be the same car.

Larry Holley is now seventy, a long-legged, boyish figure, still hale enough to work a full week in his tile business and have energy left over to ride dirt-bikes at weekends. Larry is the one everybody comes to for stories about Buddy, and it shows in a slightly haunted and impatient manner. But the same slow smile always appears as he recalls the day Buddy came and coolly asked him for $1,000 ... their trip down to San Angelo in the eighteen-wheel truck ... the single-minded fourteen-year-old, doing leatherwork in the middle of Thanksgiving dinner ... that cute little five-year-old, sawing away on his toy violin at the County Line Schoolhouse, unaware that his big brothers had silenced his bow with grease.

Larry admits that he often dreams about Buddy – dreams about their old companionship from which he invariably awakens happy and calm. And, as ever, he is sustained by the simple, absolute certainty of his Tabernacle Baptist faith. 'I know that Buddy's with the Lord, and that one of these days I'll see him again and put my arm around his shoulder, just like I used to.'

A few years ago, Larry came to Bill Griggs with tears in his eyes and handed Griggs something wrapped in clear plastic. It was the brown leather overnight-bag which Buddy had carried with him on his last journey. Since retrieving the bag from the crash site, Larry had kept it under his bed, never looking at it again. Now he said he wanted Griggs to have it, both as a mark of appreciation for Griggs's dedication to Buddy, and to ensure it a better home than some Sotheby's auction-room.

Griggs treated this most poignant and intimate relic with

almost religious reverence, taking out the contents, listing and photographing them, then replacing them, re-wrapping the bag in its plastic cover and promising himself never to open it again. I ask him to do so just once more, for the benefit of the Channel 4 film-crew I have brought with me on this visit. He agrees, with deep misgivings, on condition that the camera-crew and I shall be the only ones present.

The bag is unrolled from its plastic layers like a mummy's corpse being disinterred from its bandages. It is smaller than I expected, – two feet long and perhaps eighteen inches wide. Back in 1959, one can see, it was an extremely stylish piece of kit, doubtless purchased from one of those swanky leather shops on upper Madison Avenue. You unzip it broadside, then snap the opening rigid like the mouth of an old-fashioned Gladstone bag. On the handle is the neat binding of white adhesive tape with which Buddy made it more comfortable to carry. The glossy vermilion leather is mounted on a quarter-inch steel frame whose misshapenness indicates with what terrible force N3794N hit the ground. Before opening the bag, Griggs turns it over to show the naked strip of plaid on its underside – all that remains of the severed compartment where Buddy used to carry his .22 pistol.

The contents are then lifted out reverentially one by one – a crushed and bent tube of Colgate toothpaste, a pink and yellow toothbrush, aspirins, suntan lotion, a lint-brush, a hairbrush and a black plastic comb. The lint-brush is still clotted with the fluff which fastidious Buddy had removed from his stage-suits. The comb still has strands of his hair caught between its teeth. Each dip into the bag coats Grigg's fingers with brown dust which he will be deeply reluctant to wash off afterwards. For it is petrified Iowa soil from 1959: the very earth that took Buddy's life.

Griggs's one consuming regret is never having met and talked to Buddy, as he could easily have done back in 1957. But he feels that the omission may now have been partly rectified. Once or twice, while working alone at his office in Lubbock, he has sensed the nearness of Buddy's benign shade. 'It always happens late at night, when I'm tapping on the computer ... I suddenly get that feeling someone else is in the room. It seems to me that Buddy's standing there near my desk. He's wearing black slacks and the grey V-neck sweater he had on his English tour. And he always says the same thing: "Thanks for what you're doing."'

Among Griggs's encyclopaedic Buddy Holly photo-albums is one he is reluctant to open, let alone show to anyone else. This contains the pictures of Buddy's body as it was found on that morning of 3 February 1959. 'You can skip this book if you want to,' Griggs tells me. But I've followed my one-time inspiration and friend all this way from the end of Ryde Pier. I can hardly stop now.

It is not, as I had feared, a shocking or gruesome picture. It is just terribly, terribly sad. Silhouetted against some burst-open luggage, a long figure in a pale coat lies face-down in the snow. I remember those light-hearted words of his very first hit, 'That'll be the day ... when I die.' I realize he was a young man with everything he needed – everything except luck.

'He was an old soul,' says Maria Elena. 'He had a second passage in this world. Unfortunately, it was only a short one. If it's really true that they're out there somewhere and they can see down here, then he knows that people still appreciate his music, still love it. I say this all the time, every day. I say, "I hope that, wherever you are, you can see and hear this happening for you and that it was not in vain that you died, because what you wanted has come true. Your music really does live for ever."'

Bill Griggs delivers what is perhaps the best epitaph, both to the man and his music.

'Whenever you mention his name, it always gets the same reaction. Everybody smiles.'

INDEX

Except for the entry under his name Buddy Holly is referred to as BH